Perspectives on Credit Risk, Portfolio Management, and Capital

Readings from *The RMA Journal*

EDITORS

Michel Araten

Joseph L. Breeden

RMA is a member-driven professional association whose sole purpose is to advance sound risk principles in the financial services industry.

RMA helps our members use sound risk principles to improve institutional performance and financial stability, and enhance the risk competency of individuals through information, education, peer sharing, and networking.

Edited by Stephen Krasowski
Cover design by Arielle Morris
Text design and composition by Stephen Druding
Front and back cover photos by Shutterstock, Inc.

RMA Product Number: 0640826

ISBN: 978-1-57070-336-2

Library of Congress Control Number: 2014951178

Copyright 2014 by The Risk Management Association ("RMA"). All rights reserved. This publication is designed to provide accurate and authoritative information concerning the subject matter covered, but is not to be construed as rendering legal, accounting, or other professional advice.

Printed in the United States of America.

Contents

Chapter IV: Retail Credit Capital   229

Chapter V: Portfolio Management and RAROC   273

Chapter VI: Stress-Testing Methodologies   319

Introduction

For the last 25 years, banks have improved the quantification of the risks they assume when they extend credit or take market positions. Their objective in doing so is to better measure risk–return trade-offs, provide appropriate returns to their stakeholders, and meet the safety and stability concerns of their regulators.

Since risk has always been encountered in many different ways in retail and wholesale credit, trading activities, and investments, developing a common language for measuring risk is important. Based on the early work of Bankers Trust in the mid-1970s, economic capital became the lingua franca for measuring risk, and a risk-adjusted return on capital (RAROC) metric was introduced as a way to price and evaluate the relative attractiveness of banks' risk-taking activities.

On the regulatory side, Basel I was established in 1988 by the Basel Committee on Banking Supervision as a capital framework for international banks. It classified each asset or off-balance-sheet exposure into one of five risk buckets and assigned different levels of capital to each risk category. However, in the next decade, new products developed by banks, such as derivatives, securitizations, and subprime lending, did not fit neatly into these few risk assessment buckets, and the banks argued that this framework did not accurately measure risk. Since regulatory measures were substantially less risk-differentiated than internal assessments, regulators raised concerns that banks were beginning to practice regulatory capital arbitrage as they offloaded high-quality assets and retained poorer-quality, higher-returning assets as a way to reduce their capital requirements and increase near-term profits.

It was clear that Basel I needed replacement in the form of Basel II with its more risk-differentiated capital measures. In June 1999, the Basel Committee issued a proposal for a new capital adequacy framework to replace the 1988 Accord. The Basel II release document noted that "in developing the revised Framework, the Committee has sought to arrive at significantly more risk-sensitive capital requirements that are conceptually sound."[1] At the same time, banks also argued that internal risk measures already in use for their own decision making should find a parallel in a regulatory framework.

1

It was thus no coincidence that Robert Morris Associates changed its name in 2000 to The Risk Management Association, and its flagship publication, now called *The RMA Journal*, began publishing articles on various aspects of risk measurement as well as risk management. Appealing to a broad constituency, the articles ranged from the practical to the more theoretical and were authored by both practitioners working in banks and consultants to the industry. Many of the articles written by bankers followed the delicate balance of describing important new technologies in assessing risk that could be shared with the banking community at large without diluting any of their competitive advantages. While some of these articles were early attempts by banks to deal with these risk issues, many survive as examples of best practice and are still referred to as such today.

With the onset of the financial crisis of 2007, the critical issues around accurate measurement of risk have loomed large inside boards of banks as well as with the financial, political, and regulatory community. The enactment of the Dodd-Frank Act in the United States and the various implementations of Basel III around the globe have caught the attention of not only mega-banks but also small community banks that are striving to improve all aspects of their risk assessments.

The RMA Journal articles selected for inclusion in this book reflect some of the significant contributions that this industry has made over the 2001-14 period in advancing improvements in banks' credit risk management. They reflect the key risk parameters associated with credit extensions—probability of default, loss given default, and exposure at default—as well as how these measures may be translated into capital requirements with implications for pricing, risk- adjusted returns, and stress testing. Some of the articles candidly describe the conflicts between those measures banks use for internal decision making and the more stringent measures that regulators use for assessing regulatory capital adequacy.

This book is organized into the following broad sections:

  I. Wholesale Credit Risk Parameters
 II. Consumer Credit Risk Parameters
III. Wholesale Credit Capital
 IV. Retail Credit Capital
  V. Portfolio Management and RAROC
 VI. Stress-Testing Methodologies

Note

1. Basel Committee on Banking Supervision, "International Convergence of Capital Measurement and Capital Standards," Bank for International Settlements, June 2006.

Wholesale Credit Risk Parameters

T he section on wholesale credit risk parameters features articles dealing with the key inputs to risk measurement systems that calculate credit risk capital and provisions for loan loss reserves.

The heart of any risk management system is that which distinguishes or classifies risk into relative risk categories. A relative risk classification is used because, although it is very difficult for credit analysts to assign an absolute level of risk to any particular credit extension, they are generally able to state that transaction A is riskier than transaction B. The manner in which they assign these risks is embodied in a risk rating system.

Risk rating systems at banks were created using the examples set by the credit-rating agencies Moody's and Standard and Poor's. The internal risk-rating system introduced by Chase Manhattan Bank in the mid-1970s, for example, was based on a 10-point scale, with the last three ratings corresponding to levels of regulatory criticism. The ratings stood for the relative estimates of expected loss, effectively the combined effect of the likelihood of loss and the severity of loss. It was only after the merger of JPMorgan and Chase in 2001 that the two elements of loss—the likelihood of default and the loss given default—were separately estimated. This approach was consistent with the need to make these two elements separate inputs to credit capital models.

The first article in this section, "Effective Credit Rating Systems," by Tom Yu, Tom Garside, and Jim Stoker, describes the three elements of an effective rating system. The first is the rating scale that identifies the meaning of a rating, the scale employed, and the scope of the system. The second is the rating assignment itself and involves how ratings are assigned, who assigns them, and which tools are used. The third element is the validation or refinement of the ratings. The authors also describe how banks may differ in their approaches to rating-system design. Some may use pure judgment, others a template or scorecard, and others a pure model. To some extent this article may have been prompted by the need for banks to comply with Basel II's advanced internal ratings guidelines.

One of the most significant advances in estimating default likelihood was the pioneering effort of KMV, a consulting company. KMV demonstrated that, rather than relying on historical financial ratios, one could use the market's opinion of the riskiness of companies. In what has become known as contingent claims analysis, Robert Merton showed how the value of a firm's equity could be viewed as a call option on the firm with a strike price equal to the face value of the debt. A company could be viewed as being close to default if the market value of its assets was likely to be lower than the amount of debt coming due. The probability distribution of the market value of a company's assets was derived by converting the equity volatility of a company (obtained from the stock market) to its asset volatility and combining it with the company's leverage.

A significant number of banks were using this model beginning in the late 1990s and continue to do so today. "A Practical Review and Test of Default Prediction Models" by Jorge Sobehart and Sean Keenan, suggests that, rather than relying solely on the results of option theory models, the use of hybrid models may be more effective. The authors argue that this is especially true for firms that may be viewed as close to default. They conduct various comparisons of the results obtained, using their approach versus the pure option theory model. There should be little question that no model output should be blindly accepted without subjecting it to some sort of sanity test, and this article provides some evidence to support that view.

Recognizing that banks, in preparation for Basel II, may not have captured sufficient historical data to be able to estimate default rates for their loans, Nadeem Siddiqui and Shelley Klein suggest ways by which banks might overcome this issue in "Estimating Probability of Default from External Data Sources: A Step Toward Basel II." The avail-ability of consistent default data for banks that have been involved in multiple mergers with multiple rating systems continues to be a challenge today. The authors caution that, while external data such as that derived from rating agencies can be used, banks must first make sure that the rating philosophies are aligned and that the structures and char-acteristics of their loans and the bonds that serve as the basis of the external sources are similar. Today, however, the rating agencies have developed a significant database of de-faults for syndicated loans, so the comparisons may not be as tenuous as 12 years ago, when this article first appeared.

"Risk Grading Philosophy: Through the Cycle versus Point in Time," by Jeremy Taylor, wrestles with the critical question of which horizon banks should use when esti-mating likelihood of default. While Basel requires a one-year probability of default, it emphasizes the use of long-term averages, most likely because the Basel Committee did not want to see volatility in banks' capital, since point-in-time estimates of default prob-abilities can fluctuate. The horizon chosen is clearly an issue in aligning a bank's ratings with those of external data sources. For the most part, the rating agencies use a through-the-cycle horizon since ratings were originally designed for bond investors, who tended to be long-term holders. More recently, at least for speculative-grade credits, rating agencies such as Standard and Poor's use an 18-month horizon.

Since ratings and their associated default probabilities figure prominently in assess-ing profitability of customer relationships, it is important to be flexible in deciding how either approach should be modified in order to take into account both strategic and tac-tical decision-making. For a portfolio of credits that are likely to be traded or hedged in the market, a point-in-time approach would appear to be appropriate, while for middle market or small business lending a longer-term estimate of default may be desired.

Taylor notes that many banks use a hybrid approach where a through-the-cycle estimate is adjusted if a cycle becomes unusually pronounced.

The examination of actual ratings performance at a bank was first reported by Michel Araten, Michael Jacobs, Peeyush Varshney, and Claude Pelligrino in the article "An Internal Ratings Migration Study." This study covered a five-year period for 33,000 obligors at JPMorgan Chase that were rated on a seven-point scale corresponding to agency ratings. Both average default rates and transitions to nondefault states were noted. The article also describes the issue of dealing with withdrawn ratings where no ratings were assigned at the end of an observation period, and it offers suggestions for how to deal with this situation. This treatment remains a point of controversy today. A comparison of relative ranking accuracy, through a cumulative accuracy ratio, between the bank's ratings and those of a rating agency showed the two to be roughly similar. However, a comparison of ranking accuracy with a market-based approach using KMV's Expected Default Measure showed that market-based measures ranked more consistently than accounting-based measures.

In "Measuring the Risk of Default: A Modern Approach," authors Jens Hilscher, Robert Jarrow, and Donald van Deventer compare structural models to reduced-form models for estimating default probabilities. They argue that the structural approach that uses option-based theory suffers from a limiting assumption regarding the shape of the distribution of asset values. A reduced-form approach is more flexible with respect to including more inputs than the firm's leverage and asset volatility and, as a result, is more accurate. Today, while the reduced-form approach has increased its influence, the option-based approach continues to be more widely used in banking circles.

Jorge Sobehart and Sean Keenan examine behavioral aspects of the rating process in "Modeling Ratings Migration for Credit Risk Capital and Loss Provisioning Calculations." They posit that the perception of risk and its translation to an assigned rating by the rating agencies is impeded by the sometimes inconsistent application of judgment provided by the analyst. While numerical ratings are measured as constant ordinal differences, the probabilities of default between adjacent ratings differ by a factor of two to three times. A new or transitioned rating may result from catastrophic events, changes in regulations, or unanticipated corporate actions. Alternatively, the true value of new information is subject to interpretation, and ratings revisions can be interpreted as evidence that the previous rating had been assigned in error. Macroeconomic variables can seriously affect the perceptions of risk and the resultant ratings. The authors suggest analyzing historical time series of ratings, default rates, and macro variables and using this information to construct scenarios to allow for more robust simulations for risk capital calculations, portfolio loss provisioning, and stress scenario analysis.

The importance of validation of risk rating systems goes beyond meeting Basel II requirements. Bogie Ozdemir lays out the logic for the far-reaching benefits of validation exercises in "Validating Internal Rating Systems: The Move from Basel II Compliance to Continuous Improvement." Validation incorporates vigorous analysis of the discriminatory power of rating systems, back-testing of results, and, where appropriate, benchmarking against other systems. The increased emphasis by supervisors today on assessing whether there is an independent and effective challenge in the validation process means that management must not view it as a compliance exercise but be solidly behind it in every way.

"Loan Equivalents for Revolving Credits and Advised Lines," by Michel Araten and Michael Jacobs, tackles the measurement of exposure—one of the most critical parameters in estimating expected loss and capital, since both vary linearly with the exposure amount. While exposure for outstanding loans is assumed to be 100%, the issue is the measurement of exposure at default for partially or completely unfunded commitments—typically, revolving credits and advised lines. This exposure is denoted as a *loan equivalent amount* (LEQ) because it is equivalent to the amount outstanding. Using over 1,000 observations for 400 defaulted borrowers at Chase over a five-year period, the authors derive a regression that relates the LEQ to the rating of the loan and the remaining tenor. The logic behind the relationship is that better-rated customers are able to negotiate loan agreements with fewer covenants. The logic for the importance of tenor is that the longer the tenor, the more likely the customer will get into difficulty and draw down on the unused commitment. With so few publications containing actual bank data, this paper has become the source of LEQ estimates for many banks that have yet to assemble their data.

It should be noted that utilization is also related to the LEQ, and more recent attempts to separate correlations among utilization and rating from LEQ have shown to be promising. The most important variable that needs to be estimated is the nature and extent of covenants, since rating is actually a proxy for covenants. This data, however, is difficult to extract from historical data and one must also take into account covenant modifications.

While little LEQ data has been published, there has been substantial analysis of loss given default (LGD) data, although primarily for publicly issued bonds. "Measuring LGD on Commercial Loans: An 18-year Internal Study," by Michel Araten, Michael Jacobs, and Peeyush Varshney, is one of the few published reports to present such data for a bank—again, Chase. Analyzing loss data for over 3,700 customer defaults resulted in LGD estimates for secured and unsecured credits with some differentiation by industry. A discussion of the practical issues associated with measuring losses, along with sensitivity to discount rates and the economic cycle (downturn LGDs), should be helpful to those who have to deal with these difficult matters.

Since LGD distributions are highly bimodal, with a large number of observations at 0% and 100%, current methods seek to develop additional granularity to differentiate and capture key elements of loan structure and resolution of workouts. These include the amount of senior debt above or below the subject debt, the type of collateral obtained along with the extent of its monitoring, and whether the resolution of the workout will be through a reorganization or liquidation of the collateral and company.

Credit exposure is also obtained when banks engage in derivatives with counterparties. "Counterparty Credit Exposure from a Regional Bank Perspective," by Jeremy Taylor, provides solid advice to those banks that have somewhat smaller derivative books than the large banks. Counterparty credit exposure is a key input to market risk calculations that have become an increasingly important focus of regulators, both for interest rate risk as well as when banks engage in credit default swaps. While large banks are able to construct complex simulation models to satisfy the internal models method, smaller banks might not have similar resources and may have to settle for estimates consistent with the current exposure method.

Effective Credit Risk-Rating Systems

By Tom Yu, Tom Garside, and Jim Stoker

redit risk ratings provide a common language for describing credit risk exposure within an organization and, increasingly, with parties outside the organization. As such, they drive a wide range of credit processes—from origination to monitoring to securitization to workout—and it is logical that better credit risk ratings can lead to better credit risk management. Yet many lenders are using rating systems that were put in place 10 or more years ago.

The primary barrier to change, it seems, is not that the old rating models cannot be improved but that the process of implementation is challenging. Ratings are so tightly woven into the fabric of most institutions that they are part of the culture. And any significant change to the culture is difficult.

However, the pressures to change are mounting from both internal and external sources. Internally, it may be the desire to price loans more aggressively or to support a more economically attractive CLO structure. Externally, the capital markets desire more detailed, more finely differentiated measures of credit portfolios. For corporate lending, credit scoring has been an important accelerator for securitization.

Justification for Change

A decade of advances in quantitative measures of credit risk has led to better risk management at the transaction level as well as the portfolio level. Lenders can actively manage their portfolio risks and returns relative to the institution's risk appetite and performance targets.

At the same time, it is becoming increasingly clear that banks, in spite of their historical role, are actually disadvantaged holders of credit risk. The combination of high capital requirements and double taxation means that credit extension is typically not contributing positively to shareholder value creation. Improved risk ratings can improve the returns in this business by significantly lowering risk and process costs.

Some leading players are rethinking the business model as a credit conduit. The originate-and-hold strategy is being replaced with one of originate-package-distribute. Credit risk is being managed in much the same way as interest rate risk or equity risk. To make this strategy work, it is essential that credit risk is measured in a more standardized, accurate, and timely fashion.

Additional impetus is provided by the proposed reforms to bank regulation put forward by the Bank for International Settlements. Commonly known as Basel II, these reforms are intended to supersede the straight 8% minimum capital charge levied on banks since 1988. The expectations inherent in this reform add to the pressures for changing internal risk rating systems. The promise is that less capital will be required for banks using more advanced ratings. Many banks will find that, without a substantial overhaul, their credit risk rating system will fail to meet Basel II guidelines.

Steps Toward Change Begin with Understanding the Goal

The fundamental goal of a credit risk rating system is to estimate the credit risk of a given transaction or portfolio of transactions/assets. The industry standard "building block" for quantifying credit risk is *expected loss* (EL), the mean loss that can be expected from holding the asset. This is calculated as the product of three components:

Expected loss (EL) = Probability of default (PD) x Exposure at default (EAD)
x Loss given default (LGD).

This article concentrates on the success of a credit rating system in terms of its ability to quantify PD and LGD. For most commercial exposures, EAD is generally treated independently from the risk ratings, and this article will treat it as such.

The important risk drivers that affect PD and LGD vary from asset class to asset class. For example, the drivers of risk vary widely among retail, commercial, and asset-backed lending. Therefore, a successful credit risk rating system that covers material exposures across a bank will necessarily be quite complex, with numerous distinct models.

This points to a second goal of a credit risk rating system: It is not enough to accurately measure risk; it also must provide the bank with a unified view of its credit risk. It needs to ensure that a rating system permits the simple aggregation of risk—by obligor, portfolio, line of business, and product type—and thus allow the institution to make decisions based on solid estimation of the credit risk being taken. Simply put, being "right" is not enough. The system must be easily understood by a wide range of people and be useful for management decision taking.

For the user, this means that it should behave in an intuitive and predictive fashion. For example, a system that generates dramatically different risk ratings, without explanation for credits that seem identical to the credit officer considering the loans, damages the credibility of the model and makes it difficult to employ as a decision-support tool.

Unconstrained model development also runs the risk of creating a black-box solution; to the extent possible, a new rating system (joined with good internal training) should produce results with which people are intuitively comfortable and be capable of providing guidance on why discrepancies have arisen. At times, this will require a high-level design decision regarding the balance between complexity and clarity within the institution.

While complexity can add to a model's predictive power, it can also reduce organizational buy-in by making the system less intuitive, dramatically reducing its practical value. Good rating systems should improve process efficiency by reducing process costs and freeing time for sales and relationship management. All of these points require trust in the rating system—users must be confident that it works—with validation and back-testing as crucial elements in achieving this.

Designing a system to include all the qualities listed above is challenging, because it involves both a technical excellence during the development stage and potentially far-reaching organizational and cultural realignments.

Components of a Successful System

There are three key dimensions to a risk rating system, as seen in Figure 1. To be effective, a system must be successful in all three dimensions:

1. *Ratings scale* addresses the institution-wide metric against which all assets will be compared.
2. *Ratings assignment* addresses the actual ratings process.
3. *Validation* addresses confidence in the system, both internally and externally.

Ratings scale. A risk rating system uses an objective scale to rank credits according to risk. In defining the scale, we answer three questions:

- What does a given rating mean?
- How many ratings should there be?
- To which credits does the scale apply?

The ultimate goal is to provide a measure of the loss expected for booking a credit and the capital required to support it. By examining the ratings of any two credits in a portfolio, we would like to know which credit is riskier and the expected loss associated with each. Obviously, if we can answer the second question, we know the answer to the first. As mentioned, many credit rating systems perform well in defining credit risk on a relative basis but poorly in gauging an absolute level of expected loss of each.

Most rating systems use a two-dimensional scale to solve this problem, with the PD and the LGD being quantified separately (consistent with the proposed Basel II guidelines). The first dimension, PD, is primarily determined by the obligor characteristics. The second dimension estimates how the facility structure affects the LGD.

Figure 1
The Three Parts of a Credit Risk Rating System

Ratings Scale	Ratings Assignment	Validation / Refinement
• What does a rating mean? • How many ratings are there? • Which credits does the scale apply to?	• How are ratings assigned for each business unit? • Who assigns the rating? • What tools are used in the assignment process?	• How are ratings validated? • What data is needed for validation and model refinement? • Who is responsible for the analyses?

A key element in the definition of a ratings scale is the determination of the appropriate level of granularity. Each grade should have markedly (and measurably) different risk characteristics. If the level of granularity is too small (in other words, there are too few grades), the system will not be a useful decision-support tool for management. Conversely, too much granularity may lead to a false sense of accuracy (with models assumed better than they in fact are) or too much detail as a basis for management's strategic decisions.

Finally, an effective ratings scale must be applicable across the bank's entire credit portfolio. Banks should strive to rate all exposures, but often this is not the case. Specific credit exposures can be overlooked, such as letters of credit or the counterparty credit risk arising from trading positions.

To get an accurate profile of an institution's credit risk exposure, every credit exposure needs a comparable risk rating. The key is to use a "master scale"—a single scale to which all counterparties are mapped. It should be noted that having such a universal ratings scale does not imply that all asset classes use the entire scale. For example, you would expect corporate loans to be concentrated at the top end of the scale (with low probability of default) and retail loans to be concentrated toward the lower-middle part of the scale.

Ratings assignment. After the ratings scale is defined, it is necessary to choose an approach for assigning ratings to counterparties. This raises several issues:

- How are ratings assigned for each business unit?
- Who assigns the ratings?
- Which tools are used in the assignment process?

The answers to these questions typically differ by business unit.

Figure 2 classifies alternative ratings approaches. Banks use a mixture of these, depending on customer type. The choice between methods should depend on their cost-benefit

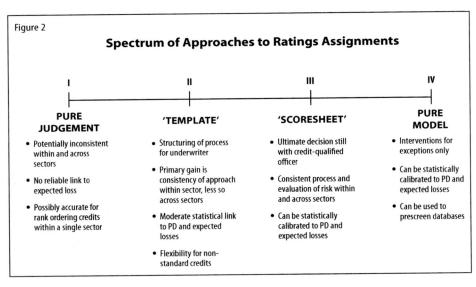

Figure 2

Spectrum of Approaches to Ratings Assignments

I	II	III	IV
PURE JUDGEMENT	**'TEMPLATE'**	**'SCORESHEET'**	**PURE MODEL**
• Potentially inconsistent within and across sectors	• Structuring of process for underwriter	• Ultimate decision still with credit-qualified officer	• Interventions for exceptions only
• No reliable link to expected loss	• Primary gain is consistency of approach within sector, less so across sectors	• Consistent process and evaluation of risk within and across sectors	• Can be statistically calibrated to PD and expected losses
• Possibly accurate for rank ordering credits within a single sector	• Moderate statistical link to PD and expected losses	• Can be statistically calibrated to PD and expected losses	• Can be used to prescreen databases
	• Flexibility for non-standard credits		

characteristics. For example, the use of extensive financial and nonfinancial (subjective) data may result in increased accuracy, but can slow the process, thereby adding cost.

Such analyses should be used only when the benefits from the marginal increase in accuracy are great. This applies to corporate lending, where many banks use a combination of financial and subjective information to drive a scoresheet approach to assigning ratings. In some cases, the scoresheets may also be supplemented by a model-based approach, such as Moody's RiskCalc. Conversely, where the marginal benefit of increased accuracy at an individual asset level is not as great—for example, in small business lending—banks are making aggressive use of pure model approaches, similar to those used for managing retail credit card portfolios.

There should be a clear articulation of responsibility for ratings assignment. The best mechanism for achieving this will differ not only from business line to business line but also from bank to bank. At some banks, ratings assignments for corporate and/or commercial credits will be undertaken by the line, by the credit function, or jointly. For retail portfolios, it's common for centralized underwriting to assign ratings. The key is to ensure that it's made clear who is responsible for assigning the relevant ratings, be it line, credit, or centralized underwriting, and that whoever assigns the rating thoroughly understands the ratings approach.

Validation. A key but often overlooked part of a ratings system is a well-defined process for ensuring it is working well. Three questions must be answered:

1. How are ratings validated?
2. What data is needed for validation and model refinement?
3. Who is responsible for the analysis?

The first two questions are answered jointly, since validation requires data. In fact, Basel II is explicit about the need to validate internal ratings with historical data. Validation—the process of ensuring that the ratings are accurately conveying the bank's credit risk—includes the following:

- **Checking accuracy of ratings.** For example, are the model's predicted results consistent with the default history of the bank? If not, are the models inappropriate, being misused, or miscalibrated (both for PD and LGD)?
- **Checking raters' performance.** For example, if there is a subjective component in the ratings process, does the rater's judgment improve the ratings or not?
- **Checking applicability of models and tools.** For example, has enough data been collected for further refinements? Are there newly available vended models that outperform the current one?

Without an effective process of validation, ratings will never provide confidence, either internally or externally (and will not be accepted by regulators for the purpose of capital allocation). At a minimum, the required data for these analyses should be explicitly specified and data-capture systems should be implemented to collect the data.

It should be noted that all the data in the world is worthless unless someone within the bank reviews and analyzes it. Banks vary in their approaches, but the responsibility for data analysis must be clearly specified. In some banks, this function is delegated back to the businesses, while in others it is centralized.

What Makes a Risk Rating System Effective?

Nearly all banks have risk rating systems, but not all systems perform well. A sound rating system should improve a bank's downstream tactical and strategic applications. Perversely, this is often an area of unexpected gain—ratings are improved for regulatory reasons but are subsequently found to pay off in other areas. Banks miss substantial opportunities if they view the development of credit ratings primarily as a regulatory compliance issue. Robust credit rating systems have the potential for significant bottom-line impact and improved shareholder value creation. Some examples of value-adding applications are given in Figure 3.

An effective risk rating system should bolster these applications and processes. Those that do so exhibit certain features:

Consistency within a portfolio. Two individual raters independently evaluating a credit package should assign the same rating (or very close), assuming that both have the same information. Inconsistency of intra-portfolio ratings negatively affects the efficiency of approvals and pricing and may generate disagreements between the line and credit functions.

Consistency across portfolios. Credit risk should be discussed across the entire organization in common terms, facilitated by the use of the central master scale. Inconsistency in the measurement of risk across portfolios undermines most portfolio-

Figure 3	
Applications That Rely on Risk Ratings	
Process/Decision	Credit Risk Rating System Role
Approval (new applications)	Measure risk Test pricing adequacy
Syndications	Pricing deal Increase market share in relation to risk appetite
Limit Setting	Assist in determining capital cost of increased concentration
Capital Management	Loss forecasting and provisioning Capital requirements
Risk Transfer	Benefits of risk transfer depends on estimate of risk
RAROC	Determine risk-adjusted profits Economic capital estimates a function of risk
Customer Profitability Measurement	Estimate of customer-level risk-adjusted profit

level decisions and processes and severely impairs the credibility and usefulness of bank-wide RAROC / SVA systems.

Granularity. To effectively distinguish between risk levels, ratings systems need a fairly high level of granularity, with increased granularity in the portfolio sub-segments having a high concentration of credit. Many first-generation rating tools with between five and 10 pass grades are unsuitable for value-adding applications, such as risk-adjusted pricing, portfolio management, and securitization initiatives. Independent of regulatory pressure, most banks have already been increasing the granularity of their risk-rating systems to meet competitive needs.

Calibration. A risk rating system should be calibrated to the bank's own historical experience. Improper calibration leads to incorrect measures of credit risk and potentially value-destroying decisions being taken. It also undermines the system's credibility, since one should expect the line to notice that the ratings are not providing accurate information on the bank's own experienced losses. Calibration, like validation, requires data and should be an ongoing process with regular refinement as increased data becomes available.

Speed and accuracy. Speed is a highly desirable goal but sometimes is obtained only at the cost of accuracy, particularly in judgmental systems. When specifically analyzed, banks are often surprised by the costs of origination, approval, and monitoring. Faster processes are favorable, since they reduce these costs and improve the customer's experience with banks. The key is to optimize the potential trade-off between speed and accuracy.

Benefits of a Leading-Edge Ratings System

Implementation of leading-edge risk rating systems can have substantial costs. These include development staff (internal and external), software/modeling costs, IT and infrastructure costs, and training costs. Given these not inconsiderable costs, banks should expect significant benefits from ratings system implementation in addition to regulatory compliance. Substantial benefits can be achieved as applications leverage a leading-edge ratings system, including a reduction in risk cost, increased risk-adjusted profitability, and cost reduction through credit process redesign.

Reduction in risk cost. Banks face two costs of credit risk: expected losses and the cost of the capital required to protect the bank against the volatility of losses. The direct benefit from introducing an improved rating system is the reduction in credit losses due to improved asset selection and the avoidance of "winner's curse," whereby a bank that systematically misprices loans suffers from negative selection.

An indirect benefit from improved rating systems is the more efficient use of economic capital through improved portfolio composition. Active management of the credit portfolio, underpinned by robust risk and valuation metrics, can dramatically improve risk-return characteristics. In many instances, it also can lead to a reduction of loss volatility—and consequently economic capital consumption—by 20% to 30%. The proposed Basel II guidelines provide an additional regulatory carrot, whereby banks with more advanced credit rating systems will also enjoy reduced regulatory capital requirements as applied to their lending activities.

Increased risk-adjusted profitability. Generally, we expect enhanced credit risk measurement to boost risk-adjusted profitability by supporting improvements in pricing discipline. Risk-adjusted pricing facilitates the cherry-picking of higher-quality credits from banks with less robust risk measurement capabilities and also ensures adequate compensation from riskier credits. It is possible to realize risk-adjusted improvements in profitability of 10 to 15 basis points of assets per year through these mechanisms. The net present value of this benefit, assuming a 15% discount rate, is 80 to 90 basis points of assets minus the fixed costs associated with the project.

Cost reduction through credit process redesign. Leading-edge risk rating systems allow banks to reduce costs in many credit-related processes. The key benefit of ratings tools is that they allow the streamlining of the entire credit process along risk-adjusted lines. Simply cutting costs across the board may, in the long term, actually increase losses as appropriate controls are compromised. Instead, efforts are reconcentrated on the areas where additional, costly assessments have the greatest payback.

The approvals process, in relation to low-risk transactions, can be semi-automated while efforts are reconcentrated on those deals for which the bank expects greater losses or there is most uncertainty. The same approach can be taken throughout the value chain—from approvals, through monitoring, to recoveries—but only if the risk inherent in each credit is well measured. Banks that have been aggressive in credit process redesign have seen large cost reductions in credit-related processes. In many instances, banks have reduced credit-related expenses by 25% to 30%.

Conclusion

Having reviewed the Basel II guidelines relating to internal credit risk models, many credit risk managers at banks globally are faced with the reality that their internal risk-rating systems fall short of what is necessary for compliance. Which options are available? What are the costs and benefits of each? The answers to these questions are constrained by available time, data, IT systems, and organizational needs.

In the perfect situation, highly customized ratings systems with internally calibrated, quantitative models can be designed and rolled out. This may be desirable for the many banks that are already partway there. For others, this may be impractical. Regardless of the approach, all models need to follow the same basic outline. The benefits generated from putting in such a system can far outweigh the costs, even without considering the regulatory advantages, and the value of such a system can only increase.

A Practical Review and Test of Default Prediction Models

By Jorge R. Sobehart and Sean C. Keenan

ompetitive, legal, and regulatory pressures continuously demand more sophisticated approaches to managing credit risk in commercial lending and investment. Quantitative credit risk models that detect a broader spectrum of stressful conditions are key to the monitoring and managing functions required for active portfolio risk management.

While such models can offer timelier, wider, and more cost-effective coverage than teams of professional analysts, their performance characteristics are not well known. Various commercial vendors now offer competitive products with claims of precise anticipation of default events and major changes in value. Recently, tests of portfolio management rules based on a commercial product, performed by JP Morgan Credit Strategy, suggest that some of these claims are incorrect or exaggerated.[1]

First There Was Altman, Then There Was Merton

By the mid-1980s, there were two main approaches to quantitative default risk modeling: 1) the statistical approach pioneered by Edward I. Altman in 1968, and 2) the contingent claims analysis, or CCA, approach of Robert C. Merton and others in 1974.

Altman's statistical approach, which is based on fundamental credit information, uses econometric techniques to determine the relationship between the event of default on obligations and market information, accounting variables, and credit opinions such as ratings.

CCA is a structural approach based on an option-theoretic view of the firm's equity and liabilities. Merton showed that a firm's equity could be viewed as a call option on the firm with the strike price equal to the face value of its debt. That is, a firm's default risk could be modeled with the same approach used (by Fischer Black and Myron C. Scholes in 1973) to price an option using stock prices and a few key parameters taken from the firm's balance sheet.

Unfortunately, even models with sound theoretical underpinnings, such as CCA, often show poor power in predicting default events in precisely those cases where these models should hold strongest. CCA models also are limited in performance during periods of volatile markets (they provide too many sell signals or "false positives" for default prediction). In addition, they are unreliable in predicting credit spreads and bond prices. This is largely the result of simplifications and abstractions required to make the CCA models tractable, but which are unrealistic and tend to seriously degrade model performance in practice.

And Then Came the Hybrids

By the late 1990s, a third approach had emerged that acknowledged not only the value of timely information like stock prices and volatility, but also the importance of fundamental credit information. This third approach led to the introduction of "hybrid" models (see note 1 at the end of this article). The key idea underlying hybrid models is that default is a contextual event.

No credit officer would ever extend credit solely on the basis of a strong stock price or low stock volatility, nor would credit extension be ruled out by a sudden drop in the market value of equity as implied by idealized CCA models. Hybrid models show that, while market equity information can be extremely valuable, it is most useful when it is coupled with an understanding and explicit consideration of the fundamental information about the firm and its business environment. A detailed examination of a firm's balance sheet, income statement, and cash flows remains a critical component of credit risk assessment.

Finally, because the additional accounting and credit information is not used to forecast equity prices but to enhance the definition of the event of default, hybrid models do not contradict any hypothesis regarding market efficiency or the no-arbitrage conditions required in CCA models. This offers great flexibility to overcoming the limitations of standard models without undermining the theoretical underpinnings of the model.

Now that commercial applications of hybrid models have become available, it is important to contrast their performance with the market-dominant CCA models. This requires answering two questions:

1. How accurately do CCA models describe actual default experience?
2. How well does this compare with the hybrid models?

Performance Testing

Alternative hybrid models have drawn the attention of financial institutions and commercial vendors for good reason: one study's conclusion that they could have provided early warning signals for such high-visibility cases as Xerox, Owens Corning, Edison International and PG&E, and many others.[2] This study, by Sobehart, Stein, Mikityanskaya, and Li, found that additional information could improve the predictive power of a Merton model, providing a more robust model of credit quality.

A second study, by Kealhofer and Kurbat, actively criticizes the hybrid nature of the model, concluding that agency ratings and additional market and financial information do not add any power to options pricing-based models,[3] findings that squarely contradict those of the first study. Despite the authors' claims, however, their empirical tests do not actually compare any version of the Merton model to a hybrid model, but rather compare their own Merton model (KMV implementation) to a handful of accounting ratios, Moody's ratings, and a simple Merton model reported in the literature.

A review of the empirical tests[4] has indicated that the methodology and conclusions of Kealhofer and Kurbat are biased as a result of several factors, including:

- The incorrect specification of the hypothesis to be tested.
- An incorrect inference about the performance of hybrid models based on an unrelated model.[5]

This article compares their version of the Merton model to the published hybrid model using U.S. nonfinancial firms, including both rated and not-rated obligors. Both models produce estimated default probabilities over a one-year time horizon, known as expected default frequency (EDF) and expected default probability (EDP), respectively.

The study's data set contains the following:

* More than 27,000 firm-year pairs of annual observations for both models for the period December 1995 to December 1999. Each pair of observations measures the obligors' credit quality at the beginning of the following year.
* 349 default events occurring during the period January 1996 to December 2000. The numbers of firm-year observations and defaults in each specific year are listed below.

Distribution of Firms and Defaults

Year	Firm-years	Defaults
1996	5,099	41
1997	5,361	50
1998	5,713	95
1999	5,755	101
2000	5,487	62
Total	**27,415**	**349**

The observations were ordered by model output—from riskier to safer—and the defaults used were those that occurred within the following 12 months of each annual observation.

Figure 1 shows the cumulative fraction of defaults as a function of the ordered population of obligors. Interpretation of this plot is straightforward; the higher and steeper the curve, the better the model is at differentiating between defaulters and healthy firms.

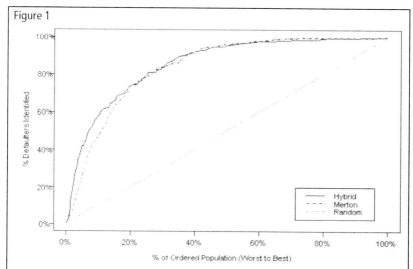

Figure 1

Power curves compare the overall default predictive performance of any default prediction model. The higher and steeper the curve, the better the model is at differentiating between defaulters and healthy firms.

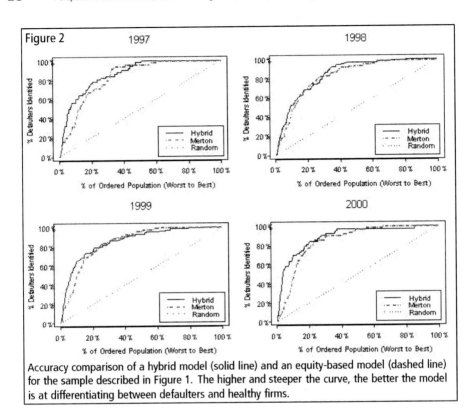

Accuracy comparison of a hybrid model (solid line) and an equity-based model (dashed line) for the sample described in Figure 1. The higher and steeper the curve, the better the model is at differentiating between defaulters and healthy firms.

Figure 2 shows similar accuracy curves for individual years, indicating that the hybrid model outperforms the equity-based model consistently.[6] Figures 1 and 2 suggest that hybrid models improve over state-of-the-art commercial applications of options pricing models, reducing the number of false positives (or sell signals).

From the practitioner's point of view, Figure 2 tells a very compelling story. More precisely, it shows that the misspecification of CCA models is more apparent for high-risk firms and becomes most severe as we approach the very point these models were designed to identify. By introducing additional credit information specifically to enhance the identification of the case-specific default point, hybrid models are able to overcome some of these limitations and can increase model performance in the critical near-default region. The result is a more reliable tool for analyzing the risk of firms in the most profitable segment of credit quality.

Why Hybrid Models Should Work Better

In the standard CCA framework ruled by idealized efficient markets, credit assessment simply reduces to identifying changes in stock prices and volatility as a reliable source of credit quality information. This results in a shortsighted understanding of credit quality based on unrealistic assumptions about the actual dynamics of the debt markets and the role of arbitrage.[7]

In the real world of lending, value uncertainty and potential arbitrage situations are rampant because most institutions' assets and liabilities do not possess the same idealized characteristics and liquidity required by CCA models. For example, unlike true option sales, the issuance of debt is not associated with any bona fide hedging activity that would tend to result in a high volume of incremental reallocative trades. Practically speaking, large denominations and thin trading in the bond and loan markets, against a backdrop of fluctuating stock prices, are inconsistent with the idealized conception of debt holders as writers of perfectly liquid options on the unobservable assets of the firm proposed in pure CCA models.

Another key problem with CCA models based on market equity stems from the fact that even fully informed equity prices are marginal prices and, therefore, primarily reflect marginal reallocative supply-and-demand conditions rather than the value of the firm's aggregate capital stock.

Differing views on the best deployment of the firm's assets can create a "control premium" and a steep supply curve for equity shares. The huge price swings that accompany takeover bids prove this point. Tightly controlled firms with inefficiently deployed assets may trade at a discount. The opposite situation, where equity trades at a hefty premium, can also occur as a result of speculative valuation, such as during the dot-com and telecom frenzies. It's unknown how much these supply-and-demand effects may be affecting market prices, so they are a potential source of uncertainty for equity valuation.[8]

This issue is fundamental in the credit risk context because commercial applications of CCA models estimate the implied market value of the firm's assets and volatility from stock prices, which are then used to estimate probabilities of default or credit spreads. Therefore, it is important to understand how the uncertainty of equity and debt markets can bias these estimates of credit quality. For example, a market correction might reflect a change in investors' preferences that could generate a sudden decrease in the firm's stock price without necessarily implying an increase in the firm's probability of default, as models derived within the CCA framework would indicate.

Anyone familiar with commercial applications of the CCA framework (such as the models in Figure 1) would notice that the swings in stock volatility over the last couple of years were not followed by a surge in defaults to the extent predicted by these models. Furthermore, equity-based models frequently assign speculative-grade ratings (probabilities of default) to well-known investment-grade corporations and financial institutions. This effect is exacerbated during periods characterized by stock market volatility. During these periods it is not unusual for equity-based models to assign a low credit score to a large fraction of the population of firms, generating undesirable sell signals or "false positive" default events as shown in Figure 2.

A hypothetical example, based on the standard Merton model, illustrates this point. An additional source of equity volatility was included to simulate the uncertainty of investors. Then, the European call option formula from the Merton model was inverted to obtain implied values of the firm's assets and volatility as a function of the true assets and volatility, as well as the par value of debt (the "exercise price" of the option).

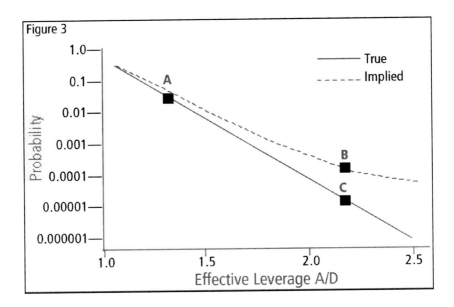

Finally, the probability of default was calculated using the true assets and volatility of the firm and the values implied from equity with the additional source of randomness. Figure 3 shows the probability of default—for a one-year time horizon—as a function of the firm's effective leverage obtained with the true value A and volatility of the firm's assets and the face value of debt D. Figure 3 also shows the probability of default as a function of the leverage estimated with the assets' value and volatility "implied" from equity using the Merton model with an additional source of noise.

Note that for highly leveraged firms (point A in Figure 3) the probabilities of default for true and implied values are similar. However, for highly capitalized firms (point C) the probability of default obtained by using implied assets and volatility assigns a lower credit quality (point B) to these firms than it should. Thus, pure equity-based models of risky debt can easily misclassify investment-grade firms as speculative-grade firms when markets are volatile. This is a consequence of the additional uncertainty introduced by the market participants, which is erroneously interpreted as asset volatility by contingent claims models.

These models will always make these errors because they are based on the assumption that market participants are perfectly informed, and stock prices can only reflect "true" changes in the value of the firm's underlying assets rather than marginal reallocative supply-and-demand conditions. Because hybrid models provide a more comprehensive credit assessment that combines market information and accounting information, they help reduce the impact of valuation uncertainty and model bias discussed above, as evidenced by their superior default predictive performance shown in Figures 1 and 2.

The Bottom Line

It seems natural that information widely used by credit analysts and loan officers should play a role in a quantitative default prediction model. Such information can improve the performance of contingent claims analysis models. But can this more traditional credit information be brought to bear on the practical monitoring and managing of risky credits without giving up the advantages in speed and coverage of a quantitative model?

The answer is a resounding yes. Hybrid models that do make use of such information outperform their market-based counterparts in terms of identifying future defaulters and avoiding false positive signals. They do this without sacrificing speed or coverage. The additional inputs they require are more easily and cheaply obtained than those needed for the CCA part of the model.

Finally, because these models can also be used to assist institutions in determining capital requirements, even a marginal improvement over an existing model can generate huge capital savings and an immediate improvement in an institution's risk-adjusted return on capital.

Notes

1. M. King, "Using Equities to Price Credit," JP Morgan Credit Strategy (London), September 2001.
2. J.R. Sobehart, R. Stein, V. Mikityanskaya, and L. Li, "Moody's Public Firm Risk Model: A Hybrid Approach to Modeling Short Term Default Risk," Moody's Investors Service, Rating Methodology, March 2000.
3. S. Kealhofer and M. Kurbat, "The Default Prediction Power of the Merton Approach, Relative to Debt Ratings and Accounting Variables," KMV Corporation, 2001.
4. J.R. Sobehart and S.C. Keenan, "Understanding Hybrid Models of Default Risk," working paper, Citigroup Risk Architecture, 2001.
5. A. Boral and E. Falkenstein, "Revisiting Mr. Merton," *Risk Professional* 3, 2001.
6. A more detailed comparison of these models is reported in S. Boras, "The Performance of Vendor Market-Based Credit Risk Measures in North America," internal report, Citigroup Risk Architecture, 2001.
7. M. Fridson, "Anomaly in Intercapital Pricing?" Merrill Lynch High Yield, October 14, 1999.
8. M. Fridson and J.G. Jonsson, "Contingent Claims Analysis," *Journal of Portfolio Management*, Winter 1997.

References

Altman, E. I., 1968, "Financial Ratios, Discriminant Analysis and the Prediction of Corporate Bankruptcy," *Journal of Finance*, September.

Basel Committee on Banking Supervision, 2001, "The New Basel Capital Accord: An Explanatory Note" and "The Internal Ratings-Based Approach (Consultative Document)," January.

Black F., and M. Scholes, 1973, "The Pricing of Options and Corporate Liabilities," *Journal of Political Economy* 81.

Kealhofer, S., 1999, "Credit Risk and Risk Management," Association for Investment Management and Research, Charlottesville, Virginia.

Merton R., 1974, "On the Pricing of Corporate Debt: The Risk Structure of Interest Rates," *Journal of Finance* 29.

Sobehart J.R., and S.C. Keenan, 1999, "Equity Market Value and Its Importance for Credit Analysis: Facts and Fiction," working paper.

Sobehart J.R., and S.C. Keenan, 2001, "The Impact of Valuation Uncertainty in the Pricing of Risky Debt," working paper, Citigroup Risk Architecture.

Estimating Probability of Default via External Data Sources: A Step Toward Basel II

By Nadeem A. Siddiqi and
Shelley B. Klein

Banks considering their strategies for compliance with the Basel II Capital Accord will likely use external data sources for estimating probability of default as part of the solution. But definitions and characteristics must be consistent, or adjusted to be so, if the external data is to be an effective and statistically useful supplement to internal data.

Banks that do not have the most sophisticated methods of calculating risk capital as required by Basel II are attempting to employ the foundation internal ratings-based (IRB) approach proposed in Basel II. To calculate regulatory capital, banks must determine the probabilities of default associated with their portfolios and then apply regulator-determined loss given default and exposure at default rates.

One seemingly simple approach banks can take is to use default probability rates available from major external rating agencies such as Standard and Poor's (S&P) and Moody's Financial Services.

However, banks need to be careful when using this data as proxies for specific loan portfolios:

1. They need to understand the method of calculating default to ensure that it matches both the bank's philosophy and processes.
2. They must be careful in matching the characteristics and structures of the loans with those of the underlying bonds from the published default studies, especially for loans below investment grade, which may require specific adjustments.
3. Some loan grades have little published default data available, and banks may need to extrapolate their default rates from available data.

Capitalizing on continuous advances in technology and analytical methods, Basel II is prompting banks to learn more about quantitative credit risk measurement. Many banks will respond by using external data to calculate risk capital.

Basel II offers three different ways of determining risk capital:

1. The standardized approach, which applies industry-based averages to different asset classes and is most suitable for very small banks that have a relatively homogenous asset base and lack the resources to meet regulatory requirements for internally calculating risk.
2. The foundation IRB approach, whereby banks need to internally estimate part of the risk calculation formula, with the rest being determined by (conservative) regulator-determined rules. This approach may be suitable for small and

medium-sized banks looking to get a foothold in the advanced approach without having the resources to commit to it fully.

3. The advanced IRB approach allows banks to fully estimate the risk and regulatory capital requirements internally. The obvious advantage of using the advanced IRB approach is that if a well-managed bank calculates its capital requirements for itself, and its risk profile requires less capital than the conservative regulator-determined charges, more capital will be freed for other uses, thus improving overall profitability.

Recent Default Activity

The poor global and domestic economic environment that prevailed in 2001 resulted in record defaults. During that year, S&P observed 216 defaults on approximately $116 billion of debt. These defaults represented a record 4.09% of all rated issuers at the beginning of the year. This default ratio surpassed the previous record of 4.01%, set in 1991.[1] In addition to a generally weak global economy, an abundance of recently issued speculative-grade debt, particularly in the leisure time/media and telecom sectors, contributed to the very high default rate.

To reflect the changing economic environment and the associated increases in defaults, yield spreads on highly speculative debt widened to a point where costs associated with issuing debt at such levels were prohibitive to most prospective issuers. To lower their cost of capital, many issuers have been forced to use alternative debt structures. In some cases, issuers provide collateral when issuing debt, or issuing securitizations, to receive higher credit ratings. A number of issuers have also issued debt with structures, including interest reserves, which ensure interest payments to investors for a number of years after issuance. Table 1 provides historical corporate default rates for the past 20 years.

The Basic Process

The risk calculation process outlined in Basel II for those institutions seeking to apply one of the IRB approaches is also composed of three parts. First, the probability of default (PD) must be obtained. Second, the loss given default (LGD) must be established. Finally, the exposure at default (EAD) must be estimated. The foundation IRB approach requires banks to estimate only the PD, while the LGD and EAD are determined by regulatory guidance.

In this article, we focus on one methodology that can be used to estimate the probabilities of default without committing substantial internal resources, to utilize the foundation IRB approach to regulatory capital calculation, as well as to check any internal calculations under the advanced IRB approach.

In risk management processes used by virtually all banks, commercial loans are assigned a credit rating. These credit ratings can be letter grades or numerical grades covering multiple states. A mapping of these bank credit ratings can then be made to bond ratings published by rating agencies such as S&P and Moody's. Once this mapping is complete, any loan can then be given an equivalent S&P rating, for example, based on

Table 1

Corporate Defaults Rates—All Ratings, 1982 through 2001

Year	Default Rate (%)	Number of Defaults	Total Debt Defaulting ($ Billions)
1982	1.26	18	0.9
1983	0.68	10	0.4
1984	0.83	13	0.4
1985	1.09	18	0.3
1986	1.69	32	0.5
1987	0.93	19	1.6
1988	1.49	32	3.3
1989	1.75	39	7.3
1990	2.86	64	21.2
1991	4.01	88	23.6
1992	1.35	31	5.4
1993	0.86	22	2.4
1994	0.62	18	2.3
1995	0.97	32	9.0
1996	0.56	20	2.7
1997	0.59	23	4.9
1998	1.26	56	11.3
1999	2.19	108	37.8
2000	2.56	132	42.3
2001	4.09	216	116.1

Source: Standard and Poor's, *Special Report - Record Defaults in 2001 the Result of Poor Credit Quality and a Weak Economy.*

the internal bank rating. Then, based on the applicant's credit rating, historical default observations from S&P may be used to estimate the probability and potential timing of default. Thus starting from existing internal bank ratings of commercial loans, probabilities of default can be attached.

A Few Kinks

While this process of obtaining default probabilities from external data vendors seems straightforward, several caveats are in order. First, most of the empirical work on corporate defaults thus far has concentrated on publicly traded bonds. Due to the private nature of the loan market, there is limited publicly available data on loan defaults. Second, since loan portfolios vary from bank to bank, even if a reasonable default database were available, it would be inappropriate to generalize these results for the entire market.[2]

What this implies is that external default data must be carefully scrutinized for suitability prior to applying it to any particular bank's portfolio. This scrutiny should center around at least two dimensions: default calculation methodology and characteristics of the instruments.

Default Calculation Methodology

At least two different methodologies have been used to estimate default probabilities in the commercial sector. S&P's standard default curves use static pools. As used by S&P, the static pool assesses the default rates of all bonds of a given bond rating, regardless of age.[3]

The S&P default rates do not take into account the age of an issuance. Default curves obtained from S&P's CreditPro database do not reflect a *new issue* bias. New-issue bias refers to the expected results of the hypothesis that an issuer that has just received a substantial cash inflow from a bond offering or loan is not likely to default in the near term, regardless of the issuer's credit rating. A new-issue bias would be expected to reduce marginal default rates in the first three years subsequent to the issuance of new debt, with the effect growing more pronounced as the credit quality declines.

To address this concern, Professor Edward Altman from New York University developed a series of default curves based on this new-issue-bias hypothesis. As stated in *Managing Credit Risk: The Next Great Financial Challenge*, "The aging effect is intuitively sound, since most companies have a great deal of cash just after they issue a bond. Even if their operating cash flow is negative, they are usually able to meet several periods of interest payments."[4] S&P also notes that "relatively few issuers default early in their rated history."[5]

Similar to S&P's default analysis, Altman grouped his analysis according to credit-rating cohorts. However, Altman's analysis differed in that his cohorts were organized by issuers with the same original rating at issuance, as opposed to issuers with the same ratings as of a random observation date (that is, static pools). He developed his default probability curves by measuring defaults in a particular period relative to the base population in the same period.

Therefore, depending on the number of observed issuers within each cohort at the beginning of the year that could possibly default during the year, the denominator used to calculate the probabilities of default may change every year. This methodology was based on the actuarial methodologies used by insurance companies and was named the *marginal mortality rate methodology* (MMR).

This methodology also differs significantly from S&P's analysis in that Altman measured the magnitude of default as the dollar value of defaults as a percentage of the total dollar value of debt rated at the beginning of the period. S&P differs in its methodology by measuring the number of issuers that have defaulted as a percentage of all the issuers rated at the beginning of the measurement period. Altman's data tends to be more volatile from year to year, especially when significant bonds default, such as the multi-billion-dollar Texaco default in 1987 or the Enron default in 2001.

The seven-year cumulative default rates implied by the two methodologies are shown in Table 2. The difference in marginal default rates over the first few years between the two methodologies is clearly visible, and the difference gets more pronounced as the credit quality declines.

Table 2

Cumulative Default Rates

Year	1	2	3	4	5	6	7
S&P Credit Pro							
A	0.04	0.12	0.18	.027	0.43	0.28	.072
BBB	0.29	.068	.098	1.52	2.04	2.42	2.84
BB	1.07	2.97	5.27	7.26	8.94	10.73	11.82
B	9.29	18.21	24.22	27.71	30.23	32.47	33.99
CCC	24.72	33.06	38.40	42.60	46.87	48.48	49.62
Altman's MMR							
A	0.00	0.00	0.03	0.15	0.21	0.23	.025
BBB	0.02	0.31	0.58	1.25	1.49	1.89	1.99
BB	0.38	1.13	3.78	5.26	7.56	8.49	10.50
B	1.16	4.15	9.75	15.30	19.21	21.62	23.82
CCC	2.06	15.6	28.51	34.53	36.52	42.71	44.91

Table 3 indicates that, historically, issuers that received funds at speculative ratings tended to avoid default for longer periods compared with issuers who may have issued debt at higher ratings but subsequently slid down the rating scale because of financial difficulties. For example, Table 3 indicates that issuers who received an initial rating of CCC and eventually defaulted have taken, on average, 3.1 years to default (CCC; "Average Years from Original Rating"). Conversely, issuers who had a last rating of CCC and eventually defaulted (but may have had a higher rating when they issued debt) typically defaulted within five months of receiving the CCC rating (CCC; "Average Years from Last Rating").

Table 3

Time to Default by Rating Category

Original Rating	Average Years from Original Rating	Last Rating	Average Years from Last Rating
AAA	8.0	**AAA**	N.A.
AA	11.9	**AA**	N.A.
A	10.7	**A**	N.A.
BBB	7.4	**BBB**	1.3
BB	5.1	**BB**	1.5
B	3.8	**B**	1.3
CCC	3.1	**CCC**	0.4
N.R.	N.A.	**N.R.**	3.3
Total	4.7	**Total**	1.1

Problems with both methodologies begin to emerge for the highly speculative issuances below CCC (CCC-, CC, and C). Whether using static pools or first rating cohorts, there is no data available for ratings below CCC. While cumulative and marginal default probability data is available from S&P for CCC-rated debt, no default rates are provided by S&P for any ratings below CCC. Default rates will therefore need to be extrapolated by banks for credit ratings below CCC. Hence, it should be noted that any comparisons made and conclusions drawn at the CCC level need to be tempered by considering the lack of data points at this rating level.

Instrument/Structure Characteristics

The second dimension that needs to be scrutinized before default probabilities can be applied to bank portfolios is the characteristics of the loans in the bank portfolio relative to those of the bonds in the published default studies. This is especially the case for speculative-rated debt, whose specific structures greatly affect the cash flow. This is probably one reason why, in Table 2, we note that the difference in default rates between the static pool and at-issuance methodologies increases as we move down the credit rating.

In addition to the added liquidity provided by the proceeds of a bond issuance, recently issued bonds, especially speculative bonds, have had structural enhancements such as interest payment guarantees for the first years of the bond's life, or in some cases they have been structured with escrow accounts containing a portion of the bond's interest payments. These factors might contribute to lower initial default rates (and in some cases higher credit ratings). These structural characteristics need to be compared to the loan structures the bank is issuing.

Corporate Bonds versus Syndicated Bank Loans

As noted above, owing to the lack of available data on the historical performance of syndicated bank loans, historical corporate bond performance data has often been used to predict the probability and timing of default that may occur.

Table 4 indicates that, while cumulative default rates for bonds and loans may even out after a number of years, syndicated loans tend to have much higher initial default rates, again especially at speculative ratings. These rates indicate that bond structures may have been substantially different from loan structures. These differences could be due to the use of more complex structures for bond issuances that are designed to pro-

Table 4

Syndicated Bank Loans versus Corporate Bond—At-Issuance Mortality Rates

	Year 1		Year 2		Year 3		Year 4		Year 5	
	Bank	Bond	Bank	Bond	Bank	Bond	Bank	Bond	Bank	Bond
Baa	0.04%	0.00%	0.00%	0.00%	0.00%	0.00%	0.00%	054%	0.00%	0.00%
Ba	0.17%	0.00%	0.60%	0.38%	0.60%	2.30%	0.97%	1.80%	4.89%	0.00%
B	2.30%	0.81%	1.86%	1.97%	2.59%	4.99%	1.79%	1.76%	1.86%	0.00%
Caa	15.24%	2.65%	7.44%	3.09%	13.03%	4.55%	0.00%	21.72%	0.00%	0.00%

Source: Caouette, John B., Altman, Edward I., and Narayanan, Paul. *Managing Credit Risk: The Next Great Financial Challenge.*

tect investors from default during the years immediately following issuances, as well as the typically shorter average maturities for bank debt compared to corporate bonds.

Unfortunately, very little data is available specifically on the historical performances of syndicated bank loans, making it very difficult to verify any of the findings presented in Table 4. Altman notes that "the marginal mortality rate results and its information content concerning the aging effect of corporate loan default rates is not conclusive."[6]

As the liquidity of the secondary whole-loan market increases in the future, so will the quantity and quality of public information available. Until then, it will remain difficult to draw meaningful conclusions, particularly at the speculative end of the credit-rating range.

Notes

1. Standard and Poor's, 2002, "Special Report: Ratings Performance 2001."
2. Altman, E. and H. Suggitt, 2000, "Default Rates in the Syndicated Bank Loan Market: A Mortality Analysis," *Journal of Banking and Finance* 24.
3. Standard and Poor's, 2001, *CreditPro 5.0 User Guide.* According to S&P, a static pool consists of all of the rated obligors on the first day of the year or a quarter and these obligors are followed from that point on. Thus, a static pool is a grouping of obligors whose members remain constant. The results presented in tables with all static pools represent a weighted average based on the number of obligors in each pool and rating category, at the beginning of each period, over a specific time period.
4. Caouette, John B., Edward I. Altman, and Paul Narayanan, 1998, *Managing Credit Risk: The Next Great Financial Challenge.* New York: John Wiley and Sons Inc.
5. Standard and Poor's, 2001, *CreditPro 5.0 User Guide.*
6. Altman and Suggitt, 2000.

Risk-Grading Philosophy: Through-the-Cycle versus Point-in-Time

By Jeremy Taylor

T he issue of cyclicality in an institution's risk-grading system is integral to the system's design and critical to how it gets used.

It's a question that peeks out from various points of discussion in the latest Basel documentation but without ever getting posed—or answered—directly. This is probably because of the innate difficulties in defining and measuring it, as well as the fact that there are both advantages and disadvantages to having risk grades that are stable through the cycle.

Basel's third consultative paper (CP3) implies that risk grade (RG) systems should reflect longer-term considerations:

> *Although the time horizon used in PD estimation is one year... banks must use a longer time horizon in assigning ratings.*[1]

But it also emphasizes the importance of risk grades that are sensitive to underlying changes in credit quality as they occur and, through appropriate stress testing, sensitive to possible downside scenarios.

RG systems are typically ordinal—for example, we know that a RG 5 borrower has a higher likelihood of defaulting than a RG 4 borrower, but we don't know how much higher. It is not until each RG is assigned a probability of default (PD) that we can say how *much* riskier a RG 5 borrower is, thus making the system cardinal.

Because cardinality is becoming increasingly necessary—for pricing, profitability measurement, capital allocations, limits setting, and so forth—it's hard to separate *how cyclically sensitive a bank's risk grade should be* from *translating risk grades into default probabilities.*

We'll begin discussing the first question by assuming static factors: a fixed translation of each RG into a PD (or PD range). Then in the following section we'll discuss how best to come up with that translation. To understand how we go from default to loss estimation, we then need to bring in *cyclicality in recovery rates.*

How Cyclically Sensitive Should a Bank's Risk Grades Be?

We should start by asking what a RG system needs to do:

1. Credit approval—to guide loan structuring, conditions, pricing, and profitability.
2. Credit monitoring at the borrower level—to guide whether additional scrutiny is required, and whether the terms or pricing of a transaction need adjusting/renegotiating as circumstances (including renewal) allow.

3. Credit monitoring at the segment/line of business/portfolio level—to guide the bank's marketing and exit activities and resource allocations, which includes limits setting and approval authorities.
4. Loss reserving and capital planning—as input into the determination of the loan loss allowance, expected loss (EL), and economic capital (EC) requirements.

For the first two roles, it's advantageous to have RGs that reflect the current point in the cycle and thus translate into PDs that are conditioned on how the industry and economy are currently performing. In deciding whether to approve a new transaction, it makes a difference whether the industry in question is nearer a peak or a trough of its cycle. This suggests a point-in-time (PIT) approach, whereby borrowers are re-graded immediately as their fortunes change, whatever the cause.

For the third role, PIT grading has advantages (such as where to look for vulnerable borrowers). At the same time, the strategic issues involved make a longer-term viewpoint more appropriate (to determine resource allocation based on how volatile an industry tends to be over time rather than on where it happens to be today).

The case for cycle-neutral, through-the-cycle (TTC) grading is clearer when we turn to the fourth role. As long as we're facing recurring cyclicality (or *mean reversion*, as we'll explore later) in the portfolio, then EL and EC should be relatively stable with any short-term ups and downs in actual losses around that mean value absorbed by capital. It's because of variability and co-variability in losses that capital is required. EL is intended to represent what the bank might lose on a given customer in a long-run average sense, irrespective of the point in the cycle at which a loan is booked. The provision for credit losses is a cost of doing business and is covered by spread income, leaving a return on the capital employed as a residual.

We'll confine our discussion to changes in credit quality driven by changes in the macro environment. This corresponds to the systematic risk component of the capital asset pricing model. Whatever ratings philosophy a bank adopts, whether PIT or TTC, it's clearly appropriate for any credit quality change that's due to company-specific (idiosyncratic) factors to trigger a grade change.

Where are banks in their ratings philosophy? A 1998 study by William Treacy and Mark Carey, both of the Federal Reserve Board, found that "…[E]very bank we interviewed bases risk ratings on the borrower's current conditions."[2] But because the categorizations are so nebulous, their conclusion regarding the prevalence of PIT grading has to be viewed cautiously. How did the responding bankers interpret the question? Was it just the RGs or also the PDs into which the grades map?

Treacy and Carey cited two likely factors contributing to a PIT orientation: 1) the greater difficulty and cost of grading through the cycle, and 2) banks' relatively short investment horizon. While these factors remain relevant, it is also the case that environmental changes since the time of their study have probably pushed many institutions toward more of a hybrid approach:

- Default and loss experience over the last few years has differed sharply from the preceding few, making a longer-term viewpoint more relevant.
- Regulators have become more sensitive to the subtleties of risk grading, including its role in the capital allocation process.

■ As banks' tools and practices for managing credit risk have grown more sophisticated, banks have paid more attention to data requirements, including shared databases of default and loss information, to allow a still better understanding of underlying patterns and trends.

All of these have had the effect of elevating the importance of RG's fourth role and of injecting into the RG process a longer-term, less cycle-dependent perspective on default estimation. However, banks have been pulled back toward PIT by the growing acceptance of statistical tools to estimate default probabilities, which are typically—though not necessarily—more sensitive to company news and fluctuating fortunes.[3] What it means in practice is that most banks incorporate elements of both and therefore lie somewhere between the extremes of PIT and TTC.

Outside anchors. TTC grading is best exemplified by the rating agencies' approach—though there's certainly not complete stability in agency ratings over a cycle. Ratings are based on a variety of longer-run considerations, both financial and nonfinancial, quantitative and qualitative. Their intent is to capture a company's ability to perform through a typical down cycle for the industry in question, which requires starting with the company's current positioning and then overlaying on that a stress test based on the long-term variability in the industry's default experience.

Banks adopting a TTC approach, or adding TTC elements to their existing procedures, will generally do so less scientifically than this. Of course, it could be very *unscientific*: Just take the long-run average PD for companies in that industry, size group, etc., and assign a RG according to PD range. But trying to "look through the cycle" as a company's performance fluctuates—more in the spirit of Basel—is a challenge. It involves separating cyclical influences from those that are secular (longer-term trend) or seasonal, separating systematic (industry- or economy-wide) factors from those that are idiosyncratic (company specific). It requires more data and analysis than PIT grading. And this is before you even get to the stress-testing part.

However, this is the direction in which Basel is pushing. A company's RG should be based on its competitiveness, financial strength, etc., and then complemented with stress testing to ensure that the rating represents "… the bank's assessment of the borrower's ability and willingness to contractually perform despite adverse economic conditions or the occurrence of unexpected events."[4] If done properly, TTC grades shouldn't change as the industry or economy cycles up and down.

In contrast, the most extreme approach to PIT grading would be to use a market-based default estimation tool like KMV's Credit Monitor or one of the competing products now available. They derive PDs that show high sensitivity to current information as embedded in equity or other public market prices. Products applying to privately held companies show less informational sensitivity,[5] though even there the trend is to try to integrate public market information (such as through peer-group comparables) to enhance predictive power and early detection.

Borrower-level implications. Under a TTC or hybrid (PIT/TTC) approach, a borrower's RG won't be fully sensitive to factors affecting the likelihood of the company defaulting in the next 12 months, such as whether the industry may be at or approaching a cyclical peak. Moving away from full-fledged PIT, there's a trade-off: You give up some

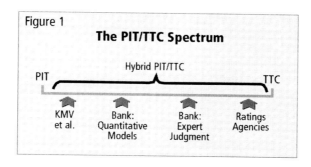

Figure 1
The PIT/TTC Spectrum

true positives (correctly called *problems*) but also some false positives (*Type II errors*, or incorrect calls). From a credit- monitoring viewpoint, the worth of the system is represented by the ratio of true to false positives together with the associated costs to the bank—earlier PIT detection (to reduce exposure and/or LGD) on accounts that go bad and extra, unnecessary monitoring on accounts that don't.

It might not be so bad to have at least some TTC-induced stability in RGs in the face of changing industry or economic conditions as long as there is some additional, early-warning architecture in place. For example:

- Increasingly, banks are obliging lending officers to explain significant discrepancies between a borrower's RG and what a measure like KMV's EDF (expected default frequency) is saying. The emphasis is on large jumps or adverse trends in EDF and on comparison against a peer group of companies, rather than on the latest-month EDF percentage per se.
- Early-warning systems may require lenders to identify in advance key indicators, either qualitative (such as Wal-Mart targeting a new region for expansion, in the case of a customer that's a retail chain in that region) or quantitative (for example, the estimated breakeven level of the crude oil price, for a refiner or a heavy manufacturer), and then to track whatever data or information is required to verify that no problems are being signaled there. These are examples of things that stress testing should pick up but are not easily adaptable to typical financial spreadsheet software.
- Limits may be imposed (on borrowers and segments, tied to their risk characteristics) as an alternative to requiring a step-up in monitoring and scrutiny. Approval authorities can be structured to do the same.
- At the industry or country level, some kind of red/green/amber system can close the door or raise the bar for transactions in cyclically vulnerable parts of the portfolio—or, going a step further, an industry override along the lines of what banks often do now at the country level.

The point of all this is that as banks step back to take a longer-term perspective, it implies that RGs will be that much less responsive to "news." While that may be desirable for portfolio management purposes, it's important for a system that looks through the cycle, or at least partly so, to be backed up by measures to ensure that relevant, company-specific problems don't get missed.

The portfolio-level implications. A purist would argue that—assuming you start with plenty of data, do your calculations correctly, and "the world" (including the composition of your loan portfolio) doesn't change—your expected losses or your capital requirements should remain stable. You may have a bad year. They happen. If losses eat into your capital base, then additional capital will have to be raised—or replaced by retained earnings—when good times return. But like a buoyant object that's pulled under water and then bobs back to the surface (*mean-reversion*, in the extreme), losses will track back to, or around, their long-run average level, corresponding to EL. *This gets to the nature of risk.* Risk isn't the likelihood of incurring a loss but rather the uncertainty and variability of expected losses—for a single borrower and, bringing in correlation effects, across all borrowers.

When there's a cyclical downturn that produces actual losses L1 above expected levels EL0, as seen in Figure 2, what does that mean for capital and for risk grading? Those higher-than-expected losses eat into some of the capital that the bank holds to protect itself against such an eventuality. Does that mean that the loss distribution shifts to the right so as to center itself on that new loss level, as shown by the dotted line? Not if we assume that cycles self-correct (mean-revert) as they have in the past—that is, weak players drop out, industry capacity gets cut back, and pricing and profitability gradually improve, reinforced by cyclical recovery in demand. The effect: Above-average losses, lower in frequency but higher in dollar impact, will be accompanied by periods of below-average losses elsewhere in the cycle. Actual losses any different from expected hit capital directly.

But the fact that cycles don't repeat themselves neatly and predictably muddies this literal interpretation. Cyclicality is trickier than seasonality. From L1, for example, things could get worse before they get better. Furthermore, maybe the world *has* changed. This corresponds to a *random-walk* view of credit markets, according to which the best estimate of tomorrow's default rate is today's, consistent with a PIT mindset. This implies a shifting loss distribution (the dotted curve in Figure 2) with required capital now covering losses out to L^{**}.

Commodity-type markets certainly exhibit TTC-consistent, mean-reverting tendencies, but others may need to be handled more carefully. Telecom and utilities going

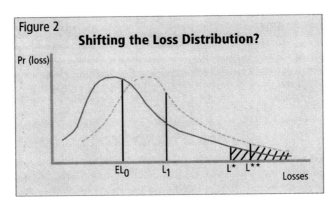

Figure 2

Shifting the Loss Distribution?

through the cold shower of deregulation, for instance, are now groping toward some new, higher equilibrium PD. It's not that cycles have disappeared, only that structural change is overwhelming cyclical effects during the adjustment period. In this situation, trying to look through the cycle and attribute a generalized worsening in performance to self-correcting cyclical factors is misleading—for both RAROC and capital allocations and for credit approval and monitoring. An institution putting in place a TTC approach, then, has to handle industries like that carefully; you may not be looking through the same cycle you thought you were, and that long-run PD value may no longer be relevant.

A hybrid approach. TTC RGs should show variability only if a cycle becomes unusually pronounced or if a company shows changes in its ability to withstand fluctuations. In *reality*, though, there's likely to be more movement in RGs under a TTC approach than this description suggests, if only because of the practical difficulties in controlling for (looking through) underlying cyclicality combined with a banker's bias to the conservative. Under PIT grading, as an industry's fortunes turn down, downgrades within that industry will have the effect of keeping the *ex post*[6] default rate for each RG roughly constant (rather than rising, as it would under TTC). However, unless there's a rigid tie-in to something like a KMV EDF (whereby PDs are translated into RGs rather than the other way around), the monitoring required, together with the administrative mechanics of putting through a RG change, mean that in *reality* some stickiness in PIT grades is likely.

So whichever approach is formally adopted, banks are likely to find themselves somewhere in between: a PIT/TTC hybrid in the mid-region of Figure 1, characterized by only partial responsiveness of RGs to changing external circumstances. And there's likely to be an asymmetry in that responsiveness, reflecting a conservative bias—faster downgrades than upgrades through a greater tendency to use reasons beyond cyclicality to explain weak performance than to explain strong performance.

How cyclicality gets picked up under alternative risk grade structures. On the spectrum of RG methodologies, a quantitative, model-based structure is likely to more closely approximate a PIT system, to the extent that it's driven by current market information and/or the most recent financials. Expert judgment systems are closer to the TTC end of the spectrum. Whether it's a Basel-type structure (based on detailed historical data and analysis and complemented by stress testing), a naïve TTC (based only on long-run averages), or just a masquerading PIT characterized by insensitivity and inertia—these are very important distinctions that credit policy needs to be clear on.

Banks have been gravitating away from the purely judgmental toward more quantitative structures, including intermediate structures like RG templates (which provide indicative financial and other measures to guide what is ultimately a RG judgment) and, further along still, scorecards (which take quantitative data plus scoring on the nonquantitative and combine them all to come up with an overall risk score). These bring in 1) PIT elements, using current financial and market information, and 2) TTC, as things like underlying cyclicality and worst-case vulnerability are assessed (template) or scored (scorecard). Just as most banks' RG systems now reflect both PIT and TTC approaches, they are now structured somewhere between the judgmental and the model-based.

Translating Risk Grades to Default Probabilities

While some of the RG functions described at the outset require only ordinality, others require going the next step to translate each RG into a PD. Basel's guidance is that "PD estimates must be a long-run average of one-year realized default rates for borrowers in the grade."[7]

Internal data should be the primary source: Looking at all borrowers in a given RG at the beginning of a given year, what percentage went into default by the end of that year? Where sample points are thin (for example, the strong risk grades), it can help to derive default frequencies indirectly through migration analysis and Markov chaining. The next step is to augment and corroborate this with external data. That could be direct observation, in the case of loss databases (like Fitch Risk Management's Loan Loss Database or Moody's Credit Research Database), assuming the grading correspondence can be reliably established. Or it might mean matching the bank's rating criteria and process with a rating agency's and then looking at the agency's historical data on defaults by rating category. Public-company tools like KMV's can add further opportunity for triangulation for companies that are in both the bank's and KMV's databases. For any external sources, recognition needs to be given to differences in things like default definitions, time horizons, and public-versus-private companies.

Finally, we should note that Basel's CP3 suggests that "...a margin of conservatism that is related to the likely range of errors"[8] should be added to whatever PD estimation the raw data provides. If a bank's RG 5 customers have historically defaulted at, say, a 1% average annual rate, then RG 5 should translate into a PD of 1% plus that margin of conservatism. This is intended to pick up things like short data periods (less than full cycle), changing underwriting standards or portfolio composition, and the use of pooled external data.

We stressed earlier the benefits of stable, cycle-neutral EL and EC calculations for instances in which portfolios are dominated by industries exhibiting recurring cyclicality. This is most easily handled by stable, TTC RGs, together with static factors for translating RGs to PDs. In Figure 3 (which pretends that shades of gray are all black and white[9]), that's the upper-left quadrant.

Figure 3

Making Adjustments Through the Cycle

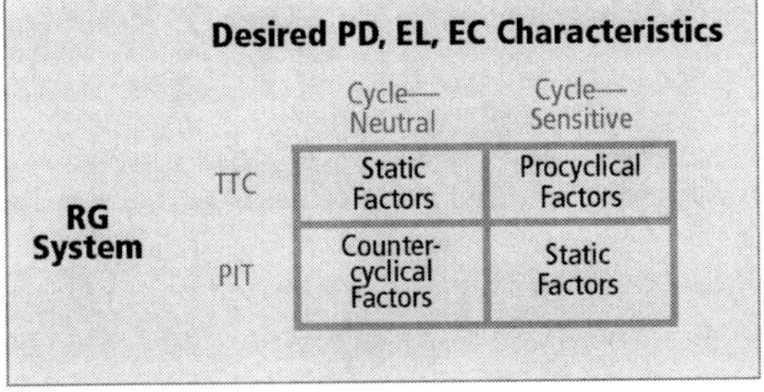

Desired PD, EL, EC Characteristics

		Cycle—Neutral	Cycle—Sensitive
RG System	TTC	Static Factors	Procyclical Factors
	PIT	Counter-cyclical Factors	Static Factors

Underlying structural change within the portfolio, for which random walk is a better description than mean-reversion of industries' default profile over time, works better with PIT grading—again in combination with the static RGPD factors that are easier to work with. This is the lower-right quadrant, and it results in the shifts in EL and EC that appropriately reflect structurally changing PDs. Alternatively, this quadrant could be selected for certain applications where a bank wishes to see ups and downs through the cycle in its EL and EC.[10]

The other two quadrants require changes in the RG-PD translation as the macro environment changes. In the upper-right quadrant, stable RGs generate PDs, ELs, and EC that move through the cycle. Those procyclical factors (for example, raising the PD for each RG in a weak economy) will be based on current or most recent default data by RG. A centralized portfolio management function could maintain and update those factors, as well as the static factors required for the upper-left quadrant.

Finally, there's the lower-left quadrant—the trickiest one. Because many banks' RG infrastructure is more oriented toward PIT grading while their preference may be for EL and EC stability in most applications, it's also potentially a very relevant one. What's tricky is the counterintuitive notion of countercyclical factors—that is, *lowering* the PD for each RG as the economy worsens, in order to offset the effects of borrower downgrades. It certainly would be a more difficult arrangement to implement and defend.

Cyclicality in Recovery Rates

Some recent research on this subject[11] points out the systematic component of loss given default (LGD) variability and the resulting correlation with default rates. Basel picks up on it as well: "Since defaults are likely to be clustered during times of economic distress and LGDs may be correlated with default rates, a time weighted average may materially understate loss severity per occurrence."[12] In a down cycle, the observed increase in defaults coincides with a drop in recovery rates as collateral values slide—though for certain types of collateral more than others and, notes Frye, for senior debt more than junior debt. The combined effect is to accentuate realized bank losses and therefore the required level of capital, an effect that isn't picked up in current RAROC models. It's particularly pronounced for real estate and project finance lending, but the phenomenon is more general.

Having adjustments in facility codes as we move through a cycle is not like adjusting RGs (that is, PIT grading) simply because most banks will base their LGD for a facility solely on its collateral classification; it's not a matter of judgment. If there's going to be adjustment, it has to be in the LGD factors (the % LGD, or LGD range, assigned to each facility code). But should there be? What Basel's CP3 proposes is that the LGD assigned to each code be based not on its long-run average but rather on bottom-of-the-cycle experience to account for cyclical volatility and the resulting systematic risk. (CP3 makes the same recommendation for EAD, although that issue doesn't have the same empirical support.) Note that this is not bringing in cyclical sensitivity to LGDs, only fixing them at a more conservative level.[13]

If we were to replicate Figure 3 for LGD, we'd have one row (with static facility codes, determined only by whatever collateral is taken) and two columns: a cycle-neutral, in the normal case of static LGD factors, and a cycle-sensitive in the alternative case of adjusting those factors procyclically (for example, raising the LGD % for each facility code in a downturn). As with PDs, moving the LGD factors while going through a credit cycle is not standard practice. Having static facility codes and static LGD factors means having static, cycle-neutral LGDs that themselves impart no variability to EL and EC.

Finally, what about the signaling role that PIT grading plays? There's no similar tool on the LGD side, but the fact that LGDs tend to be correlated with PDs suggests that monitoring for deterioration in borrower credit quality will also pick up signals relevant to recovery prospects should default occur.

Recommendations

1. PIT and TTC grading systems approach the issue of cyclicality quite differently—and there is value in both. PIT's focus on current news promotes alertness to company-specific sources of credit deterioration. TTC recognizes cyclicality as an innate and self-correcting characteristic whose ill effects are to be absorbed by capital held.
2. PIT is pretty straightforward; if things get worse (for whatever reason), you downgrade. But TTC is trickier. Basel envisages a rigorous process, something along the lines of the rating agencies' approach, of estimating and then stress testing a company's creditworthiness. This represents a challenge to bankers with 1) too many customers; 2) not enough time, data, and resources for those more complex analytics; and 3) tools more suited to PIT assessment.
3. A PIT approach to risk grading has built-in early-warning features, especially if the PD is derived from market-based information. But as bankers move closer to TTC thinking, the danger is that attention and sensitivity to changing company circumstances will be deflected. Hence the importance of stress testing in the RG process and an early-warning architecture.
4. In reality, whether a bank starts with a PIT or a TTC system, it's going to end up looking more like a hybrid. There will be some TTC stickiness and consideration of underlying cyclicality—but also some tendency to downgrade, even when problems appear to be industry-wide and likely to correct with time. This means that, in a down cycle, there will be some worsening in the weighted-average RG, consistent with a PIT approach, and some worsening (increase) in the observed default rate per RG, consistent with a TTC approach. This provides a way of defining and measuring a hybrid approach.
5. A hybrid (or anything less than full TTC) approach complicates portfolio analytics by imparting volatility to EL and EC. But that could be offset by having countercyclical factors that convert each RG into a lower PD as the economy slows to keep weighted-average PDs constant as downgrades occur.
6. Empirically as well as intuitively, there's similar cyclicality in recovery rates as in default rates. Except for the fact that there's typically little if any lender discretion in coming up with facility codes, our discussion of PDs mostly carries over to LGDs.
7. The TTC-versus-PIT issue is full of confusing crosscurrents. Both the Bank for International Settlements and domestic regulators make TTC-sounding noises.

Yet the analytical framework, the tools, and the applications of risk grading are all more oriented toward PIT. To further complicate the picture, PIT-type variability in RGs and PDs produces variability in expected losses around the long-run average—variability that capital is there to absorb, at least conceptually. Yet this (PIT inspired) variability, which causes procyclical movements in loss provisioning and required capital, is exactly what the (more TTC espousing) regulatory regime is programmed to look for.

Given these crosscurrents, the best advice is as follows:

1. Decide whether or not cycle sensitivity in PDs (and LGDs), EL, and EC is desirable. That will partly reflect how the output is to be used, but also the extent to which default and loss patterns are better characterized by random walks versus mean-reversion. It may seem like an arcane issue, but it lies at the foundation of RG structuring. Mean-reversion, corresponding to cyclically correcting markets, makes cycle-neutral PDs, EL, and EC more appropriate. Let capital absorb the ups and downs of actual losses around the long-run, expected level. But if that expected level is itself changing, making default behavior more consistent with a random walk, then cycle sensitivity is more appropriate.

2. Assess your own RG system's cyclicality, by comparing movements over time against KMV, the rating agencies, and, if possible, other banks. If the bank's culture, procedures, policy statements, and credit tools are more suited to one than the other, then decide whether that matches with the desired cycle sensitivity. Adjusting the PD (and perhaps LGD) factors is a way to realign the EC model with whatever philosophy underlies the RG system.

   Assessing where the bank should be on the PIT-TTC spectrum and where it in fact sits are highly subjective judgments, but they're the kind of questions that Basel will be prodding regulators to raise and bankers to substantiate.

Notes

1. The New Basel Capital Accord, Basel Committee on Banking Supervision, April 2003, p. 73.
2. "Credit Risk Rating at Large U.S. Banks," *Federal Reserve Bulletin*, November 1998.
3. One more PIT consideration to bring in here: the increasing granularity in RG systems, which (ceteris paribus) produces more observed variability in grading. A borrower that migrates from 5+ to 5 to 5- might have stayed a 5 through this period under a less granular system lacking the pluses and minuses.
4. The New Basel Capital Accord, p. 73.
5. Tools like Moody's RiskCalc and the Z-score, using latest-period financial ratios and growth rates, are more PIT than alternative structures that place emphasis on standard deviations and other longer-term measures.
6. This ties in with the required validation on the grading system: For a bank with a PIT approach to grading, there should be observed rough constancy in the realized default rate over time within each RG.
7. The New Basel Capital Accord, p. 79.

8. Ibid, p. 80.
9. Note also that Figure 3 links PDs to EL and EC without considering LGD or EAD, which are considered later in the article.
10. For example, some banks are moving toward EC-based approaches to limits setting. Seeing EC allocations rise as the economy slides may be advantageous for controlling harmful concentrations at the wrong point in the cycle.
11. See, for example, Jon Frye, "A False Sense of Security," *Risk*, August 2003.
12. The New Basel Capital Accord, p. 84.
13. It's a little different from the proposed treatment of PDs, whose estimation is based on the long-run average default rate by RG, plus the above mentioned "margin of conservatism." The stress-testing requirement there only identifies relative vulnerability. On average, the PD factors roughly match up with actual experience, but not so for LGD and EAD, whose factors are required by the Basel proposals to be more severe than their long-run average level.

An Internal Ratings Migration Study

By Michel Araten, Michael Jacobs Jr.,
Peeyush Varshney, and
Claude R. Pellegrino

This article discusses issues in evaluating banks' internal ratings of borrowers, drawing on six years of internal ratings data from JPMorgan Chase's wholesale exposures to perform a ratings migration analysis. While rating agencies have previously conducted these studies based on publicly rated debt, this is the first published study based on a bank's internal ratings.

Ratings migration analysis entails the actuarial estimation of transition probabilities for obligor credit risk ratings, with emphasis on estimation of empirical default probabilities. Measurement of changes in borrower credit quality over time is important as obligor risk ratings are a key component of a bank's credit capital methodology. These analyses permit banks to more accurately assess and price credit risk, as well as improve their assessment of loss reserves and portfolio capital requirements.

Key objectives of an internal ratings migration study are as follows:

- To evaluate how well a bank differentiates risk on an ordinal basis.
- To examine the consistency of obligor ratings across different lines of business (LOBs) or customer types, to suggest guidance in the risk-rating process.
- To evaluate the extent to which a bank's rating philosophy is influenced by current conditions or longer-term, through-the-cycle considerations.
- To explore how to satisfy Basel II regulatory requirements for validating the use of probabilities of default (PDs) associated with a bank's ratings.

Measurement of rating accuracy includes the notions of ordinal as well as cardinal accuracy. Ordinal accuracy tests the effectiveness of the ratings system in distinguishing credit risk on a relative basis. One can gauge ordinal accuracy by comparing agency ratings or default probability estimates (such as KMV EDFs[TM]) for a common universe of obligors. Cardinal accuracy is related to the validation of risk ratings by comparing realized default rates to assumed default rates.

Analysis of a bank's rating and default experience is carried out over a historical period by forming annual cohorts at the parent level and observing their credit rating at the beginning of the year. The number of parents in each rating category is determined at each year-end, and the transitions to other ratings categories, including default, are measured. Estimates of the transition probabilities for a given category can be derived from 1) aggregation of the transition counts in a given category and 2) computation of the proportions of these out of the total number of starting observations across all cohorts. One-year and multiyear average transition matrices can be computed for the firm as a whole as well as for individual business units. Further differentiation can be performed on the basis of public versus private status, industry group, geographic region, and loan exposure level.

Data and Methodology

The principal source of information for ratings transition data in this study by JPMorgan Chase (JPMC) was its exposure system, which tracks ratings data for the wholesale bank at the family, obligor, and facility levels. Various customer demographic and loan detail information also is available. The indicator for default is the appearance of a borrower on the system that records those borrowers deemed to be in default and for which the bank is no longer accruing interest on these facilities (nonaccruals). Supplemental information was obtained from credit surveillance reports containing comprehensive details on customers and their facilities, which are prepared when customers reach a grade equivalent to Standard and Poor's "B."

Various data filters were applied to ensure that data was of high and consistent quality. First, the study period (1997-2002) encompassed the longest historical period for which reliable and reasonably consistent data was available. Second, a size cutoff of $100 million in exposure was imposed in order to avoid observations that are more of a retail character.[1] Finally, the unit of observation is at the parent level to avoid multiple counting of distinct subsidiaries with characteristics similar to the parent's. In line with the practice of rating agencies, there is no weighting either by the value of the loan or by the number of facilities to the customer, though this data was captured and could be analyzed.

The issue of withdrawn ratings (WRs), observations for which there is no ending state, is important in ratings migration analysis in general and particularly in this study, given data and systems issues. Withdrawn ratings are observed when customers have a rating as of the beginning of a year but do not have a rating or any exposure at year-end. These are clearly non-defaulters, as the bank would have had a record of their defaulting. They represent a combination of firms that no longer need to borrow or that roll over their debt with another lender. This differs somewhat from the case of a WR in studies by rating agencies, as in some cases agencies may either decline or are asked by a company not to publish a rating.

The frequency of WRs in this study is on the order of fourfold that observed in agency studies (see Bos et al., Cantor and Mann, and Carty et al. in the References). The approach followed here, similar to one used by Standard & Poor's, is to adjust for withdrawn grades by subtracting all of the "withdrawn" observations from the denominator.[2] Ignoring all beginning ratings that transitioned to a withdrawn status will result in a conservative proportional scaling up of default probabilities. On the other hand, new credit exposures that arrive in the middle of the year and have a year-end rating also are not included in the analysis.

Withdrawn rates in a bank portfolio, particularly for low-rated credits, often reflect skilled credit risk management in denying customers continued access to credit when their quality is declining. In addition, highly rated credits may have been discouraged from refinancing if their returns are inadequate. Here, it is important to separate the assessment of ratings consistency and accuracy from credit management skills.

Many firms have evolved their rating scale and methodology over time, often as a result of mergers in which they have had to reconcile different ratings systems employed by predecessor banks. Under these circumstances, it is often a challenge to develop a database of ratings history that fairly represents a consistent ratings philosophy. This also occurred at JPMC, which revised its risk-grading methodology with a view toward promoting consistency in risk grading to facilitate comparisons with external benchmarks and to develop explicit estimates of recovery rates. Prior to this point, "split" rating categories existed, which required mapping to the new ratings scale.[3]

Care must be taken in this type of analysis to investigate whether a bank's ratings philosophy has changed over the study period. Basel II (see References) requires a clear statement of ratings philosophy for banks seeking to employ an advanced internal ratings-based (IRB) system for regulatory capital. The bank must stipulate whether a grade represents the borrower's current condition (point in time, or PIT) or the borrower's condition evaluated over a longer period of time that incorporates a business or economic cycle (through the cycle, or TTC). As previously noted by Araten (see References), "While banks may now be moving toward a mark-to-market view of the value of their portfolios, the bulk of the current historical data that a bank typically possesses is likely to be based on the TTC view." However, different business units in an organization may be more exposed to and be more influenced by current conditions than other business units. A ratings migration analysis will help expose these issues.

Results and Analysis

Exhibit 1 presents the one year average transition matrix for JPMC for about 33,000 distinct obligors covering approximately 100,000 transitions. Aggregate default rates at JPMC increase monotonically with risk grades.

This holds across all time periods and demographic measures. The transition matrix is diagonally dominated with transition rates generally decreasing with transition steps. The stability of ratings, as measured by the magnitude of the diagonal entries, diminishes with deteriorating credit quality, although not monotonically. Estimated transition matrices by individual cohort years between 1997 and 2002 are qualitatively similar with respect to ratings volatility (the diagonals), default, and withdrawn rates across grades, as compared to the overall results.

Exhibit 1

One-Year Average Transition Matrix (JPMC 1997-2002)

Rating	AAA-AA	A	BBB	BB	B	CCC	CC	Default	Total	WR	Up-Grades	Down-Grades	Up/Down Grades
AAA-AA	91.30%	5.62%	0.84%	1.03%	1.11%	0.03%	0.00%	0.08%	100.00%	14.85%	0.00%	8.70%	0.00
A	5.98%	85.91%	5.71%	1.67%	0.53%	0.09%	0.03%	0.09%	100.00%	15.45%	5.98%	8.11%	0.74
BBB	0.66%	7.02%	84.31%	6.96%	0.78%	0.11%	0.05%	0.10%	100.00%	17.19%	7.68%	8.01%	0.96
BB	0.08%	0.58%	3.99%	89.28%	4.81%	0.43%	0.26%	0.57%	100.00%	20.84%	4.65%	6.07%	0.77
B	0.12%	0.08%	0.26%	10.95%	84.07%	1.61%	1.06%	1.86%	100.00%	27.61%	11.40%	4.53%	2.51
CCC	0.00%	0.18%	0.09%	1.99%	15.10%	63.47%	9.13%	10.04%	100.00%	36.08%	17.36%	19.17%	0.91
CC	0.10%	0.10%	0.10%	1.40%	4.60%	1.40%	74.57%	17.72%	100.00%	40.84%	7.71%	17.72%	0.44
Total									100.00%	21.98%	6.88%	6.49%	1.06

Initial Risk Rating

A time trend analysis of overall default rates reveals an increasing trend during the study period that also holds by risk class and is more pronounced for investment than for speculative grades. While the investment-grade default rates do not appear to be strongly differentiated, there are too few defaults in these categories to draw a firm conclusion. This pattern holds across all time periods and demographic measures, and the lack of statistical differentiation among the investment grades is confirmed by formal tests.

Observations consisting of ratings of companies subject to default and subsequently withdrawn constitute 22% or approximately four times the proportion of the total as observed in rating agency studies (see Bos et al., Cantor and Mann, and Carty et al. in References). The withdrawn rate increases monotonically with deteriorating risk grade. This pattern holds across all time periods and demographic measures. Overall, the probability of an upgrade only slightly exceeds that of a downgrade. However, the upgrade-to-downgrade ratio is below 1 for all grades except for – rated credits, where it is 2.5.

JPMC's internal ratings can be shown to effectively discriminate credit risk on an ordinal basis, as measured by a cumulative accuracy profile (CAP) and cumulative accuracy ratio (CAR).

The CAP is a graphical representation of the effectiveness of a ratings system in detecting defaults in a population. It is "…constructed by plotting for each rating category, the proportion of defaults accounted for by firms with the same or a lower rating against the proportion of all firms with the same or a lower rating." (See Carty et al. in References.) The CAR is a summary measure, defined as the ratio of the area beneath the CAP curve and above the 45° line to the entire area above the 45° line. Overall, the CAR for JPMC is 60%.

These curves also can be used to compare different ratings systems. This comparison requires an identical population of borrowers and time periods to measure ratings. Figure 1 presents a comparison of JPMC's ratings against Moody's for approximately 1,000 com-

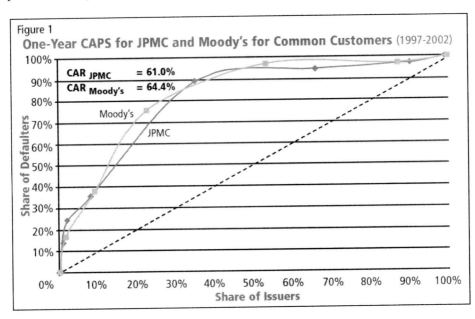

Figure 1

One-Year CAPS for JPMC and Moody's for Common Customers (1997-2002)

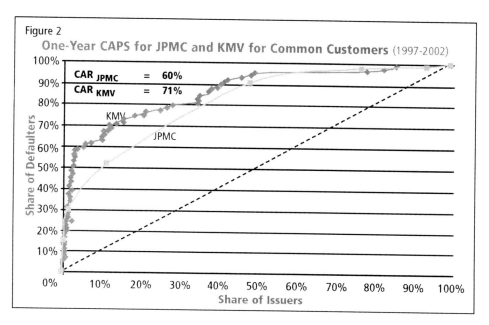

Figure 2
One-Year CAPS for JPMC and KMV for Common Customers (1997-2002)

mon customers over the study period. JPMC's ratings methodology appears just as powerful in ranking relative credit risk with a CAR of 61% as compared to 64% for Moody's. However, current market-based estimates over a one-year period have greater power to differentiate credit risk as compared to internal ratings. Figure 2 highlights a comparison of CAPs for JPMC with KMV EDFsTM for a universe of approximately 2,400 common customers over the study period. The CAR of 71% for KMV compared to 60% for JPMC demonstrates the innate ability of a market-based ratings measure to better discriminate default risk at a one-year horizon than JPMC's presumed TTC ratings system.

Cardinal accuracy, or the ability to predict the level of defaults, is measured by comparing PMC's observed default rates with its assumed default rates. The assumed rates are modified TTC rates (MTTC). They are obtained as weighted combinations of long-term average rating agency default rates and median KMV EDFs over the previous three months. Over the study period, one-year default rates for risk grades AAA to A and for CC were found to be slightly above the MTTC default rates, whereas the default rates for risk grades BBB through CC were found to be significantly below.[4] However, results of this comparison for investment-grade borrowers should be interpreted with care due to the paucity of their defaults.

Migration matrices were differentiated by various borrower demographics: line of business (investment bank—IB versus middle market—MM), public versus private in IB, and U.S. versus non-U.S. domicile in IB (Exhibit 2). While in general the transition matrices were qualitatively similar, differences were observed in the cardinal accuracy of the respective risk ratings systems.

In the LOB comparison, default rates for all risk grades in MM appear to be lower than default rates for IB, with the exception of risk grade CC. A plausible explanation may be that smaller firms reach a state of heightened vulnerability to default once a certain credit quality threshold is breached with few exit opportunities. For large compa-

Exhibit 2

Observed One-Year Default Rates (JPMC 1997-2002)

	Rating	Business Segment and Borrower Type					
		IB–All	MM	IB Public	IB Private	IB-US	IB-Non-US
Internal Rating	AAA-AA	0.06%	0.00%	0.18%	0.04%	0.00%	0.14%
	A	0.06%	0.14%	0.07%	0.06%	0.12%	0.00%
	BBB	0.12%	0.00%	0.22%	0.08%	0.15%	0.10%
	BB	0.48%	0.43%	1.04%	0.33%	0.81%	0.31%
	B	1.58%	1.17%	2.24%	1.48%	2.88%	1.11%
	CCC	10.17%	8.92%	10.59%	10.06%	14.75%	6.52%
	CC	15.42%	23.39%	19.15%	14.93%	13.75%	18.80%

nies, at the same level of credit distress there may be additional options to avoiding default. The differences observed for all grades above CC might be attributable to a more conservative grading philosophy in MM. Default rates for public borrowers in IB are higher than those for private borrowers for all risk grades. This may be due to systematic severity or leniency, with respect to grading private and public customers, respectively.

U.S. entities have higher observed default rates compared to non-U.S. entities. In particular, this holds across all grades except for, again, risk grade CC. A plausible explanation for more severe grading of non-U.S. customers could be to compensate for lower perceived quality of information. The higher default rate for non-U.S. borrowers for grade CC may be attributed to the same effect as noted in the IB versus MM comparison: a lack of exit options during times of extreme distress.

A rough indicator of ratings stability[5] or "stickiness," and perhaps the degree to which ratings are more influenced by current conditions (PIT) versus longer-term considerations (TTC), can be estimated by the percent staying in the same grade[6] over a one-year period (Exhibit 3). Here, MM with 87.6% versus IB with 85.0% remaining in the same grade shows a slightly greater propensity for stable ratings.

Exhibit 3

One-Year Transition Matrices for LOB and Borrower Types

Line of Business	Percent Same Grade (Excluding Defaults)	Upgrade/Downgrade (Including Defaults)	Percent Withdrawn
Investment Bank	85.0	1.25	22.0
Middle Market	87.6	1.04	19.5
IB—Public Corporates	83/3	0.90	6.7
IB—Private Corporates	85.5	1.40	26.5
IB—US	84.5	1.15	23.4
IB—Non-US	85.4	1.31	21.1

Withdrawn rates for public companies of 6.7% are much lower than the 26.7% observed for private companies. This rate is more in line with that reported by the rating agencies, particularly for non-investment-grade borrowers. Private-company ratings appear to be slightly more stable than ratings for public companies (85.5% versus 83.3%). This may be a sign of less current market information availability for private companies. There is also a much lower upgrade-to-downgrade ratio of 0.89 for public companies versus 1.40 for private companies. This may be due to the greater attention paid to rating-agency outlook indicators and market spread information availability for public companies.

Multiyear (2 through 5) migration matrices were also computed. They naturally are more susceptible to change, exhibiting higher default and withdrawn rates compared with average one-year transitions. While the speculative grades have the highest default rates for longer horizons, the rate of increase in investment-grade default rates is greater. As horizon increases, the investment-grade names show the most stability and speculative grades show the least stability, as measured by the percent remaining unchanged.

To better illustrate the degree of ratings consistency, both default rates and nondefault migration rates can be evaluated around various demographic details. The consistency-of-ratings approach of individual raters throughout the banking organization is of great interest. If there is concern with potential ratings bias, feedback can be given to raters to help them achieve better consistency of approach and philosophy. If current market information is available for some companies and not for others, it may be natural for the ratings for these companies to reflect more of a PIT orientation versus those private companies without such information. The performance of historical ratings may be important to validate PD estimates for Basel II. Moreover, the review of migration rates and their volatility even on a quarterly basis may help point out different ratings philosophies and potential biases by the raters.

Conclusion

This article has highlighted issues associated with conducting and interpreting a ratings migration analysis based on a bank's internal history. A ratings migration analysis allows a bank to evaluate how well it differentiates risk compared to external benchmarks, to study the consistency of its grading across segments of the organization, and to provide a basis for satisfying Basel II requirements for validating the use of PDs associated with internal ratings.

This is illustrated by a study of JPMC's risk-rating system over the last six years. This study shows how one can assess the consistency and relative performance of the ratings systems across segments of a firm. Differences can be noted that may suggest business unit review of grading policies with regard to organization, public or private entities, and geographic domicile. A ratings philosophy indicative of favoring a PIT versus a TTC approach can be better understood in the light of a migration analysis.

This study and similar ones in the future should serve as a guide to banks seeking to better understand and fine-tune their credit processes and practices.

Notes

1. Criteria for incorporating an observation in this study included any parent with a valid rating and both internal guidance and external committed facilities to its family that added up to $100 million or more.
2. The Moody's approach subtracts half of the withdrawn issuers from the denominator (that is, the total available-to-default), assuming that issues of debt exit uniformly throughout the year.
3. For a portion of the data, an old whole grade of 4 is mapped to an agency grade of BBB- to BB+ and an old grade of 6 is mapped to BB- and B+. Further analysis enabled individual assignments to a rating-agency-equivalent whole grade.
4. The AAA to A and CC rates were within a 95% confidence interval, while the BBB to CCC rates were outside the 95% confidence level, under the assumption of time-independent default rates.
5. A more quantitative treatment of stability or mobility and comparison of transition matrices may be found in Jafry and Scheuermann (see References).
6. The percent staying in the same grade calculated by excluding defaults.

References

Araten, Michel, 2004, "Current Issues in Estimating Economic Capital for Credit Risk," *The RMA Journal*, March.

Basel Committee on Banking Supervision, 2003, "The New Basel Capital Accord," April.

Bos, Roger J., Brady Brooks, and Diane Vazza, 2003, "Corporate Defaults Peak in 2002 Amid Record Amounts of Defaults and Declining Credit Quality," Special Report, Ratings Performance 2002: Default, Transition Recovery and Spreads, Standard & Poors, February.

Cantor, Richard and Christopher Mann, 2003, "Measuring the Performance of Corporate Bond Ratings," Special Comment, Moody's Investors Service, April.

Carty, Lea V., Sean C. Keenan, and Igor Shotgrin, 1998, "Historical Default Rates of Corporate Bond Issuers, 1920-1997," Special Comment, Moody's Investors Service, February.

"Internal Ratings-Based Systems for Corporate Credit and Operational Risk Advanced Measurement Approaches for Regulatory Capital," *Federal Register*, August 4, 2003 (Volume 68, Number 149), p. 45954.

Jafry, Y. and T. Scheuermann, 2003, "Measurement and Estimation of Credit Migration Matrices," Wharton Financial Institutions Center Working Paper No. 03-08, November.

Taylor, J., 2003, "Risk Grading Philosophy: Through the Cycle versus Point in Time," *The RMA Journal*, November.

Measuring the Risk of Default: A Modern Approach

By Jens Hilscher, Robert A. Jarrow, and Donald R. van Deventer

The United States is a nation of debtors. By the end of 2007, total debt outstanding by households, businesses, state and local governments, and the federal government added up to $31.2 trillion. The domestic financial sector accounted for half of this total, or $15.8 trillion.

The size of the debt market is quite large. Indeed, it exceeds both the U.S. GDP in 2007 ($13.8 trillion) and the equity market value of all domestic corporations ($15.5 trillion).[1] The primary risk of all this debt is credit risk, or the risk of default. The credit crisis demonstrated how shifts in credit spreads and market liquidity can also significantly impact debt values. Although these alternative factors are important for understanding debt markets, we will focus here only on default risk.

Investors measure default risk in many different ways, and there have been important recent innovations in this regard. The state of the art in assessing corporate credit risk is based on one of three approaches: 1) the Merton distance-to-default measure, 2) the reduced-form approach, and 3) credit ratings. We will compare and contrast these three approaches, showing that the reduced-form approach is preferred because of its generality, flexibility, and superior forecasting ability.

Merton's Distance-to-Default

For more than three decades, a common approach used to measure a firm's default probability has been the so-called distance to default. This measure is based on the pioneering work of Robert C. Merton (1974; see References), who applied contingent claims analysis to the pricing of corporate debt.

The idea is that creditors and equity holders jointly own the firm, but they do not share equally the risks of large increases or decreases in the firm's value. Creditors have a fixed claim to the face value of the debt, but equity holders' limited liability restricts them to a claim only on the firm's upside potential. If a large firm's value deteriorates to a point at which the firm's asset value is less than the face value of the debt at maturity, the firm defaults and it belongs to the creditors. The debt holders lose part of their claims, but the equity holders lose everything. On the other hand, if the firm's asset value is more than the face value of the debt, the equity holders receive the residual value of the firm over and above the debt's face value.

In effect, equity holders hold a call option on the firm's asset value with a strike price equal to the face value of the debt. Meanwhile, the debt holders own risk-free debt plus a short put option on the firm's asset value. A call option is a financial security that gives its owner the right to purchase an asset at a predetermined price, called the *strike price*, on a predetermined date, called the *maturity date*. A put option is similar, except that it gives the right to sell, and not the right to purchase. Both types of options are widely traded on equities, foreign currencies, and interest rates. And both types of options have been modeled extensively using the tools of financial engineering. Making the analogy between equity and a call option on the firm's asset value enables additional insights to be obtained through the use of these financial engineering tools.

Using this options analogy, it is easy to show that a firm's probability of default depends primarily on two factors: 1) the size of the firm's asset value relative to the face value of debt—if the debt-to-equity ratio is very high, default is likely; and 2) how volatile the firm's asset value is—if the firm is very risky, default is more likely because the risk of a sudden deterioration in asset value is high. The firm's one-year default probability therefore depends on the difference between the firm's asset value and the face value of debt, where this difference is measured in standard deviations of the firm's asset value. This is the distance-to-default measure expressed as the number of standard deviations the firm's asset value has to drop before default occurs. The larger the number of standard deviations, the smaller is the probability of default.

The approach's simplicity and intuitive appeal explain why it is the basis for commercially available corporate default probabilities offered by firms like Moody's/KMV, which first popularized the concept, and Kamakura Corporation. This approach is also often referred to as the *structural approach* because the default probability is based directly on a model for the liability structure of the firm.

Unfortunately, the simplicity of the structural approach is both a good thing and a bad thing. It is good because it is easy to understand. It is bad, however, because this simplicity implies that the model has too few parameters to match market realities. Indeed, the distance-to-default has only two key inputs: the firm's leverage ratio and the volatility of the firm's asset value.

This theory has another difficulty. For simplicity of implementation, it assumes that the firm's future asset value follows a lognormal distribution. This implies a specific linkage between the firm's distance-to-default measure and the default probability: A distance-to-default of three standard deviations implies a default probability of close to 0.1%, and at four standard deviations the default probability is practically zero.

This linkage results in a relationship between distance-to-default and default probabilities that is historically inaccurate. Kamakura Corporation has found, for example, that the actual default rate among companies with a theoretical Merton default probability of zero is actually 0.20%. Looking at the other side of the distribution of default probabilities, the actual default rate among companies with theoretical Merton default probabilities over 90% is actually no more than 10%.

In order to better match historical defaults for practical application, the theoretical Merton default probabilities are necessarily modified. The theoretical default probabilities are mapped to empirical defaults, typically using a logistic regression. A logistic regression is ordinary linear regression where the independent variable is transformed to guarantee that it always lies between zero and one. This transformation of the independent variable is needed because default probabilities lie between zero and one.

Most analysts do this mapping of theoretical to empirical default probabilities so that the ranking of companies by credit riskiness is not changed; the mapping is done monotonically, when measured by either the "ROC accuracy ratio" or the "cumulative accuracy profile." Based on these measures, the accuracy of the default model is not changed by the mapping process. However, the mapping does change the relationship between actual and expected defaults.[2]

A final concern about the distance-to-default measure is that it appears less applicable to retail and small business clients. This is because, as commonly implemented, the distance-to-default measure requires the use of traded equity prices. Retail and small business clients would not have publicly traded equity. One vendor's early attempt to modify and use Merton's model for unlisted companies was ended after a decade without commercial acceptance. To our knowledge, no commercial product using the Merton model has ever been employed for retail risk assessment.

Reduced-Form Default Probabilities

An increasingly popular approach to measuring default probability is the reduced-form model. This model is more flexible than Merton's structural model because it allows for more factors to affect the probability of default. The approach has its origins in Merton (1976; see References), who used a default intensity to value put and call options on a firm that may go bankrupt at any point in time, suddenly driving the stock price to zero. However, at that time, Merton was not interested in analyzing credit risk, but rather in valuing options on stocks whose prices exhibit large jumps. About 15 years later, applying this approach to credit risk, Jarrow and Turnbull (1992 and 1995; see References) introduced the reduced-form model.

The idea of the reduced-form approach is straightforward; corporate default may be triggered by many different factors, and default may happen at any point in time.[3] For example, a firm that has no debt outstanding may not have enough cash to make salary payments to its staff, therefore causing a default. The Merton model does not allow the firm to default because it has no debt. Other examples of cash-flow-induced defaults include a firm that runs out of cash to make office lease payments or an unprofitable firm unable to raise additional capital to offset its losses. A firm that needs cash may find that the market for its assets has suddenly shut down (for example, the CDO market in 2007) or a firm that has borrowed too much may run out of funds for repayment. In addition, the reduced-form model allows the firm's debt-to-equity ratio and other important firm liabilities to change across time. This is not true for Merton's model.

As just explained, the reduced-form approach can incorporate many different inputs, including the inputs from the Merton approach. As such, it can never be less accurate than the Merton approach. In theory, this is a distinct advantage. The reduced-form approach chooses the inputs by estimating their relative importance in fitting historical defaults, thereby generating better predictions of future defaults. The reduced-form approach is more general because, unlike the structural approach, it does not assume a particular model of the firm's liability structure. It therefore does not limit the model's inputs to only the firm's leverage and volatility. The reduced-form probability of default is calculated using all available information at a given point in time.

Another advantage of the reduced-form approach is that it can be used to estimate the probability of default not only over the next month but over any period of time—the next year or even the next five years. Creditors care about these long-horizon default probabilities because they can be used to help predict financial distress and avoid related investment losses. For example, it would have been helpful to know that Countrywide's default probability was high enough to cause financial distress before its equity value dropped dramatically in the fall of 2007.

In a 2008 paper, Campbell, Hilscher, and Szilagyi (see References) agree that default probabilities should be estimated over long horizons: "Over a short horizon, it should not be surprising that the recent return on a firm's equity is a powerful predictor, but this may not be very useful information if it is relevant only in the extremely short run, just as it would not be useful to predict a heart attack by observing a person dropping to the floor clutching his chest."

Comparing Structural and Reduced-Form Models

One way to evaluate the accuracy of these two approaches is to ask which one—the reduced-form or the distance-to-default—better predicts historical defaults. Two studies, by Campbell, Hilscher, and Szilagyi and by Bharath and Shumway (see References), show that the reduced-form approach has been better able to predict U.S. corporate defaults.

Both studies also find several additional variables that increase the default-prediction accuracy of the Moody's/KMV method of using only the distance-to-default approach. This result is not surprising. Simply put, both studies find that additional measures of firm characteristics add predictive value. Commercially, the Kamakura Corporation has also reported similar results with its reduced-form and Merton models in its technical guides for each of the four versions of the models.[4]

Given the high predictive accuracy of reduced-form models and the ability to continually update them, it is surprising that so many practitioners in the financial markets are still mainly using the slow-moving distance-to-default-based default probabilities.

Credit Ratings

All of this brings us to the third, and probably most widely used, default risk measure of publicly traded debt securities: the bond's credit rating. A credit rating is simply an ordinal ranking of companies by credit risk, typically using 20 rating categories. These groups could be labeled from 1 to 20 or from CC to AAA.

The default probabilities associated with each rating category are unknown, although they can be subsequently estimated. The implication is that all firms within a given rating category have the same default probability. In contrast, in a reduced-form or structural model, each company in a given rating category would have a different default probability. Of course, the hope is that the firms falling into a particular rating category would have similar default probabilities as measured by these other techniques, but this need not be the case.

Rating agencies typically publish historical default statistics by rating category. The assumption implicit in these statistics is that the default probabilities are constant across time. Indeed, a common practice in modeling defaults is to use the historical one-year default rate for a given rating—say, CCC—across time despite the fact that the historical CCC default rate has varied from zero to 44% over the U.S. experience. The economic implication of the constant default rate assumption is that there is no business cycle. Of course, this is a fatally flawed assumption in light of U.S. economic history.

A further complication in the rating categories is the lack of a horizon associated with a given rating. For a short-term horizon (say, one month), a BBB company in a good economy has nearly the same default risk as an AAA company: zero. In the longer term (a year or more), this is certainly not the case, if the ratings have been assigned correctly.

There is another aspect of the rating process that lowers its accuracy: The rating agencies are reluctant to change a rating "too often."[5] If a company's risk suddenly rises and then falls 30 days later, the rating agencies, feeling their clients are opposed to a rating that falls and returns to its original level so quickly, will wait until they think there is no risk of a reversal before assigning a rating change. This wait-and-see approach is a reason why reduced-form models outperform agency ratings as predictors of default across all measured time horizons.[6] Another reason is that the size of the company is the single most statistically significant factor in determining a company's rating. Since company size is also used in estimating reduced-form default probabilities, further consideration of the rating process will not increase the accuracy of the default probabilities.[7]

The imprecision of credit ratings has exacerbated the currently troubled credit environment. Many institutions have policies that restrict investment to either only AAA debt or only investment-grade debt. Historically, it was very difficult to receive an AAA rating from one of the major rating agencies, such as Standard & Poor's, Moody's, or Fitch. However, over the last few years, senior tranches of repackaged portfolios of debt securities (CDOs) have often received AAA ratings even though the constituent parts were often of much lower credit quality.

The Financial Times reported on December 18, 2007, that these high ratings were seriously flawed, and they were suddenly and severely downgraded in one abrupt adjustment. As a result, many investors were forced by their own investment policies to dump these troubled securities on the market in a manner guaranteed to result in poor execution of the trades. Consequently, many investors are shifting to an investment policy that relies on independent valuations and independent default probabilities in order to move more skillfully and quickly as an asset becomes troubled.

Of course, agency ratings are not available for retail borrowers, for small business borrowers, and for many listed corporations. But enterprise risk management depends on estimates of their default risk as well. To use the credit-rating approach, internal ratings need to be "mapped" to agency ratings in a consistent manner. This is often done by equalizing default rates across internal-rating and credit-rating categories, but there is still a problem. If CCC annual default rates averaged 27% but have varied from 0% to 44%, which default rate in this range should be used to map to an equivalent internal rating? Shouldn't the business cycle be considered? Regardless of the approach used, the result is often a highly arbitrary process.

Conclusion

Best practice in risk management requires continuous improvement and perfect transparency. Risk managers are seeking an enterprise-wide ability to manage risk, as the default probabilities across all borrowers—from retail to corporate to sovereigns—rise and fall with the macroeconomic factors driving the business cycle.

Financial institutions are now turning away from company-specific over-the-counter derivatives like credit default swaps to hedge these risks. Instead, they are turning to macro factor risk hedges using derivatives on interest rates, stock price indices, foreign exchange rates, and home price futures. Only a reduced-form approach to credit risk modeling allows a risk manager to achieve this objective with the essential speed and accuracy required.

Notes

1. Source is the Board of Governors of the Federal Reserve System, flow of funds statistics.
2. For more on this point, see D.R. van Deventer, L. Li, and X. Wang (2006).
3. The Merton approach, by contrast, initially assumed that default occurs only at the end of a single period. Recently, Merton models have been generalized to allow defaults across time by employing the insights of F. Black and J. Cox (1976).
4. See R. Jarrow, M. Mesler, and D.R. van Deventer, Kamakura Risk Information Services Technical Guide, Versions 1 (2002), 2 (2003), 3 (2005), and 4.1 (2006).
5. This constraint was stated clearly in a presentation by Moody's Investors Service at a conference sponsored by PRMIA and DePaul University, Chicago Mercantile Exchange, February 28, 2008.
6. As reported by D.R. van Deventer, L. Li, and X. Wang (2006).
7. See R. Jarrow, L. Li, M. Mesler, and D.R. van Deventer, Kamakura Risk Information Services Technical Guide Version 4.1, February 2006.

References

Bharath S. and T. Shumway, 2008, "Forecasting Default with the Merton Distance to Default Model," *Review of Financial Studies* 21, no. 3.
Black F. and J. Cox, 1976, "Valuing Corporate Securities: Some Effects of Bond Indenture Provisions," *Journal of Finance* 31, May.
Campbell, J.Y., J. Hilscher, and J. Szilagyi, 2008, "In Search of Distress Risk," *Journal of Finance* LXIII, no. 3 (December).
Jarrow, R., M. Mesler, and D. R. van Deventer, 2006, Kamakura Default Probabilities Technical Report, Kamakura Risk Information Services, Version 4.1, Kamakura Corporation memorandum, January 25.
Jarrow, R. and S. Turnbull, 1992, "Credit Risk: Drawing the Analogy," *Risk Magazine*, 5 (9).
Jarrow, R. and S. Turnbull, 1995, "Pricing Derivatives on Financial Securities Subject to Credit Risk," *Journal of Finance* 50, March.
Merton, R.C., 1974, "On the Pricing of Corporate Debt: The Risk Structure of Interest Rates," *Journal of Finance* 29.
Merton, R.C., 1976, "Option Pricing When Underlying Stock Returns Are Discontinuous," *Journal of Financial Economics* 3, January- March.
van Deventer, D.R. and K. Imai, 2003, *Credit Risk Models and the Basel Accords*, John Wiley & Sons.
van Deventer, D.R., K. Imai, and M. Mesler, 2004, *Advanced Financial Risk Management: An Integrated Approach to Credit Risk and Interest Rate Risk Management*, John Wiley & Sons.
van Deventer, D.R., L. Li, and X. Wang, 2006, "Another Look at Advanced Credit Model Performance Testing to Meet Basel Requirements: How Things Have Changed," *The Basel Handbook: A Guide for Financial Practitioners*, 2nd ed., Risk Publications.

Modeling Ratings Migration for Credit Risk Capital and Loss Provisioning Calculations

By Jorge R. Sobehart and Sean C. Keenan

 eliable loss prediction requires both robust estimation methods and accurate data. This article presents a way to leverage rating-agency data that can provide greater flexibility and stability of results in simulation-based estimates of future portfolio losses.

Based on a simple behavioral model that quantifies the structural relationships in historical default frequencies and transition rates for different ratings,[1] this technique leads analysts to hypothetical transition matrices for portfolio loss simulations that preserve the basic relationships observed in the historical transition and default rates reported by the rating agencies, allowing for unlimited sampling. The matrices can also be linked to macroeconomic factors to mimic the dynamics of credit cycles and economic shocks, allowing for richer descriptions of plausible future scenarios and what-if scenario analysis that goes beyond the limitations of historical data.

The Basel II capital adequacy framework provides strong incentive for financial institutions to use internal risk management systems to measure risk and determine sufficient regulatory and economic risk capital. While commercial risk measurement tools can be used as part of an overall solution, institutions must tailor them to their own portfolio specifications. Further, some of the development and implementation of the new systems will fall to their own risk management teams.

In many cases, whether they use commercial models or internal methodologies, analysts continue to rely on major rating agencies' data for default rates, ratings migration rates, and other key statistics. Despite recurring and somewhat troubling issues regarding the meaning and consistency of ratings, regulators tend to be more accepting of methodologies based on agency data because of the agencies' long and well-documented ratings histories. This data may indeed be deeper and may conform better to an accepted standard than banks' own internal ratings histories, yet the depth of agency data generally falls short of what's needed for the Monte Carlo-based economic risk capital estimation techniques in widespread use today.

The Shortcomings

The simplest portfolio loss model assumes that ratings transition probabilities are stable across obligor types and across the business cycle and that a single set of average historical ratings transition and default rates is all that's needed to characterize potential future losses. However, there is ample evidence that credit migration and the ratings process depend on a number of factors, such as the state of the economy—for example,

55

the probability of downgrades and defaults is greater in a downturn than in an upturn. Moreover, historical data is volatile; thus, the average-rate approach will understate potential tail loss—the very thing we want to measure with precision.

A slightly more sophisticated alternative is to use observed annual historical-rating transition rates as a sample from which to draw plausible future credit migration scenarios to simulate the forward loss distribution. The main drawback of this method is the small number of historical-rating scenarios on which to draw. Accurate Monte Carlo simulations for large portfolios usually require tens—or even up to hundreds of thousands—of random draws. However, because historical scenarios number only in the tens, the simulated loss distribution will tend to be lumpy as tail losses bunch up around the worst year from the historical period. Clearly, this problem cannot be overcome by increasing the number of Monte Carlo simulations.

A Behavioral Model of Risk Perception

A different approach is to directly model the relationship between transition probabilities and macroeconomic factors and then simulate plausible ratings migration patterns over time by generating various macroeconomic conditions. To do this, we need a behavioral model of how risk ratings are assigned. Let's begin with the observation that ratings are *opinions* of credit quality, representing different degrees of belief in the credit quality of the firm. Agency statistics, such as default and transition frequencies, are merely by-products of this rating assignment process, rather than properties inherent to the ratings themselves.[2]

Analysts' judgments, meanwhile, are based on a combination of qualitative and quantitative comparisons of the credit risk they perceive. Even if specifically attempting to arrive at a default probability calculation, the analyst cannot be sure of the precise relationship between the risk factors affecting the obligor and his or her own mental model of risk perception, which may lead to errors in risk assessment. Thus, even with complete and perfect information on the obligor's risk exposure, the analyst would still face "model risk" because of judgment. Any qualitative comparison between two risk exposures is clearly probabilistic in nature since it relates to uncertain events.

Unfortunately, analysts' perceptions of the probability of default, expected losses, and future ratings revisions are not publicly available and therefore cannot be tested. However, we can construct a behavioral model for the average perceived risk that can be calibrated with historical default and transition rates associated with a given risk perception (rating at a given point in time) assuming that the ratings are unbiased estimates of the average (ex ante) analyst's perception of the risk criterion.

The basic argument underlying the model presented here is that, at the fundamental level, the risk-assessment process is based on a relative comparison between perceived risk severities for pairs of risk exposures—the obligor's risk exposure and that of its peers, or a mental estimate constructed by the analyst. More precisely, let E be the obligor's risk exposure with severity $p(E)$ (for example, the expected probability of default) and R be the resultant average risk perception (risk rating). If the absolute perception of two risk exposures differs by a just noticeable amount when separated by a given relative increment of risk severity, then when the risk exposures are increased, the perceived risk increment must be proportionally increased for the difference in perception to remain just noticeable. From this relationship, we find that the relation between the severity $p(E)$ and the risk perception R becomes approximately:

Equation 1

$$\log\left(\frac{p}{1-p}\right) = \frac{1}{a}(R-b) + c$$

Here, the parameter a is the psychological *sensitivity* to variations of the risk exposure, and b is a reference value for the maximum risk severity corresponding to the maximum risk exposure. The term c reflects judgment errors for individual risk exposures. In the following we focus only on the average risk perception, neglecting the error term c.

Equation 1 depends on the time horizon over which the risk is being assessed. For a given time horizon T, the parameter $b(T)$ in Figure 1 provides the reference risk rating used in the comparison of risk exposures, and the parameter $a(T)$ provides the sensitivity of the risk perception to changes in risk severity. If we assign a cardinal value to agency ratings (for example, AAA=0, AA+=1, AA=2, etc.), then the parameter $a(T)$ provides the number of notches required to increase the odds nearly threefold (actually an increase in a factor $e = 2.73$).

For the moment, let's assume that the probability of default is an unbiased estimate of the analyst's perception of risk severity and that the historical default rates are unbiased estimates of the (ex ante) probability of default for a given risk perception (in the

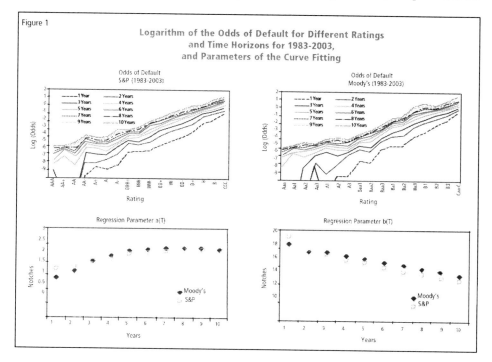

Figure 1

Logarithm of the Odds of Default for Different Ratings and Time Horizons for 1983-2003, and Parameters of the Curve Fitting

next section we introduce a different risk perception criterion and analyze the consistency between the two). The upper panel of Figure 1 shows the empirical relation between the risk perception R (rating) and the average default rate for corporate issuers for different time horizons during the period January 1983 to December 2003 for Moody's and S&P ratings, expressed in terms of the logarithm of the odds of default: $\log(P_d /(1-P_d))$ given the default rate P_d.

The quasi-linear trend between ratings (perceived risk) and the logarithm of the odds of default is an example of the Weber-Fechner law observed in psychology and physiology, which indicates that intuitive human sensations tend to be measured in relative terms leading to logarithmic or power functions of the stimulus. For example, normal conversation may appear two times as loud as a whisper, whereas its true acoustic intensity is actually hundreds of times greater. The familiar decibel scale used in audio equipment relates perceived loudness to the objective concept of intensity in the same way that the risk perception R (rating) measures the likelihood of default.

Notice that if Equation 1 were strictly true, this would indicate that the separation between rating grades had a consistent meaning in terms of the relative change in the likelihood of default. For example, a one-notch downgrade would indicate an e-fold increase in the likelihood of default from the previous rating, and a one-notch upgrade would indicate an e-fold reduction in the likelihood of default. In general, this is not the case, but the approximation holds reasonably well.

The lower panels of Figure 1 show the parameters of the fitting for Equation 1 for both rating agencies. For short time horizons, the linear fitting provides a rating dispersion of the order $a(T=1\ year) \sim 1.5$ notches for an e-fold increase in the odds of default and a rating reference $b(T=1\ year) \sim$ 18-19 notches (roughly a CCC/Caa rating). These values are consistent with the notions that agency ratings are reasonably accurate within one or two notches for short-term horizons and that CCC/Caa ratings show similar characteristics to defaulters.

The proximity of fitted parameters for both leading rating agencies shown in Figure 1 is remarkable. Another important aspect of Figure 1 is that the linear relationship between the empirical log of the odds and ratings breaks down at the top of the rating scale where defaults are extremely rare. This casts doubt on whether investment-grade analysts are responding primarily to changes in perceived default risk, as discussed in the following section.

Transition Risk as Perceived Risk

Obviously, given the sheer number of rating assignments relative to the number of defaults, it might be unreliable to infer the behavioral underpinnings of the rating scale on the basis of default risk alone. In fact, the rating scale may have a more consistent basis in transition risk.

From the investor's perspective, the likelihood that a rating may be raised or lowered over a particular time horizon creates risk primarily associated with the obligor's performance. But from the analyst's perspective, revisions to ratings may also reflect the inaccuracy of the initial rating. In noncontroversial cases, revisions may result from catastrophic events, changes in regulations, or unanticipated corporate actions. In other cases, the true value of new information is subject to interpretation, and revisions of ratings (their timing and magnitude) can be interpreted as evidence that the previous rating had been assigned in error. Common signals of inaccuracy include complaints from issuers and investors, persistent inconsistencies between ratings and credit spreads, and, most importantly, frequent revisions of ratings that appear to be reactive instead of anticipatory.

Agencies and financial institutions measure ratings volatility over time with ratings transition matrices. The elements of the transition matrix represent the likelihood of either remaining in the same rating or moving up or down to a new ratings category. Transition matrices give us an independent set of frequencies with which to calculate the odds ratios for revisions needed to test our behavioral model of perceived severity using this new risk perception criterion.

The test is straightforward. Instead of assuming that the perceived severity is the obligor's default probability, let's assume that it is the transition risk. Given a time horizon T, for each initial rating R we simply calculate the odds-ratio of a downgrade of W-R notches to a worse rating (higher value in notches) W using the empirical transition frequencies as proxies for the transition probabilities (rating revisions) $P_{RW}(T)$. We then approximate the logarithm of the odds-ratio of ratings revisions for each position as a linear function of the magnitude of ratings revisions using the following extension to Equation 1:

Equation 2

$$\log\left(\frac{P_{RW}}{1-P_{RW}}\right) \approx \frac{1}{a_d}\left((R-W) - b_d\right)$$

Here $a_d(R,T)$ and $b_d(R,T)$ are empirical parameters for downgrades to be determined for each initial rating R and time horizon T. These parameters have a similar interpretation to those in Equation 1. Note that when $W+b_d \sim b$, Equation 2 resembles Equation 1. The equation is identical for upward revisions of R-B notches from rating R to a better rating B with parameters $a_u(R,T)$ and $b_u(R,T)$. For each initial rating (a particular row in the rating transition matrix), Equation 2 for upgrades and downgrades is an inverted V-shaped function. If the V-shaped pattern were symmetric, the parameters $a_u(R,T)$ and $b_u(R,T)$ for upgrades and downgrades would be the same ($a_u=a_d$ and $b_u=b_d$). In this situation, the separation between ratings grades would have a consistent and homogeneous meaning in terms of the relative change in the severity of ratings transitions. For example, a one-notch revision of credit quality could be nearly three times as frequent as a more severe two-notches revision of creditworthiness.

Figure 2 shows the average of S&P one-year historical transition rates from a given initial rating to any other rating for the period 1983-2003.[3] An almost identical pattern is exhibited for Moody's data. In Figure 2, the small symbols represent the empirical rating transition frequencies and the lines represent the model in Equation 2. Figure 2 also shows the transition element $(1-P_{RR})$ from a given rating to any other rating including the default state. Notice the divergence between the model estimates and the actual rates for extreme, and rare, transitions (several notches).

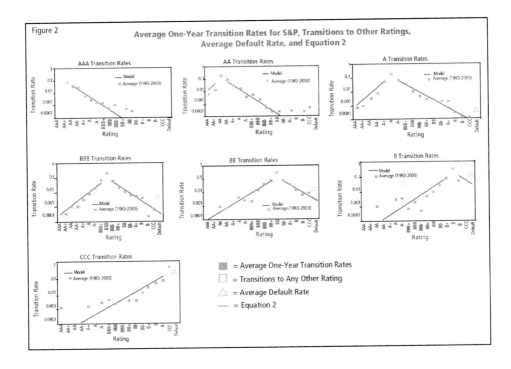

Figure 2

Average One-Year Transition Rates for S&P, Transitions to Other Ratings, Average Default Rate, and Equation 2

The overall impression one gets from Figure 2 is that the linear approximation (2) holds remarkably well for the average transition rates. The approximation is not as good for individual years because of the large variability of the transition rates over time. For the BBB/Baa rating, the inverted V-shaped pattern seems symmetric. However, for investment-grade firms, analysts seem to be more reluctant to upgrade ratings than to downgrade them, creating asymmetries in the scale, $(a_u < a_d)$. In contrast, for the segment of very low credit quality, analysts seem to be less biased to either downgrade or upgrade firms, although the fit is relatively poor. From Figure 2 we can infer that the sensitivity to downgrades is roughly constant, while upgrades become increasingly more difficult as credit quality improves (the better the credit quality, the steeper the line for upgrades).

One of the most striking features of Figure 2 is the relationship between the default frequency and the line implied by the behavioral model in Equation 2. In each case, the empirical default rate (open triangles) lies above the line and represents one of the largest deviations from the model. That is, the expected default rate based on the credit migration pattern is significantly lower than the observed default rate. One explanation is that transition rates reflect expected losses as opposed to default risk. Note, however, that the recovery value implied from the extrapolated transition rates is much lower than the average reported by the agencies.

Another plausible explanation is that analysts have full control over the assigned ratings, and therefore transition rates between ratings are affected mainly by analysts' decisions. For example, the decision to maintain a rating may not necessarily reflect a stable credit quality outlook for the issuer, but its purpose might be a reluctance to further limit the firm's access to credit markets. In contrast, analysts have no control over which issuers actually default on their obligations, and therefore inconsistencies between the assigned ratings and the transition rate to the default state could easily arise.[4]

Credit Migration and Portfolio Risk

The model introduced here provides a simple yet sound means of constructing ratings transition matrices that preserve the basic relationships observed in the historical transition and default rates reported by the rating agencies. As discussed above, this is critical since there is a limited number of historical transition matrices—a data set inadequate for providing the wide spectrum of scenarios required to obtain robust Monte Carlo simulations for economic capital and reserves at the high confidence levels required. The ability to construct ratings migration scenarios with internally consistent structural relationships and variability for different economic conditions (obtained, for example, from the distribution of fitting errors for Equations 1 and 2) can help to analyze situations beyond the limitations of historical data. Moving one step further, by associating the time paths of the key parameters

$$a, b, a_d(R,T), b_d(R,T), a_u(R,T)$$
$$\text{and}$$
$$b_u(R,T)$$

with macroeconomic and credit market data, transition matrices generated using Equation 2 can be linked to the dynamics of credit cycles and economic shocks, allowing for the kind of what-if scenario analysis and stress testing required for the active management of credit risk.

The steps for the simulation of ratings migrations can be summarized as follows:

1. Obtain historical time series of ratings migration matrices and macroeconomic variables.
2. Construct the models in Equation 1 and 2 for each ratings transition matrix.
3. Regress the structural coefficients of the model and the standard deviation of unexplained errors on lagged macroeconomic variables to identify systematic drivers of credit migration.
4. For each macroeconomic scenario, simulate random ratings migration patterns using the structural models 1 and 2 and the distribution of unexplained errors.

Simple econometric models for the coefficients in Equations 1 and 2 and the standard deviation of unexplained errors using lagged multiple regression analysis illustrate this process. The selected descriptive variables are the annual GDP growth rate, relative changes in short-term lending rates, and the ratio of the number of speculative-grade issuers over the total number of issuers lagged two years. The latter variable describes the relationship between debt issuance and credit quality, as well as the overall dynamics of the credit cycle. Even this limited set of variables can allow for the analysis of regional diversification in credit portfolios by simulating ratings migration for individual countries conditioned on their current position in their economic cycle.

Figure 3 shows the evolution of the historical and estimated one-year default rates for S&P and the standard deviation of the scenarios produced by the model for selected ratings for U.S. issuers. Similar results are obtained for Moody's ratings.

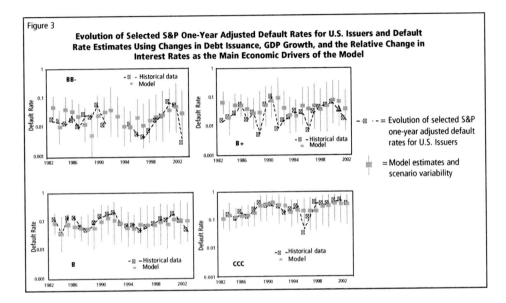

Figure 3

Evolution of Selected S&P One-Year Adjusted Default Rates for U.S. Issuers and Default Rate Estimates Using Changes in Debt Issuance, GDP Growth, and the Relative Change in Interest Rates as the Main Economic Drivers of the Model

From the viewpoint of forecasting default rates, the accuracy of this simple model may seem relatively modest. However, its purpose is not to forecast specific outcomes, but to generate large numbers of plausible scenarios consistent with given macroeconomic conditions. From the portfolio simulation viewpoint, the additional uncertainty allows for a realistically wide spectrum of alternative what-if scenarios for given values of the economic drivers through the credit cycle or for stress scenarios. This is exactly what is really needed for economic capital simulations, since the main goal of portfolio simulation is to study the tail end of the loss distribution, and the characteristics of this tail are often driven by the irregularities and small-sample-size effects found in published transition data.

Conclusion

Current financial institutions' credit risk assessment processes often include inputs both from quantitative, statistical models and from traditional fundamental analysis. Frequently, however, models for estimating portfolio loss provisions and economic risk capital retain a dependence on key rating-agency statistics such as default rates and transition rates. Unfortunately, this historical data is still generally insufficient for robust estimation of portfolio losses through Monte Carlo techniques.

The behavioral model offered in this article is capable of quantifying the empirical distribution of default rates and transition rates for different ratings categories in a sensible and parsimonious way. The model can be used to construct a rich set of ratings transition scenarios that go beyond the limitations of historical data, while preserving the empirically observed structural relations between ratings transitions and default rates. It also provides a link between economic conditions and credit migration scenarios defined in terms of transition and default frequencies. These capabilities allow institutions to conduct more robust and more controlled Monte Carlo simulations for risk capital calculations, portfolio loss provisioning, and what-if and stress scenario analysis.

Notes

1. Agency studies have recently acknowledged that ratings themselves may be insufficient for predicting future migrations and default rates.
2. Agencies typically direct researchers to the historical rating statistics, but do not go so far as to say that these performance statistics were what the ratings originally intended to express.
3. This covers the entire history of ratings on the numerically modified scale.
4. However, a change in rating can produce additional financial distress through ratings trigger covenants in the firm's obligations.

Validating Internal Rating Systems: The Move from Basel II Compliance to Continuous Improvement

By Bogie Ozdemir

More banks are realizing the importance and urgency of improving and validating their internal credit-rating systems. Some banks *must* do this to gain Basel II compliance, while many others want to do it to keep their compliance options open and to leverage best-practice risk management in making improved business decisions.

Improving business decisions is an important goal for validation programs because internal rating systems have become a core information system, feeding risk data into the MIS and economic-capital-based systems that banks use to make strategic and tactical decisions, including performance measurement, risk-based pricing, limits setting, and incentive compensation.

Validation programs are hard to get right, however, and they involve a lot more than running one or two technical tests, such as a discriminatory power test. Statistical procedures are not enough to gain Basel II compliance. And they certainly are not enough to gain the risk management and business benefits of an improved rating system—including better credit surveillance and a near-term reduction in credit losses.

Over the years, efforts to help banks build validation strategies have helped us understand the most common validation pitfalls and how banks can avoid them to turn their rating system investments into competitive advantage.

Surprisingly, the technical and data issues are rarely the real hurdle. Instead, the hurdle is much more like a classic management conundrum: setting the right goals, understanding the issues, putting the right people in place, and making sure different pieces of the organization work together to a common end.

Senior managers do not need a Ph.D. in mathematics to set their organizations on track to a sound validation and ratings improvement strategy, but they do need a solid game plan.

Set the right goals. Do not aim only for compliance with Basel II, but shoot for business benefits.

Basel's Pillar 2 has prompted banks to improve their internal rating systems, but it also set many banks on the wrong track. Improving rating systems is seen as a cost of doing business—a compliance hurdle rather than a source of potential business benefits.

Yet improving a bank's risk-rating system offers immediate business gains. A recent study suggests that moderately improving a rating system to better screen new midmarket loans can generate a $5.6 million gain for a medium-sized U.S. bank.[1] This number relates only to the improved loan screening during origination. It does not include the significant gains the bank would make from improved risk-based pricing, better capital allocation, and other competitive benefits.

Critically, gaining competitive benefits from the bank's rating system depends not only on improved ratings accuracy, but also on the confidence that the bank and its senior management have in their rating system when making important decisions. In the aftermath of the credit crisis, which caused many banks to lose confidence in their lending practices, renewed trust in their systems may help management regain some of that lost willingness to lend.

Even those banks determinedly focused on compliance now need to move on from Pillar 1 and pay attention to Pillars 2 and 3. The Pillar 2 supervisory review makes many demands concerning credit stress testing and the quality of the bank's capital adequacy assessments. It also obliges banks to forge a link between the ratings used to calculate regulatory capital and the credit risk information that management uses to make business decisions.

Pillar 3 compliance will concentrate minds even more. Banks will have to publish information drawn from their internal rating systems for the benefit of investors and bank analysts. That information had better be right because it will drive the bank's share price up or down. Analysts also will monitor how trustworthy the bank's credit information turns out to be over time, making an accurate and robust rating system a business imperative.

In truth, this is exactly what the regulators are hoping to see: banks translating Pillar 2 implementation into better risk management and business benefits, rather than writing Basel II down as a regulatory tax.

Take time to understand what validation really is.

It's tempting to think that rating-system validation consists largely of a handful of technical tests. This is simply not true, not for regulators and not for banks keen to secure potential business benefits.

In fact, regulators use the term *mosaic of evidence* to refer to the many different dimensions of internal-rating-system validation. Much of that mosaic is not really technical testing at all. The mosaic includes the conceptual soundness of the rating models, how the rating system is operated day to day, and a series of very technical tests that must be interpreted within this wider context.

Figure 1 illustrates how all the components of validation work together. Take the example of a rating system that produces inconsistent probability-of-default estimates for similar borrowers because there is a problem with the rating system's conceptual soundness. The specific reason for this might be that some of the ratings are based on a shorter time horizon than others (that is, they are more point-in-time) or there might be some systematic biases for obligors in certain industries. If this rating system allows lenders to override the system without sufficient limits or monitoring, it also will suffer from an operational weakness.

It's likely that any outcomes analysis tests (see the box, *Outcomes Analysis*) run by this bank will show the rating system is not distinguishing effectively among borrowers or performing as well as external benchmarks. To respond to these technical test results

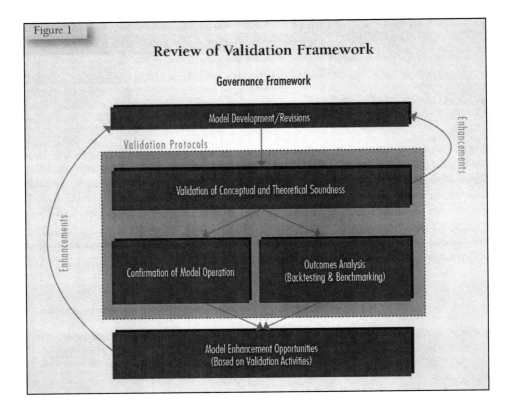

Figure 1

Review of Validation Framework

Governance Framework

Model Development/Revisions

Validation Protocols

Validation of Conceptual and Theoretical Soundness

Confirmation of Model Operation

Outcomes Analysis
(Backtesting & Benchmarking)

Enhancements

Model Enhancement Opportunities
(Based on Validation Activities)

and mend the system, managers will first have to grasp how the test results relate to potential conceptual and operational weaknesses.

This explains why validation is more than simply back testing and also why senior managers are a vital part of the validation process. They can encourage staff to stand back and take a critical view of how rating models are used in a business and operational context.

Building internal validation capabilities is an ongoing part of a bank's core competence.

For banks that regard validation procedures as a set of specialist technologies to be applied once a year, it is tempting to outsource rather than create their own validation skills. This is a mistake. Validation is a procedure that goes to the heart of the bank's core competence: differentiating between borrowers.

Regulators insist that validation is an ongoing activity. So if banks do not run the show themselves, they must bring in expensive external consultants annually to run their "black boxes." Of course, it can make sense to work with industry experts who already have the tools, data, and expertise needed to power up a ratings validation program. But banks should demand that these external experts help their staff build a validation factory that the bank can run itself.

OUTCOMES ANALYSIS
What Are the Key Technical Backtesting and Benchmarking Tests?

Backtesting

1. *Discriminatory power of rating system.* These tests assess how good the bank's system is at distinguishing default and recovery risk—in other words, whether defaults come from risk ratings with high estimated probabilities of default (PD). Do higher realized losses after a default correspond to high loss given default (LGD) estimates?

2. *Calibration test.* This test asks whether the PD and LGD levels assigned to a rating are consistent with the actual default and recovery experience. Are any apparent discrepancies statistically meaningful?

3. *Long-run PDs.* Do the PDs assigned to risk ratings reflect the bank's long-run default experience? The challenge here is that the internal default rate time series, from which the PDs are estimated, may not cover even a single full economic cycle. How can the bank use internal and external data jointly and robustly to mend this problem?

4. *Downturn LGDs.* How can the bank adjust its LGD estimates to account for the interdependencies between default rates and recoveries? The correlation between PDs and LGDs is not taken into account when estimating Basel's credit capital (or in many commercially available economic capital models). This results in an underestimation of the bank's capital requirement. Using downturn LGD is one way to compensate for this underestimation.

5. *Realization of risk-rating philosophies.* The bank needs to validate whether it is actually following its stated risk-rating philosophy, whether this is "point in time" or "through the cycle." An unnoticed divergence from the intended philosophy will have serious implications for how the bank interprets and manages its risk and capital.

6. *Risk homogeneity of obligors in each risk rating.* How does the bank know, for example, that a "risk rating 5" in one region or sector is the same as a "risk rating 5" in a different region or sector?

   If default rates differ, it might be a sign that the risk ratings are not risk homogeneous. The bank needs to have a strategy for testing, quantifying, and mending this kind of problem.

Benchmarking

7. *Benchmarking performing loans.* These tests benchmark internal ratings against external ratings for the same borrower, where these are available, and against third-party models that produce PDs, LGDs, and implied ratings for unrated entities. The agreement between internal and external ratings should be monitored over time to identify systematic trends and changes in trends.

(continued)

8. *Benchmarking defaulted loans.* Are the bank's realized default rates, migration rates, and LGDs consistent with relevant industry experience?
9. *Benchmarking the backtesting performance.* It can be a big challenge to make sense of backtesting results. They are not meaningful in isolation. Banks need to benchmark the results to determine the performance of their rating systems on a relative scale. To make an apples-to-apples comparison, however, the bank must first adjust the results to account for differences in portfolio composition, risk-rating philosophy, and so on.

Banks should require that external experts arrive with an open-book mentality, including offering open source code for validation models and tests, training bank staff in how to validate ratings, and showing how the results of tests can be built into a program of continuous rating system improvement.

Validation is not a backroom issue. Teams must challenge and improve organizational practices.

Validation is almost useless if it is limited to technical tests performed by "quants" whose results stay largely within the validation group, mainly because rating systems often go wrong for organizational and business reasons. To understand what is broken and how to put it right, banks have to build robust connections between validation personnel and other bank functions.

For example, validation tests often reveal that the actual default rate associated with the lowest origination (pass) rating grade in a portfolio is much higher than the probability-of-default estimate associated with the rating grade made by the bank's rating system. The reason lies with business pressures. Lenders are motivated to award pass grades and originate new loans even when the loans are higher risk than permitted by the bank's official policies. To address this issue, the bank may need to reexamine its policies within a risk-return framework to determine whether the bank has established an economically rational cutoff point in terms of the riskiness of the lowest passing grade.

Questioning a bank's rating system often provokes internal controversy. The Basel II regulators require that validation groups be able to "effectively challenge" the designers of the risk-rating systems. That means validators must be given a minimum level of power and independence—for example, in terms of reporting lines.

It also is important to build the right mix of people into the validation group. Quantitative talent plays a role, but the group must also contain personnel from the front line of the credit group and from the business lines.

Lastly, validation groups should not simply be delivering test reports. They need to be talking to other bank functions and communicating with senior management in the language of the banking business. Otherwise, the team, in partnership with senior management, cannot persuade the wider bank to alter its practices to improve the accuracy and consistency of ratings.

Validation is not a once-a-year activity. It is part of a continued improvement program.

Regulators require that certain validation activities be performed at least once a year (for example, outcomes analysis). With the right kind of validation factory in place, however, it is quick, easy, and cost effective for banks to use validation tools to continually monitor and improve their rating systems through the year.

This is especially true of the key performance indicators (KPIs) that regulators encourage banks to put in place. KPIs should cover many aspects of the credit rating system and credit risk reporting. For example, one class of KPI might track the tendency for the bank's lending officers to override the bank's rating system by lender and industry segment. That way, management can see where and why overrides are happening across the bank's key portfolios.

Other KPIs might track the degree of dissonance between the bank's internal ratings and the benchmark or external agency ratings (or the ratings computed on a sample of the portfolio using a third-party model). For example, as macroeconomic conditions deteriorate, can the bank spot and justify a gap that opens up between the bank's internal ratings and those of the rating agencies? Figure 2 shows what shape this gap might take in various situations.

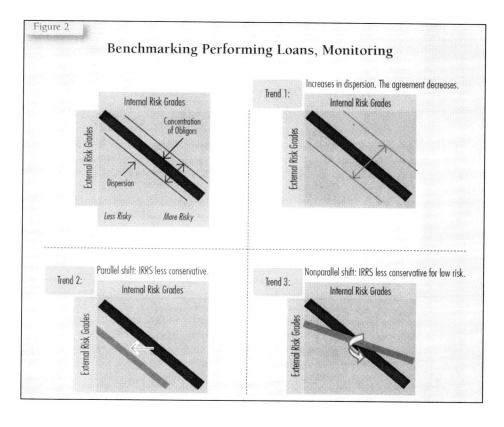

Figure 2

Benchmarking Performing Loans, Monitoring

Management also may want to set up a KPI that compares realized default rates and realized loss-given-default rates for recently defaulted loans with the default and loss rates predicted by the bank's rating system or with historical averages.

Increasingly, leading banks find it useful to monitor KPIs up to once a month and to run a large subset of validation procedures up to four times a year. For these banks, an initial ambition to build an annual Basel II rating validation procedure with business benefits has resulted in a continu-ous improvement program for their rating systems.

Conclusion

Banks need to shed the idea that validation is simply a series of technical tests to help them comply with regulations. That idea will lead them to treat validation as a yearly expense rather than as a system of continual improvement for one of their core competitive competencies.

Too limited an approach may not even deliver compliance, given the regulators' insistence that banks examine a wider mosaic of evidence, including rating concepts and operations. Furthermore, the limited approach will look increasingly irrelevant as the regulators put more emphasis on compliance with Pillars 2 and 3.

A more ambitious program means validation cannot be confined to the backroom but must reach out into the bank. Experience shows that senior management must help set the right goals, put the right people in the right place, and make sure the different pieces of the organization work together toward the common goal. That goal is not just regulatory compliance, but a continually improved rating system that reduces credit losses in the short term and sustains long-term bank profitability and competitive advantage.

Note

1. See Janet Mitchell and Patrick Van Roy, "Failure Prediction Models: Performance, Disagreements, and Internal Rating Systems," National Bank of Belgium Working Paper 123, December 13, 2007.

References

Miu, Peter and Bogie Ozdemir, 2005, "Practical and Theoretical Challenges in Validating Basel Parameters: Key Learnings from the Experience of a Canadian Bank," *Journal of Credit Risk*, Fall.

Ozdemir, Bogie and Peter Miu, 2008, *Basel II Implementation: A Guide to Developing and Validating a Compliant, Internal Risk Rating System*, McGraw-Hill Professional Books.

Loan Equivalents for Revolving Credits and Advised Lines

BY MICHEL ARATEN AND MICHAEL JACOBS JR.

When a bank makes a credit commitment, it provides a borrower both with immediate cash and the future availability of cash. Forms of commitments vary, as do restrictions on their continuing availability. Credit risk measures, such as expected loss and volatility of loss, are expressed as percentages of the amount drawn at the time of default. At any point in time, it's likely that the current amount drawn will remain outstanding in the future.

The exposure, or the additional amount drawn arising from the unused commitment, is of concern. In this article, *loan equivalent exposure* (LEQ) is defined as the portion of a credit line's undrawn commitment that is likely to be drawn down by the borrower in the event of default.

While it is important to recognize that an option has been provided to the borrower to draw down on bank lines that would presumably be less expensive than the borrower's current funding source, even when the borrower has not defaulted, it is not the intention of this article to price this option. Instead, this article reviews the bank's exposure at default, regardless of the borrower's motivation for draw-downs.

Reliable estimates of LEQs are important in aggregating and analyzing a bank's effective credit exposure across different types of facilities as well as in assessing risk capital requirements. Although internal historical bank data should be used to estimate LEQs, methodological hurdles must be overcome in order to obtain estimates of these factors. Such hurdles include paucity of defaults from high-credit-quality borrowers, data integrity issues, and lack of additional demographic variables that would aid in interpreting the data.

A significant overstatement of risk and capital requirements can come from using a conservative assumption that the LEQ is on the order of 75% (BIS II) or even greater. Although there is no agreement in the industry concerning which factors, a priori, should contribute to a higher LEQ, there are a number of commonsense assumptions. It is generally understood that if a borrower's credit deteriorates, it may be shut out of existing funding sources and will seek replacement or additional cash to fund its operations. At the same time, if covenants permit, a bank will protect itself by seeking to cut off unused commitments. In effect, the LEQ measures the outcome of the race between the bank and the borrower with regard to the draw-down of unused commitments in adverse circumstances.

One view is that since investment-grade borrowers enjoy fewer restrictive covenants, they should have high LEQs. It has also been argued that high LEQ factors should be used for non-investment-grade borrowers; because this type of borrower has a greater probability of default or financial distress, it is more likely to draw down a greater proportion of the unused credit over a given horizon. As a mitigant to this view, covenants are generally more restrictive for non-investment-grade borrowers.

In return for credits being successfully renegotiated after covenants are violated, borrowers may be required to sell assets. This could well result in a reduction of both usage and commitments. In other instances, a lender may actually find it prudent to increase and, at the same time, restructure its commitment to enhance the borrower's viability. Here, the unused credit would be increased—but with severe accompanying restrictions that prevent the borrower from drawing down these funds without the bank's permission. The LEQ measure, then, could be low in the event of default if there weren't an increase in commitment.

The tenor of the commitment is an important dimension of evaluating LEQs. The longer the time to maturity, the more time available for adverse credit migration—as well as greater opportunity and need for a borrower to draw down unused lines. Other factors that could affect differentiating estimates for LEQs include the nature of the obligor's business, access to commercial paper markets, whether there are borrowing-based limits restricting full commitment, the size of the commitment, and the current usage percent.

A Citibank study[1] covering 1987-91 examined 50 facilities that were generally rated BB/B or worse and then extrapolated these results to better-graded facilities. The estimated LEQs, though expressed as a percentage of the normally unused commitments, decreased with decreasing credit quality.

The study on which this article is based directly determines the LEQs on defaulted facilities. The study included 1,021 observations on 408 facilities for 399 defaulted borrowers at Chase over a five-and-three-quarter-year period ending in December 2000. Key results, based on historical draw-downs relative to unused amounts after properly filtering the universe of defaults and deciding upon an appropriate measurement procedure, are as follows:

- LEQs for revolving credits (RCs) averaged 43% across all ratings and time-to-default measures.
- LEQs show a highly significant increase relative to time-to-default across all ratings categories. One-year RC LEQs average 32%, while five-year LEQs are 72%. This may be due to a rating migration effect and a greater opportunity to draw down and implies that LEQs should be tenor adjusted in credit models.
- LEQs generally decrease as credit quality worsens, although unlike the time-to-default relationship, this is not as robust. An explanation may lie in tighter covenants and cutbacks in commitments for poorer ratings. In general, LEQs for BBBs and better average 62%; for grades between BBB- and B+ they average 48%, and for B and worse the average is 27%.
- The high volatility of estimated LEQs is seen in both the barbell-shaped distribution of LEQs, with observations clustered at 0% and 100%, and the relatively high standard deviation of 41.4%, with little variation across most grade and time-to-default categories. This implies that LEQ volatility should be incorporated into credit risk capital models.
- Estimated LEQs do not seem to be differentiated by lending organization (middle market versus large corporate), RC commitment type, size of commitment, do-

mestic-versus-foreign borrowers (although data is less robust for foreign borrowers), or by industry.

- There are some LEQ differences based on percentage utilization. Since utilization rates track to risk grades (worse grades tend to have higher utilization), this does not provide significant explanatory power.
- As expected, LEQs for advised lines for periods up to one year are lower than LEQs for RCs and average 17%.

Analysis of Revolving Credits

This section examines the relationship between the estimated LEQs and various facility and obligor characteristics. Characteristics of interest are risk ratings, time to default, usage levels, commitment levels, facility types, borrower industry, borrower domicile, and lender organization.

The data set of 834 facility years and 309 facilities implies that, on average, there are two to three years of LEQ measurements prior to default per facility. With 321 obligors, there were very few cases of multiple facilities to a given obligor. The average LEQ in the sample is 43.4%, with a relatively high standard deviation of 41.4%. The distribution is bimodal, with 39% of the sample in the 0-10% range and 26% of the sample in the 90-100% range. This is partly a consequence of the truncation procedure. Since there were more observations (28%) truncated to 0% than those truncated to 100% (14%), excluding all truncated observations would have the effect of increasing the average LEQ to 50.7%. Given the conservative practice of truncating negative LEQs to 0, it was deemed best to utilize all the data.

Analysis by Risk Grade and Time-to-Default

Table 1 shows the average and count of estimated LEQs by time-to-default (rounded up in time to the nearest year) and risk grade (10-point facility scale).

We can see the relative paucity of data at the higher risk grades (BBB and better) and longer times-to-default (four to six years). The strongest pattern that emerges is the increase in average LEQ with longer times-to-default, monotonically from 32.9% to 71.8% going from one year to default to five years to default and greater, respectively. This pattern also holds across risk-grade categories for which we have a reasonable amount of data, grades BBB+ to B-, although not in a strictly monotonically increasing pattern.

The relationship between LEQ and credit quality is seen to be an inverse one, as the rightmost margin of Table 1 shows a decrease in average LEQ from investment grades to speculative grades. However, the pattern is not monotonic and is less pronounced across time-to-default categories. The decline in LEQ with increasing risk grade is most evident in the shorter time-to-default categories, years one and two.

Various forms of regression and different candidate variables were explored. It was found that a relatively simple form provided good explanatory power with all the coefficients highly significant.[3] A regression equation for LEQ in percent based on time to default (TTD) in years and facility grade (FG) on a scale of 1 to 8 was derived:

$$LEQ = 48.36 - 3.49(FG) + 10.87(TTD)$$

Table 1

Average LEQ by Facility Risk Grade and Time-to-Default for Revolving Credits

(number of observations in parentheses)

Facility Risk Grade	Time-to-Default (in years)					
	1	2	3	4	5-6	Total
1 (AAA/AA-)		12.1% (1)				12.1% (1)
2 (A+/A-)	78.7% (3)	75.5% (6)	84.0% (1)			77.2% (10)
3 (BBB+/BBB)	93.9% (1)	47.2% (7)	41.7% (5)	100% (2)		55.5% (15)
4 (BBB+/BBB)	54.8% (18)	52.1% (20)	41.5% (9)	37.5% (3)	100.0% (2)	52.2% (52)
5 (BB)	32.0% (81)	44.9% (84)	62.1% (45)	76.0% (17)	68.3% (4)	46.4% (231)
6 (BB-/B+)	39.6% (129)	49.8% (100)	62.1% (37)	62.6% (25)	100.0% (4)	50.1% (295)
7 (B/B-)	26.5% (86)	39.7% (22)	37.3% (5)	97.8% (2)		30.7% (115)
8 (CCC)	24.5% (100)	26.7% (14)	9.4% (1)			24.6% (115)
Total	32.9% (418)	46.6% (254)	62.1% (103)	68.7% (59)	71.8% (59)	43.4% (834)

Applying the equation to the various facility grades and time-to-default categories yields a smoothed table as seen in Table 2.

Other Variables Considered

While other variables were considered both in various forms of regression and in simple cross-tabulations, these were not found to be significant:

- *Lending organization.* While there appeared to be some differences in LEQs between large corporate and middle market organizations, these were better explained by facility grades.
- *Domicile of borrower.* Only 53 out of the 834 observations were for borrowers outside the U.S., and their LEQ was 39% versus 44% in the U.S.
- *Industry.* There was a fair amount of variation in LEQs by industry. The higher LEQs (ranging from 77% to 50%) were seen for governments, insurance, business services, and energy.
- *Type of revolver.* Distinctions in LEQs by long-term, short-term, and convertible revolvers were 43%, 49%, and 31%, respectively.

Table 2

Regression Model Predicted LEQ by Facility Risk Grade and Time-to-Default for Revolving Credits

Facility Risk Grade	Time-to-Default (in years)					
	1	2	3	4	5-6	Total[2]
1 (AAA/AA-)	55.7%	66.6%	77.5%	88.4%	99.4%	60.5%
2 (A+/A-)	52.2%	63.1%	74.0%	85.0%	95.9%	57.0%
3 (BBB+/BBB)	48.7%	59.6%	70.6%	81.5%	92.4%	53.5%
4 (BBB+/BBB)	45.2%	56.2%	67.1%	78.0%	88.9%	50.0%
5 (BB)	41.8%	52.7%	63.6%	74.5%	85.4%	46.6%
6 (BB-/B+)	38.3%	49.2%	60.1%	71.0%	82.0%	43.1%
7 (B/B-)	34.8%	45.7%	56.6%	67.6%	78.5%	39.6%
8 (CCC)	31.3%	42.2%	53.2%	64.1%	75.0%	36.1%
Total[1]	38.6%	49.5%	60.5%	71.4%	82.3%	43.4%

1—Evaluated at the sample average of 5.9 for facility grade.
2—Evaluated at the sample average of 1.44 for time-to-default.

- *Commitment size.* Overall, LEQs did not show any strong pattern with respect to commitment size. Commitments in excess of $25 million had 50% LEQs, but so did commitments below $1 million. Commitments between $10 million and $25 million had LEQs of 34%, while commitments between $1 million and $10 million had LEQs averaging 44%.
- *Percent utilization.* Percent utilization showed significant distinctions in LEQs. However, utilization was closely related to facility grade, as the weaker grades had higher average utilization.

Analysis of Advised Lines

This section looks at the relationship between the estimated LEQs and various facility and obligor characteristics for advised lines. By definition, advised lines are cancelable at any time by the bank, require approval prior to draw, and are generally reviewed annually. If the line is not cancelled, the borrower may draw down on it and, if credit conditions are deemed stable, the bank may renew the line.

Characteristics of interest are risk ratings, time to default, usage levels, commitment levels, facility types, borrower industry, borrower domicile, and lender organization.

All observations have been part of the analysis, including those with times to default in excess of one year. LEQs for these observations imply that the bank has voluntarily renewed the advised line.

There were 187 observations for 87 obligors for 87 facilities. The average LEQ in the sample is 38% with a relatively high standard deviation of 42.6%. The distribution is bimodal, with 47% of the sample in the 0-10% range and 22% of the sample in the 90-100% range. Excluding all truncated observations would have the effect of increasing the average LEQ to 47%. Again, given the conservative practice of truncating negative LEQs to 0, it was felt best to utilize all the data.

Table 3 shows the average and count of estimated LEQs by time to default (rounded back in time to the nearest year) and risk grade.

We can see the paucity of data at the higher risk grades (BBB and better). The strongest pattern that emerges is the increase in average LEQ with longer times to default. The relationship between LEQ and credit quality is seen to be an inverse (although not monotonic) one, as the rightmost margin shows a decrease in average LEQ from 52% to 18%, going from BBB+ to CCC, respectively.

Table 3
Average LEQ by Facility Risk Grade and Time-to-Default for Advised Lines
(number of observations in parentheses)

Facility Risk Grade	Time-to-Default (in years)					Total
	1	2	3	4	5-6	
2 (A+/A-)	17.2% (2)	23.8% (2)				20.5% (4)
3 (BBB+/BBB)		2.7% (1)	2.7% (2)			2.7% (3)
4 (BBB+/BBB)	0 (1)	51.1% (5)	50.0% (2)	56.3% (2)	100.0% (1)	51.7% (11)
5 (BB)	32.6% (18)	43.0% (30)	49.5% (14)	71.8% (11)	78.1% (1)	46.5% (74)
6 (BB-/B+)	8.8% (23)	39.4% (25)	66.4% (11)	81.1% (3)	70.7% (1)	35.4% (63)
7 (B/B-)	16.9% (13)	38.1% (9)				25.6% (22)
8 (CCC)	10.0% (10)	100% (1)				18.2% (11)
Total	17.1% (67)	41.4% (73)	54.5% (28)	73.4% (19)	82.9% (3)	37.9% (187)

Given that advised lines are cancelable by the bank and that careful review is made periodically, LEQs should be primarily based on one year time-to-default results. With only 67 observations, it may be best to consider a flat LEQ regardless of grade. Alternatively, to reflect the pattern of decreasing LEQs as grades worsened, a slightly higher LEQ could be assessed for risk ratings of BB and better.

Conclusion

The following conclusions are offered:

1. This analysis offers a foundation to better risk-differentiate facilities based on their specific attributes. The importance of carefully screening and cleaning data cannot be overemphasized.
2. It is clear that, while there is a high volatility of LEQs for revolving credits, LEQs are influenced by both rating category and time to default. Maturity can be an effective proxy for time to default, as the longer the maturity, the greater the opportunity in time for ratings to downgrade and borrowers to draw down on unused facilities. Table 2, derived from the regression, can serve as a smoothed lookup table based on facility grade and maturity.
3. While other factors may also be important in better differentiating LEQ, the lack of meaningful data has restricted its exploration here. For example, borrowing base facilities may set an effective lower limit to drawing capability than the legal commitment.
4. While less robust, the results for advised lines reconfirm the need to assess LEQs for these facilities, although the risk of drawdown is less and should be based on the one-year results.
5. Credit capital models are currently based on uncertainty of default and volatility of loss severity. They could be expanded to incorporate volatility of LEQ using these estimates.

Notes

1. See Elliot Asarnow and James Marker, "Historical Performance of the U.S. Corporate Loan Market: 1988-1993," *Journal of Commercial Lending* 10, no. 2 (Spring 1995), pp.13-32 and private communication.
2. Some revolving credit facilities could be used for off-balance-sheet exposures (for example, letters of credit). When such instruments were issued, they were counted as a drawn outstanding and reduced the unused.
3. Overall $R2 = .11$ with a standard error of 39.1%

Values	Intercept	Facility Grade	Time to Default
t-values	6.1	-3.0	7.8
p-values	.0000	.0027	.0000

Measuring LGD on Commercial Loans: An 18-Year Internal Study

By Michel Araten, Michael Jacobs Jr., and Peeyush Varshney

his article presents findings associated with an extensive internal loss-severity study for the JPMorgan Chase (JPMC) wholesale bank. The recently completed loss given default (LGD) study draws on 18 years of loan loss history at JPMC for 3,761 defaulted borrowers at its several heritage organizations.

Estimates of LGD are key parameters in a bank's risk-rating system that impact facility ratings, approval levels, and the setting of loss reserves, as well as developing credit capital underlying risk and profitability calculations. LGD can be measured as either the net charge-off rate (accounting LGD), or the present value of cash losses (economic LGD), with respect to the initial book value of a defaulted obligation.

Analysis of JPMC's loss history entailed compilation of quarter-end book balances, charge-offs, recoveries of charge-offs, and cash flows for all customers that defaulted in the period 1982-99, with losses determined through 2002. LGD was computed for JPMC as a whole and was differentiated by business unit, industry group, geographic region, cohort year, and collateral type. Some findings of the study are as follows:

- Overall, the average accounting and economic LGD values were found to be 27.0% and 39.8%, respectively. An annual discount rate of 15% was used to compute the economic LGD.
- Differentiation by business unit revealed that, while the JPMC investment bank (IB) unit's borrowers had an economic LGD of 40.4%, the middle market (MM) and private bank (PBG) organizations' borrowers had economic LGDs of 40.3% and 34.5%, respectively.
- The distribution of LGD was seen to be bimodal, with large concentrations at 0% and 100% and with a high standard deviation (on the order of the mean).
- Economic LGD was found to be lower for secured (40.9%) as compared to unsecured facilities (50.5%) for a large subset of the population.
- The average time to final resolution and the average time a loan remained in a nonaccrual status were computed to be 2.4 years and 1.8 years, respectively—again with significant variability.
- Results by industry and geographic region showed wide variation in LGDs but were deemed not statistically significant enough to be of use other than as rough guidance.
- LGDs for unsecured credits were shown to be well correlated with the economic cycle, while LGDs for secured credits were not.

There have been a number of LGD studies by rating agencies and academics, but these have been focused principally on large syndicated bank loans, often in the high-yield market. The last comprehensive study describing a bank's internal experience was that of Asarnow and Edwards (see References), covering 831 defaults over a 24-year period ending in 1993 and resulting in an LGD of 34.8%.[1]

Measurement Issues

Most banks, including JPMC, place loans on a nonaccrual status either on a discretionary basis when payment default is likely, or automatically after the loans are 90 days past due principal or interest payment. In a number of cases, this automatic designation resulted from operational errors that needed to be corrected. On occasion, loan payments were credited to the wrong account or loans were renewed without updating maturity indicators.

Care was thus taken to cleanse the data in order to eliminate these operational errors. For example, all "short lived" nonaccruals (defined as six months or less on nonaccrual with no charge-off) with a subsequent return to accrual status were carefully reviewed. This procedure, which was designed to eliminate spurious defaults, has been consistently applied for all related historical studies, such as the evaluation of loan equivalents and probabilities of default.

Another measurement issue is the treatment of borrowers who default on facilities to lenders other than JPMC. In these relatively few cases, payments to JPMC continued, even when borrowers were in bankruptcy. For the purposes of this study, these cases were not counted as defaults. Since the LGDs of these facilities are zero, including them would result in a lower overall LGD but a higher probability-of-default estimate.

Issues of determining exposure amount also arise in the computation of LGD. The aggregation of all defaulted facilities to an obligor was chosen as the unit of observation for the practical reason that, in many cases, neither the workout process nor JPMC's historical nonaccrual systems allocated charge-offs and recoveries to individual facilities.

In addition, all forms of cash flows attributable to a given initial exposure at default—such as payment of back interest, liquidation of collateral, or payments of principal—were included and were not treated differentially. At the same time, all forms of cash outflows, such as additional facilities defaulting and additional advances to a defaulted customer under an existing facility, were incorporated. In these instances, the exposure profile during default could be an increasing one, possibly resulting in a discounted LGD being greater than 100%. A size cutoff of $100,000 in initial balance was imposed to filter out observations of a more retail character.

Both accounting and economic LGD values were determined for each obligor. Accounting LGD is defined as the net charge-off rate (the sum of charge-offs minus recoveries), while economic LGD is defined as the present value of cash losses. These are both determined relative to the initial book balance. In principle, losses should include all workout costs, and cash recoveries should include any noncash payments (such as equity, warrants, and property).

Workout costs were not tracked in this study, but a previous study determined that they add approximately 1% to the economic LGD. Noncash payments were captured to the extent that they were recorded as recoveries of charge-offs. Economic cash flows are measured based on changes in book balance, coupled with accounting charge-offs and recoveries.

A "vulture" discount rate is used to discount these cash flows, as opposed to the original contract rate on the loan or a cost-of-funds rate. The rationale for using a vulture rate is that it appropriately accounts for the riskiness of distressed-instrument cash flows. An alternative to discounted cash flow analysis is to measure the trading value of distressed debt shortly after default (see, in the References, Altman and Kishore and Fitch Risk Management). However, except for a relatively few large corporates, most of the defaulted customers do not have debt that is traded publicly; and even if they did, the use of such prices is predicated on the efficiency of the market for such debt.

Determination of when the workout is finally resolved and no further payment in cash or in kind is received also presents difficult measurement issues. In some cases, this period could be rather lengthy. Excluding those observations that were not determined to be finally resolved would reduce the number of observations and also result in lagged LGD estimates. Only those customers who defaulted no later than the fourth quarter of 1999 were included as observations in this study. This allowed up to three years—that is, through the fourth quarter of 2002—for additional charge-offs and recoveries to manifest themselves. Recoveries as well as additional charge-offs likely to be recorded beyond this three-year period needed to be estimated. These adjustments were made based on benchmark profiles of cumulative recoveries and charge-offs over different periods following default.[2]

There were also a small number of observations with LGDs below 0% (0.5% of observations), partly as a result of gains in asset sales. This feature of the LGD distribution, with a relatively large amount of outliers on both ends of the domain, results in statistical difficulties—in particular, the variance of the LGD blows up. "Windsorizing" the data, or effectively capping and flooring the LGD distribution at appropriately chosen quantiles,[3] addressed this problem.

To further analyze the determinants of loss severity, observations were segmented along line of business (LOB), borrower industry, geographic region, cohort date, and type of primary collateral. The main LOBs were investment bank (or "large corporate"), middle market (or "regional / small business"), and private bank (private high net worth). As there had been a number of reorganizations over this period, historical LOBs were remapped to these designations.

A separate LOB presenting special issues is the emerging-markets business. Nonaccrual information for emerging markets was occasionally incomplete—in some cases, loans appeared to be paid off, but in fact the asset was moved elsewhere on the bank's books, resulting in a possible understatement of LGD. Recoveries following country rescheduling events were often arbitrarily allocated to individual loans. In other cases, it was not possible to track loans to resolution, so missing observations added to the thinness of data. For this reason, data on emerging markets was broken out separately.

Determining whether collateral was received and how it was categorized also raised measurement issues. Our analysis was developed at the obligor level. Collateral, however, is obtained at the facility level. It is thus possible that some facilities to the same borrower were secured with collateral, while other facilities were unsecured or had different types of collateral.

JPMC credit surveillance reports (CSRs), prepared when customers near a criticized status ("B"), were consulted to determine whether the exposure was secured and, if so, the primary collateral designation. CSRs were not available for all defaulted borrowers, as historically they were generally prepared for larger exposures and for those borrowers with more problematic workout issues. A sub-sample of 1,705 obligors with CSR or collateral information at the time of default was used to differentiate secured versus unsecured LGD.

It should be noted that management of bank loans is a dynamic process. At origination, the loan may have been unsecured, but somewhere along the workout process collateral is often obtained. To improve the distinction between secured and unsecured LGDs, it would be highly desirable to determine when collateral was received.

Results of the Study

Table 1 gives the overall results of the study for 3,761 resolved defaults in the period from the first quarter of 1982 to the fourth quarter of 1999, encompassing all JPMC heritage organizations. The average net charge-off is 27.0%, with a standard deviation of 37.9%, while the average economic LGD is 39.8%, with a standard deviation of 35.4%. The average time to final resolution and the time to zero book value are 2.4 and 1.8 years, with standard deviations of 2.3 and 1.6 years, respectively.

The economic LGD was computed using a 15% annual discount rate. Table 2 shows a sensitivity analysis of overall average economic LGD. Using a discount rate of 10% or 5% yields averages of 36.2% or 31.9%, respectively. A good argument can be made to vary the discount rate to reflect varying investor yield requirements during different

Table 1
Summary of Overall LGD Study Results JPMC
Resolved Defaults (1Q82-4Q99)

Description	Mean	Standard Deviation
Net Charge-Offs	27.0%	37.9%
Discounted LGD @15%	39.8%	35.4%
Gross Charge-Off Rate	30.8%	37.7%
Time to Final Resolution [Yrs]	2.4	2.3
Time-to-Zero Book Value [Yrs]	1.8	1.6

Table 2
Sensitivity Analysis of Overall LGD
JPMC Resolved Defaults (1Q82-4Q99)

Discount Rate	Economic LGD
5%	31.9%
10%	36.2%
15%	39.8%

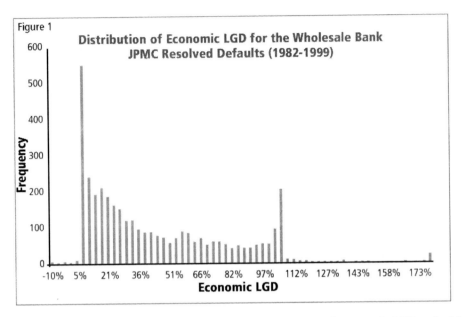

Figure 1

Distribution of Economic LGD for the Wholesale Bank JPMC Resolved Defaults (1982-1999)

parts of the economic cycle. Figure 1 shows the distribution of economic LGD to be bimodal, with 0.5% (8%) of observations at 0% (100%) and below (above), highly abnormal with a pronounced positive skew.

Table 3 breaks the results out by business unit, although given the high standard deviations of LGD, these results should be interpreted with care. The highest economic

Table 3

LGD by Business Unit
JPMC Resolved Defaults (1Q82-4Q99)

Business Units	Obligor Count	Average Time-to-Resolution (Years)	Net Charge-Offs Mean	Net Charge-Offs Standard Deviation	Discounted LGD Mean	Discounted LGD Standard Deviation
Large Corporates (U.S.)	676	3.33	23.8%	34.2%	41.6%	30.9%
Large Corporates (non-U.S.)	268	2.58	22.9%	33.8%	37.3%	33.2%
Real Estate	719	2.23	29.8%	36.6%	42.0%	33.7%
Emerging Markets	394	3.04	25.8%	39.5%	42.2%	35.6%
Middle Market	1,264	2.15	30.0%	40.4%	40.3%	38.4%
Private Banking	310	1.66	25.4%	40.9%	34.5%	38.3%
Other	130	1.35	15.6%	30.1%	23.1%	28.2%
Total	3,761	2.43	27.0%	37.9%	39.8%	35.4%

LGDs are seen in real estate and emerging markets, with respective averages of 42.0% and 42.2%, and the lowest is in the private bank, at 34.5%. The LGD results for large corporate (U.S.) and middle market are 41.6% and 38.7%, and the average time to resolution is 3.03 years and 2.07 years, respectively.

Table 4 summarizes the differentiation of LGD by industry type. Among those groups having reasonably large numbers of observations, manufacturing wholesale (46.3%) and retail (43.3%) have mean economic LGDs notably above the overall average, while communications (34.4%) is markedly below. Finance companies and lessors, while having a relatively low sample representation (68 obligors), seem to be significantly above the overall mean economic LGD (47.1%). Energy, with a mean economic LGD of 46.8%, also has a relatively high loss severity, even without including some of the recent large losses. Communications, another sector in which large loss severities of late are not reflected in this data, has mean economic LGD lower than the overall average of

Table 4					
LGD by Industry					
JPMC Resolved Defaults (1Q82-4Q99)					
		Net Charge-Offs		**Discounted LGD**	
Industry	**Obligor Count**	**Mean**	**Standard Deviation**	**Mean**	**Standard Deviation**
Automotive	29	37.9%	40.2%	52.5%	39.8%
Utilities	20	36.8%	59.1%	49.0%	50.8%
Finance Companies & Lessors	68	34.5%	38.3%	47.1%	38.1%
Energy	102	31.4%	35.6%	46.8%	35.7%
Mfg Wholesale	246	33.8%	42.5%	46.3%	38.4%
Retail	279	32.2%	37.9%	43.3%	34.8%
Metals & Minerals Mfg	44	26.8%	41.0%	42.4%	39.5%
Construction	104	29.8%	38.8%	41.0%	38.5%
Real Estate	864	26.3%	36.0%	38.6%	34.0%
Transportation	98	23.9%	35.1%	38.2%	31.5%
Consumer Services/Entertainment	86	27.7%	38.5%	38.0%	35.9%
Communications	86	21.5%	29.6%	34.4%	29.3%
Other	1,735	25.0%	38.0%	38.2%	35.3%
Total	3,761	27.0%	37.9%	39.8%	35.4%

34.4%. Again, while there is clear variability in average LGD across industries, potential lack of statistical significance in the averages should be kept in mind.

Table 5 differentiates LGD by presence and type of collateral for a sample of the population having CSRs. This sample of 1,705 borrowers has about 75% of the names coming from the 1990-99 period and the rest from earlier periods. The CSR-based 1,705 observations had somewhat higher overall LGDs of 43.3% versus the remaining non-CSR-based 2,056 observations that had a 36% LGD. In this context, we observe that about 75% had some form of security associated with their loans and experienced an economic LGD of 40.9%. Unsecured exposures to obligors had, as expected, a significantly higher economic LGD of 50.5%.

Nine buckets of primary (mutually exclusive) collateral types are shown, with the economic LGD ranging from 35.8% for cash and marketable securities to 53.0% for other. Accounts receivable and inventory lie between these, with economic LGDs of 35.1% and 40.9%, respectively; the latter are not distinguishable from the overall average. Mortgages/liens on real property are between these, with an economic LGD of 39.4%. LGD is higher for unsecured as compared to secured exposures and increases as the quality of the security decreases. The magnitudes of LGD for secured suggest sample

Table 5					
LGD by Categories of Collateral **JPMC Resolved Defaults (1Q82-4Q99)**					
		Net Charge-Offs		**Discounted LGD**	
Type of Secured Collateral [Primary]	**Obligor Count**	**Mean**	**Standard Deviation**	**Mean**	**Standard Deviation**
Cash & Marketable Securities	36	23.7%	37.1%	35.8%	33.8%
Nonmarketable Securities	11	15.8%	29.7%	44.9%	54.7%
Accounts Receivable	126	24.3%	34.6%	35.1%	32.4%
Inventory	60	31.9%	34.5%	40.9%	32.2%
Accounts Receivable & Inventory	66	30.9%	41.6%	41.6%	38.6%
Fixed Assets / Machinery & Equipment	71	32.1%	36.8%	42.3%	34.2%
Mortgages / Liens on Real Property	706	25.0%	32.5%	39.4%	31.2%
Blanket Lien	120	33.2%	34.2%	47.2%	32.7%
Other	83	41.4%	48.8%	53.0%	41.8%
Total Secured	1,279	27.7%	35.3%	40.9%	33.4%
Total Unsecured	426	40.3%	42.5%	50.5%	38.1%
Total	1,705	30.8%	37.2%	43.3%	34.6%

selection bias (it seems to be generally higher than the overall sample) and possibly incomplete characterization of collateral types (for example, one would expect much lower LGDs for cash collateral).

Another issue of concern is that 75% of the CSR sample consists of secured customers, while most of the loans are unsecured at origination. This points to the difficulty in associating an LGD with an unsecured exposure, as a good portion of them will wind up as secured at the time of default. Estimates of LGDs for unsecured loans should take into consideration the likelihood of obtaining security during the workout process.

Table 6 summarizes the LGD by cohort year. The net charge-off rate and economic LGD for 18 years follow the expected pattern with respect to the trend in business cycles

Table 6					
		LGD by Cohort Year			
		JPMC Resolved Defaults (1Q82-4Q99)			
		Net Charge-Offs		**Discounted LGD**	
Year	**Count**	**Mean**	**Standard Deviation**	**Mean**	**Standard Deviation**
1982	223	34.2%	38.2%	53.3%	30.5%
1983	181	22.0%	35.4%	43.5%	31.3%
1984	144	22.0%	35.0%	41.9%	29.1%
1985	134	26.8%	37.2%	46.0%	33.6%
1986	446	28.1%	42.3%	42.2%	39.4%
1987	281	26.4%	38.8%	39.4%	37.3%
1988	214	31.0%	40.6%	41.9%	37.6%
1989	268	40.3%	40.8%	53.5%	37.5%
1990	352	37.7%	41.5%	48.0%	36.5%
1991	439	27.3%	38.1%	38.7%	35.3%
1992	255	23.0%	32.2%	33.3%	31.9%
1993	167	24.3%	33.5%	33.1%	31.4%
1994	101	11.6%	25.6%	22.7%	25.0%
1995	54	15.0%	29.3%	24.2%	27.4%
1996	131	12.7%	26.4%	21.4%	26.5%
1997	124	14.3%	27.7%	23.2%	26.7%
1998	131	19.7%	32.4%	28.2%	33.3%
1999	116	23.3%	37.6%	30.4%	37.1%
Total	3,761	27.0%	37.9%	39.8%	35.4%

over the last two decades. LGDs are higher during recessions (53.5%, 48.0%, and 38.7% in the respective years 1989 to 1991) and lower during the expansion periods (24.2%, 21.4%, and 23.2% in the respective years 1995 to 1997). The credit cycle is also reflected in the larger number of defaulted obligors in recession years. Note that the volatility of LGD also has a negative correlation with the rate of economic growth. This further implies that the positive correlation of LGD with default rates is accentuated during bad years.

Empirical Analysis of LGD and Default Rates

The preponderance of theoretical arguments and empirical evidence supports the hypothesis that LGDs, on either individual instruments or for segments of the market, should increase with some measure of the default rate (see, in the References, Altman and Kishore, Altman et al., and Hu and Perraudin). In this study, a more refined analysis of the relationship between LGD and the business cycle is presented for bank loan LGDs.

Figure 2 shows the average annual LGD for unsecured U.S. large corporate borrowers plotted against the average Moody's all-corporate default rate for the period 1984-99. Given this segmentation, acceptable correlations between LGD and the state of the economy can be derived, as shown by the following estimated regressions for these 15 data points:

$$LGD = 0.35 + 7.18 \text{ x Default Rate}$$
$$(0.0001) \ (0.0556)$$
$$R^2 = 0.25 \text{ Adjusted } R^2 = 0.20$$
$$LGD = 1.16 + 0.16 \text{ x In (Default Rate)}$$
$$(0.0001) \ (0.0069)$$
$$R^2 = 0.44 \text{ Adjusted } R^2 = 0.40$$

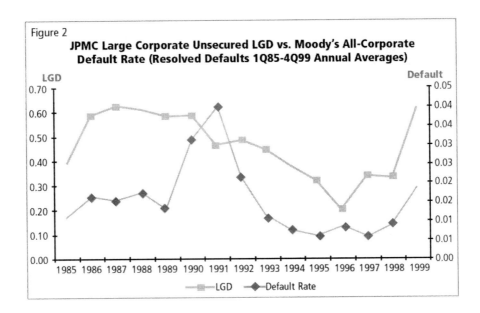

Figure 2
JPMC Large Corporate Unsecured LGD vs. Moody's All-Corporate Default Rate (Resolved Defaults 1Q85-4Q99 Annual Averages)

The coefficients on either the default rate or its logarithm are positive and significant in both regressions (at the 10% level at least) and the r-squares are in line with empirical evidence regarding this relationship (Altman and Kishore; Hu and Perraudin). The relationship is stronger in the log-linear regression compared to the linear regression with an r-squared of 44% versus 25%, respectively. The fitted relationships are illustrated in Figure 3. While these results are broadly in line with existing empirical evidence, there are some differences worth noting.

The r-squares relating secured exposures to the business cycle for the same period were about 2%, showing virtually no correlation. While values of collateral are expected to rise or fall with economic conditions, this was not observed here.

Altman et al. measure recovery as the market value weighted-average annual recovery of a broad sample of domestic publicly traded corporate bonds at default for the period 1982-2000. The economic variable used in the basic univariate regression is the weighted-average annual default rate in the high-yield market. Used as a regressor, it is able to explain anywhere from 45% to 60% of the variability in recovery rates, depending on the model specification.

There are several reasons why the relationship here is somewhat weaker. First, bank loan LGDs have greater variability than recovery rates on bonds. Second, there is a more direct connection between the default and recovery rates on bonds in the same high-yield sector, as compared to LGDs for JPMC and the default rate on the entire corporate sector. Finally, it can be argued that discount rates should be more punitive at less favorable points in the cycle, and the absence of such an adjustment serves to reduce the correlation observed in this regression.

Hu and Perraudin perform an analysis of bond recovery and default rates that has greater comparability to what is done here. They look at recoveries on the entire

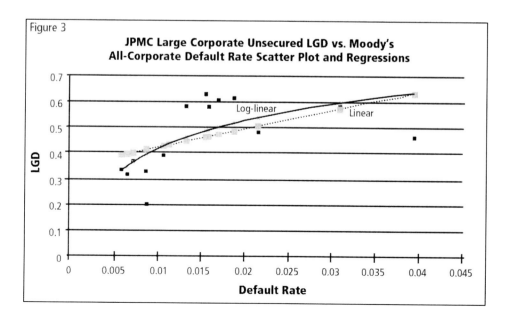

Figure 3

Moody's universe of public bonds, versus the issuer-weighted default rate, at quarterly intervals from 1982 to 1999. The authors obtain correlations ranging between 21% and 31% depending on the model, which is a significantly weaker relationship than recorded here.

Conclusion

Measurement of LGDs for bank loans requires great care in treatment of archival data, particularly if the historical period is to encompass several economic cycles. Consistent definitions of default, cleaning up of spurious indicators of default, choice of discount rates, and identification of secured versus unsecured exposures are critical to the forensic analysis of loss severities. The dynamic character of bank loan management requires tracking of exposure and collateral received throughout the life of a loan. LGDs have high volatilities, and LGDs for unsecured loans exhibit relatively high correlation with the economic cycle. These relationships need to be incorporated into the determination of capital requirements for bank portfolios.

Notes

1. Included in the definition of default were loans classified as "doubtful," and the discount rate used was the contractual lending rate.
2. Based on the analysis of an early part of the data set, a charge-off or recovery would be scaled upward by the inverse of the average proportion of total amounts received during the years following default. These adjustments were applied to approximately 8% of the observations.
3. This was done at the .01 and 99.99 percentiles, resulting in bounds of -10% and 176%, respectively.

References

Altman, Edward I. and Vellore M. Kishore, 1996, "Almost Everything You Wanted to Know About Recoveries on Defaulted Bonds," *Financial Analysts Journal*, November/December.

Altman, Edward I., Andrea Resti, and Andrea Sironi, 2001, "Analyzing and Explaining Default Recovery Rates," ISDA, December.

Asarnow, Elliot and David Edwards, 1995, "Measuring Loss on Defaulted Bank Loans: A 24-Year Study," *Journal of Commercial Lending* 77, no. 7.

Fitch Risk Management, 2001, North American Loan Loss Database, October.

Hu, Yen-Ting and William Perraudin, 2002, "The Dependence of Recovery Rates and Defaults," Bank of England.

Keisman, David, Karen van de Castle, and Ruth Yang, 2000, "Suddenly Structure Mattered: Insights into Recoveries from Defaulted Loans," *Credit Week*, May.

Counterparty Credit Risk Exposure from a Regional Bank Perspective

BY JEREMY TAYLOR

he measurement and management of counterparty credit exposure, or CCE, have evolved along with the industry over the past 10 years or so.

During that time, we have seen derivatives structuring become more complex and derivatives systems grow more powerful. It should come as no surprise that measurement tools—the metrics for quantifying the amount of credit exposure and the risk management practices surrounding how those metrics are used—have kept step with that evolution. Significantly, these developments are market, not regulator, driven. As in other banking areas, regulators are moving to keep up with leading practices at the largest institutions.

Trends in CCE Measurement

What has changed in the market and the industry when it comes to CCE measurement? For one, the industry has seen derivatives become more widely accepted. In the process, more complex structures for derivatives have allowed market risk to be hedged more inventively and effectively.

At the same time, available derivatives systems have become more powerful in their ability to mine market and bank data in order to measure and differentiate risk. Over time, the tools used to measure other aspects of a bank's portfolio risk were adapted to the credit exposure exercise. Hence, value at risk (VaR), a tool for measuring the price risk in a portfolio, has been applied to the measurement of CCE.

What this last point highlights is this: While we are focusing on the measurement of credit risk exposure, the underlying dynamics are related to market risk. We are measuring how much the underlying market variable—for example, an interest rate or an exchange rate—might move in an extreme scenario and what impact that movement would have on the value of a position or a portfolio. Indeed, it is useful to remember that when looking at a derivatives position, market risk and credit risk are conceptually (though not in practical terms) mirror images of each other. If a position moves against the bank, that is market risk. If that position moves in the bank's favor, it is credit risk.

Again, the market-risk drivers of VaR determine the dollar amount in either case, subject to a certain confidence level and holding period.

Role of the Regulators and Basel II

There is no doubt that regulators' expectations are rising. On the credit side of the current Basel proposals is the internal ratings-based (IRB) approach, requiring banks to collect loss-related data and to adopt more sophisticated analytics to support how they estimate credit losses and their variability. Also, regulators are pushing for more stress testing, back testing, and the like. On the CCE side, there is a parallel move toward more risk-sensitive methodologies for measuring credit exposure to derivatives counterparties, as reflected in what Basel II calls the internal models method, going well beyond the current exposure method (CEM) of Basel I. The CEM calculates exposure by using add-on factors that reflect underlying market volatility, to multiply by the notional dollar amount of a derivatives position.

It certainly appears that there is more regulatory oversight than ever. However, it is important to remember that regulators are really responding to developments in the market and, in particular, to developments at the top end of the market, where the larger players are developing tools to become more risk sensitive in their approach to measuring credit exposure. The size and complexity of their derivatives portfolios, and the attendant risks they take on, have required them to make this effort.

Midsize Banks and Their Options

Large institutions have been proactive in recognizing the need for more risk-sensitive CCE measures and for adapting market-risk tools to the CCE exercise. But what is appropriate for a top-tier institution is not necessarily the optimal solution for a smaller bank, whose portfolio typically is less complex and is subject to corresponding differences in its risk profile. Therefore, we will likely continue to see a significant divergence in terms of actual market practice, even as we see a consensus on best practice emerge over time.

When approaching a CCE exercise, the size and complexity of a bank's derivatives book are critical factors. Nonlinear derivatives positions, which reflect optionality in structure, mean that a linear transformation will be less useful because there is no way to differentiate, for example, at-the-money versus away-from-the-money positions. This is a drawback of using fixed add-on factors, as in the CEM.

Much of the difference in approach revolves around available resources. Naturally, large institutions have deep in-house resources to develop CCE tools and to use them effectively. However, for a regional/midsize bank with a derivatives operation, the required data feeds, the computational resources, and the in-house support are quite daunting.

For example, unlike the exercise of computing mark-to-market valuation, there are various ways a bank can calculate potential future exposure (PFE), which is an important component of CCE. PFE indicates how much further a position might move in the bank's favor (subject to a certain confidence level) over the remaining life of a contract, which is added to the existing valuation to obtain CCE. The exercise is problematic because it requires a variety of different assumptions and can be approached with varying degrees of sophistication and systems requirements, all of which may differ given the size and scope of the institution.

These factors militate against standardization of CCE measurement across the industry. A midsize bank is likely a Tier 2 dealer, in OCC terminology; the bank is marketing derivatives to a small business or less sophisticated commercial customer base and not running an open book. Midsize banks have less need for the more powerful simulation approaches employed by the larger Tier 1 players, whose approaches constitute best practice in the market today.

A CCE Approach That Moves Toward "Best Practice"?

In trying to anticipate how the underlying market variable might move and the impact such a move would have on a derivative's value, there is no doubt that a simulation approach represents today's best practice. Simulations are aimed at identifying a point on the exposure distribution—for example, the 99th percentile.

I believe regional banks are moving in this direction, but with important qualifications. RMA's recent survey on this topic indicated that a surprising number of large institutions are still using add-on factors, corresponding to the CEM laid out in Basel I. Although the add-on factor can be computed to incorporate current market volatility data, this approach is less powerful and less sensitive compared with running daily simulations on each position, as is the practice among leading practitioners. However, banks that are Tier 2 dealers marketing derivatives to a less sophisticated customer base may find that "plain vanilla" derivatives account for so much of their book that some sort of add-on approach may be appropriate, given other considerations.

A second component is emerging in the area of best practice: stress testing to probe that 1% tail. What are the most extreme scenarios (market outcomes) that would produce very large buildups of credit? These scenarios should reflect the institution's particular product and market alignment. They should be based on large historical movements and on possible, even if unlikely, future movements. They should incorporate not just volatility but also correlation effects. By looking at specific, discrete outcomes, stress testing complements the more rigid and sterile results of simulation modeling by itself.

As suggested earlier, for a small derivatives player a simulation-based approach may be more than is necessary; alternative, less powerful methodologies may suffice, at least until the portfolio reaches critical mass. For example, a scenario-based approach incorporates certain key features of a simulation approach but less onerously. Revaluations are still being done on individual positions—similar to a simulation model but unlike an add-on approach.

A scenario-based approach differs from a simulation-based approach in that it views the underlying market variable as a deterministic process, rather than as a random variable whose outcome is to be simulated. For example, for an interest rate derivative, yield curve scenarios could be constructed to reflect parallel upward and downward shifts, yield curve twists, and so on. These would be constructed to represent, say, "99% events." This contrasts with running Monte Carlo simulations to capture, more richly, the range of possible yield curve movements—say, 1,000 simulations—then selecting the one that gives the 990th highest exposure result.

The scenario-based approach is less computationally intensive, requires less middle- and back-office support (for setting and testing the required assumptions, for example), and is more transparent, meaning that it is easier to visualize and understand the specific drivers of more extreme outcomes compared with the "black box" of a simulation model—especially for a bank whose credit and marketing personnel may be less familiar with the complexities of derivatives markets. Set against these considerations is the loss in precision compared with a simulation approach. For some institutions, that trade-off may make sense.

One of the most important aspects of Basel II is that it encourages institutions to continue to upgrade but without requiring that a bank adopt a particular approach. Last year's Notice of Proposed Rule Making (NPR) for the U.S. implementation of Basel II did the same. Industry participants recognize an emerging consensus as to best practice in CCE: a simulation approach complemented by stress testing. But again, there are a number of important considerations—the existing data and human capital infrastructure, the complexity of a bank's portfolio, etc.—that will determine how far and how fast an individual institution will choose to move along the path toward best practice.

Monitoring Credit Utilization

So far we have focused on how CCE can be measured and computed. It is appropriate to finish by bringing in the exercise of setting credit limits for derivatives customers (counterparties); calculation of CCE then determines utilization of those limits.

Limits are set to reflect not just the bank's assessment of a customer's creditworthiness but also the customer's anticipated credit (that is, CCE) needs. This exercise is complicated by the connection between those two factors, something we in the industry call wrong-way and right-way risk, meaning that the exposure amount correlates with the default probability.

Wrong-way exposures tend to get more attention in the literature (try Googling them!). What is interesting, however, is that right-way exposure is, and should be, more important than wrong-way. That is because when derivatives are structured correctly to hedge a customer's risk, they create right-way exposure.

A few years ago, I was involved in the setup of an energy derivatives program. We quickly recognized that for an energy producer hedging its price risk, higher commodity prices would mean both higher credit exposure to the customer and a lower default probability. This is an important mitigating factor, but one that is extremely difficult to model. If oil prices rose, the bank's credit administration certainly recognized the positive influence of right-way exposure on creditworthiness, even if it was not something we were able to quantify and explicitly capture in our credit management setup for this program.

Moving beyond this one issue, though, the same general observations can be made for monitoring and reporting CCE as for direct loans. We need to recognize the value of the following: full daily reporting of positions, including customer aggregations across products; the ability to reflect enforceable netting rights; and the ongoing dialogue between not just the front and middle office but also involving credit and line officers.

Best practice in CCE is not just the choice of measurement methodology, with back testing to validate that choice, but also how the resulting metric gets applied, monitored, and reported as part of the overall credit management process.

Consumer Credit Risk Parameters

Events of the last decade have dramatically altered the landscape for retail lending analytics. Credit scoring and loss forecasting have been slowly evolving over many decades, but the introduction of Basel II pushed top lenders to make huge new investments in data capture, retention, and analysis.

The U.S. mortgage crisis exposed the inherent weaknesses in many of the core models being used in the industry, including the just completed work on Basel II. In response, we have seen a new round of regulation, data gathering, and model building in support of stress testing, along with a push for mid-tier lenders to create these models. The trend is clear. Lenders of all sizes must evolve and become more data-driven and model-based in their account decisioning and portfolio management.

This section contains articles on credit risk modeling for retail loan portfolio forecasting and account management. Although loan-level models can be aggregated for portfolio forecasting, few of these models have the necessary structure to create monthly forecasts with macroeconomic inputs. For this and many other reasons, the models and corresponding literature tend to split along the lines of aggregate modeling for portfolio forecasting and loan-level models for account management.

The first articles in this section discuss core concepts in portfolio modeling. The next set of articles focuses on account-level modeling. The final article merges the two concepts to create loan-level forecasts.

When the first article of this section, "Retail Loan Portfolio Dynamics: Becoming a Better Vintner," by Joseph Breeden, was written in 2002, retail lending analytics consisted of credit scores, roll-rate models, and a few lenders making vintage plots. Actual vintage analysis was almost nonexistent, as were stress testing and economic capital models. This article describes the core concepts of portfolio dynamics and introduces the reader to a class of models capable of quantifying the drivers of portfolio dynamics.

In the decade since publication, age-period-cohort (APC) models have become part of the lexicon of retail lending analytics. Although in use in demography and other fields for more than 100 years, APC is a new introduction to retail lending that can model vintage-aggregate data for portfolio answers. The concepts introduced in this article are discussed in great detail in the APC literature.

Breeden's second article, "Portfolio Forecasting Tools: What You Need to Know," is essentially a sequel. The reader is taken through the modeling components needed for portfolio forecasting, elements of scenario design, and the range of models in use in 2003 for portfolio forecasting. Very little has changed. Notably, the cons listed for roll-rate models are exactly the reason those models failed during the U.S. mortgage crisis. Roll-rate models were the dominant forecasting technique in use during the crisis.

The article ends with a plea for more companies to create real forecast models. That plea has only recently been heeded. The head of credit risk for a large mortgage lender stated loudly at a meeting in 2004, "Why should I worry about forecasting? I never lose money when I foreclose on a home. I don't even *do* a forecast. I just write down a number!" He retired three years later.

"Leveraging Aggregated Credit Data in Portfolio Forecasting and Collection Scoring," by Jeffrey Morrison and Andy Feltovich, jumps ahead to 2010. After the crisis, forecasting and stress testing of retail portfolios had attained the emphasis they deserved. This article discusses new ways that credit bureau data could be aggregated and used for the purpose of portfolio forecasting. The authors' key argument is that aggregate bureau data can mirror the same information as economic data, but is generally available much faster than the various government-reported indices.

Much of the article is dedicated to better collections management, since this is one area where portfolio forecasting becomes actionable and of quantifiable value.

"The Role of Credit Scores in Consumer Lending Today," by Elizabeth Mays, changes focus to account decisioning and the models that best support it. The article is the introductory chapter of the author's book[1] and provides a good overview of the uses of scores and how they are created. For loan acquisition, bureau scores are compared to custom scores. In account management, specific discussions are provided for behavior scores, recovery scores, and the champion-challenger process for score management.

As brought out in all these articles (this one was written in 2003), progress in the industry has been incremental, not revolutionary. May's article describes the early use of survival models, which would naturally include Cox proportional hazards models. In the following decade, some organizations have tested more advanced modeling techniques, but more than 90% of all industry scoring models are still built with logistic regression. The reason is that logistic regression served the needs to which it was put. Events of the last five years are beginning to change that perspective.

"Looking Behind the Credit Score: Beware of Shifting Risk," by Barrett Burns, directly tackles the issue of monitoring risk beyond a rank-order credit score. With specific examples observed throughout the mortgage crisis, the article shows how credit risk could change dramatically even as the scores were still rank ordering. Effective rank ordering was the stated design goal for the scores, but the article warns that loan origination and pricing require knowledge of how the score-odds relationship changes through the economic cycle. Although much of the article is a snapshot of how conditions were changing in 2010, the style of analysis and review is informative.

"Consumer Risk Appetite: How Consumer Demand Drives Credit Quality," by Joseph Breeden, revisits data from events just prior to the U.S. mortgage crisis to study patterns in consumer behavior. The severity of the mortgage crisis was a result of everything going wrong at once, but we need to remember that mortgage was not the only asset class that suffered. This article looked for causes beyond a decline in house prices and found that consumer demand is not static through the economic cycle. In fact, at any given score level, more fiscally responsible consumers choose not to borrow when conditions do not look favorable, such as during times of rising interest rates or when house prices are either rising too fast or falling. Only the risky consumers remain.

This notion of macroeconomic adverse selection as an initial trigger of the mortgage crisis has also been discussed in academic publications examining other asset classes. Breeden's key premise is that credit risk can change in ways that cannot be seen by scoring factors, and these changes may be essential in understanding the credit cycle.

The article is accompanied by a letter to the editor in which a reader asks whether the Housing Affordability Index could explain shifts in consumer demand. After running tests, the author reported back that credit risk for new originations is also poor when house prices are falling, even through affordability is improving. This seems to further support the idea that consumer risk aversion is behind much of what we observe in the credit cycle for new originations.

The final article in the section, "Pricing Loans with Real PD Forecasts," by Joseph Breeden, combines the lessons from the portfolio forecasting articles with those from the loan-level scoring articles. This article describes a new generation of loan-level models. With the data, techniques, and computation now available, lenders can skip the process of guessing at cutoff scores for new originations and instead directly forecast monthly or lifetime loss probabilities given current economic conditions or scenarios for the future.

This proposed convergence of forecasting and scoring is already under way and lenders are creating stress-test models, but those models have not yet become operational. This article encourages lenders to make that next step to operationalizing loan-level forecasting.

Note

1. See Elizabeth Mays, *Credit Scoring for Risk Managers: The Handbook for Lenders,* Thomson Southwestern Publishing, 2004.

Retail Loan Portfolio Dynamics: Becoming a Better Vintner

By Joseph L. Breeden

Maturing portfolios should result in fine wines, not bad whines. To help ensure they do, some organizations are using new techniques for quantifying the drivers of portfolio performance. These new techniques analyze retail loan "vintages," groups of accounts originated in a given time period.

Surprise is the enemy of any business. Stock value, securitization, lending capital, strategic planning, and government oversight all rely on portfolio visibility. Unexpected shocks to receivables or losses are always punished by investors and regulators.

Yet, eliminating surprises is not simply a matter of publishing more data. The difficulty is in extracting cause-and-effect from performance data to explain why the portfolio is performing as observed. Is it the economy? A new originations score? The natural maturing of the portfolio?

The lack of such information not only worries investors and regulators, it also forestalls effective portfolio management. In the fall of 2000, many risk managers were observing degradation in their portfolios and wondering, "Is it us, or is it the economy?" Months were lost before the bankruptcy shock became apparent as a real industry-wide event. That time should have been used for action rather than self-doubt.

At the onset of the Asian economic crisis of 1997, many financial institutions suffered from terminal indecision. Retail loan portfolios in Asia had grown rapidly with aggressive expansion into lower-income consumer segments and new products. As such, they were untested in an economic crisis.

When the Thai interest rate shock began, officials denied that it could spread through the economy. On May 10, 1997, IMF Managing Director Michel Camdessus stated, "I don't see any reason for this crisis to develop further."

In the spring of 1997, banks saw unusual activity in their portfolios, but could not tell whether the Chinese New Year, lax originations, or economic impacts were at fault. The result was management committee meetings consisting mostly of finger-pointing and no concrete action. At some organizations, five months passed before any concrete actions were taken—far too late to be effective.

Even as the Federal Reserve declared the U.S. recession of 2001 over, bankers were aware that the consumer debt burden was at all-time highs (Figure 1). Banks navigating these rocky shoals needed tools that would make the dangers clear with sufficient time for correcting course.

Many different causes operating on different time scales drive retail loan portfolios. Originations quality, account maturation, seasonality, management actions, competition, and the macroeconomic environment are some of the factors affecting portfolio

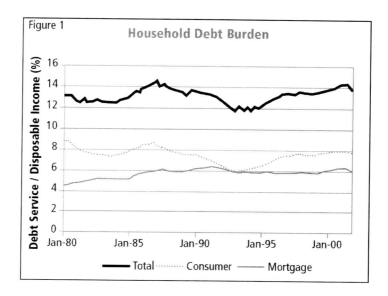

Figure 1
Household Debt Burden

performance. This article reviews the most important effects, the common ways of looking for them, and some new approaches to understanding portfolios.

Originations Quality

Credit bureau scores are the dominant method for assessing quality at origination.
However, many factors, such as negative selection and application systems failures, can
create surprises.

To monitor the quality of new originations, the most common approach is called
vintage analysis.

A retail loan vintage is a group of accounts originated in a given time period. For example, all new customers from 2001 make up the 2001 vintage. Vintage groupings can
be monthly, quarterly, or annual, depending on the application and the amount of data
available. The OCC's ALLL guidelines call for lenders to consider vintage analysis at least
intuitively when studying homogenous loan pools.

Like a bottle of wine, consumer vintages mature with age. By plotting multiple vintages
together against months-on-books, we can make comparisons for similar maturities.

The difficulty with vintage plots is that effects other than originations quality can influence the result. Changes in the economic environment, product policies, collections
systems, and more can mask the result being sought. In the hypothetical example in
Figure 2, can we conclude that the 2001 vintage is intrinsically higher risk and lower
quality? Recent changes in the economic environment could be at least partly responsible for the worsened performance.

The sudden rises seen in the 2000 and 1999 vintages suggest environmental impacts
could be affecting all vintages. With such ambiguity, quantifying cause-and-effect is a
daunting task.

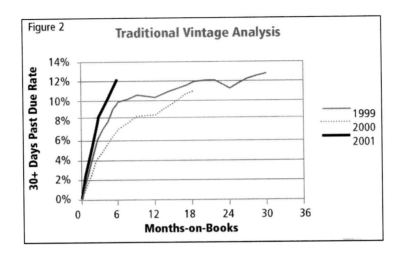

Figure 2 — Traditional Vintage Analysis

Vintage Maturation

Vintage analysis as just described is intended to provide a visual method for adjusting vintage performance for the maturation process. The maturation process itself is often valuable information. Figure 3 shows the maturation curves for two consumer segments. Aside from exhibiting different overall delinquency risk, the segments differ in when the risk is greatest. Such differences have implications for timing loss reserves and collections staffing.

The shapes of the maturation curves can vary by consumer segment and product. Policies specific to an institution can introduce unique features in the curves. For exam-

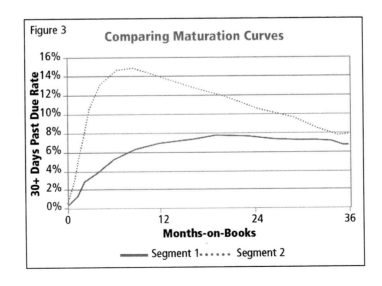

Figure 3 — Comparing Maturation Curves

ple, credit cards that carry an annual fee will show a spike every 12 months in the maturation curve for attrition. Quantifying the maturation curve is an essential starting point for understanding a portfolio.

The standard approach for measuring a maturation curve is to align the historical vintages by months-on-books and compute the average at each point. This will provide a rough estimate of the maturation process.

When Originations Change

The difficulty with averaging algorithms is that they cannot adapt to changes in originations or the environment. Consider a case where originations quality improved steadily over a four-year period. An average across vintages would not represent the true maturation process because vintages of different risk are being observed at different months-on-books.

Figure 4 shows a hypothetical example built with an improving originations scenario, from which we can see that the averaged curve does not decrease as it should. Relying upon a distorted curve such as this could lead management to a false prediction of future loss levels and overly pessimistic loss reserves. If the maturation curve in Figure 4 were used to generate an 18-month delinquency forecast, vintage delinquency rates would be overestimated by an average of 49%. The total portfolio loss forecast would be overestimated by 66%. In practice, few portfolios are so seriously wrong, but this is due to the use of intuition and hand-crafting of the forecast. As an automated tool, this approach falls far short. Actual performance will follow the true curve, independent of the average.

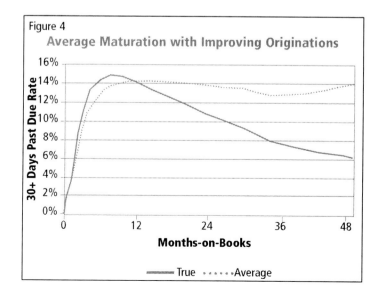

Figure 4
Average Maturation with Improving Originations

The maturation curve estimation process is analogous to a vintner sampling old bottles of wine to see what his new vintage will taste like when it matures. If the older vintages were made from sour grapes, he might sell the vineyard before realizing the quality of his new wines.

When the Environment Changes

Changes in the environment can distort the averaged maturation curve as well. Using an environmental scenario similar to what occurred through the 2001 recession, the averaged maturation curve would again be distorted similarly to what was shown in Figure 4. With a scenario that the environment will improve over the next few years, the averaged maturation curve would be as shown in Figure 5.

The practical consequence of Figure 5 is that data obtained in the years following the bottom of a recession can mislead the analyst into an overly optimistic view of how the portfolio will mature. Conversely, studying data from 1999 through 2001 could give an overly pessimistic view of how the portfolio will mature.

These examples demonstrate that a maturation curve obtained through a months-on-book average of vintages is useful for understanding the portfolio, but has questionable accuracy in detailed portfolio forecasting.

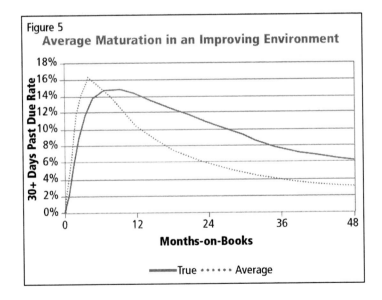

Figure 5
Average Maturation in an Improving Environment

Macroeconomic Environment

All bankers understand that the economy drives their businesses. If the economy grew at a steady rate with no booms or busts, performance could be predicted with precision. The variability of the vineyard would be replaced with the reproducibility of the brewing tank.

Measuring the impact of the environment is arguably the most challenging of portfolio modeling tasks. The two most common approaches are *total portfolio analysis* and *vintage-level analysis*. A few organizations go a step further to computing *maturation residuals*.

Total portfolio analysis is the simplest and most widely used. This once standard approach of directly comparing total portfolio performance to macroeconomic variables by way of econometric models has been widely discredited. Changes in segment mix, changes in credit policies, and the maturation of the portfolio all contribute to confound the estimation of macroeconomic impacts.

A more effective approach to measuring economic impact is to compute a vintage-level average. By aligning the vintages by calendar month rather than months-on-books and computing the average, we can easily eliminate biases from portfolio growth.

Some organizations take this analysis one step further. The vintage average is still vulnerable to biases due to portfolio maturation. By computing the vintage residuals relative to the maturation curve (maturation residuals) and averaging those for each month, we can estimate a time series of environmental impacts.

Average residual for month t =
average across all vintages at month t of
(vintage performance - expected maturation value)

Few organizations actually compute the vintage residuals because of the possible instabilities in the estimate. In a portfolio with changing originations criteria or product policies, distortions will appear that may mask economic impacts.

Figure 6 shows the results of these three approaches for a hypothetical portfolio. It shows the growth of a product launched in January 1998 and measured with quarterly vintages. A real-world example of environmental impact was included to show the rise in risk through 2001 and the onset of the recession (solid line). As the environment de-

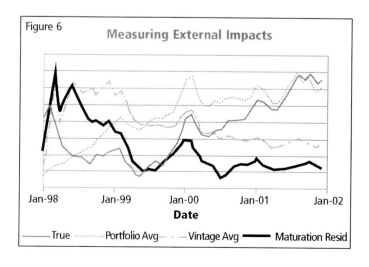

Figure 6   **Measuring External Impacts**

Date

——— True ········ Portfolio Avg — - —Vintage Avg ▬▬ Maturation Resid

graded, new bookings were curtailed and originations criteria were tightened. This scenario, while hypothetical, rings true for a number of portfolios. Comparing the three approaches, which does the best job of finding the external impact?

The total portfolio approach looks best until you realize that this is just a lucky accident. The example was of a new and growing portfolio; thus, losses just happened to coincide with a worsening environment.

Neither of the other two approaches would have even noticed the recession. Although the maturation residuals seem like a good idea, the poor quality of the maturation estimation (Figure 4) makes the maturation residuals one of the worst results. Since long-term trends are crucial for macroeconomic comparisons, none of these approaches reproduces the environmental impacts sufficiently to support econometric modeling.

Even going outside the portfolio to industry averages can leave management in doubt. Has the industry shift to subprime lending or aggressive pricing for prime lending contributed to an observed rise in delinquency?

During the 1995 Mexican peso crisis, loan rewrites were extensive in Argentina—so much so that it became difficult to determine when the crisis might be over. Was the dramatic drop in slow debt just due to the rewrites, or was the economy improving? In retrospect, it became clearer that rewrites had created an artificial lull, but not in time to assist policy decisions. Figure 7 shows the actual slow debt rate for consumer lending in Argentina. The dashed line represents what might have happened without the rewrite programs.

Recognizing the rewrite wave in the Argentina data is crucial to making econometric models for that market. In the absence of that industry insight, the double peak in slow debt leads to misleading correlations to macroeconomic data. Industry data alone is not a complete answer for understanding external impacts on a portfolio.

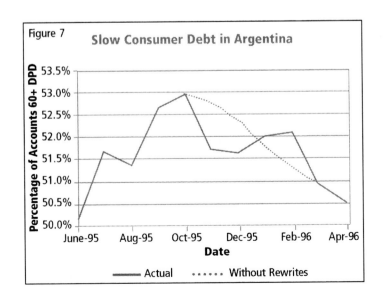

Figure 7   **Slow Consumer Debt in Argentina**

Seasonality and Other Shocks

Portfolio analysis cannot be complete without a detailed study of seasonality. Intuitively, it is the simplest component of portfolio performance to understand. Credit card use always rises at Christmas time. Delinquency usually falls during tax refund season.

The most common way to view seasonality is to make a cyclic or polar plot versus month of the year. Figure 8 provides an example of delinquency rate in a cyclic plot. This example shows the growth of a new portfolio from 1997 through 2001. The natural maturation of that portfolio introduces an overall trend in the data. Further, events in 2001 create a dramatic rise. Figure 8 does show the customary tax-time drop in delinquency, but the end-of-year drop is suspicious. Creating an average measure of seasonality is somewhat helpful qualitatively, but not quantitatively.

For this example, where portfolio maturation transitions smoothly into a recession, the worst distortions can be removed by first *detrending* the data. Detrending is always a good idea in computing seasonality, but it is not always completely effective. The complexity driving many portfolios introduces more instability than a polynomial or moving-average detrending can correct.

The final step in understanding portfolio performance is to analyze consumer response to credit policy changes, systems changes, and other management actions. Ideally, these effects should be quantified by maintaining control groups. During any change, some subset of the portfolio should be managed under the old policies so that response specific to the new policy can be observed separately from maturation, seasonality, and the environment.

Unfortunately, accidents happen. Failures in payments processing or collection systems can cause unintended shocks to the portfolio. Some policies are enacted with a "no going back" attitude, making the impact universal. In such cases, the only available approach is to understand in detail all the fundamental drivers of the portfolio first.

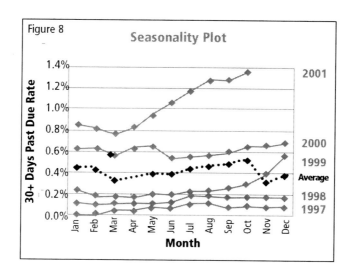

Shocks due to unique events will become apparent only after stripping away the known effects of maturation, origination changes, seasonality, and environmental impacts.

Solutions

Is there no better way to predict the quality of a bottle of wine? Well, with wine, perhaps not, but the situation in consumer lending is not hopeless.

Data. The simplest way to get better answers is to collect more data. Vintage-level data is essential, but more of it is needed. The industry standard seems to be to save only two to four years of performance data. When archiving account-level data, these limitations are natural. However, analyzing portfolio performance does not necessarily require account-level data. All of the preceding analysis can be done from vintage-level aggregated data, preferably monthly vintages. For a typical portfolio, even 10 years of monthly vintage cohorts with monthly performance reporting take on the order of tens of megabytes of data.

Data storage in relational databases at the account level is a leading reason that institutions do not do more vintage-level portfolio analysis. Portfolio-wide analysis requires touching every account in the database, which is the worst-case scenario for relational database performance. For portfolio analysis, a separate database with a time-series orientation is preferable. Recent developments suggest that this vintage data is even sufficient to support internal-ratings-based (IRB) models under the proposed Basel II Accord.

Additional data is useful in portfolio analysis because the portfolio can be observed under a broad range of conditions. The simple approaches described earlier fail most dramatically for portfolios measured only through part of a cycle—an economic downturn or a trend to tighter originations. Observing the same portfolio through several changes in originations policy or several economic cycles allows the trends to be averaged away.

New technologies. Additional data, while a long-term goal for many organizations, is unavailable in the short term. In such cases, more sophisticated analysis is required. The techniques described in the first half of this article are basic. Practitioners have experimented with numerous refinements and can do better than the estimates shown. Nevertheless, the underlying weaknesses persist.

Some organizations are starting to use new techniques that have been developed recently for quantifying the drivers of portfolio performance. *Decomposition approaches* attempt to simultaneously separate maturation and exogenous effects, such that the components are independent and unbiased. While analogous to principal component analysis in linear regression, decomposition uses an approach that is adapted to the nonlinearity of the components and the different time dimensions of months-on-books and calendar time.

Such nonlinear decomposition techniques leverage research in scientific fields involving nonlinear dynamical systems and nonlinear partial differential equations. Rather than treating each vintage as an independent forecasting problem or just looking at the total portfolio, the vintages are used as probes. Each vintage measures how consumers mature with time and how consumers respond to their environment. The added complication is that the probes are uncalibrated, because each vintage varies in composition.

These new techniques analyze the data from the vintages as if it represented a sur-face—as, say, the surface of a pond. Changes in the environment ripple across the vin-tages. The maturation process appears as a large wave running down the vintages in a different direction. Nonlinear partial differential equations provide a natural framework for analyzing such overlapping waves. The major components of portfolio performance (originations quality, maturation, and environmental impacts) are extracted in a mutu-ally independent fashion.

The result is a view of the maturation process without the distortions of originations or the environment, quantification of originations quality independent of the environ-ment, and a better measure of environmental impacts than is available from industry-wide data. Most importantly, this analysis can be performed on the short, noisy data sets common among retail lending institutions.

Analysis of commercial loan portfolios has been revolutionized over the last decade through the introduction of sophisticated mathematical techniques. Because of the fun-damental differences between commercial lending and retail lending, commercial port-folio management techniques have a poor track record when applied to retail loans. Using techniques from nonlinear time-series analysis and partial differential equations, retail portfolios can now be analyzed with the fidelity prevalent in commercial lending.

Figure 9 shows a re-analysis of the same data shown in Figure 6 extracting the exter-nal impacts. This result shows how external effects are extracted independently of mat-uration and originations quality to produce a much higher fidelity result than any of the standard algorithms. The error bars are largest in the first portion of the curve, where there are very few vintages.

There are numerous, substantial benefits to be realized from this new technology. Since the real, underlying maturation curves can be isolated for specific portfolio seg-ments, portfolio caps and score cutoffs can be set so that the long-term profitability of the total portfolio can be maximized. By isolating the response of the portfolio to macroeco-

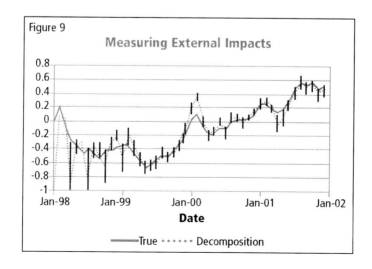

Figure 9

Measuring External Impacts

nomic and other secular developments, we can make accurate estimates of portfolio response to stress scenarios. Since the impact of past management actions can now be estimated accurately, effective contingency plans can be developed and the identification of specific situations can be made earlier in the process as these situations unfold.

This technology also improves the accuracy of loss forecasting, which, in turn, helps ensure that adequate reserves are maintained and that corrective actions are taken well in advance of deteriorating conditions. Improved loss forecasting also facilitates the allocation of capital to loan portfolios and can either free excess capital for use elsewhere within the organization or identify undercapitalized situations. Finally, it can serve as an independent check on business forecasts and alert senior management to situations where managers may be either too optimistic or too pessimistic regarding their expectations.

Wouldn't a vintner love a recipe for how the grape, the weather, and the cask combine to produce a bottle of wine? In retail lending, that is becoming a reality.

Portfolio Forecasting Tools: What You Need to Know

BY JOSEPH L. BREEDEN

T he world of portfolio forecasting is never static. The demands placed on forecasting continue to grow along with the challenges. At the same time, improved internal data availability, new external data sources, and new modeling techniques offer hope of meeting these demands.

What Is Forecasting?

Almost every activity in lending involves some form of forecasting. For the present discussion, let's focus primarily on retail loan portfolio forecasts. This is a pooled analysis of some performance metric of interest, such as attrition or prepayment, balances or utilization, delinquency, losses, fees, up-sell or cross-sell, recoveries, etc. The goal is to predict monthly performance from one month to several years into the future.

In this definition of forecasting we are including the annual budgeting process, delinquency and loss forecasts by credit risk, revenue forecasts by marketing, profitability forecasts by finance, collections inventory forecasts, and lifetime value forecasts, just to name a few.

Any forecast is relative to a scenario for marketing and sales plans, management policies, and the macroeconomic environment, whether implicitly or explicitly. To make the best business decisions, we want to be able to explain how these assumptions drive the forecasts. Forecasts should therefore be scenario-based because they are more useful.

Excluded from this discussion are scoring models. Scoring models usually focus on ranking account-level behavior over a period of time, such as delinquency in the next two years. Scoring models are usually designed to provide a rank-ordering of accounts rather than to predict specific performance metrics in a given macroeconomic environment. Although extremely important in account decisions, scoring models are not designed to address the portfolio forecasting questions just described and are best left to a separate discussion.

Areas of Current Industry Focus

Portfolio forecasting methodologies are under constant revision. The current high-volatility environment is steering development efforts toward the following goals:

- Predicting over long time horizons—more than six months forward.
- Modeling at the vintage level.
- Incorporating macroeconomic factors into the models.

- Incorporating management scenarios into the forecasts.
- Modeling profit over the life cycle—timing mismatches between revenue and loss.

What good is forecasting? What is the return on investment for better forecasts? With scoring models, the answer is simple. Many companies make claims such as, "Using our score will immediately lower attrition by an average of 13%. Our clients have saved on average $3 million." If you are trying to implement a better internal forecasting process, what should the sales pitch be?

The problem is that a forecast methodology is only as good as what you do with it. Accurate scenario-based forecasting should drive better strategic decision making. Unfortunately, the classic sentiment is, "If we made a good decision, it was due to our keen business insight. If we made a bad decision, it was the fault of the forecast."

Improved strategy is perhaps the highest value an organization can obtain, yet it is the most difficult to quantify. Who would admit that they would have made a poor decision if not for the forecast?

To make the case for the value of forecasting, perhaps the best place to look is the newspaper. The year 2002 was full of interesting news. During that period, you could have read the following items on consumer lenders:

Bear Stearns's David Hochstim lowered his rating to "peer perform" from "outperform," citing "an inability to confidently forecast the extent of an increase in losses and earnings." The stock value fell $1.5 billion that day.

"…announced unexpected credit losses in its large finance subsidiary that caused a one day loss in market value of $3.4 billion."

"We have been on a great ride over the past nine years with the economic expansion and a lot of our modeling never picked up on negatives in the credit cycle. So it has been a challenge to get these models to look at the risks associated with the bad times."

Clearly, shareholders understand the value of greater performance visibility. On a personal level, portfolio managers know that setting and meeting realistic targets can only be to their benefit. But perhaps most important, accurate forecasting has the potential to become the core of strategic planning, budgeting, and decision making.

Knowing where you've been. When planning a journey, you need to know where you've been before you can decide where you want to go. Managing a portfolio is no different. For example, you cannot predict whether an economic recovery will bring lower losses until you know the extent to which macroeconomic changes have affected your portfolio in the past.

Every portfolio metric is impacted to some degree by the same forces: originations quality, life cycles, seasonality, management actions, and the environment. Quantifying these impacts allows them to be included in a forecast or to change them in a scenario.

Originations Quality

What is the intrinsic quality of an account or a consumer? An account opened in a bad environment can be expected to perform worse than an account opened in a good environment, but it seems that such behavior should be assigned to the environment, not the account. Credit scores usually have a similar goal. Most scores are designed so that a change in the environment does not change the relative ranking of accounts.

Naturally, credit scores are the primary tool for measuring account quality. Experience has shown that scores usually capture 60% to 80% of a vintage's quality, depending upon the product and segment. However, other issues can also play a role in explaining originations quality. Loan-to-value, first- versus second-lien position, product mix, channel mix, and geographic mix are just some of the other factors that can drive quality.

Some factors driving quality are less predictable or controllable, such as system breakdowns and adverse selection due to things like competitor actions. For this reason, score monitoring must always be accompanied by direct measurement of quality from the performance data with proper adjustments for changes in the environment and differences in maturity.

Keep in mind that a simple vintage plot does not convey this kind of information. Although a visual comparison of vintages is useful, vintage plots are ambiguous as to the cause of the differences between vintages.

Recent vintage quality. Economic cycles tend to create industry-wide reactions. Although every portfolio has its unique aspects, similar patterns in vintage quality can be observed through most. Figure 1 shows a schematic representation of how vintage quality has changed over the last several years. Again, this is not vintage performance, but rather the component of performance attributable to the intrinsic quality of the accounts.

Much discussion has surrounded the *2000 vintage* for its poor performance. Credit scores and economic conditions are not enough to explain this performance. In fact, none of the usual metrics revealed anything abnormal.

The best hypothesis seems to be adverse selection. As the economic shocks began in early 2000, better-quality consumers in any given score band became more cautious about taking on debt. The result was a vintage of unexpectedly poor quality.

Conversely, 2001 and 2002 were years of directed action. Most portfolio managers dramatically tightened their criteria because of the worsening economic environment and worrying delinquency trends. The resulting higher-quality vintages typically will

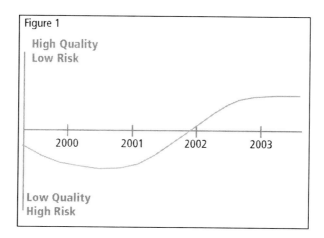

Figure 1

not dominate portfolio losses for several more years, yet the reaction of being conservative in a bad economic period is quite common.

Anecdotal evidence suggests that this trend may be reversing. As managers see better economic prospects ahead, they may again start loosening underwriting criteria in a battle for market share. The established pattern repeats.

Life Cycles

Fundamental to any portfolio is an understanding of the life cycles in any performance metric. New accounts follow a natural life cycle. A credit card account that starts empty will tend to mature by building a balance and increasing the risk of delinquency. When environmental impacts are removed, almost all performance metrics show accounts maturing relative to months-on-books.

The maturation process is one of the most predictable aspects of the portfolio. When cleaned of variation in originations quality and environmental impacts, it provides an immediate boost for portfolio forecasting efforts.

The specific shape of the maturation curve varies across products and demographic segments. Figures 2 and 3 show examples of maturation curves. Prime versus subprime creates one of the strongest disparities in the shape of maturation curves. Figure 2 compares charge-off rates for prime and subprime credit cards.

Subprime products in general tend to peak high and fast compared to prime products. It may be a bit optimistic to have subprime drop below prime even after years of maturing, as shown in the figure, but one can always hope. Although subprime loss rates can be quite high, the good side is that the origination-to-attrition cycle is short, and therefore the portfolio can be actively managed. For prime products, the lag between origination and peak delinquency is so long that course corrections are very slow to affect portfolio performance. Today's prime portfolio performance is often a remnant of the actions of previous management.

With prepayment rates, the patterns tend to be reversed. Prime auto loans, for example, will show important levels of prepayment in the first few years as the lowest-risk

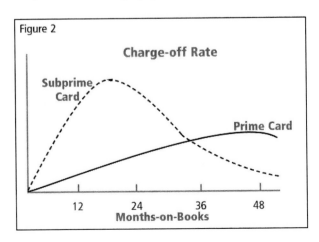

Figure 2

Charge-off Rate

Subprime Card

Prime Card

12   24   36   48
Months-on-Books

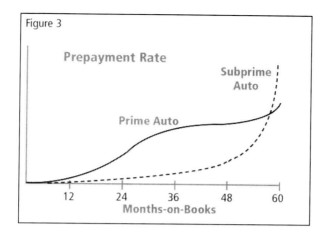

Figure 3

customers pay off their loans. With subprime, few consumers have surplus funds with which to make advance payment, so loan payoffs tend to occur predominantly at the end of the term.

Life cycles are important in understanding portfolio performance, because yesterday's accounts perform *differently* tomorrow, even if nothing in their universe changes. Accounts booked today may have peak revenue or delinquency up to several years in the future. Although conceptually simple, this effect creates a great deal of confusion when interpreting performance data.

Changes in originations criteria today can dominate the portfolio years into the future under a different economic environment. Many lenders have poor vintages from 2000 dominating their portfolios today. For those same portfolios, a recovery in 2004 would coincide with a portfolio composed largely of today's high-quality bookings. Timing originations policies to the environment is one of the most difficult aspects of portfolio management (see Figure 4). Underwriting criteria are set by calibrating to the most recent year or two of data. (This is how credit scores are commonly used.) New accounts are originated, and peak delinquency risk may not occur until several years into the future. This can, and often does, make origination policies exactly out of phase with the environment, where the worst loans mature in the worst environment and the best loans mature in the best environment.

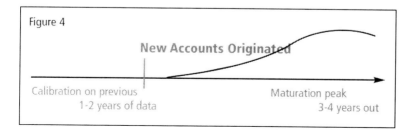

Figure 4

Seasonality

Maturation curves and originations quality describe vintage performance in isolation. Consumers live in the real world, so we must consider shocks to this idealized behavior. Seasonality, management actions, and macroeconomic impacts all have the power to alter the observed vintage performance.

Seasonality is the most obvious of all portfolio impacts. Holidays, tax refunds, summer vacations, and back-to-school spending are the most common examples. Almost all portfolio metrics show the effects of seasonality. Seasonality is not difficult in concept, nor particularly difficult to measure. The key to success is keeping long time series. A two-year rolling database is insufficient to provide a reliable estimate. Seasonality can be masked by recurring policies. For example, the timing of line increases to Christmas spending can exaggerate the effect.

Seasonality doesn't tend to vary significantly across demographic segments, which can provide additional clues about seasonal patterns.

Management Actions

Every portfolio history includes course corrections. This is what management is paid to do. Yet management actions can confound any portfolio analysis. Embedded in the portfolio performance metrics are changes in collections policies, credit line assignment, system outages, database changes, and so on.

These effects must be identified and extracted so that the forecast does not implicitly assume a replay of past actions. Few organizations maintain detailed logs of policy changes.

This must change with the Basel II focus on operational risk, but it is also extremely valuable to forecasting and management.

Measuring these impacts and extracting them is much easier when a process is employed that first removes the portfolio variability caused by origination changes and vintage maturation.

Macroeconomic Impacts

The business cycle is not dead. Intuitively, everyone knows the economy drives portfolio performance. Quantification, however, is quite difficult. Long time-series are essential.

Originations volume and quality, vintage maturation, management actions, and seasonality must all be removed before macroeconomic impacts become clear. Yet, early warning of these changes is extremely valuable, allowing managers to implement contingency plans.

Industry-wide indices can help, but they can be masked by industry-wide management trends. For example, the recent move to higher-quality originations will affect any industry-average performance metric. Therefore, an accurate internal measurement is always essential to understanding how macroeconomic impacts are affecting the portfolio.

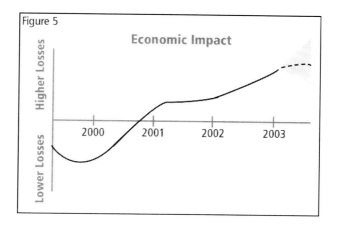

The current macroeconomic environment for losses continues to be difficult (see Figure 5). Many portfolios are at recent highs for losses driven by macroeconomic factors. This is not to say that total portfolio performance is at its worst. Some of the better-quality vintages from 2001 may be starting to bring down overall loss rates. Nevertheless, most portfolios show the outside environment's contribution to losses to be at recent highs. The real question, of course, is where do we go from here?

Measurement

The preceding discussion lays out the components of historical behavior that should be measured and understood. The key to success is to estimate them such that they are roughly independent of each other. Achieving statistical independence in the measurement is not easy, but very valuable. This article has not focused on how those pieces are measured, but a thorough discussion of that subject can be found elsewhere.[1]

Predicting where you're going. Historical analysis is necessary, but everyone's burning question is, "Where is the portfolio headed?" Even though the components driving portfolio behavior are obvious and universal, a broad range of techniques exists for incorporating these features into a forecast. Further confounding the effort are an endless number of hybrids incorporating aspects of different techniques.

For these reasons, no overview can be truly exhaustive, but we will try to review some of the dominant techniques in use and under development. Forecasting techniques differ greatly in their handling of scenarios. Some provide explicit and extensive support for scenarios, while others operate more as a black box with no obvious controls. Nevertheless, all forecasts make certain assumptions about the following:

- New originations quality and volume.
- New management actions.
- Economic conditions.

A forecasting approach that does not allow users to input scenarios for these items must be either assuming "no change" or creating scenarios using some form of extrapolation. Therefore, all forecasting approaches should be viewed as scenario based. The only question is whether you can change the scenario.

What follows is a short encyclopedia of forecasting techniques, providing a brief description along with the pros and cons of each. Although some are more sophisticated and seemingly more capable than others, the correct choice of forecasting technology is a multifaceted question that will be addressed later.

Cohort Averages

Accounts are segmented into many small cohorts based on a range of criteria. Recent historical averages are computed for each segment and taken as a prediction of future performance.

Pros:

- Extremely simple.
- Doesn't require much historical data.

Cons:

- Extremely inaccurate. Should be used for monitoring only.
- Doesn't provide insight into what drives a portfolio.
- Can't incorporate any scenarios or outside factors, since no historical dynamics have been learned.

Cohort averages had to be included in this list because they are so simple to create. However, they are so prone to failure that no important decision should be based solely on a cohort average forecast.

Industry-wide Forecasts

Many industry-wide forecasts and data have become available from consortia, bureaus, or other vendors. These can be used as a proxy or starting point for an internal forecast.

Pros:

- Useful when internal data is short or noisy.
- Useful as a guide for new products.

Cons:

- Not specific to the portfolio. Incorporates industry trends in booking mix, originations quality, and economic impacts that may not be appropriate for individual portfolios.
- Availability for near-prime, subprime, and regional portfolios limited to just a few variables.

Industry-wide indices or forecasts work best when integrated with an internal forecasting methodology in order to overcome data shortcomings.

Roll Rates

The classic roll-rate model is a structural model of the net rate at which accounts roll through delinquency buckets (see Figure 6). Predictions are made by computing a moving average of historical roll rates.

Pros:

- Simple to implement.
- Easy to manipulate.

Cons:

- Slow to adapt to changes in originations quality and economic conditions. Best in a steady-state portfolio.
- Usually adjusted intuitively to account for future changes in the environment.

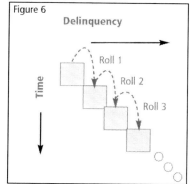

Figure 6

Markov Models

Roll-rate models are a simplified subset of the broader class of Markov models. State transitions are modeled by transition probabilities (see Figure 7). Probabilities are usually computed as a moving average on the historical data.

Pros:

- May be used to model revenue and delinquency.
- Are a logical extension of roll-rate models.

Cons:

- More difficult with line-of credit products.
- Require additional models to adjust weights for life cycles, seasonality, management actions, or economics.

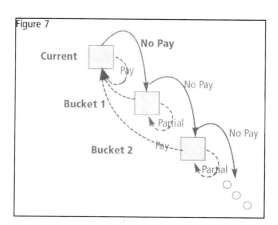

Figure 7

Markov models have seen some limited use, but generally they are not flexible enough to be used across the range of portfolio forecasting problems.

Vintage Models

Vintage models start by estimating rates as a function of months-on-books by computing average curves from the historical data. Vintage models are often used as the starting point in hybrid approaches.

Pros:

- Provide an immediate boost in accuracy because life cycles are essential elements and comparatively easy to estimate.
- Apply to many variables: roll rates, utilization, attrition, etc.

Cons:

- Must be adjusted for the quality of each vintage.
- Require intuitive adjustment for economic impacts.
- Many groups find vintage models technically difficult to implement in full detail with good accuracy.
- Macroeconomic impacts are usually the confounding factor.

Neural Networks, Etc.

Many sophisticated statistical approaches have been tested on consumer loan portfolios. Desktop computing power has ushered in an era of nonlinear models for many applications. Neural networks, etc., really refer to the many nonlinear statistical techniques available in the common statistics packages today.

Pros:

- Able to estimate a broad range of nonlinear functions.

Cons:

- No innate knowledge of consumer loan dynamics.
- Often constructed as a black box providing no insight into what drives the prediction.
- Extremely difficult to modify intuitively.
- Offer few real successes to point to.

The current generation of nonlinear statistics packages is probably best suited to account-level scoring. To be effective in portfolio forecasting, these seemingly sophisticated techniques are best hybridized with a more structural approach that understands retail lending. Unmodified off-the-shelf implementations are rarely useful.

Nonlinear Decomposition

As a categorical term, *nonlinear decomposition* is not in wide use. As defined here, it refers to techniques that attempt to quantify all the historical components first (originations quality, life cycle, seasonality, management impacts, and economic impacts) and then combine those components at the vintage level to create a forecast.

Many different approaches are in use within this category. They cover the spectrum from completely manual and labor-intensive techniques to fully automated modeling engines and many stages in between.

Pros:

- Can be designed to capture nonlinearities.
- Can be applied to any variable of interest.
- Can provide a coherent mathematical structure for incorporating intuition and scenarios.

Cons:

- Require specialized knowledge of consumer lending.
- Not available in mass-market statistical packages.
- Technically difficult to implement.

Econometric Models

Modeling macroeconomic impacts is of great interest for portfolio forecasting. Although in some texts *econometric modeling* is even defined to include simple regression, here we are interested in relating macroeconomic variables to portfolio performance. The goal is to understand and predict the economy's impact on the portfolio. A wide variety of models are used to create this relationship.

Pros:

- The economy is the most important uncontrolled driver of portfolio performance. Any model can serve as a qualitative guide.

Cons:

- Finding a good portfolio-performance measure to predict is difficult. To get a clean signal, the many other portfolio drivers need to be removed.
- Getting a long enough time series to model is a challenge. Most businesses have two to five years of history stored, representing less than one economic cycle.

Which Technique Is Right for Me?

This is the most obvious question, but it does not have a one-line answer. Instead, consider the following factors when choosing a modeling technology.

How much data history do you have? All historical data can be normalized for today's conditions. Keep all you can. You don't need account-level data to support these modeling activities. Segments by vintage and demographics are usually sufficient.

When data length is a problem, the modeling will need to focus on capturing the life cycles and vintage quality. This is usually 70% of the battle. Scenario-based tools can substitute best guesses where data is missing.

How complex are your products? When revenue and loss timing are matched and environmental impacts are small, simple methods may work well enough. These cases are rare, but for some subprime card portfolios the life cycle plays out in a single calendar year, removing the uncertainty of long-term impacts.

Today, 95% of the portfolios contain all the component dynamics described in the section on historical analysis. As such, simple approaches are likely insufficient to provide the detail needed to support modern portfolio management.

What is your access to technical resources? Small portfolios usually lead to small modeling budgets. Most portfolios have some stray pieces that are not sufficiently valuable to invest in large forecasting efforts. In such cases, a simple roll-rate model in Excel® may be sufficient. Conversely, do not scrimp on analyzing and understanding products that constitute 90% of your business. Money spent on gaining knowledge is rarely wasted.

When did you last review your process? Much has changed in data availability, forecasting technology, and external resources. If your forecasting technology has not changed in a few years, it's time to reexamine your approach.

What does your forecast explain? Part of evaluating your forecasting technology is deciding what you want to achieve. Baseline and scenario-based forecasts are clearly high value. Perhaps equally valuable is being able to explain the factors contributing to a forecast.

Figure 8 shows an example of a portfolio where the forecast was $500 million. This could be a prediction of delinquent receivables 12 months in the future. If you don't know where that number comes from, it's difficult to assess how much impact management can have on it.

By running through a contribution analysis, you might learn that 72% of delinquencies are "baked in." That is, if no accounts are originated, no policies change, and the economy does not change, this is the level of delinquency one would expect.

Twelve percent of the delinquency will arise from accounts booked during the upcoming 12-month period. Delinquency is expected to decrease 15% due to recent changes in the quality of accounts being originated. Miscellaneous policy changes will

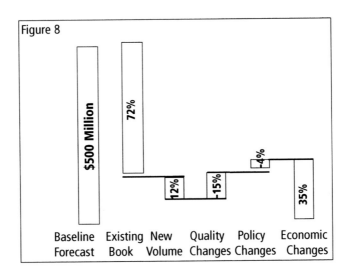

Figure 8

decrease delinquency by an additional 4%. Lastly, a worsening economy is expected to add 35% to the delinquent volume.

Although a hypothetical example, this is quite representative of the contributions to 2002 delinquency and loss performance experienced within the industry. A 15% to 35% contribution from the economy was normal. Projecting decreased delinquency due to improvements in originations quality is also normal.

A contribution report like that in Figure 8 can be produced from any forecasting technology that is explicitly scenario-based. The columns in your report will correspond to the scenario inputs in your forecasting software. The trick is simply to compare how performance changes when you take the scenario from "no change" to your "best case" assumptions.

How Accurate Is Your Forecast?

Before changing to a new forecasting methodology, you need to be able to quantify the accuracy of your current methods. Although the concept is simple, you will again need to consider a range of possibilities.

Which forecast? Accuracy will vary by product, segment, variable, and more. Choose a reference set for assessing forecast accuracy.

Over what horizon? Short-term forecasting (less than 6 months) is much easier than long term. If your primary goal is to support the annual planning process, use an 18-month horizon.

Are you flying to the forecast? Do not credit the model for unplanned actions taken during the year to meet the target. Consistent benchmarks are essential.

What should you be accountable for? Errors should be attributed to cause. Most portfolio forecasting groups do not pick the economic scenario. It is often chosen by senior management or a staff economist. Many management actions may be out of the forecaster's control. Decide whether you want to condemn a forecast for failing to predict a change in the economy. The contribution report can help decide what caused the observed performance and which forecast components should be enhanced.

Adopting Forecasting Tools

What are people using? This question is never easily answered. It depends on which group you talk to and what their objectives are. A survey about Basel II modeling will give an answer very different from asking about how forecasts are made for the operating plan.

Figure 9 is a personal assessment of what is being used for portfolio forecasting in retail lending across all product types. This is based on informal conversations with more than 30 portfolio forecasting teams over the last two years, reflecting only what they chose to reveal. The results are merely conceptual.

Roll-rate models are shown as being ubiquitous, because the groups not using them have simply moved on and no longer need them. Although the most interest lies in creating econometric models, it is unclear how many of these efforts have significant resources or will successfully reach completion.

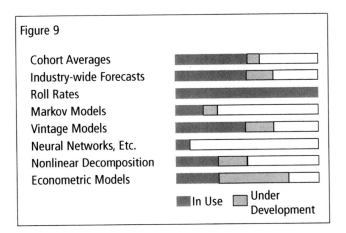

Figure 9

Nearly all groups employ multiple forecasting techniques and are looking for ways to combine the strengths of each into a single model.

Preparing for the Unexpected

Creating a single baseline forecast cannot prepare you for the unexpected. A single forecast won't show your portfolio's sensitivity to changes in the economy, marketing plans, or management policies, and it has limited value for strategic planning.

To be prepared, you must consider a range of possible scenarios and consider the consequences of each. Running multiple scenarios allows management to better conduct several strategic activities.

- Set trip wires for action by agreeing in advance on how far is too far.
- Form prearranged contingency plans when trip wires are triggered so that calm decisions can be deployed in stressful situations.
- Integrate forecasting with economic capital estimation. Portfolio forecasting includes all your best information about the future of the portfolio. Why not include that when estimating economic capital?

Scenarios on Autopilot

Any scenario-based forecasting system can be used to test a range of possible future scenarios and create distributions of possible outcomes. In some cases, the user may want to move from creating scenarios by hand to putting them on autopilot. The basic idea is to wrap an automated scenario generator around the existing scenario-based forecasting system and accumulate the forecasts on the other end.

Monte Carlo simulation is the standard approach for generating large numbers of scenarios. However, most uses of Monte Carlo simulation are much simpler than what one faces in retail lending. A Monte Carlo simulator predicting stock market returns can assume that the time series has no autocorrelation and that everything is random.

Consumer portfolios are much more complex, as was made apparent in the discussion of historical analysis. Consumer life cycles, existing vintage quality, and seasonality are not random forces. They are extremely predictable with the correct tools. Marketing plans and management policies are hopefully not random. The only piece of portfolio performance that should be controlled via Monte Carlo simulation is the impact of the external shocks.

Furthermore, external shocks from the economy or competitive pressures are not purely random events month to month. These shocks are strongly autocorrelated. An upward trend in delinquency like that shown in Figure 5 takes time to reverse and return to levels of 1999, even under the most optimistic scenario.

For these reasons, any off-the-shelf Monte Carlo simulation package will probably need to be modified to produce plausible scenarios for external impacts. Those impacts are then combined with the best-guess scenarios on marketing and management plans to run the necessary simulations. The process is not inherently difficult, but, as usual, retail lending has unique quirks that must be considered when designing a solution.

Where Does Forecasting Get You?

Forecasting is not just a cost of business or a regulatory requirement. Forecasting is at the heart of an effective business strategy. Increasing visibility of future profits aids management and investors.

Basel II is also not the final word on forecasting. In fact, almost any methodology discussed here could be used to meet the rather minimalist forecasting requirements of Basel II. It is probably better to think of Basel II as the second step on a staircase of unknown height. Demand for better forecasting will continue to grow, and eventually the regulatory guidelines will begin to leverage the much better forecasting techniques already available in retail lending.

Lastly, recent advances in computer hardware, data availability, and forecasting techniques are creating new profit opportunities for those who push ahead. This statement could have been written 10 years ago or 10 years from now. The essential point is that opportunities will always exist to improve profitability if one gains a better understanding of what drives the portfolio.

Note

1. See the article "Retail Loan Portfolio Dynamics: Becoming a Better Vintner" elsewhere in this volume.

Leveraging Aggregated Credit Data in Portfolio Forecasting and Collection Scoring

By Jeffrey S. Morrison and Andy Feltovich

Aggregated credit data can play an important role in a collections environment when individual credit data is lacking.

The collections environment is a resource-intensive business where only companies making the most efficient use of their operations survive—especially in troubled economic times, when many see their liquidation rates decline.

The days of turning a profit by focusing only on the age of the account and certain dollar volumes are gone. In a recession, consumers are worried about losing their jobs—and with good reason. Many workers are standing in long unemployment lines, and others are underemployed. Moreover, consumers are saving more money; the national saving rate has been on a significant upward trajectory since 2008. It is no wonder that in a recession we see liquidation rates falling, even with well-trained collectors whose organizations are already moving toward an analytically based risk collection mindset.

Senior officers who run collection agencies are currently wrestling with two issues: 1) the direction of liquidation rates and volumes over the next few years, and 2) how best to leverage or mine potential data sources to increase the return on collection efforts.

The first issue is strategic, requiring a realistic examination of external factors affecting profits over some forecast horizon. These external factors include not only economic conditions like the unemployment rate, house price depreciation, and real disposable income, but also risk factors specific to the credit markets. The second issue is tactical, requiring the uncovering of unknown customer information that can enhance the effectiveness of the entire operation and return on investment.

The purpose of this article is to provide insight into both the strategic and tactical concerns. First, we will examine the individual relationships between liquidation and external factors, both economic and credit, along with their use in a portfolio-level econometric forecasting model. Second, we will present evidence that the use of aggregated credit information at the zip code level adds considerable value when prioritizing accounts for maximum collection effectiveness.

Portfolio Forecasting

Recently, TransUnion conducted a study in which an index of portfolio liquidation rates was correlated with a variety of economic and credit variables to determine which factors drove collection effectiveness.

The index was created to reflect the percentage growth in liquidation rates as measured from a base period just before the recession of 2001. For example, a liquidation index of 110 would reflect a 10% growth in liquidation rates compared with the base period.

The study examined collection efforts across two recessions: 1) a relatively light economic downturn in 2001, caused in part by a burst dot-com bubble and the terrorist attacks on 9/11, and 2) the severe recession that began in late 2007, when housing prices took a sudden downturn.

On the economic side, the variables correlated with the liquidation index were the traditional measures of economic activity: disposable income, saving rate, unemployment rate, GDP, consumer confidence, and other variables specifically geared to the housing industry.

From a credit perspective, more than 60 important aggregate measures related to the recent credit environment were examined, including the average number of active installment trades per consumer and other credit characteristics such as average balances, delinquency rates, and credit limits.

In each case, statistical tests were performed to determine if the correlations were significant. In addition, an examination was undertaken to determine whether trends in economic or credit variables preceded a movement in the liquidation index.

The results of the study were informative. New vehicle registrations had the highest correlation (0.81) with the liquidation index, followed closely by home ownership (0.77), affordability of housing (−0.74), and unemployment (−0.73). The vehicle registration series was found to lead collection effectiveness by one quarter, while the remaining variables mentioned above were contemporaneous (occurring within the same time period).

From an economic perspective, the results were, as expected, heavily weighted on changes in the housing market, specifically the impact of negative equity generated by falling house prices. On the credit side, trends associated with lenders approving new installment loans were correlated most strongly with the liquidation index. For example, the average number of active installment trades per consumer showed a correlation of −0.83 to movements in the liquidation index. Particularly interesting was the finding that changes in the average number of installment trades led collection activity by two quarters.

Further, average mortgage delinquency rates (60/90/120 days past due) followed closely behind, with correlations near −0.80. Movements in the delinquency data, unlike the installment trade characteristic, did not exhibit a strong lead in collection activity, but were more contemporaneous.

With the above results in mind, two predictive models were developed, one using only aggregated credit data and the other only economic data. In Figure 1, note that the line with the higher R-squared (a measure of statistical fit) of 0.83 reflects the general finding that aggregated credit characteristics are significantly more predictive than information based solely on economic measures. Furthermore, the validation portion of Figure 1 representing a two-quarter holdout period (from the third quarter of 2009 to the fourth quarter of 2009) shows that the economic model incorrectly predicted an upswing in the liquidation index.

Credit data was more predictive than economic data for two reasons. First, when we use credit data to predict liquidation, we are observing directly the same environment faced by collectors: loan defaults in the credit market. So when the average number of

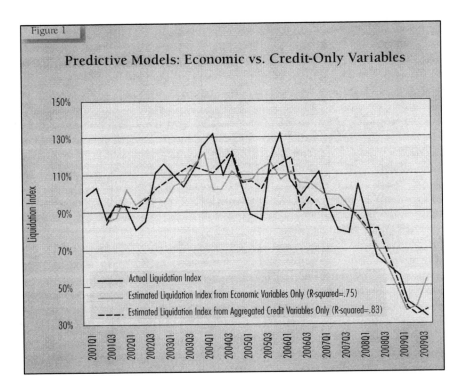

Figure 1

Predictive Models: Economic vs. Credit-Only Variables

Actual Liquidation Index
Estimated Liquidation Index from Economic Variables Only (R-squared=.75)
Estimated Liquidation Index from Aggregated Credit Variables Only (R-squared=.83)

installment loans goes up during an economic downturn, we see what consumers see: an increase in their debt burden constrained by the fact that lenders are reducing credit limits in other areas to minimize their exposure to risk. Second, credit data is timely, accurate, and not subject to revisions. Economic data typically is revised on a regular basis, so a model's historical numbers using economic data are not set in stone.

Nevertheless, economic data is still very important in predicting liquidation, especially during a recession characterized by dramatic changes in house prices, home ownership, and employment. To illustrate this point, a hybrid portfolio forecasting model was developed using both credit and economic data. Although credit variables explained much of the variation in the liquidation index, the model did improve significantly with the addition of certain economic variables.

Taking the credit model developed earlier, we added two relevant economic series: home ownership and interest rates. This hybrid model resulted in the R-squared moving from 0.83 to 0.88, with all the original variables remaining significant. Here, the home ownership rate was found to be the most important variable after installment trades. Home ownership and interest rates were selected as candidates because of their high correlation with the liquidation index and their low correlations with each other, along with economic considerations centered around the housing sector.

As mentioned earlier, the model found an inverse relationship between liquidation and the average number of installment loans—heavily weighted with the most recent recession.

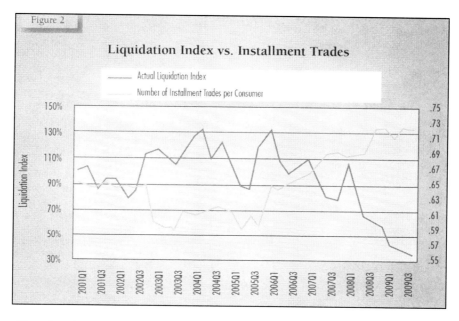

Note that there was not much movement in installment trades in the weaker recession of 2001, but beginning in 2006 we saw lenders approving consumer installment loans at a record pace. As Figure 2 illustrates, the most recent recession saw a growing demand for installment credit as economic conditions began to worsen, creating a more difficult collections environment compared to the 2004-05 period of economic prosperity.

Not included in this study was an attempt to capture internal factors such as changes in the average number of collectors or variations in collection strategies over the course of the historical period—something strongly recommended for most forecasting exercises of this type. Still, the results support industry findings that credit and economic conditions both have an impact on collection effectiveness. That said, the final step in the forecasting process is to feed economic and credit assumptions into the model to produce a base-level outlook for collection effectiveness over some planning horizon.

Collection Scoring

Although portfolio forecasting helps answer strategic questions often asked in a recession, it does not offer a great deal of immediate tactical assistance other than to point out that a downward trend in liquidation may be due to external rather than internal reasons. The fact is that collectors constantly need the best information about their book of accounts, regardless of the business cycle and their volume.

The good news is that the same types of aggregate credit data that were so helpful in portfolio forecasting can be used within a traditional data-scoring framework to solve a common but important challenge: What do we do about "no hits?" These no-hits, consumers for whom little or no credit information is available, cannot be scored using traditional credit-scoring models, but can add up to a sizable revenue stream for collectors.

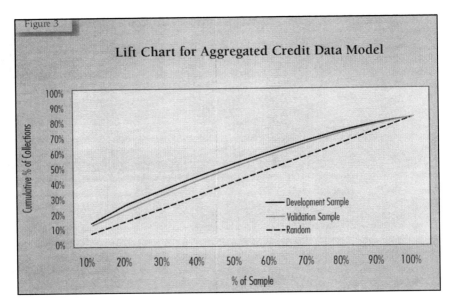

Lift Chart for Aggregated Credit Data Model

In a recent study, TransUnion conducted research to determine if it was feasible to build a recovery score for a no-hit population using *only aggregated* credit bureau data at the zip code or county level. The population of accounts was obtained from third-party collection agencies between January 1 and September 21, 2006, and the payment performance was monitored for 12 subsequent pay periods (12 months). A good account was defined as one where a total of $50 or more was collected over a 12-pay-period window.

The results were compelling. With a KS statistic (a rank-ordering measure where higher is better) near 20, the aggregated scoring tool did a good job in separating consumers whose debt obligations could be collected from those consumers whose obligations could not. Granted, this level of separation power is below what might be found using scoring models in which individual credit characteristics are known, but remember that we were working only with consumers who were previously invisible to most modeling attempts.

Some of the variables that drove this no-hit separation power were average amount past due on trades currently 60 or more days delinquent, average balance of new bank cards, and average credit limit/high credit of active retail trades per retail borrower. All data in the model was aggregated at either the zip code or county level. Owing to the large amount of data available for aggregation at the zip code level, scoring this previously invisible or hidden population became a straightforward process.

Conclusion

Aggregated credit data can play an important role both strategically and tactically in the collections environment. Strategically, a portfolio-level forecasting model can help senior managements better understand the varying relationships across the business cycle and indicate whether they can expect a continuation of depressed liquidation rates in an economy recovering from severe recession.

Although the volume of accounts sent to collection agencies will rise during times of high unemployment and nonpayment rates, a collection department can experience less success as consumers watch their last dime and contemplate the possibility of job loss or a reduction in income. An effective portfolio-level forecasting model should combine credit and economic factors to properly evaluate collection revenue and quantify how it may change based on what-if scenarios such as a move toward a stronger recovery or a double-dip recession.

However, aggregated credit data is also helpful to collectors because it can identify local credit conditions clustered around common demographics. This is especially true for consumers with little or no credit history. For example, if the consumer is living in a zip code where the mortgage delinquency rates are climbing or always high, the chance for collection may be significantly less than for those in zip codes where the delinquency rate is relatively low and stable.

By identifying opportunities where few existed given a lack of individual consumer credit data, aggregated models may offer the lift needed by many collection agencies to finally turn a profit in a recessionary environment.

The Role of Credit Scores in Consumer Lending

BY ELIZABETH MAYS

e've seen a revolution in the financial services industry as lenders have embraced automated decision-making and model technologies to speed loan decisions and manage credit risk. Although credit scoring has been used by lenders since the 1950s, it's become pervasive throughout the consumer lending arena and has expanded to products like residential mortgages and small business loans.

Credit scoring has become the standard method used to evaluate the credit quality of residential mortgages since the introduction of automated decisioning technologies by the government-sponsored enterprises (GSEs), Freddie Mac, and Fannie Mae in the mid-1990s.

A 1997 article published by the Federal Reserve Bank of Philadelphia noted several benefits from credit scoring.[1] First, it provides great efficiencies and time savings in the loan approval process. The article cited a study indicating the traditional approval process for small business loans can take as much as 12 and a half hours over as long as two weeks. This time can be reduced to under an hour with the use of credit scoring.

A second benefit of credit scoring is reduced subjectivity in the loan approval process. With traditional underwriting, the standards to which applications are held can vary depending on who the decision maker is. Human judgment is affected by past experiences. With credit scoring, lenders can ensure they are applying the same standards to all applicants regardless of race, gender, or other applicant characteristics.

Another study[2] noted an additional benefit of credit scoring over traditional underwriting: Score models permit the loan decision to take into account more factors than a human making the decision judgmentally.

Former Federal Reserve Chairman Alan Greenspan stated in an October 2002 speech to the American Bankers Association, "Credit scoring technologies have sharply reduced the cost of credit evaluation and improved the consistency, speed, and accuracy of credit decisions."

The benefits of credit scoring don't just apply to the loan acquisition process but to credit scores used for account management as well. That is, using credit scores for loan collection and modification decisions, line management, and loss recovery strategies can speed these decisions, remove bias from them, and help lenders make the right decisions.

In the same speech, Chairman Greenspan further noted, when discussing credit scoring technologies, "Their use also has expanded well beyond their original purpose of assessing credit risk. Today, they are used for assessing the risk-adjusted profitability of account relationships, for establishing the initial and ongoing credit limits available to borrowers, and for assisting in a range of activities in loan servicing, including fraud detection, delinquency intervention, and loss mitigation. These diverse applications have played a major role in promoting the efficiency and expanding the scope of our credit-delivery systems and allowing lenders to broaden the populations they are willing and able to serve profitably."

This article explains how lenders use credit scores and then discusses the methods and techniques for building and applying them.

Use of Scores in Loan Acquisition

Many lenders (certainly the vast majority of large lenders) have their own proprietary custom acquisition scores. A custom score is one that is built for a specific product using a lender's own data. A custom score will often contain characteristics based on data from the loan application, such as monthly income or the debt-to-income ratio, while generic scores are based only on credit bureau data.

Generic scores are built using a wide array of consumer credit data and typically don't focus on a specific loan product or specific set of borrowers. The most well-known example is the FICO score.[3] The FICO score is based on models built by a leading scorecard developer, Fair Isaac Company, and is designed to rank the likelihood that an applicant will go 90 days delinquent on any consumer credit loan or account within the next two years.

Lenders who use custom scores may still use generic credit scores to make quick decisions about the highest-credit-quality customers. In this case, the generic score is reviewed, frequently in combination with other data provided by the applicant, to get a preliminary risk assessment.

If the borrower appears to pose very low risk, the loan may be funded with little or no further review. If the generic score leaves any question that the applicant presents little risk, more information is obtained so that the custom score can be calculated. As an example, many indirect auto lenders will commit to fund a borrower's loan on the basis of a high FICO score as long as certain other lending parameters are not exceeded. For applicants with lower FICO scores, additional information is obtained and the custom score is calculated before a decision is rendered.

In the residential mortgage arena, the GSEs use scoring to determine the amount of documentation the borrower must provide to certify income and liquid asset holdings. If the credit risk is evaluated as being low, applicants need to provide less documentation on their income and assets.

In addition to using credit scores to make decisions on individual loan applications, the generic credit score is a standard data requirement for lenders bidding on loan packages available for sale. Also, the credit rating agencies, such as Fitch and Standard and Poor's, require that lenders desiring to securitize consumer loan packages provide credit scores along with other data elements before a loan package can be rated.

Credit scores are frequently used to set prices for loan packages and individual loans. Even "prime" lenders who lend to borrowers with generally good credit histories frequently segment their populations into tiers and set prices based on credit quality.

In an article detailing the use of credit scores, William Makuch noted, "The value of a loan is nothing more than its expected future cash flows discounted appropriately to incorporate the uncertainty and volatility of cash flow."[4] The most complex pricing models specify all expected future cash inflows and outflows and the timing of each. Scores or score-based models can be used to predict the incidence of credit losses and are an important component of such models.

Account Management Scoring

Scores are used at each stage in the life cycle of a consumer loan. Behavior scores, or account management scores, are distinguished from acquisition scores by their inclusion of characteristics representing the borrower's own payment pattern on the loan in question. The number of times a borrower has gone delinquent, the seriousness of the delinquency, and even the point during the month when payments are typically received are all very predictive of future behavior.

Because they include variables related to the borrower's demonstrated willingness and ability to pay on the particular loan under consideration, behavior scores tend to be even more predictive than acquisition scores. Acquisition scores, of course, are based only on data available at the time the loan is originated.

For nondelinquent loans, behavior scores are frequently used to set limits for credit card products and home equity lines of credit. A typical strategy for setting overdraft limits consists of using a matrix where behavior score ranges form the rows and average balance forms the columns.[5] Overdraft limits are then set for each cell in the matrix in an attempt to control not just the likelihood of delinquency or default (measured by the behavior score) but overall profitability, which is related to both the default incidence as well as the loss in the event of default.

Behavior scores are also used in the residential mortgage area for streamlined refinancing programs. Borrowers who have shown a pattern of paying on time and have excellent behavior scores may be eligible to refinance their mortgage without having to provide the income and asset documentation that is typically required. Behavior scores are also used to "cross sell" products to existing borrowers. For example, a lender may use a behavior score generated for the mortgage portfolio to select borrowers for a favorable offer on a credit card.

One of the most important uses of behavior scores is for the collection of delinquent accounts. Borrowers with poor behavior scores are contacted earlier in the month and the method of contact (phone calls versus letters, etc.) may be varied with the score. Frequently, strategies are developed that use scores in combination with outstanding balance (or loan amount minus expected collateral value in the case of collateralized loans) to decide whom to contact and how frequently to attempt the contact.

Champion and challenger strategies became common in the collections area in the 1990s. With a champion and challenger strategy, a given score or score strategy is designated as the "champion." It is considered the accepted way of doing things. New, untried strategies are the "challengers" and are tested on a selected sample of loans. The outcome (loan performance) is observed and compared to the performance of the loans to which the champion strategy was applied. If a given challenger strategy is found to beat the champion, it is implemented as the new champion strategy.

Behavior scores are also used to determine strategies for handling seriously delinquent accounts. Scores that predict the likelihood a borrower can recover from serious delinquency may be used to select loans for modification programs or other special treatment.

Loss forecasting is another area to which scores are being applied. Acquisition scores may be used to generate loss forecasts for accounts that have not been on the books long (say, less than a year). For accounts that have a long enough payment history to observe, a forecast may be generated using behavior scores that reflect the borrower's payment pattern.

Finally, recovery scores are another type of behavior score used to estimate the likelihood that all or some portion of a bad debt will be recovered by the lender. After an account has gone seriously delinquent or even been charged off, recovery scores can be generated to rank accounts in terms of the likelihood that some of the debt will be collected. Recovery scores help lenders make sound decisions concerning which accounts to retain and attempt to recover themselves versus which to sell to debt collection agencies or other third parties.

New Credit Scoring Methods and Applications

Although regression analysis remains the most frequently used method for building credit scoring models, many techniques have been tested, including a number of nonstatistical methods such as neural networks, genetic algorithms, and linear programming.[6]

Several studies have been undertaken to determine if one or more of these techniques results in more powerful scorecards. Most methods have been found to produce acceptable results and none has been proven a clear winner as far as ranking borrower credit risk is concerned, but certain techniques may have advantages over others, depending on the situation.

Regression techniques have an advantage over neural networks given the ease with which the effect of characteristics on the outcome variable can be interpreted and explained. Because it is easy to determine the incremental effect of a given change in each characteristic on the outcome variable, generating adverse action reasons for rejected applications is straightforward. Understanding the magnitude of the effect of each predictive variable on the outcome variable also helps risk managers develop appropriate lending policies. Neural networks, on the other hand, have become fairly commonplace in the fraud modeling arena where such interpretability is not as important.

Meanwhile, credit scores are now being used to forecast portfolio default rates and credit losses—and even to estimate profitability at the loan level. Historically, credit scores have been used to rank the relative risk that borrowers would go seriously delinquent or default. The score's ability to assign more low scores to loans that eventually went bad than to loans with good outcomes was the main concern among developers and users of scores. Although some attention was paid to the default odds of various score ranges when the score cutoff was set, scores were not typically used to predict the default rate for a given set of loans or to estimate the likelihood that a particular loan would default.

Scores are no longer being used just as risk-ranking tools. The models that form the basis for scores can be used to generate, for each loan, the predicted probability that an event, such as default, will occur. These can be used to generate loss estimates at the loan level that can be used for loss forecasting and provisioning, as well as for estimating the amount of credit losses that must be covered by the price set for the loan at origination.

The emphasis of risk management at financial services companies has changed from one of loss avoidance to one of profit maximization. Lenders are willing to take on more risk and offer products they may have avoided in the past as long as they feel comfortable they understand the risks involved and have properly priced for them. Understanding the risks requires that lenders generate estimates of risk-adjusted profitability. A modeling technique called survival analysis is useful in estimating loan-level profitability and is making inroads in the risk management arena.

Survival analysis has been widely applied in other areas, such as the biomedical field. It is a regression technique much like logistic regression (the method traditionally used to build credit scoring models). But instead of predicting the likelihood that an event such as default or early payoff will occur within a specified period of time, it predicts the likelihood the event will occur at *numerous points in time.*

With this approach, the model uses data on the performance of loans in each period (typically monthly) from the point of their origination up until some given point in time. The output from the model is a forecast of the probability the event will occur at each month during the loan's life. These probabilities are important inputs into profitability models because they tell us the likelihood of receiving each future payment. Models can be built to predict default, early payoff, and utilization in the case of lines of credit, to give a full accounting of cash flows over the life of the loan.

An additional benefit of survival models is that they can also incorporate the effect of changes in the economy over the life of the loan. In addition to borrower-level characteristics, economic variables are likely to be very significant predictors of the rate at which loans go bad. Variables such as the unemployment rate, market interest rates, and collateral values (for secured loans) have all been found to be important predictors in consumer credit models. These variables may be included as "time-varying covariates"—that is, variables whose values can change during the period of time that loan performance is observed.

There are two advantages to including economic variables in our credit models in addition to the traditional consumer characteristics. First, analyzing the model results aids our understanding of how consumer loans perform in good times and bad times. Second, the risk effects related to the economy can be decomposed from the risk effects related to the borrowers themselves, such as credit history variables and variables that measure ability to pay. This permits us to obtain a more accurate assessment of the effects of borrower risk drivers on loan outcomes because the effect the economic environment can have on them has been removed.

This focus on bringing in new sources of data and using new modeling techniques to explain borrower behavior promises to be a fruitful area for continued research in the credit scoring arena.

The Future of Credit Scoring

The early years of the second millennium promise to be exciting and dynamic ones for the field of credit scoring. Risk managers are turning more and more to quantitative techniques to understand risks and manage their portfolios.

The credit scoring field is growing and new and better techniques are being brought to bear every year. Increasingly, lenders are bringing the expertise to build and use models in-house as they recognize the competitive advantage of having first-rate models and using them well. Lenders who recognize these advantages early and use scoring and modeling to their best advantage will gain the biggest benefit to their bottom lines.

Notes

1. See Loretta J. Mester, "What's the Point of Credit Scoring?" *Business Review*, Federal Reserve Bank of Philadelphia, September/October 1997.
2. David J. Hand, "Modeling Consumer Credit Risk," *IMA Journal of Management Mathematics*, vol. 12, 2001.
3. The FICO score is called the Beacon score at Equifax and Empirica at Trans Union.
4. See William M. Makuch, "The Basics of a Better Application Score," in Elizabeth Mays, editor, *Handbook of Credit Scoring*. Glenlake Publishers, 2001.
5. See Lyn Thomas, David Edelman, and Jonathan Crook, *Credit Scoring and its Applications*. Society for Industrial and Applied Mathematics, 2002.
6. See Chapter 5 of *Credit Scoring and Its Applications*. For another article describing these methods, see chapter eight of *Handbook of Credit Scoring*.

Looking Behind the Credit Score: Beware of Shifting Risk

By Barrett Burns

A s the economy shifts, the consumer risk levels indicated by credit scores shift as well. This phenomenon is analogous to a variance in automobile mileage. The EPA can rate the mileage performance of a particular vehicle, but the actual mileage will fluctuate under different road conditions.

Similarly, the meaning of credit scores can shift with changing environmental conditions. In the context of credit score performance, "environmental conditions" are defined as substantive changes in the ways consumers manage their debts. Exotic mortgage products and high-risk payment strategies—coupled with unsound underwriting methods such as unverified income, inflated appraisals, and so on—have primarily created and driven these changing conditions.

This shift is particularly noticeable in mortgage lending, but it can also be seen in credit card and auto loans. When reading news accounts of tightened requirements for government and private lending, we must remember that while a consumer's credit score may have remained unchanged, the risk it represents has not. Such changes have the potential to alter a credit score's ability to identify those consumers who will pay their debts on time and those who won't.

Lenders relying on credit scores in any part of their business need to regularly assess whether the credit score they are using adequately captures these changing conditions and also determine if a recalibration of the score is needed to align their risk management strategies with the new ways consumers are managing their debt.

Despite indications that an economic recovery is in the making, mixed signals remain and it is too soon to know if it will take hold. Furthermore, a recovery will not reach out to all consumer segments equally, which complicates the risk manager's role in implementing prudent growth strategies.

The credit card industry is one example—along with consumer real estate and auto lending—where opportunity may present itself if lenders combine heightened risk management with in-depth analysis. As credit card delinquencies and charge-offs drop, lenders are able to reduce reserves earmarked for loan losses.

In this environment, issuers prepare for growth opportunities and search for new customers so that a hidden momentum or trajectory in the consumer's environment, when combined with credit scores, can serve as a useful barometer of borrowers' future performance.

Bank Cards

VantageScore Solutions examined risk levels of both new (those originated in the first three months of the performance period) and existing accounts in the bank card sector for five consecutive two-year periods for the most common VantageScore credit tiers. The VantageScore range is from 501 to 990, where a higher number indicates lower risk.

Figure 1 represents the percentage of consumers who became 90 or more days past due on new bank card accounts at each score band for the two-year periods depicted. Our analysis uncovered a significant increase in risk across all credit tiers during the time frame of June 2007 to June 2009. This result represents a dramatic change from the four previous two-year periods, when risk increased in the subprime bands (500 to 639) but rose only slightly in the prime tiers (700 to 899) and remained relatively stable with super-prime (850 and higher) credit consumers. A similar increase in risk was found within existing accounts.

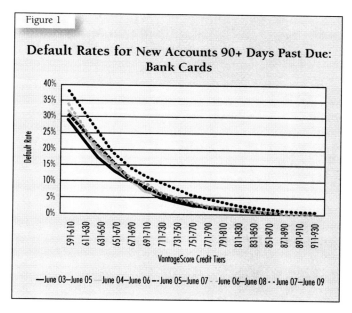

Figure 1

Default Rates for New Accounts 90+ Days Past Due: Bank Cards

—June 03–June 05   June 04–June 06 --- June 05–June 07   June 06–June 08 · · June 07–June 09

Consumer Real Estate

Reflecting the mixed signals in the economy, our research found that risk has increased at an accelerated pace for prime and super-prime credit tiers in all product sectors, even while risk levels have recently improved for subprime consumers with mortgage loans.

While risk also increased for the subprime and near-prime tiers (591 to 690)1 for the first four periods, it's encouraging to see an improvement during the time frame of June 2007 to June 2009 in the 591-to-610 tier.

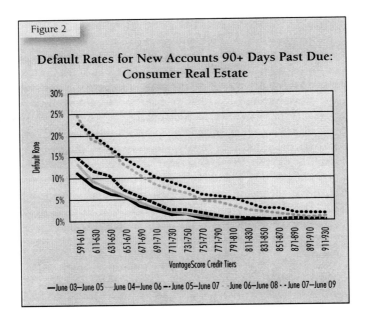

Figure 2

Default Rates for New Accounts 90+ Days Past Due: Consumer Real Estate

VantageScore Credit Tiers

— June 03–June 05   June 04–June 06 – – June 05–June 07   June 06–June 08 · · June 07–June 09

Upper-level score bands (790 and higher) demonstrate no increase in risk during the first three periods, as depicted by the overlapping lines on the graph. However, a dramatic rise in risk is seen for all credit levels during the June 2006 to June 2008 time frame. During this period, risk increases most quickly at the subprime end of the scale, jumping an eye-popping 55%. The prime and super-prime bands also experience an increase in risk, but at a slower rate. This result is reversed when the most recent time frame of June 2007 to June 2009 is added. The prime and super-prime tiers see an average 100% increase over the previous period.

The effects of growing default levels as a result of increasingly-high-risk mortgage products offered to unqualified consumers may be one driver of the risk profile depicted in Figure 2.

During this period, it is important that any scoring model like VantageScore continues to rank-order consumers correctly, allowing risk managers, lenders, and others to continue to distinguish high-credit-quality consumers from poor-credit-quality consumers.

Auto Loans

As we examine auto loans (Figure 3), our findings confirm that risk levels continue to climb for new loans in this sector. In the June 2003 to June 2005 period, consumers in the 591-to-610 credit tier had a nearly 14% likelihood of becoming 90 days or more past due on their auto loan.

Those same consumers represented approximately a 12.5% likelihood of becoming delinquent during June 2004 to June 2006, meaning that risk actually decreased for consumers at this credit band for this period. Interestingly, the opposite trend took place

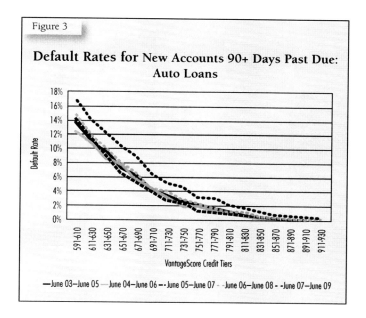

Figure 3

Default Rates for New Accounts 90+ Days Past Due: Auto Loans

VantageScore Credit Tiers

— June 03–June 05 — June 04–June 06 – • June 05–June 07 - - June 06–June 08 • • June 07–June 09

within the next time frame (June 2005 to June 2007): Risk worsened for this lowest credit tier, rising beyond 14% for the first time.

During these same periods, risk remained relatively stable at above the 700 VantageScore level, but we noticed a dramatic change by the June 2006 to June 2008 period: Risk had increased for all consumers, after being nearly identical in the prime and super-prime credit tiers.

In the super-prime category, the rate of increase slowed, but still represented the first time that risk had grown there. This result can be attributed to the recession and to economic issues in the real estate sector that were beginning to affect the auto sector.

During the June 2007 to June 2009 period, subprime risk increased from approximately 14.5% to 17%. Risk has now increased at all credit levels.

Shifting Payment Priorities

Just as we've seen shifts in risk, we've also seen shifts in how consumers pay their debts. For consumers who have at least one delinquent loan, mortgage payment as the priority is changing.

According to past payment hierarchy, consumers who were financially pressed have generally paid their mortgage first, allowing auto loans and credit card accounts to become delinquent. However, VantageScore Solutions has discovered a shift in recent consumer behavior: Some consumers are becoming delinquent on mortgages but remaining current on auto loans and credit cards owing to a need for transportation and purchasing power.

Comparing data for December 2006 and December 2009, VantageScore Solutions found that a smaller percentage of consumers remained current on their mortgages while having other delinquencies in their credit file (Figure 4). This result represented a

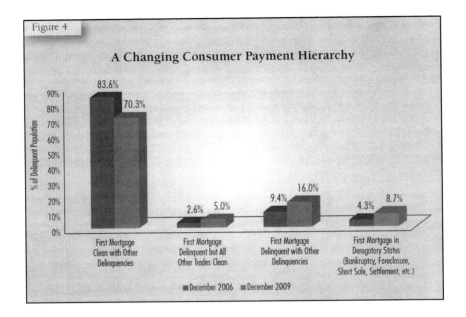

Figure 4

A Changing Consumer Payment Hierarchy

16% drop in mortgages remaining current. Additionally, the percentage of consumers who had a delinquent mortgage while maintaining all other debts in good standing increased by more than 90%.

News reports and industry statistics reflect our findings, indicating that fewer Americans fell behind on their credit card bills in May 2010, representing the fifth straight month of improvement in this category. Equifax statistics for the same month tell us that the number of consumers who were at least 60 days behind on bank card accounts dropped to 4% from 4.2%. This is a significant improvement from the May 2009 peak of 4.8%.

According to an Experian Automotive analysis, the 30-day car loan delinquency rate fell 1.06% from the first quarter of 2009 to the first quarter of 2010 (from 2.82% to 2.79%), while the 60-day auto loan delinquency rate dropped slightly from 0.79% in the first quarter of 2009 to 0.78% in the first quarter of 2010.

Portfolio Exposure and Securitization

Even as risk shifts and credit markets begin to show faint signs of recovery, private-label mortgage securitization, a vital component in lending, is lagging behind. This result can be attributed partly to portfolio exposure, which has increased because of higher consumer default levels over the past six years.

As shown in Figure 5, lenders using a 1% default strategy in 2003 would have set a cutoff of 750 for a VantageScore credit score (solid red arrow). In 2009, the same cutoff would have resulted in a 2.5% default scenario (dashed red arrow), representing about

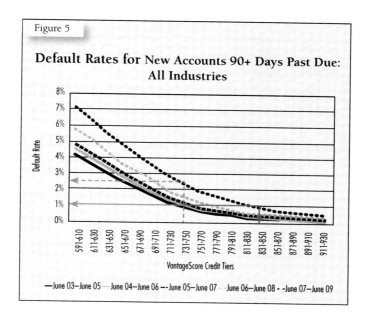

Figure 5

Default Rates for New Accounts 90+ Days Past Due: All Industries

VantageScore Credit Tiers

—June 03–June 05 ⋯⋯ June 04–June 06 –·– June 05–June 07 ⋯⋯ June 06–June 08 – ·– June 07–June 09

two and a half times the risk for the same score. To maintain the 1% risk level in this example, lenders would need to move the cutoff to approximately 850 (blue arrow).

We are now at a point in the credit cycle where lenders have strengthened their balance sheets. Moreover, many of the credit challenges have been stabilized and some are even showing improved trends.

VantageScore Solutions' findings on shifting risks, whether in auto loans, credit card accounts, or mortgage loans, reflect the need for lenders to regularly assess whether their credit scoring and risk management strategies are keeping up with these changing conditions.

Additional analyses by VantageScore Solutions reveal that there are 60 million creditworthy borrowers whose credit scores are either stable or improving in the United States. Of this total, 7 million borrowers cannot be identified using standard scoring methods. Within the 60 million, we found 10.6 million consumers whose overall credit quality is improving and whose risk profiles are consequently very attractive.

Conversely, our research showed 11 million consumers who are likely to represent a drop in credit quality over the next 12 months. Being aware of shifting credit risk will help separate profitable opportunities from those segments requiring increased risk mitigation.

Risk managers now are poised to carefully grow their organization's revenue stream. As more risk has been driven into the system and credit policies are being revised, it is important for risk managers to review cutoff strategies, revalidate the credit scoring model being used, and ensure that it scores more people. This will create a broader applicant population to fit target markets and enable lenders to identify the potential customers who have been improving their creditworthiness in this environment of shifting risk.

As lenders consider how to move beyond recession-based management strategies and intelligently reenter the world of originations and portfolio profit maximization, adjusting strategies to account for the increased risk levels while taking steps to adapt in this volatile environment will promote success in the credit markets.

Note

1. VantageScore Solutions chose these credit-tier ranges only for the purposes of research and general analysis. Lenders are likely to determine their own credit score tiers in accordance with their own credit and risk management strategies.

Consumer Risk Appetite: How Consumer Demand Drives Credit Quality

By Joseph L. Breeden

"What is your bank's risk appetite?"

You may have heard—or asked—this question frequently as the banking sector reworks its risk management controls following the financial crisis and recession.

But when was the last time you asked a friend at a dinner party, "What is your risk appetite?"

It would be an unusual dinner party indeed if someone were to answer that question. However, if you were to ask, "Is this a good time to buy a car?" or "Would you buy a home now?" you would probably receive an immediate reply.

Intuitively, consumers constantly assess and balance their risk appetite. It often takes the form of deferred consumption—for example, a decision to buy a car next year rather than now.

In their underwriting, credit scoring, risk-based pricing, and loan decisions, few lenders incorporate the fact that consumers have a risk appetite just as banks do—and that it changes over time.

Why do changes in consumer demand matter? We looked at this question in an attempt to find explanations for credit cycles in the mortgage industry. The results were surprising.

Measuring Credit Cycles

Before discussing their relationship to consumer demand, we need a robust way of measuring credit cycles. The most common approach is to look at trends in credit scores. However, consumer credit scores respond to influences from many different factors—and often with significant lags.

When lenders nationwide were concerned about their exposure and cut the open-to-buy on home equity lines for consumers, credit scores fell. When the economy went into recession and unemployment rose, credit scores fell again. But when consumers were offered products they could not manage effectively, such as subprime option ARMs, their scores did not change until one to three years later, when they became unable to manage their finances.

Therefore, scores can move or not move for many reasons. But for measuring credit cycles, we need to answer the question, "What is the credit risk of loans being originated by lenders, independent of the economy?" Vintage-based[1] methods for analyzing loan performance provide a simple answer to this question. Age-period-cohort,[2] dual-time dynamics,[3] panel data,[4] and survival and proportional hazards[5] models all allow for

141

comparison across vintages, while normalizing for changes in the economic environment and age of the loan.

Figure 1 shows the volume and aggregate credit quality of all mortgage loans originated in each month since 1990. This measure of credit risk, originally published in a study in 2008,[6] was obtained by applying dual-time dynamics to an industry-wide mortgage data set. By adjusting for the age of the loans and the economic environment they lived through, the study obtained a pure measure of credit risk.

The graph's left axis shows the relative credit risk of loans originated in different time periods. Zero is the average credit risk for the industry through the period covered by the data set. Positive numbers show to what degree high delinquency levels were experienced for a specific vintage relative to the average. Negative numbers indicate less-than-average delinquency.

The right-hand axis shows the volume of mortgages originated for these vintages. Taken together, the credit risk and volume measures show a strong relationship and indicate three clear cycles. In 1992-93, a large volume of low-risk loans were originated. In 1994, volume dropped to 1990 levels and credit risk spiked to twice the normal levels. In 1998, another boom in origination occurred with very low credit risk. And not long after, in 2000-01, a comparatively low volume of loans were originated—but, again, with twice the normal credit risk.

In 2002-03, volume grew dramatically on loans of extremely low credit risk. By 2004, however, volume had started to fall and credit risk was rising steadily. The study of this cycle, performed in 2006, was the source of the early warning that the mortgage industry was headed into a crisis. In fact, the credit risk of loans originated through 2006-08 continued to rise rapidly to levels not seen before.

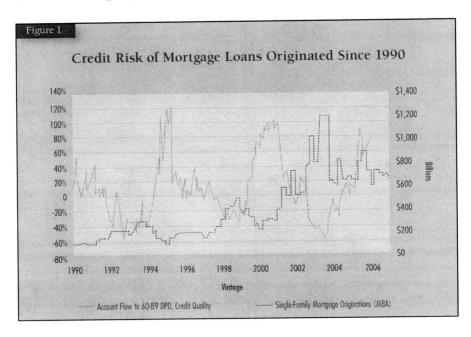

Figure 1

Credit Risk of Mortgage Loans Originated Since 1990

— Account Flow to 60-89 DPD, Credit Quality   ----- Single-Family Mortgage Originations (MBA)

The results shown in Figure 1 are independent of the drop in housing prices in 2007 and the recession in 2009. Those environmental effects were separated during modeling. We also tend to assume that the recent deterioration in credit quality was due to the boom in nonconforming mortgage securitizations, which peaked in 2006. However, the rapid deterioration in 2004 and the previous peaks suggest something more than just the influence of the securitization market. The question is, what caused these credit cycles?

Explaining Credit Cycles

The most logical hypothesis to test is whether changes in underwriting standards could account for these credit cycles. Fortunately, for the same period covered by our study, the Federal Reserve Board (FRB) has been conducting its Senior Loan Officer Opinion Survey (SLOOS). The FRB-SLOOS provides a widely quoted measure of whether banks are loosening or tightening their underwriting standards. Figure 2 shows time series for FRBSLOOS underwriting standards plotted against the measure of credit risk.

The surprising result from this graph is that there is no relationship between industry measures of underwriting standards and the credit risk being originated. The actual correlation is 0.01. However, the same FRB-SLOOS report shows the results of a survey that asked lenders whether consumer demand is increasing or decreasing.

Figure 3 compares the consumer demand revealed by the survey to the credit risk originated. In this case, there is a very strong anti-correlation: When consumer demand is strong, *credit risk is low*. Using a simple moving average of the FRB-SLOOS index, the correlation to industry-wide credit risk is 80%.

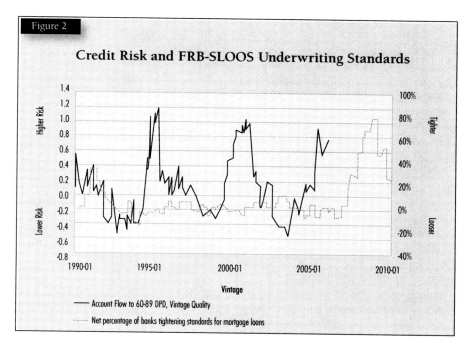

Figure 2

Credit Risk and FRB-SLOOS Underwriting Standards

—— Account Flow to 60-89 DPD, Vintage Quality

------ Net percentage of banks tightening standards for mortgage loans

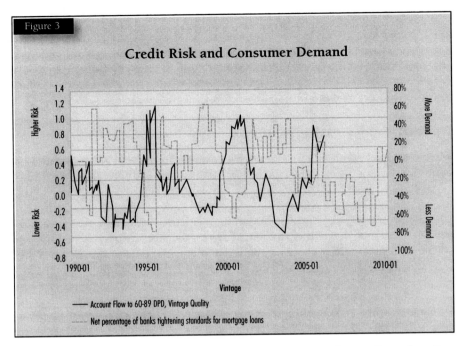

Figure 3

Credit Risk and Consumer Demand

Vintage

— Account Flow to 60-89 DPD, Vintage Quality

---- Net percentage of banks tightening standards for mortgage loans

This finding represents a dramatic step forward in our understanding of credit cycles, but we don't yet have an explanation for why consumer demand changes so dramatically. Our investigation now turns to macroeconomic data.

Let's compare credit risk by vintage to the economic conditions at the time the loan was written. Figure 4 compares credit risk to the interest rate offered on a 30-year conventional mortgage. Figure 5 compares credit risk to the year-over-year change in housing prices. Each of the variables captures aspects of the credit cycle. When these variables are taken together, we again get an 80% correlation to credit risk.

The relationship here makes intuitive sense. We find that when interest rates have been falling over the previous two years, the credit risk for loans originated will be low. Conversely, in periods when interest rates are rising, comparatively risky loans will be originated.

With housing prices, the relationship is a bit more complex, but equally intuitive. When home prices are rising faster than about 6% per year or falling at any given rate, comparatively risky loans will be originated. When home prices are flat or rising only slowly, low-risk loans will be originated.

Psychological studies have shown that people can be grouped broadly into those who are conservative and those who are risk takers. Either behavior can be beneficial in various aspects of life; however, from a lender's perspective, fiscally conservative consumers are at lower risk of default.

Keep in mind that these credit cycles were not anticipated by standard credit scores. In 2001, it was common to hear lenders say, "Our score tracking is flat. We didn't change anything. Why is the 2000 vintage so bad?" The same comments were heard early in

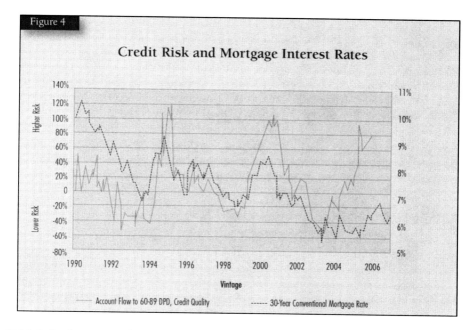

Figure 4

Credit Risk and Mortgage Interest Rates

Account Flow to 60-89 DPD, Credit Quality   30-Year Conventional Mortgage Rate

2006. Indeed, score tracking again showed no change until economic problems began in 2007.

This situation is not the fault of credit scores, but it does reflect a process we call *macroeconomic adverse selection*. Credit scores measure risk according to past financial

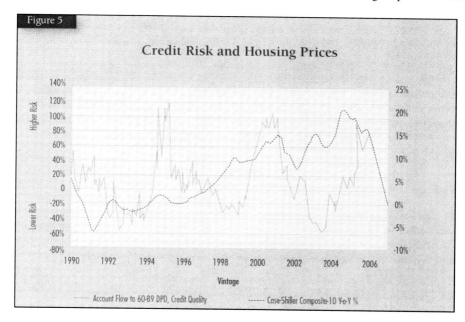

Figure 5

Credit Risk and Housing Prices

Account Flow to 60-89 DPD, Credit Quality   Case-Shiller Composite-10 Y-o-Y %

performance. However, there is no mechanism to determine whether past success came from being fiscally conservative or from taking risks that paid off. Our study suggests that changes in economic conditions cause shifts in the pool of consumers interested in obtaining loans.

Some lenders have worked to incorporate macroeconomic factors directly into their scores, presumably to capture this same effect. These macroeconomically driven scores are certainly the exception to the rule among today's lenders.

The preceding analysis was done for mortgages. However, another recent study[7] found a similar adverse-selection effect using panel-data methods analyzing home equity loans. Additional studies have shown similar yet more muted effects in auto lending and student loans. Least affected were credit cards, although the impact was still noticeable.

Managing through Credit Cycles

For those who attempt to manage portfolio credit risk, our analysis paints a dark picture. Credit scores do not measure consumer psychology. Much like the disclaimers in reports of stock market performance, past consumer performance is no guarantee of future results.

Furthermore, the use of credit scores assumes that the same pool of consumers is interested in borrowing as was present when the scores were built, and this is clearly not true. Therefore, attempts to manage the bank's risk appetite through changes in underwriting policy alone are unlikely to succeed during peaks of the credit cycle.

If there are no "good consumers" interested in obtaining a loan, adjusting underwriting will not cause good loans to appear. Underwriting is a process of selecting the best applicants, but it does not change the pool of applicants. For portfolio management, understanding the credit cycle from a macroeconomic adverse-selection perspective is at least as important as improving the underwriting process.

In fact, that is the actionable message here. When interest rates are rising or housing prices are either increasing rapidly or falling, lenders need to worry about the risk of macroeconomic adverse selection causing risky loans to be booked.

Depending on market conditions, this concern can take the form of increasing loan pricing to cover the likelihood of higher losses or reducing lending volume when loan pricing cannot be changed. This is more manageable when only select markets show house prices appreciating too rapidly or falling. When the problems are nationwide, as in 2005-08, the only answer may be to accept that long-term survival is more important than preserving near-term market share.

The Next Credit Cycle

The relationships between credit cycles and either the FRB-SLOOS or macroeconomic factors allow us to create models that predict consumer risk appetite and the credit risk of loans being originated by the industry, regardless of underwriting criteria.

Given the most recent results of the FRB-SLOOS consumer demand index, we would conclude that loans originated in 2010 were extremely low risk and trending toward average risk through 2011. This prediction is shown in Figure 6, along with a comparison to the historical credit risk measure for mortgages.

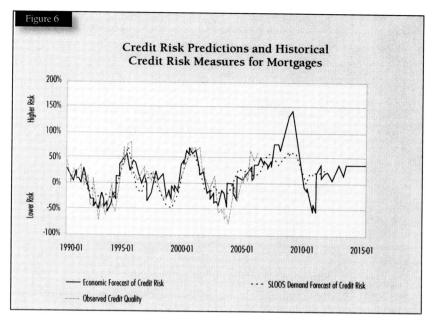

Figure 6

Credit Risk Predictions and Historical Credit Risk Measures for Mortgages

—— Economic Forecast of Credit Risk   - - - SLOOS Demand Forecast of Credit Risk
······ Observed Credit Quality

We also looked at the predictions from a macroeconomic model using mortgage interest rates and housing prices. That model does a better job of capturing the extremely high credit risk known to have been booked in 2007-09.

Figure 7 shows one possible economic scenario for the next few years, which anticipates a slow rise in mortgage interest rates starting in 2012 and a gradual increase in

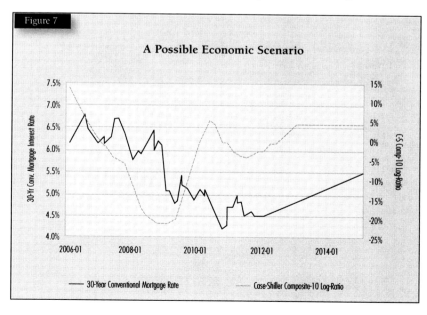

Figure 7

A Possible Economic Scenario

—— 30-Year Conventional Mortgage Rate   —— Case-Shiller Composite-10 Log-Ratio housing prices. With that scenario, we would anticipate a gradual deterioration into the next credit risk cycle, occurring in 2014. However, based on current scenarios, the next credit risk cycle may be significantly muted compared to those observed since 1990.

Overall, when looking for early-warning indicators of the next credit cycle, pay careful attention to the economic climate, consumer demand, and the performance of new loans.

Create your plans now for how you will change strategy when those warnings arrive. Remember, credit risk begins with consumers' risk appetites.

Notes

1. A *vintage*, also known as a *static pool*, is a group of accounts originated in the same time period. The performance of each vintage is tracked separately and compared using vintage analysis techniques, such as dual-time dynamics.
2. See N. D. Glenn, *Cohort Analysis*. Sage Publications, 2005.
3. See J. L. Breeden, *Reinventing Retail Lending Analytics*. Riskbooks, April 2010.
4. See E.W. Frees, *Longitudinal and Panel Data: Analysis and Applications in the Social Sciences*. Cambridge University Press, 2004.
5. See T. M. Therneau and P. M. Grambsch, *Modeling Survival Data: Extending the Cox Model*. Springer-Verlag, 2010.
6. See J. L. Breeden, L. C. Thomas, and J. W. McDonald, "Stress-testing Retail Loan Portfolios with Dual-time Dynamics." *The Journal of Risk Model Validation*, 2(2), summer 2008.
7. See P. Calem, M. Cannon, and L. Nakamura, "Credit Cycle and Adverse Selection Effects in Consumer Credit Markets: Evidence from the HELOC Market." Federal Reserve Bank of Philadelphia Working Papers, No. 11–13, March 2011.

Letter to the Editor

A reader responds to "Consumer Risk Appetite: How Consumer Demand Drives Credit Quality," written by Joseph L. Breeden, Ph.D. In this interesting exchange, Dr. Breeden responds to each point raised by Bob Merkle, president and CEO, Cash Flow Insights, Unionville, Pennsylvania.

Dr. Breeden:

Your article is very interesting. I especially like your insight into how the banking industry shapes credit scores through common actions when under stress. You explained beautifully a factor of which I have been subliminally aware.

I have a couple of personal observations from when I was marketing consumer credit at major banks that might cause some of the risk cycles you describe.

1. The marketing channel greatly impacts the quality of the applicant. For example, appli-cations taken in a branch have the highest credit quality and lowest tele-marketing. Banks manage their lending businesses by budgeting/targeting a certain growth every year. As demand for a product slows, banks increase their dependence on the lower quality application channels. These channels are more expensive because of the cost associated with the higher disapproval rate, so they are used less when demand is strongest. Therefore, banks cause a great deal of the credit quality cycle through their own behavior as demand changes. Your Figure 1 brought this to mind.

Dr. Breeden responds: I have definitely observed this too. When lenders say, "Grow 40%, but don't drop your cutoff scores," it sounds like an attempt to achieve responsible growth, but it really just directs marketing to use tools invisible to the credit scores in order to source the volume requested.

Based upon what I observed through the mortgage crisis, I believe this to be a contributing factor. As consumer demand fell but growth targets stayed high, marketing would need to shift to riskier loans. I do not see it as the only factor, but certainly an important contributor.

2. As rates decline, the percentage of applicants who are refinancing increases. These essentially proven risks (and often the new mortgage reduces the payment required, reducing the probability of default even more) improve the perceived/experienced risk associated with their new cohort. This probably explains why decreasing rates correlate with lower risk. Does your data allow home pur-

chase and refinance applicants to be analyzed separately, and even better separate cash-out applicants from the other refinancing applicants? If it does, you can correlate the risks of each pool to the amount of rate decline. (It takes a certain decline to make refinancing economic.)

Dr. Breeden responds: When this initial analysis was done, I saw the same credit cycles in new purchases and refinances, prime and subprime, traditional (30-year fixed) and nontraditional (option ARM), but the magnitude of the effect varied. I am currently working with a refreshed data set to revisit this analysis and hope to have results to report later in the year.

3. Rapidly increasing or decreasing home prices change the home affordability index a great deal. Would this index be a better measure to use related to risk? An improvement in the affordability index can easily bring more first-time home buyers into the market, increasing the pool of "untested" applicants and, therefore, the risk of the cohort.

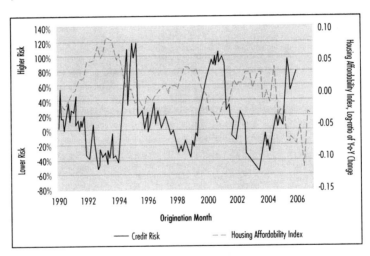

Dr. Breeden responds: This is a very interesting suggestion. The National Association of Realtors kindly provided time series of the Housing Affordability Index covering the time period in this analysis. Shown in the figure is a comparison between their composite index with an optimized transformation (three-month moving average of the log ratio of the 24-month year-over-year change). Conceptually, this is approximately the percentage change in the index over a two-year window, with a three-month smoothing.

Using this as a model to predict credit risk, R2 equals 0.54. For comparison, R2 equals 0.8 using the best transform of the FRB-SLOOS mortgage demand index and credit quality, and R2 equals 0.8 for the best model of house prices and interest rates. Given the uncertainty in all these estimates, these numbers do not prove conclusively that any of them is the winner. However, I suspect that the Housing Affordability Index does a good job of capturing increased consumer demand based upon individual financial considerations. What it might be missing relative to the other models is consumer fear of buying into falling housing markets. Combining those two effects might provide the best model overall, but any of these models will provide a very good intuitive guide to potential shifts in the credit cycle.

4. Finally, I have a question about the FRB-SLOOS data. Does it contain information on the percent of loans approved that were exceptions to the applicable lending criteria? In my experience, the policies are rarely changed, but the willingness to accept marginal applicants (the exceptions to policy) changes frequently in order to meet volume goals. This would be a second cause of risk increasing as demand declines. If this data were available, you would have a much better analysis than the one you used related to credit quality changes.

Again, thank you for an excellent, thought-provoking article.

Dr. Breeden responds: *To my knowledge, the FRB-SLOOS data only includes the survey questions around "loosening underwriting standards" and "increasing consumer demand." What you suggest would be interesting to test, but I am not aware of industry-wide data available to study the question.*

Pricing Loans with *Real* PD Forecasts

BY JOSEPH L. BREEDEN

"The world is changed."
– Galadriel from *The Lord of the Rings*

Every two years, at the end of August, the Credit Scoring and Credit Control Conference is held in Edinburgh, Scotland. The event routinely draws industry and academic participants from over 30 countries, many of whom present their latest research into retail lending analytics. No other conference on this subject matches the breadth and research quality of the "Edinburgh Conference."

Observing how it has changed provides a measure of how the industry is changing.

The first conference I attended seemed focused on the minutia of logistic regression scoring, and I was bored.

Then came the Basel II accord, first published in 2004.

The banking industry's weight shifted like a sumo wrestler. Banks changed their focus from creating more credit scores to modeling probability of default (PD). However, the initial retail lending PD models were rudimentary (if they could even be called models).

Challenges in implementing Basel II, and the use test requiring that the models actually be employed in areas beyond regulatory compliance, led researchers, both academic and industry, to create real probability models. The next several conferences saw an explosion of research into how to predict PDs, and traditional scores alone did not satisfy that need.

At the most recent conferences, "scores" that are based on duration models, survival models, Cox proportional hazards models, and age-period-cohort (APC) models have taken center stage, with many academics and practitioners accepting some variation of them as "the answer." But what was the question again?

What is the score's special purpose?

Models do not exist to provide accurate rankings or forecasts. The justification for any model must be that it increases profits. Historically, one modeling technique has been the unquestioned leader in return on investment: logistic regression.

The logistic regression scores have been the workhorse of the banking industry and have always been advertised as providing stable rankings, not ratings. They are intended to predict whether Mary is a better credit risk than Frank, but not whether they will both default in the next recession. If all we wanted to do was rank Mary and Frank, logistic regression would be fine, but that doesn't provide the loss probabilities necessary to help price the loans.

In sample, every logistic regression score does predict PD. That forecast can be thought of as a combination of the odds of default for the entire training data set (the population odds) and the unique risk of the individual relative to all others in the set (the idiosyncratic risk). Practitioners decades ago discovered that the population odds were highly unstable out of time, but the idiosyncratic risk was stable enough for decision making. So every major bank in the United States has designed a process around creating scores that provide rank ordering. However, are they still solving the problem that needs to be solved?

Several decades ago, with wider margins and practically no risk-based pricing, a ranking was good enough. The manager could simply choose to accept the best two-thirds of applicants or set a cutoff score intuitively based on past experience. Profits increased.

"The world is changed"

The introduction of Basel II was widely described as a "full employment program for analysts." That's not a great value proposition. Although Basel II started the conversation about predicting probabilities, the U.S. mortgage crisis was what raised the volume.

The crisis had many causes. Almost every level of the banking industry has been implicated in the debacle, but the simple truth is, if the loans had been priced for the true risk being assumed, the crisis would never have gone beyond a bad case of indigestion.

Every lender now does risk-based pricing, but if the models are based primarily on logistic regression scores, where does the risk get assessed? Pricing risk is not about whether Mary ranks higher than Frank. The issue is whether both, either, or neither of them will default during the lifetime of the loan.

To price a loan at origination, we need the most accurate forecast possible of the discounted cash flows for the life of the loan, adjusted for default and attrition. That's a lot to ask of a cutoff score bolted on to a rank-order score.

In most organizations where analysts create risk-ranking scores, someone else is left to estimate the margin—and the actual risk of loss—at each score point. Almost universally, those estimates are still done with moving-average score-odds calibrations. Inherently backward-looking, averaged odds unavoidably underestimate the losses going into each recession and overestimate the losses following a recession. The risk ranking did not fail in the mortgage crisis, but the score-odds calibration failed spectacularly.

"Risk-based pricing optimizes the past, and therefore only serves to ensure that we have the worst loans in the worst economy and the best loans in the best economy," a seasoned portfolio manager once noted.

The underlying problem is that rank-order scores were never the solution required for risk-based pricing of loans. But as the discussions in Edinburgh showed, the solutions exist, and the banks and portfolios with the least entrenched legacy structures are moving the quickest to adopt them.

To free the industry of perpetually failing risk-based pricing, we should consider the following five-step program.

Five steps to usable risk-based pricing

1. Abolish scores. Analysts need to create probability models from the start.
2. Eliminate cutoff scores. Speak in the language of minimum margin and maximum PD.
3. Incorporate time in the models. Analysts need to adopt some form of duration model with monthly performance data. Fixed observation windows from which "good" or "bad" are assessed are so last century.
4. Include attrition within the lifetime loss probability. To convert monthly, conditional probabilities to a cumulative lifetime loss, calculations must incorporate whether the loan will pay off early.
5. Use near-term economic scenarios. Yes, pricing really is about the future and we really need to be honest about the fact that future economic conditions drive our business.

Why not throw macroeconomic data into the scorecard?

The field is strewn with the models of analysts who tried before you—and fell on their swords.

Logistic regression scores are synonymous with data sets that allow for a short origination window (say, six months) and a fixed observation window (such as the subsequent 48 months). Having a short origination window means that you cannot apply any model that estimates loss timing, because the loans are not spread over a wide enough period to remove economic variations.

Having a fixed observation window with a cumulative good/bad assessment means that you cannot correlate to macroeconomic variation during that window. More history is needed to distinguish macroeconomic variations than is typical in scores.

The right approach is to spread the originations across many years, and use all the available observations until the loan attrites, defaults, or remains active today.

Even with the right data, even with a monthly logistic regression model, properly called generalized linear regression (GLM), you should expect problems. The APC literature explains that when age, vintage, and time are mixed within a single model, a specification error arises in the linear component. Some researchers call this colinearity, although it is across multiple dimensions rather than within a dimension. The APC literature discusses ways to treat this and should be required reading before attempting this.

Taking that APC book to a mountaintop and meditating on scoring for a while will also reveal some deeper truths about what's wrong with scores even for risk ranking. Logistic regression scores treat all "bads" as equal, but is a default at the height of the mortgage crisis the same as a default during the preceding period of rapid growth? The answer is no, but any economic variation occurring during the observation will be "explained" by whatever trends are present in the scoring variables. Scores are designed to fail out of time because they do not understand that time exists.

What's the minimum requirement for a probability model?

The model must capture loss and attrition timing, meaning the life cycle as a function of the loan's age for the loan product considered (as done in survival models). It must either measure net macroeconomic impacts (as done in APC models) or incorporate properly transformed, consumer-oriented macroeconomic data as a function of calendar date. And it must incorporate loan-specific scoring factors (as in Cox-PH models, generalized linear models, or generalized linear mixed models [GLMM]) or incorporate them in a staged approach as with APC scoring.

What if I don't trust our economist to drive pricing?

I don't either. If you want to get really depressed, buy several years of back issues of *Consensus Economics* and track the accuracy of the various economists. You will find optimists, pessimists, and herd followers, but even a herd follower is helpful for the next six months. Beyond six to 12 months, don't let any economist drive your pricing. Use a mean-reverting model or something similar to relax from the economist's scenario 12 months from now on to the long-run average.

If all that sounds like wishful thinking, then at least take current economic conditions and use a mean-reverting model to relax on to the long-run average. The result will be far more relevant than any backward-looking score-odds calibration.

What if I can't change our systems and management structure?

The systems question is the easier one. Loan origination or management systems that use scores can still be fed scoring outputs from these models. After creating your favorite PD model, zero-out the macroeconomic factors and integrate the PD model over whatever horizon is desired. That is a rank-order model that is not time-varying, but it was built to understand time and integrate with a fuller PD model. The result is far better than a score.

For the cutoff score, reinstate the macroeconomic scenario to determine the loss probability for each score point. Then proceed as normal.

As for the management structure where a credit team builds scores, credit policy sets cutoffs, and finance sets pricing—it's time for some group therapy. Credit needs to build probability models, credit policy needs to incorporate macroeconomic scenarios and set cutoff probabilities to maintain maximum allowable loss rates, and finance needs to determine maximum allowable losses for the established price points and margin targets.

Is anyone actually doing this?

The Federal Reserve is using such models for stress testing under its Comprehensive Capital Analysis and Review (CCAR) program. Its documents suggest that the Fed is using GLM-style regression to estimate models on loan-level data with repeat observations. Among its inputs are the usual scoring factors, the age of the loan, and macroeconomic factors. Although the CCAR models are a lowest-common-denominator model, other published work from the Fed is more sophisticated and in the same vein.

In general, lenders in Europe appear to be at a more advanced stage than their American counterparts. Cox PH and GLM appear regularly in discussions of their modeling practices, and PDs are a common part of loan origination.

Within the U.S., the PD models discussed here are standard fare for stress testing and forecasting, yet they rarely penetrate loan pricing, where they are needed the most.

We buy scores from vendors. How does this affect us?

Vendor scores traditionally provide a risk ranking and leave pricing (and implicitly estimating probabilities) to the lender. If you're not building scores, chances are you're not building a probability model either and are just setting cutoff scores to manage originations.

Today, that would be called standard practice, but certainly not leading practice. To stay in the risk-based-pricing game, you will need a probability model. Whether you hire a statistician to make a probability model wrapped around a vendor score or buy a probability model from a vendor, here are some questions you can ask.

- *Is the model built to consider when the loan defaults?* Defaults for young loans are much more costly than defaults for old loans.
- *Does the model consider economic conditions when the loan defaulted?* A default during a good economy is not the same as a default during a bad economy.
- *How is a lifetime-loss forecast created? Which economic scenario is used?* Loan pricing for lifetime losses cannot be based solely on current economic conditions.
- *Is the model specific to the product being offered?* A product-independent bureau score is usable as input to a probability model, but the probability of default is very specific to the product, features, and terms offered.

How do I start?

If you build your own models, you already have everything you need. You just have to start from the beginning.

At a minimum, the input data must record each month, for each loan. Did the loan attrite or default this month? The data needs to be spread over time. Short training sets, frequently refreshed, are part of the problem, not part of the solution.

With monthly performance data in hand, every major stats package has the routines needed. Survival models—Cox PH, APC, and GLM—are all well-established methods.

Admittedly, there are caveats associated with their use. Questions are surfacing about whether Cox PH properly handles the linear specification error. GLM and GLMM are so flexible that poorly structured models can be created—with poor results.

Overall, it would be wrong to suggest that creating such models is a trivial undertaking. Challenges, dead ends, and pitfalls await, but the race to price with real PD forecasts is already under way. The question is, have you left the starting gate yet?

References

1. Banerjee P. and J. Canals-Cerdá, 2012, "Credit Risk Analysis of Credit Card Portfolios under Economic Stress Conditions," Federal Reserve Bank of Philadelphia Working Paper No. 12-18, June.
2. Bellotti, T., 2013, "Using Survival Models for Profit and Loss Estimation," Proceedings of the Credit Scoring and Credit Control Conference XIII, Edinburgh, Scotland.
3. Bellotti, T. and J. Crook, 2013, "Forecasting and Stress Testing Credit Card Default with Dynamic Models," *International Journal of Forecasting*, 29:4, 563-74.
4. Board of Governors of the Federal Reserve System, 2012, "Comprehensive Capital Analysis and Review 2012: Methodology and Results for Stress Scenario Projections," March 13.
5. Breeden, J., 2013, "Incorporating Lifecycle and Environment in Loan-Level Forecasts and Stress Tests," Proceedings of the Credit Scoring and Credit Control Conference XIII, Edinburgh, Scotland.
6. Breeden, J., 2013, "A Mean-Reverting Model to Create Macroeconomic Scenarios for Credit Risk Models," Proceedings of the Credit Scoring and Credit Control Conference XIII, Edinburgh, Scotland.
7. Chisholm, K., 2013, "Treacle and Knicker Elastic: A Parsimonious Hazard Function for a Consumer Credit Portfolio," Proceedings of the Credit Scoring and Credit Control Conference XIII, Edinburgh, Scotland.
8. Credit Scoring and Credit Control Conference, Edinburgh, Scotland (available at http://www.business-school.ed.ac.uk/crc/ conferences).
9. Crook, J. and D. Osipenko, 2013, "Modelling the Profitability of Credit Cards for Different Types of Behavior with Panel Data," Proceedings of the Credit Scoring and Credit Control Conference XIII, Edinburgh, Scotland.
10. Dobson, A. J. and A. Barnett, 2008, *An Introduction to Generalized Linear Models, Third Edition*, Chapman & Hall.
11. Holford, T., 2005, "Age-Period-Cohort Analysis," *Encyclopedia of Statistics in Behavioral Science*, Wiley.
12. McDonald, R. A., A. Matuszyk, and L. C. Thomas, 2010, "Application of Survival Analysis to Cash Flow Modeling of Mortgage Products," *Journal of the Operations Research Society*, 23:1, 1-14.
13. McNeil, A. J. and J. P. Wendin, 2007, "Bayesian Inference for Generalized Linear Mixed Models of Portfolio Credit Risk," *Journal of Empirical Finance*, 14:2, 131-49, March.
14. Melnitchouk, V. and A. Vashurin, 2013, "Vintage Decomposition of Federal Financial Institutions Examination Council (FFIEC) Charge-Off Mortgage Data for Credit Risk Research and Education," Proceedings of the Credit Scoring and Credit Control Conference XIII, Edinburgh, Scotland.
15. Thomas, L. C., 2009, *Consumer Credit Models: Pricing, Profit and Portfolios*, Oxford University Press.

Wholesale Credit Capital

iven the divergent risks that can arise from credit, market, operational, and reputational sources, it is important to compare these risks using a common measurement scale. While bankers have long understood the concept of average or expected loss in calculating their provisions for credit losses, they were also aware of the large fluctuation in their annual losses. There could be many years when credit losses were small and seemed predictable, but the nature of banking and its ties to the economic cycle gave rise to a few years when losses were many multiples of the average level.

This variability in loss rates drove the need for capital, and consultants sometimes used the term "unexpected loss" as a synonym for capital requirements. Unexpected loss is actually the standard deviation of loss, and capital is usually several multiples of this quantity. The key question of how many standard deviations are required for capital adequacy can be answered by specifying the level of confidence such that losses could not exceed available capital.

Economic capital requirements were determined through models that simulated many scenarios characterized by correlated borrower defaults. For each default outcome, exposure and loss severities for individual borrowers were combined and aggregated to form a probability distribution of total losses. Initially, banks focused on pure defaults and ignored situations where the credit quality of borrowers weakened but they did not default. Since loan books didn't have to be marked-to-market based on credit deterioration, they considered default-only models adequate.

However, as secondary markets for loans and credit default swaps began to be developed, bankers realized they could hedge their losses. The benefit from hedging could only be determined if bankers were able to calculate their losses using a mark-to-market approach, even if they were not required to do so for accounting purposes. As a result, bankers began to migrate their economic capital models to mark-to-market models.

The regulators also began to focus on the banks' models and followed their development with their own capital models to be used for regulatory capital purposes.

159

The article "Current Issues in Estimating Credit Capital for Credit Risk," by Michel Araten, discusses the numerous choices surrounding input measurement, capital modeling, and management implementation and how these choices can lead to divergent decision-making.

Determination of input parameters revolves around how to measure historical defaults associated with ratings and point-in-time versus through-the-cycle philosophies, LGD and LEQ measurement challenges. In contrasting default-only (DO) versus mark-to-market (MTM) economic capital models, it is noted that DO models are easier to build while MTM models have many more switches to tweak. As a result, given the wide variety of approaches to gathering inputs, deciding how to structure credit capital models, what to include in them, and how to apply the result of these calculations in decision making, it is not surprising that divergent estimates of capital, minimum pricing, and profitability are obtained.

In "Economic Capital, Performance Evaluation, and Capital Adequacy at Bank of America," by John Walter, a case study reveals several basic principles shared by all economic capital frameworks and provides a practical illustration of how economic capital can work for any financial institution. The article offers a discussion of the financial theory of allocating equity capital among different businesses for the purpose of evaluating business performance and capital adequacy. In addition, the author offers a detailed look at the measurement system itself, including each of the four different sources of risk—credit, country, market, and business—that together determine the amount of capital assigned to an activity.

"Economic Capital for Counterparty Exposures," by Evan Picoult, describes the key differences between estimating credit exposure for loans versus exposure to counterparties who are engaged in derivative transactions. Credit exposure is the amount owed by borrowers at the time of default, and while it may vary if there are unfunded commitments, the variation is subject to the control of the lender and the borrower.

Counterparty exposure is based on the fluctuations and changes in market rates of the underlying interest or foreign exchange contracts and their translation into market values at the time contractual payments are due. To estimate economic capital for market risk, one must simulate a whole set of market rates and associated factors and translate them into a probability distribution of loss associated with the underlying contracts, taking into account correlations among the rates.

The author also distinguishes between approaches for a counterparty such as a corporate end-user with only a single contract versus that of a market maker with multiple contracts that may involve legal netting or offsetting of exposures. The requirements for validating market risk models have become substantially more demanding in the wake of Basel III, the Dodd-Frank Act, and the many concerns of supervisors as to the applicability of historical data.

"Economic Capital versus Regulatory Capital," by Michel Araten, reviews the numerous ways that regulatory parameters, which are subject to the highly conservative assumptions required by regulators in the Basel framework, are different from those used for economic capital modeling. While the Basel framework expected that regulatory parameters would be subject to a use test—namely, that these parameters would also be used in determining economic capital and in making portfolio decisions—many practitioners found this impossible to implement.

For example, PDs based on long-term historical data could hardly be used when evaluating the benefits of hedging loans with market-based instruments, such as credit default swaps. However, with the recent emphasis on stress-test results being used as critical criteria for banks' dividend payments and stock buybacks, the pendulum has shifted to a focus on regulatory and stress-test parameters, and their effect on regulatory capital and stress-test outcomes is becoming paramount in decision making.

Charles Monet's "Back to Basics: What Is Economic Capital All About?" pokes holes in common concepts about economic capital. While banks target levels of economic capital based on loss volatility that could deplete book capital, the primary reason for bank defaults is poor liquidity and an inability to staunch the loss of confidence. This has certainly been brought out in the recent financial recession, with Lehman Brothers being a prominent example.

The author suggests that market-based measures, such as the market value of equity relative to its earnings momentum, through operational and business risk elements, are more informative. Interestingly, many banks use KMV's market-based measures to determine the likelihood of customer default but fail to use similar measures to determine their own capital adequacy. The author also criticizes the use of the same hurdle rate for all lines of business in assessing whether returns are adequate. Rather, different lines of business could have different hurdle rates based on peer comparisons. Thus, the cost of equity for a credit card business could be compared to that of monoline credit card companies, and the cost of equity for an investment bank's line of business could be compared to that of a pure-play investment bank competitor.

"Convergence of Economic Credit Capital Models," by Michel Araten, describes the results of a benchmarking exercise conducted by the International Association of Credit Portfolio Managers and the International Swaps and Derivatives Association. For a given portfolio, economic capital estimates across banks can differ due either to different views of the input parameters, such as PD and LGD, or the way the various models treat these inputs, or both.

In an attempt to determine how modeling differences may affect economic capital estimates, a hypothetical portfolio was created with specified or fixed parameters. Banks were asked to use their vendor-based or internal models to run the portfolios, and comparisons were made across banks. When banks ran their models under the assumptions that losses were to be determined based on a "default only" outcome without any mark-to-market intermediary valuations, substantial agreement among the models could be obtained as measured by the standard deviation of results.

However, when banks used their mark-to-market models, not only were the results more varied across different types of models, but within the same type of model, such as a standard vendor-based model, there were significant differences. The mark-to-market models had more switches that different banks chose to flip in different ways, leading to a lack of strong convergence. Similar benchmarking exercises continue to be employed throughout the industry to ascertain best practices.

"Stressed LGDs in Capital Analysis," by Gary Wilhite, focuses on both economic capital and regulatory capital treatment of LGD. While capital models generally assume volatility in idiosyncratic LGDs, resulting in U-shaped distributions, observers noted that higher LGD levels were usually obtained during economic downturns. Since the Basel formula did not incorporate variability in LGDs, the regulators specified that stressed or downturn LGDs should be used as inputs to the regulatory capital calculation.

This article discusses the supervisory formula that was originally proposed by the regulators in cases where historical data was insufficient to conservatively estimate downturn LGDs, and it makes a number of practical suggestions for incorporating stressed LGDs. Today, downturn LGDs continue to be an area of extreme focus from both regulators and bankers as its effect on regulatory capital is critical.

"Sources of Inconsistencies in Risk-Weighted Asset Determinations," by Michel Araten, evaluates the reasons why different banks could have varying estimates of risk-weighted assets (RWA) and regulatory capital for the same set of loans. Under the advanced internal ratings-based (AIRB) approach, banks are free to use their own internal estimates of PD, LGD, and EAD, subject to supervisory review. This article demonstrates numerous instances where banks may come up with different estimates of these parameters, depending on how they conduct the forensic analysis of their default data.

In addition, different risk management processes at banks will also lead to different outcomes and result in divergent estimates of AIRB parameters. Recognizing the sources of these differences is important, as regulators are moving toward non-risk-sensitive measures, such as leverage, in light of observed inconsistencies in RWA estimates across banks.

Current Issues in Estimating Economic Capital for Credit Risk

BY MICHEL ARATEN

Measuring inputs, model structure, and management applications of economic capital entails numerous choices that can lead to divergent decision making. A discussion of these key issues is presented here, along with insight obtained from studies at JPMorgan Chase and elsewhere, for those institutions seeking to implement processes for estimating economic capital.

The theory and practice of estimating economic capital for credit risk have advanced significantly over the past five to 10 years. During that time, state-of-the-art portfolio credit risk assessment models, such as those from KMV and RiskMetrics, have been introduced, banks have developed their own internal models, and regulators are rising to the challenge of keeping up by reforming their own regulatory capital models.

Markets have reacted by accommodating the appetite for risk mitigation with explosive growth in hedging instruments, including single-name default swaps, structured baskets, and related indices. While there is some convergence around approaches to model development, many open questions surround three major issues: measurement of inputs, model structure, and management applications of economic capital. The manner in which these issues are treated creates significant differences in the way banks determine capital and how they use capital in decision making.

Measurement of Inputs

Key drivers of economic credit capital models consist of probabilities of default (PD) associated with risk ratings, loss given default (LGD), loan equivalents (LEQs) for unfunded commitments, correlations, and market spreads. Recently, particular focus has been placed on PDs and LGDs.

Risk ratings and default probabilities. Risk-rating assessments can emphasize a longer-term view that incorporates a business or economic cycle (*through the cycle*, or TTC), or they can place greater emphasis on current borrower conditions (*point in time*, or PIT). TTC ratings tend to be more stable and represent the primary rating philosophy followed by the ratings agencies. To measure ratings stability, Moody's reports that it "tracks the frequency of rating changes, the frequency of ...large rating changes... [and]... rating reversals."[1] PIT ratings are often influenced by current market indicators, such as market spreads, or by default estimates provided by RiskMetrics (Credit Grades), KMV (EDFTM), and other firms.

163

It is difficult to determine where banks or their individual credit analysts base their ratings along the continuum from PIT to TTC. Credit assessments of companies with public debt or publicly traded equity may be more influenced by market publicized events than are assessments of companies without public debt or public equity. This leads to serious issues regarding ratings consistency within an institution. Jeremy Taylor of Union Bank argues that "[while]...banks have been pulled back toward PIT...[and are]...more sensitive to company news....most banks lie somewhere between the extremes.[2]

The view of this author is that while banks may now be moving toward a mark-to-market view of the value of their portfolios, relying more heavily on current market indicators, the majority of banks have rating philosophies that lie somewhat closer to the TTC end.[3] Analysis of ratings migrations, similar to one conducted at JPMorgan Chase (JPMC), may help a bank determine how consistent it is with regard to different internal-ratings philosophies.[4]

These distinctions are important when estimating PDs. Banks emphasizing longer-term views of economic capital requirements will associate historical average PDs with their TTC ratings. Banks employing a PIT approach will use more current estimates of PDs as input. Volatility in input PDs will create volatility in capital.

Loss given default. Measures of loss given default are usually obtained from a forensic analysis of a bank's nonaccrual and charge-off history. There are numerous methodological issues that impinge on data quality—for example, ensuring that defaults are properly recorded, that collateral is identified, and that all sources of recoveries, such as liquidation of securities received in workouts, are included in the calculations.

Cash flows are reconstructed from these records so that their present value, discounted at an appropriate rate, can proxy for the economic recoveries. One issue is the choice of the discount rate. Alternatives include a funding rate, the original contract rate of interest, and a distressed (or "vulture") rate. The distressed rate represents the yield that investors are likely to seek should the bank wish to sell the exposure rather than work it out on its own. The distressed rate represents an appropriate opportunity cost and is aligned with ratings-agency estimates of secondary loan prices on defaulted securities approximately one month after default.

A recent study conducted by JPMC of more than 3,700 defaults over an 18-year period found an overall LGD of 40% based on a 15% discount rate.[5] This rate was chosen to approximate an average distressed rate over that period. To illustrate sensitivity to the discount rate chosen, a 10% discount rate would result in an average LGD of 36%, and a 5% discount rate would result in an average 32% LGD. A good argument can be made that the discount rate should vary, depending on the point at which the firm estimates itself to be in the economic cycle.

Historical analysis of loss severities based on the type of collateral received offers guidance for assessing LGDs in the current portfolio. Ratings agencies publish differentiated historical results for bond LGDs, based on their senior, junior, secured, or unsecured characterizations. These descriptors do not change over the life of the bonds.

The management of bank credit, however, is substantially more dynamic. Although a bank loan may have been unsecured at the outset, that does not preclude obtaining additional protection when the borrower's credit deteriorates. In fact, unsecured loans can become secured, and the package of collateral initially granted at origination often can be improved. This was observed in the internal study at JPMC, where a relatively large proportion of defaulted loans was deemed secured at the time of default, yet a good number of these were not secured at origination. An argument could thus be advanced that the LGD associated with a newly originated unsecured loan needs to take into consideration the likelihood of the bank obtaining security.

Model Structure

Issues concerning model structure primarily concern whether to use "default only" (DO) or mark-to-market (MTM) models to generate probability distributions of loss. Overall portfolio capital is determined for both models by associating a point on the loss distribution (in excess of expected loss) with a cumulative loss probability. This point is usually related to a desired minimum agency rating standard.

The DO model measures losses associated solely with defaults. The MTM model incorporates loss from defaults as well as loss from valuation changes (when a loan's value is marked to market either due to upward or downward migration of risk or when credit spreads change). Both approaches require an assumed horizon over which to aggregate their respective loss measures. Common practice is to set the horizon to one year, although the rationale for this choice merits further exploration.

Default-only models. DO models are aligned with balance-sheet and profit-and-loss accounting-related measures in that loan accounting is on an accrual basis. In this approach, losses associated with defaults can be made to match reasonably well with credit costs that appear in the form of charge-offs or provisions. Capital can then be associated with volatility of accrual-reported income over the coming year. The issue here is how to treat risks associated with maturities in excess of one year. Various schemes have been advanced, including extending the horizon and annualizing the results or term-adjusting the capital by term-adjusting the default probabilities.

Mark-to-market models. MTM models are aligned with an economic view of valuation losses, both realized and unrealized, that are associated with changes in credit quality and credit spreads. If the portfolio is actually marked to market or "shadow marked," capital can be associated with the volatility of these values. However, if balance sheet and income statements are reported externally on an accrual basis, there will be an inconsistency that may affect the way return on equity (ROE) or shareholder value added (SVA) is viewed. While internal management reporting could be made consistent with the MTM view, this could create divergent internal versus external performance measures and incentives.

Difficulties arise in developing the market spreads for the large portion of the portfolio that is relatively illiquid and has only indirect market comparables. One approach is to estimate the current spread used to originate or renew the loan based on its credit characteristics and market environment today rather than on when it was originated. This measure relates closely to a valuation based on a theoretical economic opportunity cost.

In MTM approaches, one typically finds capital charges associated with longer-dated high-investment-grade exposures to be relatively high, as these have the greatest potential for valuation losses upon a downgrade. Client managers often have difficulty understanding the steep capital term structures for these clients, and even senior credit officers may be concerned that such charges will discourage building a high-quality portfolio. Many of these issues would disappear if the exposures were marked to market at origination.

Furthermore, although 2003 was an unusual year with regard to 40-50% decreases in market-based PDs, other periods have demonstrated significant volatility in default rates and attendant capital requirements. These estimates fuel the debate behind the procyclical effects of using an MTM approach. Despite these difficulties, momentum appears to be building toward MTM capital measures to better represent the total opportunity costs—if not the realized ones—associated with credit quality changes. Banks that are active users of risk-mitigation alternatives available in credit markets will use an MTM approach because it more closely matches the risk valuations they see in the markets.

DO models are easier to build, and related measures of total portfolio capital by different banks will generally be quite similar.[6] MTM models have many more switches to tweak, and the divergence in reported portfolio capital can grow based on these modeling choices. In a joint study conducted by the International Swaps and Derivatives Association and the Institute of International Finance in 1998 and published in 2000,[7] it was clear that, even with standardized portfolios, there were significant differences in the way participant banks set key parameters and in how they ran their models. For MTM models in particular, growing sophistication in how and what to model is leading to even greater divergence.

The following are details of what and how to model:

- Using a single overall set of market credit spreads (in conformance with a theoretical no-arbitrage view across markets) or using multiple sector-oriented actual market credit spreads for valuation.
- Introducing into the valuation analysis the option borrowers have to prepay facilities.
- Correlating loss severities across defaulting facilities in the portfolio to conform to the empirical view that lower recovery rates are found to be associated with higher levels of systemic defaults.
- Incorporating defaulted loans into the modeling of performing loans to reflect the uncertainty of their recovery rates and their correlation with systemic defaults.
- Incorporating uncertainty around LEQ estimates.
- In addition to adding credit default swaps into the models, incorporating baskets and tranches of structured transactions with specific identification of assets in the portfolio and associated "waterfall" rules governing tranche losses.
- Expanding the normal correlation of asset values of borrowers in various countries to model the effect of country default events. This would include simultaneous borrower defaults occasioned by country-transfer risk events associated with single country defaults or domino effects across regions.
- Including retail-oriented assets, such as credit cards, auto loans, and mortgages, into commercial loan portfolio models.

Management Applications of Economic Capital

Practices vary widely as to how decisioning is affected by economic capital and whether the type of decision being made warrants alternative measures of economic capital.

Relationship profitability and pricing decisions. In deciding whether a customer relationship meets an overall target risk-adjusted return on equity or has positive SVA, credit capital needs to be assessed at the customer level. The assessed capital is usually derived in such a way as to be additive—across customers and lines of business—to the aggregate amount of capital. These measures reflect capital allocation based on the portfolio mix at a point in time. In addition to performance measurement and incentive compensation decisions, these measures are used to make strategic decisions with regard to customer relationships or classes of customers.

Often, however, these capital factors also are used to decide whether to extend additional facilities to a customer or to withdraw from unprofitable relationships. Firms that use the same capital factors for pricing or profitability models and for determining whether a proposed transaction is SVA positive do so under the assumption that the transaction will be approved. However, once the transaction is part of the portfolio, the allocated capital could very well change if concentrations shift. Other firms recognize the need to conduct an analysis of the incremental effect associated with a particular transaction. They derive the incremental capital associated with a portfolio consisting of the old portfolio *plus* this transaction.

Capital attribution. Once overall portfolio capital has been determined, there may be wide variation in the approach to assigning capital to individual exposures based on their risk contribution. Most banks measure risk contribution to *portfolio variance*, assuming that the number of standard deviations required to reach the confidence level criterion is constant. A few banks assess contribution to *tail risk*, a more direct measure of capital. Borrowers with different correlations or with different maturities may have significantly different capital charges based on the approach followed.

In determining the actual capital associated with individual exposures needed for performance measures, such as SVA, banks may be reluctant to "export" these actual capital charges. Internal management accounting systems may not support the direct feed of the individual capital charges as new exposures appear or old ones roll off, thus requiring an almost daily rerunning of the model.

While there are technical solutions to this problem, including the incorporation of marginal "deal analyzers," more fundamental objections are sometimes raised. The user community of relationship managers may perceive actual capital charges as derived from a black-box model. These charges may be challenged based on the fragility of the input assumptions, especially those dealing with correlations. Moreover, it will be difficult for users attempting to estimate the relationship or deal profitability on their own without access to the underlying model.

These practical and cultural concerns are addressed through indirect capital factors that are extracted from the models' output based on regressions or through incremental runs of the models. Thus, capital charges for individual exposures are collapsed into factors that may be functions of risk rating, tenor, industry, and country. While these charges also may be perceived as a black-box outcome, they may be more acceptable since they can be incorporated into more familiar spreadsheet tools. Broader factors, while crude approximations to the model's estimates of risk contribution, satisfy "directionally correct" viewpoints of users.

The trade-offs in approaches to implementation will reflect the degree to which separate portfolio management functions have developed independent roles in the organization. The value of hedging activities is best measured at the portfolio level by directly reestimating overall portfolio risk capital. Therefore, some organizations may have parallel measures of economic capital, depending on whether the purpose is to measure the effects of risk mitigation or relationship profitability. The degree to which banks continue to expand their roles in intermediating credit exposures with the goal of retaining as little as they can on their balance sheets will determine the extent to which they will emphasize direct measures of risk contribution.

Diversification benefits. There is little argument that the benefits of diversification in a credit portfolio should be passed to all the exposures within that portfolio. Divergent views arise about what should constitute a portfolio. Should middle-market or retail credits be included in a large corporate credit portfolio or should these portfolios be evaluated on a stand-alone basis?

Charles Smithson distinguishes *stand-alone* capital from *marginal* capital by explaining that the former examines the capital required as if that business existed by itself, while the latter represents the incremental amount of capital if that business were added to the existing portfolio. Based on the nature of the decision taken, he argues that "it is generally agreed that stand-alone capital is appropriate for measuring performance of business unit managers...[while] marginal capital is the appropriate measure for evaluating acquisitions or divestitures...."[8]

There are strongly divergent views on the larger context of assessing economic capital across credit, market, operating, and business risk. A survey of 31 financial institutions by the BIS Working Group on Risk Assessment and Capital concerning risk integration and risk aggregation notes that "risk aggregation and economic capital methods are still in early stages of evolution."[9] Conflicting views of the efforts to reduce all risks into a single number are reported, but the survey notes the conceptual appeal of providing a single metric along which all types of risk can be measured and traded off.

Stress-related scenarios as well as statistical correlations measured across the types of risks are used to estimate overall risk levels and assess diversification. There is an especially wide variation of methods to aggregate across risk types. The use of stress scenarios to explore the interaction of these risks can be illuminating, primarily at the major business level.

Conclusion

Formal and informal efforts to compare credit capital models and related measures across firms are continuing. Some of these efforts, such as the QIS associated with Basel

II, have been initiated by regulators trying to better tune changes in regulatory capital requirements to economic capital practices.

Associations or consortiums of banks, such as The Risk Management Association and the International Association of Credit Portfolio Managers, have pursued quantitative and qualitative surveys as benchmarking exercises. Given the wide variety of approaches to gathering inputs, and deciding how to structure credit capital models, what to include in these models, and how to apply the result of these calculations in decision making, it is not surprising to see divergent estimates of capital, minimum pricing, and profitability.

Continued sharing and publicizing of historical analyses, model developments, and implementation practices can only improve risk assessment and capital model methodologies. Such efforts may well turn out to be one of the more valuable contributions to risk mitigation in the banking community.

Notes

1. See Moody's Investor Services, "Special Comment: Measuring the Performance of Corporate Bond Ratings," April 2003.
2. See Jeremy Taylor, "Risk-Grading Philosophy: Through the Cycle versus Point in Time," *The RMA Journal*, November 2003.
3. See Michel Araten, "Development and Validation of Key Estimates for Capital Models," in *The Basel Handbook: A Guide for Financial Practitioners*, Michael Ong, ed., December 2003.
4. See Michel Araten, Michael Jacobs, Peeyush Varshney, and Claude Pellegrino, "An Internal Ratings Migration Study of JPMorgan Chase Bank," December 2003.
5. A discount rate of 0% would result in an accounting-based net charge-off measure of 27%.
6. See H. Ugur Koyluoglu and Andrew Hickman, "Reconcilable Differences," *Risk*, October 1998.
7. See "Modeling Credit Risk: Joint IIF/ISDA Testing Program," February 2000, available at http://www.iif.com/pub/publication.quagga?id=18&ref=main.
8. See Charles Smithson, "Economic Capital: How Much Do You Really Need?" *Risk*, November 2003.
9. See Basel Committee on Banking Supervision, "The Joint Forum: Trends in Risk Integration and Aggregation," Bank for International Settlements, August 2003.

Economic Capital, Performance Evaluation, and Capital Adequacy at Bank of America

BY JOHN S. WALTER

A case study of the economic capital system used by Bank of America reveals several basic principles shared by all economic capital frameworks and provides a practical illustration of how economic capital can work for any financial institution.

This article begins with a discussion of the financial theory of allocating equity capital among different businesses for the purpose of evaluating business performance and capital adequacy. It then provides a detailed look at the measurement system itself, including each of the four different sources of risk—credit, country, market, and business—that together determine the amount of capital assigned to an activity.

Institutions using *economic capital methodology* have coined the term to distinguish it from other measures of capital adequacy—in particular, regulatory and accounting concepts of capital. The term *economic* also encapsulates an ambition, like that of the "dismal science," to describe and measure on a consistent basis the range of phenomena that drive a bank's risk-return decisions. A consistent and comprehensive economic model accomplishes two goals:

1. It provides a common currency of risk that management can use to compare the risk-adjusted profitability and relative value of businesses with widely varying degrees and sources of risk.
2. It allows bank management and supervisors to evaluate overall capital adequacy in relation to the risk profile of the institution.

With increasing dialogue among practitioners, regulators, and academics, best practices have gradually emerged, setting standards for calculation in most aspects of economic capital.

Advances continue, especially in the areas of operational risk and consumer credit risk, but the overall field has matured to the point where supervisors have begun, with the upcoming implementation of the new Basel Capital Accord, to adopt and codify the industry's best practices in the regulatory capital framework.

Market Value Definition of Risk

Over the past decade, economic capital has steadily progressed toward market value models. Most commercial portfolio frameworks have by now discarded first-generation economic capital models based only on default risk, although these models persist in some cases for consumer portfolios. Given the goal of ensuring capital adequacy for a certain level of solvency, the volatility of market value is the best measure of a bank's risk and therefore its capital requirement.

Ultimately, shareholders are interested in the total return on their investment in the bank's stock and its risk in market value terms. They compare the return earned on their investment to a required return based on its risk. Bondholders also care about market values. The value of their fixed-income investment is a function of the credit spread of the bank, the level of interest rates, and the expected cash flows of the debt. Since both stockholders and bondholders evaluate their investments based on market values, management should evaluate its opportunities with the same market value discipline. Defining risk in market value terms reinforces this discipline by aligning the interests of business managers with those of shareholders and bondholders.

The values of debt and equity are intimately related, as they are both derivative claims on the underlying assets of the company. According to the Merton model, the equity of a firm is equivalent to a call option on the firm's value, with the debt being the strike price. The equity holders have the option to "buy" the firm's assets and any other value of the franchise by repaying the debt. Equity holders will not exercise this option and will default on their obligation to the debt holders if the total asset and franchise value falls significantly short of the amount owed to creditors.

The firm's leverage in market value terms (that is, the difference between the market value of assets and the book value of liabilities) and the volatility of its market value are therefore the primary determinants of a company's default probability and required credit spread. The measure of risk that drives both the value of debt and equity, then, is the volatility of asset values.

The distinction between a market-value-based measurement of risk and an accounting earnings-based measurement of risk is important. Given the need to maintain a low likelihood of default, a high credit rating, and the resulting ability to finance the firm's activity, the most relevant measure of risk for determining capital adequacy is the volatility of a bank's market value.

Just as a bank's overall capital requirement is driven by the volatility of its market value, capital allocations to the bank's individual activities should depend on the contribution of each to the overall market value volatility. However, since most bank businesses do not mark their portfolios to market, risk managers cannot directly track the volatility of market values; rather, model-driven estimates of market value volatility or even the volatility of earnings must serve as surrogates.

Accounting for Diversification

For an economic capital model to apply to the entire bank as well as its individual activities, it must consider not only the volatility of market value for each activity, but also how that value changes with respect to that of all other activities.

The logic for this diversification adjustment is straightforward: The less cyclical exposures generate diversification benefits for the bank as a whole that enable the bank to operate with less equity capital. A capital allocation based on risk contribution confers this benefit to business activities that enhance diversification, thereby encouraging their growth. Omitting this effect would clearly overstate the risk of the bank.

Finance theory tells us that investors' required returns are a function of non-diversifiable risk. One of the primary goals of the economic capital framework is to measure and compare business performance across activities with widely varying degrees of risk. Shareholder value added (SVA) is calculated by comparing each business's return to the bank's cost of equity. Because the bank's cost of equity is based on systematic risk, the risk measure used for calculating SVA must be based on risk contribution rather than on stand-alone risk. Otherwise, a second process would be required to determine differentiated costs of equity for each business.

Strictly speaking, the risk contribution approach outlined above measures the exposure to internally undiversified risk rather than truly systematic or non-diversifiable risk. However, when this approach is used by large diversified financial institutions, any differences in the theoretical cost of equity after adjusting for risk contribution of individual businesses are likely to be well within the measurement error of the risk measures themselves.[1]

Capital Adequacy

For capital adequacy purposes, the overriding goal of allocating capital to individual businesses is to determine the bank's optimal capital structure—the amount of equity that is required to maintain the bank's internal standard of solvency (that is, its target credit rating) given the overall level of risk. This process involves estimating how much the risk of each business contributes to the total risk of the bank and hence to the bank's overall capital requirement.

Ultimately, the *economic* capital based on risk should be compared to the *actual* capital held by the bank. A sensible risk-based capital adequacy framework should match the measured risk with the financial resources available to cover that risk. The financial resources available to cover the total amount of losses over a given horizon include not only book capital, or common equity, but also loan loss reserves and income generated during the period.

Banks consider expected or average level of loss to be a cost of doing business. Margins on loan products, for example, are set at a level sufficient to cover operating costs as well as expected loss and to provide a favorable return on capital. As a result, expected loss is not included in the measurement of risk, but is thought of as a direct charge against current period earnings.

To determine capital adequacy, best-practice institutions measure capital based on *unexpected loss*, or volatility around expected loss, and compare their estimate of required capital with financial resources available to cover unexpected loss—common equity and loan loss reserves. Since expected loss is covered by future margin income, *expected loss* is not included in the measurement of economic capital. Likewise, future margin income is excluded from the financial resources available to cover losses.

Performance Measurement

For performance evaluation purposes, risk-adjusted return on capital (RAROC) systems assign capital to businesses as part of a process to determine the risk-adjusted rate of return and, ultimately, the SVA of each business. The objective in this case is to measure a business's contribution to shareholder value after fully adjusting for risk, and thus to provide a basis for strategic planning, ongoing performance monitoring, product pricing, and tactical portfolio management decisions.

The RAROC for each business is its net income divided by its required economic capital. Often, the calculation adjusts *accounting net income* to replace *provisions* with *expected loss* and to remove timing distortions inherent to the accounting process. If the RAROC is higher than the cost of equity—shareholders' required rate of return—then the business is creating value for shareholders.

RAROC is a clear and consistent indicator of profitability. However, the exclusive use of RAROC or any rate of return to evaluate performance can discourage profitable investments. A rate of return does not measure how much value an activity creates or destroys; it only indicates its rate of profitability. To maximize shareholder wealth a bank must undertake any new project that, over its expected life, yields a RAROC that exceeds the cost of capital. Managers rewarded solely on RAROC are likely to reject value-increasing projects that will lower their average return.

To avoid this problem and create the right investment incentives, a bank should evaluate performance according to the SVA of a business. SVA is calculated by subtracting the cost of equity capital from the operating earnings of the business. Like RAROC, SVA uses economic capital as the "currency" for risk and therefore allows comparison of activities with varying risk characteristics. It overcomes the limits of RAROC by incorporating the size of the investment, not just its rate of return.

Rewards to managers should depend on the incremental improvement in shareholder value added rather than its absolute value. This levels the playing field, encourages turnarounds of poorly performing businesses, and avoids rewarding the inheritance of a highly profitable operation.

Economic Capital at Bank of America

Bank of America defines risk as volatility in the firm's market value. The key elements of this definition are its comprehensiveness and its emphasis on market value rather than earnings. Bank of America calculates risk in four major categories—credit, country, market, and business—but the particular categorization is less important than its guiding principle: There must be "a place for everything, with everything in its place."

Capitalization and confidence levels. Two estimates describe a bank's risk profile: expected loss and unexpected loss. As illustrated in Figure 1, expected loss is the average

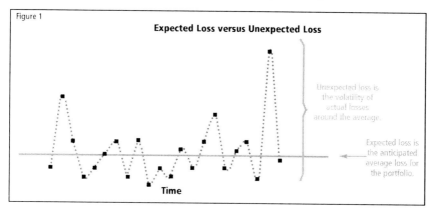

Figure 1

Expected Loss versus Unexpected Loss

Unexpected loss is the volatility of actual losses around the average.

Expected loss is the anticipated average loss for the portfolio.

Time

rate of loss expected from a portfolio. If losses equaled their expected levels, there would be no need for capital. Unexpected loss is the volatility of losses around their expected levels. Unexpected loss determines the economic capital requirement.

To prevent insolvency, economic capital must cover unexpected losses to a high degree of confidence. Banks often link their choice of confidence level to a standard of solvency implied by a credit rating of A or AA for their senior debt. The historical one-year default rates for A firms and AA firms are approximately 10 and 3 basis points, respectively. These target ratings therefore require that the institution have sufficient equity to buffer losses over a one-year period with confidence levels of 99.90% and 99.97% (Figure 2).

Bank of America's reference points for the allocation of economic capital are a target rating of AA and the related 99.97% confidence level for solvency. This confidence level requires that economic capital be sufficient to cover all but the worst three of every 10,000 possible risk scenarios with a one-year horizon. To ensure consistent treatment and the unbiased evaluation of businesses, the bank applies this common standard to all businesses and risk categories.

Risk contribution. The theory underlying the economic capital framework requires each portfolio's capital allocation to reflect its "contribution" to the volatility of the bank's market value as opposed to its own stand-alone volatility. The calculation therefore includes both the stand-alone volatility of an exposure and its correlation with value changes for the rest of the portfolio. As long as correlation is less than perfect, the capital allocation will be less than what would be necessary if the activity were a stand-alone business. This approach will not only capture the diversification benefit to the

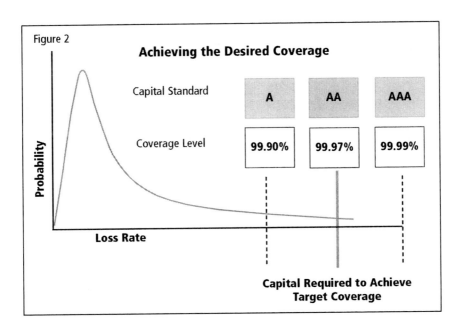

Figure 2

Achieving the Desired Coverage

overall firm of holding a portfolio of risks, but it will also allocate that benefit to the individual activities that contribute to the diversification.

The calculation of risk contribution as opposed to stand-alone risk is also necessary for the aggregation of capital across businesses. A bottom-up approach, including the diversification effect, allows the aggregation of capital at several levels and in various dimensions without distorting the results. For example, a customer relationship manager may evaluate the capital required across all businesses and types of transaction for the customer.

Credit risk. All businesses with borrower or counterparty exposure receive capital for credit risk, or the risk of loss due to borrower defaults or deteriorating credit quality. For commercial portfolios, credit risk capital is calculated for individual loans. For consumer portfolios, the large number of loans makes it cost effective to calculate credit risk only down to the "risk segment" level. Risk segments are homogenous groups of loans based on product, credit score, delinquency status, and other attributes.

Several factors determine the credit risk capital requirement. The most important are the exposure amount, the borrower's default probability, the estimated loss given default, the remaining tenor, and the correlation to other exposures in the portfolio.

The Bank of America credit risk capital model measures the default risk using an analytic formula for correlated binomial events. The model calculates the volatility of loss for an exposure based on estimates of the expected value and volatility of three factors: exposure given default, loss given default, and the binomial default indicator (yes or no).

Like that of many other institutions, the system relies on a portfolio risk model. Portfolio effects, such as correlation and capital multipliers, are determined by applying the Moody's KMV Portfolio ManagerTM software to the total credit portfolio, including both consumer and commercial assets. This approach accounts for the specific portfolio composition, diversification, and concentrations of the institution.

Implementation of the model across a wide range of applications requires the estimation, using the Portfolio Manager results, of marginal correlation factors based on product, location, market segment, industry, and credit quality. Capital multipliers, which scale the volatility contribution to the capital requirement, are determined in a similar fashion. The Bank of America model uses capital multipliers based on credit quality in order to capture the varying shape of the loss distribution for different segments and adapt to changes in portfolio composition between model updates.

The portfolio risk model also is used to set the capital requirement for migration risk. Migration risk is estimated by comparing the capital requirement based on market value changes with that based only on default risk. The migration risk component is a function of remaining term and credit quality.

Country risk. Country risk is the risk of loss—independent of the borrower's financial condition—on foreign exposures due to government actions. Causes of these potential losses include foreign exchange controls, large-scale currency devaluation, and nationalization of capital investments. Country risk is attributed to all businesses with international exposures.

Country risk capital is driven by the sovereign default probability and the borrower's conditional probability of default given a country event. Internal country risk ratings are used to determine the sovereign default probability. The conditional likelihood of default varies within three main categories: transfer exposures, local currency exposures, and trade exposures.

Country risk and credit risk are similar concepts, so the country risk approach closely parallels the method for default risk. The treatment of borrower concentration is different, however. The total amount of unexpected loss for the country, instead of for each borrower, drives the concentration effect.

Market risk. Market risk is the risk of loss due to changes in the market values of the bank's assets and liabilities caused by changing interest rates, currency exchange rates, and security prices. It arises from outright positions in securities or derivative transactions, structural interest rate risk, and private equity investments.

Bank of America estimates market value at risk (VAR) on a global level and for each of its trading desks using a historical simulation approach. The economic capital assignment is based on the contribution of each trading desk to the global VAR during the quarter. Before the allocation of capital, the daily VAR contribution is scaled to a one-year horizon and 99.97% confidence level to ensure consistency with other capital allocations.

A traditional variance/covariance VAR model, using the historical volatilities and correlations of venture capital and stock market indexes, is used to determine the capital requirement for the bank's equity portfolio. For interest rate risk, a Monte Carlo model simulates interest rate scenarios, their effects on cash flows, and ultimately the market value of equity.

Business risk. Business risk is the risk of loss from non-portfolio activities. These activities include origination, servicing, distribution, trust, asset management, and the activities of any other fee-driven businesses. This category is one of the few where risk measurement is not yet market-value based. Business risk comprises two categories: operational risk and strategic risk.

Bank of America measures operational risk using a loss distribution approach (LDA), where operational risk is the risk of loss due to inadequate or failed internal processes, people, and systems or due to external events. The bank uses the Basel categorization, which divides operational risk into seven subcategories. The model's foundation is a database containing the bank's internal history of operational loss events and their financial consequences.

Publicly disclosed industry data, scaled for relative differences in size and quality of controls, supplements the internal data where it is insufficient for statistical models. The LDA model relies on estimates of frequency and severity distributions for each risk category and a Monte Carlo engine to combine them into an aggregate loss distribution, incorporating insurance deductibles and program limits.

Strategic risks and general economic risks, such as those relating to competition, operational leverage, product and technological obsolescence, and business strategy and execution, must also be covered in a comprehensive capital allocation framework. The bank uses a top-down approach for measuring strategic risk, which is based on the volatility of non-portfolio earnings for each business. Non-portfolio earnings are the net income for each business adjusted to remove the effects of credit risk, country risk, market risk, and operational risk.

Recognizing the historical nature of both of the above methods, Bank of America's business risk model also includes a qualitative adjustment to reflect changes in the control environment and inherent risk of the business over time. A self-assessment process that evaluates exposure to reputation, execution, people, processing, technology, legal, regulatory, and external risks determines this qualitative adjustment.

Intangible assets. In addition to the capital assignment for operational and strategic risks, Bank of America also includes a capital assignment for goodwill and other intangible assets. The capital assignment for intangibles largely reflects the considerable regulatory capital penalty for these assets. As opposed to the other components of capital, the capital assignment for intangible assets is motivated by their regulatory burden.

Inter-risk diversification. Capital requirements are determined separately for each of the above risk categories. However, the worst possible losses due to credit risk, market risk, country risk, and business risk are not likely to occur simultaneously. Simple addition of the capital requirements implies perfect correlation across risk categories, which is an incorrect and extremely conservative assumption.

Rather than lower the capital requirements within the individual models by using lower confidence levels or other parameter adjustments, Bank of America explicitly measures the inter-risk diversification effect. A correlation matrix for losses in each risk category is the backbone of this approach. The model treats correlation estimates based on historical data conservatively. The application of the correlation matrix creates an offset to the capital requirements for the individual risk categories and reduces the bank's overall economic capital requirement.

Conclusion

Over more than a decade, the methods employed by financial institutions to calculate economic capital have advanced to encompass nearly all areas of risk, including operational and strategic risks. They have expanded beyond accounting-based principles to consider the volatility of market values. Looking ahead, improved technology, increasing amounts of better-scrutinized data, and research by both professionals and academics will continue to drive advances in the field.

The new Basel Capital Accord has increased awareness and confirmed the importance of economic capital by adopting and codifying some of the practices in the industry. This convergence of regulatory capital to economic capital should not stifle further innovation and improvements. As a powerful tool for performance evaluation and capital adequacy, economic capital will continue to evolve to suit the needs of the industry.

Note

1. Less diversified (not always smaller) institutions would need to carefully evaluate the use of a single cost of equity in their SVA calculations. If they use a stand-alone risk measurement approach, a single cost of equity would not be correct from a financial perspective. If they use risk contribution, it may or may not work, depending on the specifics of their portfolio.

Economic Capital for Counterparty Credit Risk

By Evan Picoult

ike all forms of credit risk, counterparty risk is the risk that an obligor will be unable or unwilling to meet its contractual obligations.

The primary distinguishing feature of counterparty risk is that the magnitude (and the sign) of the credit exposure to a counterparty on any future date is uncertain. It depends on the market value of the contracts with the counterparty on that future date, which in turn depends on the potential future state of the market, which cannot be known with certainty today.

The potential credit exposure that a firm may have to each of its counterparties at each future date depends on the potential state of market rates at that future date, the effect that changes in market rates have on the value of the contracts with the counterparty, and the effect of any legally enforceable risk-mitigating agreements (such as netting, margin, or option to early termination) on the exposure.

Firms with Counterparty Risk

The parties that enter into derivative contracts have a range of characteristics. At two extremes are simple end users and very large market makers:

1. The simplest end user will enter into one or at most a few derivative contracts to hedge a single market rate (for example, the U.S. dollar/Japanese yen exchange rate). If such a firm enters into more than one derivative, it will do so in a single direction (for example, to hedge the risk of a fall in the yen) and for roughly the same tenor.
2. A very large derivative market maker will enter into many different types of OTC derivative contracts (such as forwards, swaps, and options) on a very large set of underlying market rates (including yield curves, spot exchange rates, equity indices, specific equities, the credit risk of specific obligors, and commodity prices), in different directions (buying and selling), for different tenors, and with a large number of counterparties.

Many market participants have characteristics that fall in between a simple end user and a very large derivative market maker. The nature of the counterparty's portfolio is part of the context that needs to be assessed in ascertaining the appropriate method for measuring counterparty exposure and economic capital for counterparty risk.

178

Contrasting Lending Risk and Counterparty Credit Risk

Counterparty credit exposure differs materially from loan portfolio exposure in several respects:

- The magnitude and the sign of future credit exposure depend on the future state of the market, which is not certain. At best we can describe the potential range, or *probability distribution*, that market rates could have at a future date, given their historical volatilities and correlations. Consequently, the potential future exposure to a counterparty can best be described *statistically*, as a potential exposure profile over time, measured at some high confidence level. In contrast, the exposure of a bullet loan is certain.

> ### Counterparty Risk
>
> Counterparty risk is the risk that the counterparty to a trade(s) could default *before* the final settlement of the transaction's cash flows. A firm would experience an economic loss if the counterparty to a forward or derivative trade defaulted prior to settlement and if the contract (or portfolio of contracts) with the counterparty had a positive economic value at the time of default. Counterparty risk occurs in contracts such as derivatives (e.g., forwards, swaps, options) and security finance transactions (e.g., repos and reverse repos) that have cash flows that settle at *future dates*.
>
> Counterparty credit risk is sometimes referred to as *presettlement* risk (PSR) to differentiate it from *settlement* risk, a different and much more common form of credit risk. Settlement risk is the risk to a firm, in a contractual exchange of financial assets, that a counterparty could fail to make its payment to the firm on a *settlement date* while the firm made its payment to the counterparty—i.e., the risk of an "asymmetric exchange." Settlement risk is a general risk that exists in any type of exchange of financial assets.

- For a very large derivative market maker with multiple counterparties, not every derivative counterparty of the bank can have a positive mark-to-market value at the same time. Some counterparties will have trades that are, on net, in offsetting directions to the net trades of other counterparties (in other words, some counterparties may want protection for a decrease in the yen, others for an increase in the yen). In contrast, a bank has credit exposure to all of its loan obligors at the same time.

- The market value of a forward or swap with a counterparty could potentially be positive or negative, depending on the future state of the market. Consequently, unlike with a loan, either party to a forward or a swap could potentially have a credit loss to the other. This complicates the assessment of the proper cost of credit risk, since counterparty risk is often bilateral (depending on the future state of the market, either party could have a credit loss if the other defaulted).
- Various types of legally enforceable and risk-mitigating agreements, such as netting, margin, and the option to early termination, can materially reduce potential exposure and risk and need to be included in the simulation of these quantities.

Measuring Counterparty Exposure

The first step to measuring economic capital (EC) for counterparty risk is to identify the method for simulating the potential exposure to each counterparty over time. A second step is to identify the method for measuring the EC for counterparty risk from either a default-only or a potential-loss-of-economic-value perspective. In essence, the calculation of EC for counterparty risk will require a *double level of simulation*:

1. The simulation of potential exposure due to the potential changes in market rates.
2. The simulation of the types of credit events (such as default, recovery, and change in general and counterparty-specific credit spreads) that will generate losses.

Let's begin by describing a method for measuring the potential credit exposure of a counterparty with multiple transactions.

Counterparty Exposure and Potential Future Replacement Cost

A firm can avoid the surprise of a potentially large exposure to a counterparty at a future date by defining and measuring its counterparty exposure as a potential exposure profile over the remaining life of the transactions with the counterparty.

The immediate credit replacement cost of a single transaction, viewed in isolation, is the larger of its current value or zero. The potential market value of the transaction at a future date may be significantly different from its current value. Two factors can cause the market value of a transaction to change over time:

1. For a contract with multiple cash flows (such as a swap or an interest rate cap), the contractual fixing of floating rates, the expiration of options, and settlement of cash flows over time will change the *sensitivity of the market value* of the remaining unrealized cash flows to *changes in market rates.*
2. Changes in market rates will cause changes in the market value of the transaction's remaining unrealized cash flows.

The measurement of value at risk (VAR) for market risk normally assumes a static portfolio of contracts and measures the effects on market value of potential changes in market rates. In contrast, the measurement of the potential future credit exposure of a transaction, or a portfolio of transactions with a counterparty, requires that we simulate both the *potential changes in market rates over time* and the *contractual setting of floating rates, the expiration of options, and the settlement of cash flows over time.* Note that the latter is not an attempt to model trader behavior, but rather is the modeling of the effect of each transaction's contractual terms and condition over time.

The two most common ways of measuring potential exposure of a counterparty with multiple transactions are a *simple transaction* methodology and a more precise and sophisticated *portfolio* methodology.

Simple-Transaction Method of Measuring Counterparty Exposure

The simple-transaction method defines the counterparty exposure of each transaction as a *single number*—a prudent measure of its potential future market value, defined at some high confidence level. In this method, the potential exposure of a transaction is the sum of two terms—the transaction's current market value and a prudent estimate of its *potential increase in value*, measured at a very high confidence level. Standardized tables can be defined that approximate the potential increase in the value of each transaction per unit of notional principal.

The best way to represent the potential exposure of each transaction is by the transaction's *exposure profile* over time. The exposure profile describes the potential replacement cost of the transaction at a set of future dates, at some confidence level. The exposure profile will tend to vary in magnitude over time, which is very different from the credit exposure of a bullet loan, which is a fixed number over time. *The simple-transaction exposure method makes an approximation by condensing the time-varying potential exposure of a transaction into a single number.* That number might be the peak or the average of the transaction's exposure profile over time, calculated at some confidence level.

In a simple-transaction method, the total exposure of a counterparty with many transactions is calculated as simply the sum of each transaction's counterparty exposure.

There are two basic shortcomings inherent in the simple-transaction method:

1. The trade-off between ease of implementation and precision. Any practical implementation of the simple-transaction method will rest on the calculation and firmwide dissemination of tables of the potential increase in the value of each transaction. These tables invariably employ approximations to make them simple to implement.
2. Its inability to accurately *calculate* and *represent* the potential exposure of a portfolio of multiple contracts with a single counterparty. *Under the simple-transaction method, the total exposure of a portfolio of many contracts with a counterparty is simply the sum of each contract's potential exposure.* There are several flaws in such a calculation of portfolio exposure:

   ▪ The transactions with the counterparty may have *different tenors*. The peak exposure of each transaction's exposure profile would consequently occur at different times. As a consequence, the sum of each transaction's potential peak exposure tends to overestimate (sometimes dramatically) the potential peak exposure of the portfolio.

- When a counterparty has entered forward and derivative contracts on different underlying market rates, it is unlikely that changes in these market rates will be perfectly correlated. Calculating the total potential exposure of each transaction in isolation ignores the diversification of having transactions with sensitivity to different market rates.
- The counterparty may have done transactions in offsetting directions. Consequently, it may not be possible for all transactions with the counterparty to increase in value at the same time.
- The simple-portfolio method cannot properly calculate the effect of a netting agreement.

In summary, the exposure profile of a counterparty will tend to be less—and potentially dramatically less—than the sum of the potential exposure of each transaction. The shape of the exposure profile to the counterparty will tend to be very different from the arithmetic sum of the shapes of each transaction's potential exposure.

For a simple end user with only a few transactions in the same direction, portfolio diversification is not a material issue. Consequently, the simple-transaction method of calculating potential exposure will not be a bad approximation. In contrast, for a large market maker with many transactions in either direction and on many underlying market rates, the simple method will be grossly inaccurate. Portfolio simulation is the only accurate method for measuring the potential exposure of such obligors.

Counterparty Portfolio Simulation Method and Counterparty Exposure Profile

In 1991, Citibank developed a portfolio simulation method for calculating a counterparty's pre-settlement exposure. Following is the essence of that simulation method.

1. **Simulate thousands of scenarios of changes in market factors over time.** For each simulated scenario, begin with the current level of market rates. It is necessary to simulate as many market rates as are required to value the contracts in the portfolio. For a large financial firm, this may require simulating thousands or tens of thousands of market rates.

   Each simulated scenario should consist of a simulation of the potential value of market rates at a set of future dates. For example, start with today's market rates and simulate market rates at each day over the next week, each week over the next month, and each month over many years (depending on the types of contracts traded, this might be 10 or more years).

   The simulation of long-term changes in market rates can be done with varying levels of sophistication and subtlety. At a minimum, it should take into account the long-term volatilities and correlations of all simulated market rates and should make some assumption about how spot rates drift toward their expected forward value.

2. **Calculate the potential market value of each transaction at each future date of each simulated path.** For each simulated path, calculate the simulated market value of each contract at the current date and at each future date for which mar-

ket factors are simulated. The simulated market value at each future date will depend on the revaluation algorithm appropriate to the contract, the contract's terms and conditions, the number of remaining unrealized cash flows of the contract, and the particular path over time that market rates had been simulated for that scenario (which will affect how floating rates were set, etc.).

3. **Calculate the potential exposure of each counterparty at each future date of each simulated path.** For each simulated path, at each simulated future date, employ the appropriate *aggregation rules* to transform the simulated market value of each contract into the simulated exposure of the portfolio of transactions with the counterparty. The aggregation rules need to take into account the *legal context,* including the effect on exposure of any enforceable risk mitigants that have been entered into, such as netting agreements, margin agreements, or option to early termination agreements.

4. **Calculate the counterparty's exposure profile.** The exposure profile of a counterparty is the current immediate exposure and the potential future exposure, calculated at some confidence level at a set of future dates. The *exposure profile* is defined in the context of the existing set of forwards and derivatives transacted with the counterparty, the risk-mitigating legal agreements that have been entered into, and the assumptions and methods underlying the long-term simulation of changes in market factors. An example of a counterparty's exposure profile is shown in Figure 1, which measures the potential exposure of the current set of transactions and assumes no additional transactions with the counterparty.

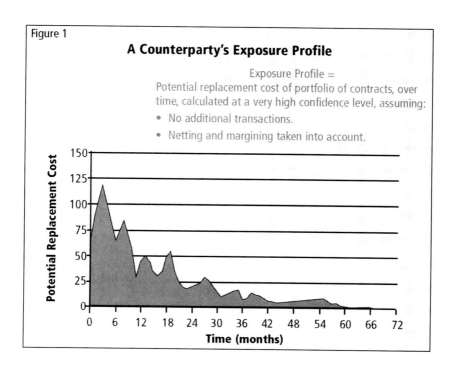

Figure 1

A Counterparty's Exposure Profile

Exposure Profile =
Potential replacement cost of portfolio of contracts, over time, calculated at a very high confidence level, assuming:
- No additional transactions.
- Netting and margining taken into account.

For the purpose of monitoring and limiting the potential credit exposure to a counterparty, the exposure profile should be calculated at a high confidence level, such as 99%. For other purposes (see below), the expected positive exposure profile should be calculated.

Deriving Economic Capital

As illustrated in Figure 2, economic capital is derived from the calculation of the probability distribution of potential loss over some time horizon. Two key features of a loss distribution are the expected loss (EL) and the unexpected loss (UL), where UL is defined as the difference between the potential loss at a high confidence level (such as 99.97%) and the EL. EC is the UL measured at a specified confidence level.

EC depends on the shape of the potential loss distribution and the confidence level at which the UL is measured. All other things held constant, the *wider the width of the potential loss distribution* (that is, the more uncertainty in the amount of the potential loss), *the larger the EC*. The shape of the potential loss distribution will depend on several things:

- The type of risk (market risk, loan portfolio credit risk, counterparty credit risk, operational risk, etc.).
- The definition of *loss* (for example, economic loss versus accounting loss).
- The time horizon over which the potential loss distribution is simulated (such as one year, three years, or lifetime of the portfolio).

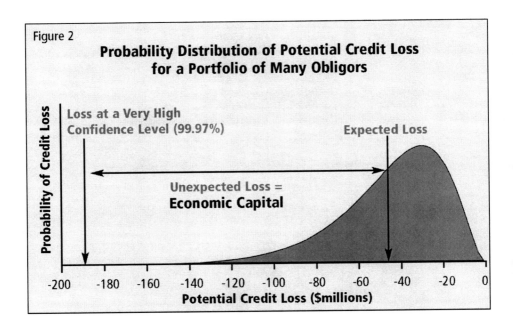

Figure 2

Probability Distribution of Potential Credit Loss for a Portfolio of Many Obligors

▧ The degree of *concentration* or *diversification* of the underlying portfolio's risk exposure.

Economic Capital

Economic capital (EC) is a measure of risk. It is the potential *unexpected loss of economic value* of a portfolio or business, over some *long time horizon* (e.g., one year), at some *high confidence level* (e.g., 99.97%). EC can be defined for a *specific* risk type or across the *full range* of risk types of a business. It can be calculated at different organizational levels of a firm on a stand-alone or marginal basis.

Economic Capital for Loans

Before describing how to measure EC for counterparty risk, let's summarize the definition and calculation of EC for lending risk. This will lay a necessary foundation for the discussion of counterparty credit risk and also enable us to highlight the unique features of EC counterparty risk by contrasting it to that of loans.

EC for a portfolio of loans can be measured from two different perspectives of loss: a *default-only* perspective or an *economic-loss* perspective. A default-only perspective measures the potential loss due to default and recovery. An economic-loss perspective measures not only the potential loss due to default but also the potential decrease in the imputed market value of the loans in the portfolio that did not default, occurring as a result of changes in market spreads and the risk rating of the obligor. The measurement of risk from an economic-loss perspective is especially important to the degree that a bank actively manages the credit risk of its loan portfolio. However, for reasons of space, EC is considered here only from a default perspective.

To measure from a default-only perspective the potential loss distribution of a loan portfolio over a one-year horizon, one needs to simulate hundreds of thousands of scenarios of potential defaults and recoveries of the loan portfolio over some time horizon, such as a year. For a given time horizon, the width (and hence the EC) of the loss distribution will be driven by several factors:

▧ Uncertainty over *how many* obligors will default over the specified time horizon.
▧ Uncertainty over *which* obligors will default over the specified time horizon. This matters particularly if there is homogeneity in the obligor exposures (in other words, if some obligors have small exposure and some have very large exposures). The lumpier the portfolio (for example, the more risk concentration in a few obligors), the wider the loss distribution.
▧ Uncertainty over *how much will be recovered* from each obligor in the event of default (which properly should be simulated from a distribution of potential recovery values for each type of risk mitigant).
▧ The correlation of default.

There are several ways of simulating the potential loss distribution from a default-only perspective, but these will not be covered in this article.

Economic Capital for Counterparty Risk: General Principles

The economic capital for counterparty credit risk is derived from the probability distribution of potential loss, as illustrated in Figure 2.

An essential difference between the potential loss distribution due to lending risk and the potential loss distribution due to counterparty risk is the uncertain exposure of the latter. If the future state of market rates could be known with certainty, the credit exposure arising from counterparty risk would be known with certainty. Under that condition, we would have certainty about the magnitude and value of all future cash flows between each counterparty and our firm, and measuring EC for counterparty credit risk would be no different from measuring it for loans: Given our assumed omniscience about future market rates, we would know exactly how much credit exposure (if any) we had to each counterparty at each future time.

Of course, we do not know what the future state of markets will be. However, for each simulated path the market could take over time, we can measure what corresponding exposure (if any) we would have to each counterparty at each future point in time. Consequently, whether we define credit loss from a default-only perspective or a loss-of-economic-value perspective, for each simulated path of market rates over time, we can calculate a potential loss distribution for forwards and derivatives using the same methods developed to measure the potential loss distribution of loans. The final total loss distribution due to counterparty risk would be the weighted sum of the loss distributions calculated for each simulated path of market rates.

Economic Capital for Counterparty Risk: Default Only, Full Simulation

In more detail, to calculate EC for counterparty risk under a default-only perspective, we need to follow these steps:

1. **Simulate thousands of paths of changes in market factors over time.** This step is identical to the first step in calculating a counterparty exposure profile on a portfolio basis.
2. **For each simulated path of the market, calculate the potential exposure to each counterparty at many future dates.** This is identical to the second and third steps in the calculation of a counterparty's exposure profile on a portfolio basis.
3. **For each simulated path of the market, calculate potential loss by simulating counterparty defaults, at many future dates.** In more detail, for each simulated path of the market, we can generate thousands of simulations of potential defaults and recoveries of counterparties over time. Each simulation of potential default would be similar to what is done for lending risk: At each future date of the simulation, we would randomly make a draw to determine how many coun-

terparties were simulated to default and make another draw to ascertain which counterparties were simulated to default. For each defaulted counterparty, a loss could occur if our firm had a simulated positive exposure to the counterparty at that point in time. If a default was simulated and the counterparty had a positive exposure, we would make another simulation of the loss in the event of default. The result of tens of thousands of simulations of defaults and recoveries for each simulated path of the market would be a probability distribution of potential loss. Note that, for a given path of the market, not every counterparty simulated to default will have a positive exposure.

4. **Repeat the simulation of potential defaults and recoveries for each stimulated path of market rates.** By taking into account many potential paths of market rates, we introduce another stochastic element into the calculation of the final loss distribution due to counterparty exposure.

5. **Calculate the final loss distribution by appropriately aggregating the potential loss distribution for each simulated path of the market.** Economic capital from a default-only perspective would then be derived from the loss distribution by measuring its UL at the appropriate confidence level.

Economic Capital for Counterparty Risk: Default-Only Using Loan Equivalent

The method of calculating EC for counterparty risk described above is a "full simulation" method in that it entails the *joint simulation* of potential changes in exposure and in default and recovery. One could ask if it is possible to define a *loan equivalent* for EC for counterparty risk. In other words, can we define a *fixed exposure profile* for each counterparty, such that the EC calculated under the simulation of defaults and recoveries (but without simulating changes in exposure) is identical to the EC calculated under full simulation? Note that this definition of loan equivalent would not require an identical loss distribution as derived from full simulation, only the same EC at the specified confidence level.

One could ask if the loan equivalent for EC could be defined as the *expected positive exposure* (EPE) profile of the counterparty (that is, the average positive exposure of the counterparty at a set of future dates). One problem in using the EPE is that it ignores the contribution to EC from the uncertainty of the potential exposure. As explained earlier, all sources of uncertainty in exposure and default increase the width of the potential loss distribution and thus increase the EC. On the other hand, for a large market maker, not all counterparties will have a positive exposure at the same time. Consequently, it is not intuitively obvious how good a "loan equivalent" the EPE is.

Two years ago, this author wrote a proposal to an International Swaps and Derivatives Association (ISDA) working group that recommended we define a quantity called "alpha," a scaling factor to transform the EPE into a good loan equivalent. I defined alpha as the ratio of two quantities A/B, where:

A = The EC for counterparty risk measured with full simulation, as described above.
B = The EC for counterparty risk measured assuming a constant exposure profile for each counterparty equal to its EPE.

I proposed that alpha should be measured as a function of various characteristics of a firm's counterparty portfolio. In other words, alpha should be measured as a function of:

- The effective number of independent counterparties.
- The effective number of independent market rates that affect potential exposure.
- The default probability of each counterparty.
- The correlation of default across counterparties.

Within the ISDA working group, Eduardo Canabarro (at the time, with Goldman Sachs) developed a very efficient method to measure alpha as a function of the characteristics of the counterparty's portfolio. Tom Wilde (Credit Suisse First Boston) was able to replicate Canabarro's simulation results analytically. Here is a high-level summary of our findings:

- In the limit of a very large portfolio, with highly diversified exposure to an unlimited number of counterparties and an unlimited number of independent market rates, alpha will equal 1.0 and the EPE is an exact value of the loan equivalent.
- For more realistic portfolios of large derivative markets that are exposed to a large but realistic number of effective counterparties and effective market rates, alpha will equal about 1.10.
- For end users with only a few counterparties and exposure to only one or two market factors, alpha will be higher.

Economic Capital for Counterparty Risk: Other Issues

The process discussed here assumed zero correlation between the potential future state of market rates and the probability of a counterparty defaulting. In general, that assumption is reasonable for most counterparties.

However, under some circumstances, the correlation between changes in market rates (potential exposure) and counterparty default are clearly nonzero. A sophisticated methodology would incorporate the correlation of default and exposure where feasible.

References

ISDA-LIBA-TBMA, 2003, "Counterparty Risk Treatment of OTC Derivatives and Securities Financing Transactions," recommendations submitted to the Models Task Force of the Basel Committee on Banking Supervision, June 25 (available at www.isda.org).

Canabarro, E., E. Picoult, and T. Wilde, 2003, "Analysing Counterparty Risk," *Risk*, September.

Economic Versus Regulatory Credit Capital

BY MICHEL ARATEN

Much of the debate over the proposed regulatory credit capital requirements known as Basel II centers on the benefits of its greater risk differentiation compared to the Basel I regime. Offsetting these benefits is the increased need for documentation and validation, as well as the extensive data systems development required to capture and record both data and computations.

In a number of financial institutions, these systems requirements are developing a life of their own and nosing out the priorities previously accorded to important risk management and reporting projects associated with economic capital. At some smaller institutions, managements that were beginning to make significant investments in economic capital modeling are rethinking their approaches. Some, who are increasingly burdened with Basel II qualification requirements, are considering abandoning their economic capital models to rely simply on the parameters and capital arising from Basel II.

Given that this was never the intent of regulators and industry participants, it is important to step back and review the differences in objectives, methodologies, and uses of the two frameworks. These differences must be respected, and while some features of the Basel II regulatory framework are aligned with economic capital motivations, they do not substitute for economic capital frameworks.

Objectives of Basel II versus Economic Capital

The stated objectives of Basel II are to strengthen soundness and stability, maintain sufficient consistency, ensure competitive equality, and promote stronger risk management practices at the financial firms subject to regulation.

Objectives in developing economic capital are to 1) provide a consistent and comprehensive risk management tool to measure, control, and mitigate risks; 2) establish a consistent and comprehensive return-on-capital framework; 3) provide risk-adjusted measures of business, product, and client performance; and 4) optimize investment of capital across competing long- and short-term opportunities.

While a number of these objectives overlap, the standards relative to the development of key parameters that underlie these frameworks can be significantly different. The key to these differences lies in the decision context underlying the use of credit capital estimates.

Figure 1 illustrates broad objectives, the types of decisions undertaken, and the range of parameters and modeling choices that may be available. Portfolio management, performance measurement, and profitability improvement objectives are affected by

189

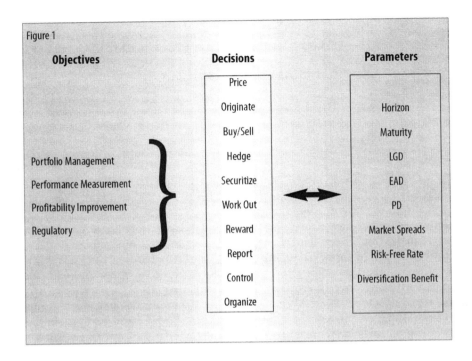

Figure 1

Objectives	Decisions	Parameters
	Price	
	Originate	Horizon
	Buy/Sell	Maturity
Portfolio Management	Hedge	LGD
Performance Measurement	Securitize	EAD
Profitability Improvement	Work Out	PD
Regulatory	Reward	Market Spreads
	Report	Risk-Free Rate
	Control	Diversification Benefit
	Organize	

multiple decisions and alternatives undertaken that require economic capital modeling approaches. These include 1) originating and pricing transactions; 2) buying, selling, or securitizing loans and securities; 3) hedging risks; and 4) working out or selling distressed assets. At the same time, capital enters into decisions as to how to reward, report, control, and organize business units. Economic capital provides a common language and metric for weighing and trading off the risks associated with these decision alternatives.

Those with more advanced economic capital models will find that parameters are either estimated differently or excluded completely when it comes to regulatory capital. Advanced modelers may need to weigh the interactive effects of choice of horizon and the maturity of their credit exposures. As will be described in greater length below, how one evaluates probabilities of default (PDs), loss given default (LGD), and exposure at default (EAD) will have a significant impact on regulatory or economic capital determination. Firms that incorporate market and contractual spreads, the risk-free rate, and diversification benefits in their economic capital modeling will find their economic and regulatory capital determinations out of alignment.

Much has been discussed in the industry regarding the "use test" wherein supervisory standards stipulate that ratings used for regulatory capital must be the same ratings used to guide day-to-day credit risk management activities. The same standards do recognize, however, that banks may use parameter estimates for risk management that are different from those used for regulatory capital but they must provide a well-documented rationale for the differences.

Parameter Estimation

The beginning point for PD estimation is usually an obligor rating with an estimate of the associated default rate. Obligor ratings will reflect the philosophy of the bank as to how ratings respond to changes in the credit cycle. Banks with a through-the-cycle approach will tend to have relatively stable ratings that will be combined with somewhat more variable PDs that reflect the current risks. Those banks with a point-in-time rating approach will move their ratings around more frequently, but reference stable historical PDs.

Basel II expects PDs to reflect "a long-run average of one-year default rates for borrowers in the grade."[1] However, banks that have an active portfolio management function incorporating dynamic hedging of credit risks will wish to incorporate PDs that are more reflective of current conditions. Their PD estimates may be based on current market spreads or derived from current equity prices. The regulatory view dilutes the benefits of third-party guarantees in its treatment of the likelihood of both parties defaulting. It does this by rejecting the double-default framework if the underlying obligors are financial institutions. And, as a result, it will significantly reduce the capital reduction benefit of guarantees for corporates.

Most banks, however, will find there is a substantial and valuable reduction in credit risk associated with these transactions. The objective in economic capital modeling is to reflect the risks as best as can be prudently measured, as these risks will need to be traded off against the revenues that may be generated. Conservatism for its own sake will lead to lost opportunities that should have been pursued.

Both regulatory and internal validation measures place emphasis on the historical analysis of outcomes associated with obligor ratings, known as "back testing." If risk mitigants are not recognized in the rating process and in the setting of PDs for regulatory purposes—but actually do provide added value—unnecessary noise will be introduced in the validation of PDs.

Of particular concern is the assignment of ratings and PDs associated with "low default" segments of the portfolio. For certain financial entities, defaults are quite scarce, and, if they happen at all, they occur over vastly different credit regimes. Thus, the observed data is unreliably thin and cannot serve as a basis for validation. Relative ratings and market spreads may be useful linchpins for individual firms. Whatever validation standards the regulators may wish to see followed may not serve the risk management objectives of the organization.

In addition to an analysis of historical default rates or back testing, the regulators look to "developmental evidence" and benchmarking for validation of PD estimates. Developmental evidence supports the basis for associating ratings with key financial characteristics and judgmental factors. Here, the requirements for the documentation explaining the underpinnings of the internal rating should serve as an important validation tool both for economic as well as for regulatory purposes, though the time frames may well be different.

Benchmarking will have less import to the firm's internal ratings processes, but will be examined by regulators for dispersion effects, as was done in the recent examination of a Basel II rehearsal exercise known as QIS4. Internal assessments across firms for the same type of risk may be more or less conservative, but as long as the firm employs these measures in a consistent, prudent manner, these are legitimate individual expressions of risk assessment.

LGD estimates for economic and for regulatory capital should not be very different, though it depends on how *default* is defined. In some instances, facilities are so well structured that even when borrowers declare bankruptcy and are unable to pay third-party debt, they continue to pay principal and interest on the bank's facilities. In this case, the bank may choose to consider this as a default event and will have assessed the risk of bankruptcy and default in its obligor rating. As a result, the historical LGD will effectively be zero and will reduce the overall estimate of LGD. Since LGDs have a linear impact on regulatory capital, and PDs have a nonlinear impact, it is not clear whether the regulatory capital framework would concur in including this event as a default.

Since bank loan management is a highly dynamic process, steps are usually taken to improve a bank's position prior to an actual default. For well-structured facilities, banks are often able to encourage borrowers to sell assets to pay down debt when covenants are breached or if borrowers require extensions of maturity. Should the borrower eventually default, the LGD will be measured against the exposure at the time of default. Expressed as a percentage of exposure at default, the LGD will be high relative to its measurement of exposure prior to the sale of assets and the pay-down of debt. Some banks will, therefore, vary the LGD at different points in the relationship with the borrower. Supervisors, however, will assess validation against the historical exposure at default.

In the same way, when debtors run into problems and breach technical covenants, banks may also obtain security for loans that were originally unsecured. At the time of default, the observed LGDs will be associated with a secured loan. In other instances, a bank may not be successful and, at the time of default, the loan will remain unsecured and its LGD will be higher. In determining which LGD to apply to newly originated unsecured loans, the bank may want to take into consideration the likelihood that such loans will become secured and assign an LGD associated with a secured loan. In these instances, a regulatory approach will require the application of the historically determined unsecured LGD to unsecured facilities without recognizing the potential for obtaining additional security.

The use of "downturn LGDs"—that is, LGDs associated with downturns in the economy—is an issue of diverging practice between regulatory and economic capital modeling. While in some instances it can be shown that recovery rates are depressed during recessionary times, this may not apply to all loans.[2] In addition, different segments of the portfolio may incur stress periods at different times over the business cycles. Advanced economic capital models may well take the relationship between stress periods and LGDs into consideration, but will not necessarily adopt the approach being promulgated by regulators.

Capital Models

The Basel II AIRB capital model assumes an infinitely granular portfolio—that is, one that does not have country, industry, or individual obligor concentrations. It also assumes a single-factor correlation structure relating to systematic risk. Most bank portfolios tend to have concentrations, and more sophisticated economic capital models provide multiple systematic factors based on specific obligor or industry characteristics.

To test the sensitivity of regulatory-versus-economic models to portfolio composi-

Figure 2		
Capital Sensitivity to Key Parameter Changes		
Parameter	Basel II Capital	Economic Capital
Create two subportfolios	0%	7%
All exposures in one country	0%	40%
All exposures in one unassigned industry	0%	5%
Increase PDs by 20%	6%	6%
Increase LGDs by 20%	20%	14%
Increase tenors by one year	11%	15%

tion, a hypothetical portfolio was assembled that resembles a large bank's corporate portfolio. This $100 billion portfolio consists of 3,000 borrowers with diverse exposure amounts, credit quality, maturities, industry, and country composition, as well as specific systematic correlation factors.

Sensitivity tests were run to see the impact on portfolio capital defined at the 99.9 percentile, with the results displayed in Figure 2. One test shows that, for economic purposes, when the overall portfolio is divided into two sub-portfolios and the capital for the two portfolios is separately determined, capital is increased but there is no change in regulatory capital. Similarly, when all exposures are assumed to be in a single country or in a single industry, regulatory capital is unaffected but economic capital can increase markedly.

In other sensitivity analyses, such as increasing PDs, LGDs, or tenors, we find different results for economic versus regulatory capital.

The allocation of capital as a function of the EAD to individual transactions for regulatory purposes is strictly a function of PD, LGD, and tenor of the transaction. Firms, however, will employ various measures to allocate capital, including results that are more closely associated with concentrations. Some firms will set limits on their one-obligor or industry concentrations that are not just a function of notional exposure but also a function of allocated capital. An important feature of economic capital models is that, in assigning capital to individual exposures, they do take into consideration portfolio composition effects.

Conclusion

It should be clear that regulatory capital is not a substitute for economic capital modeling. Supervisory review of internal capital practices at large banking organizations has been in place for over five years. As noted recently, "the capital goals of supervisors and institutions are not necessarily identical (nor should they be)—but they are complementary."[3]

Given the various purposes to which economic capital modeling has been applied, it is important that firms continue to expand their efforts in improving the sophistication of their internal models. The parameters underlying the supervisory estimates should not always match those employed in the firm's day-to-day risk management practices. While supervisory requirements may spur some institutions to improve their modeling practices, they should not supplant the use of economic capital models.

Notes

1. Basel Committee on Banking Supervision, "International Convergence of Capital Measurement and Capital Standards," updated November 2005.
2. See Michel Araten, Michael Jacobs, and Peeyush Varshney, "Measuring LGD on Commercial Loans: An 18-Year Internal Study," *The RMA Journal*, May 2004.
3. Remarks by Susan Schmidt Bies, Board of Governors of the Federal Reserve System, at the International Center for Business Information's Risk Management Conference: Basel Summit, Geneva, December 6, 2005.

Back to Basics: What Is Economic Capital All About?

By Charles Monet

conomic capital has come a long way since its original invention in the late 1980s. JP Morgan was the first firm to disclose its economic capital framework, using its 1999 annual report to do so. Now, every large financial firm has an economic capital framework. These principles are at the root of the Basel II capital rules for credit risk and operational risk.

Financial firms should reconsider the principles of economic capital frameworks in two key areas:

1. **Amount of the firm's economic capital.** Most firms' economic capital frameworks are based on the assumption that bankruptcy occurs when the firm's book equity declines to zero. This decline in book equity is linked to a default probability implicit in the firm's credit rating.

   Based on this assumption, firms have built models of extreme downside losses—losses the firm might expect to incur once every 1,000 to 3,000 years. These extreme losses, combined across the various risk categories or business units, define the economic capital. The level of economic capital is assumed to have a close linkage with the required level of the firm's actual book equity.

2. **Cost of economic capital.** By multiplying the economic capital by an expected return on equity (ROE), firms integrate the cost of equity capital into the management accounting framework. This allows managers to consider the cost of economic capital with respect to strategic decisions (for example, expanding a line of business) and tactical decisions (particularly loan pricing).

   For simplicity, most firms use the same expected return on equity across business units. The logic for this approach is that each business is equally risky because each has the same default frequency. If each business is equally risky, a constant expected return on equity seems to make sense.

Both assumptions are deeply flawed. As a result, most banks' economic capital systems are unsuitable for determining the appropriate level of book equity or for measuring the cost of capital for business activities.

Determining the Level of Capital for the Firm

There are three reasons why the level of economic capital is not directly related to potential loss scenarios that would absorb 100% of the firm's book equity:

1. Book equity has little to do with the firm's default probability. The focus should be on the firm's market value, not its book value.
2. Financial firms often go bankrupt because of inadequate liquidity, not because of a decline in book equity to zero. Recent bankruptcy events illustrate this point.
3. It is not meaningful in most cases to model 99.9% downside events. We should focus on less extreme losses because they are more credible to managers and easier to validate.

Book equity has little to do with a firm's default probability. One way to approach this point is from a theoretical perspective. KMV and others have developed models to predict default frequency for firms. These models do not focus on the level of book equity. Instead, they focus on market equity and market volatility.

As an illustration, Table 1 depicts the level of book equity for several wholesale-oriented investment banks compared with the volatility of their net income. The table focuses on wholesale-oriented investment banks because they use mark-to-market accounting for most of their assets; therefore, it excludes Merrill Lynch and Morgan Stanley because they have significant retail lending activities that are not marked to market. To be conservative, we compute the default distance based on pretax income, rather than income after tax. That is because taxes would not be available to offset losses if losses were a sizable proportion of book common equity.

Table 1 computes the distance to default for these investment banks, defined as the ratio of book equity to the volatility of earnings. The distance to default is between 29 and 34 standard deviations. A default distance of 30 is not credible.

Naturally, we should consider the impact of skewness and kurtosis. Interestingly, quarterly earnings for these three firms from 2000 to 2004 showed zero skew and lower kurtosis than a normal distribution. This occurred despite a severe downturn in the equity markets. Therefore, an adjustment for skewness and kurtosis is speculative.

This shortfall should not stimulate us to search for additional skewness. Instead, we should take a fresh look at our model of the default process. If we focus on market value rather than book value, we arrive at a much more credible default model. (See Table 2.)

Table 1				
Book Equity Compared with Volatility of Net Income				
	Book Equity at 12/31/04 (in millions)	Annualized Standard Deviation of Quarterly Pretax Income 2000–2004 (in millions)	Ratio (default distance)	Moody's Senior Unsecured Credit Rating
Goldman Sachs	$25,079	$725	34.6	Aa3
Lehman Brothers	$13,575	$462	29.4	A1
Bear Stearns	$8,543	$252	33.9	A1

Table 2			
Effect of Incorporating Market Value and Volatility of Market Value			
	Share Price Volatility (in percent) Based on 60 Months 2000–2004	Default Distance (1 ÷ percent volatility)	Implied PD, Assuming Normal Distribution
Goldman Sachs	36.8%	2.7	0.33%
Lehman Brothers	41.1%	2.4	0.75%
Bear Stearns	32.7%	3.1	0.11%

This analysis is illustrative and makes none of the important adjustments that would be appropriate for an accurate estimate of PD. The point is, at least these default distances are in the right order of magnitude. We do not have to add arbitrary layers of conservatism to explain our results. That is why this approach has been a solid foundation for default models such as KMVs.

Financial firms do not go bankrupt when losses exhaust book equity. We can use past bankruptcies of financial firms to test the hypothesis that financial firms default when equity has been reduced to zero through losses. Two notable bankruptcies are Enron and Refco. We treat Enron as a financial firm because its default was driven by its trading activities, not by its other energy businesses.

Enron defaulted on December 2, 2001. Financial statements (including restatements for Raptor) were issued on November 19, as of September 30. Those statements showed the following:

- Net income of negative $644 million in the most recent quarter.
- Year-to-date net income of $225 million.
- Common equity of $9.6 billion.
- Tangible common equity of $6.05 billion.

There were severe accounting problems at Enron. However, it is not the case that the accounting problems at September 30 meant that equity was actually near zero at September 30. The inclusion of Raptor and similar transactions had reduced equity by about $1 billion. The subsequent investigation did not reveal other transactions that would have reduced owner's equity by $6 billion.

It is also not the case that trading losses caused book equity to drop from $6 billion at September 30 to zero by December 2. Trading losses were $200 million per month in the third quarter and could not have accelerated to $3 billion per month in October and November.

Enron defaulted because it lost its liquidity. Debtors lost faith in the credibility of the company's management. Enron did not have the liquidity cushion that we expect with a well-managed investment bank. Such a cushion would have allowed it to continue for a sustained period of time without rolling over its debt.

Refco provides a similar picture. Prior to its default on October 17, 2005, the most recent financial statements were dated May 31. August 31 financial statements were not issued. However, financial disclosures in a press release dated October 10 stated that the company continued to be profitable through August 31. The May 31 financial statements showed the following:

- Net income for the most recent quarter was $43 million.
- Common equity was $188 million. Additional capital was provided by $600 million of senior subordinated notes (uncollateralized) due in 2012.
- Goodwill was $744 million.

Having been through a leveraged recapitalization in the recent past, Refco was thinly capitalized on a tangible basis. However, there were no operating losses. The bankruptcy resulted from a liquidity crisis as secured lenders refused to roll over secured financing transactions without additional collateral.

These two stories paint a consistent picture. Trading firms default when the market loses confidence in their managements' credibility. The immediate cause of default is a loss of liquidity. The erosion of book equity through operating losses is not the cause of default.

It is not meaningful, in most cases, to try to estimate 99.9% downside events. We have no idea of how to model losses when the systematic risk variable has a 99.9% downside. We can look back 100 years to the Great Depression. Some 25% of the workforce was out of work.

Farmers could not make mortgage payments. Banks tried to sell farms to pay off the mortgages, but farms were worth nothing because there was no demand for farmland. Wages were cut and cut again. This is only a 99% downside. What should we assume for a 99.9% downside?

We should focus instead on losses where we have an idea of how to model the risk. This is probably a 95% downside (worst in 20 years) at most. When we consider losses beyond that confidence level, we should presume that the economic paradigm changes. We cannot guess the economics of that new paradigm.

A second problem is that managers are not accountable for losses that might occur one year in a thousand. First, they do not expect to be around when such a loss occurs. Second, if it does occur, it will be a systemic event, and they will be able to say that everyone was crushed, not just them. However, we can hold managers accountable for losses that might occur during their working life, perhaps once in 20 years.

A third problem is that extreme loss estimates, by definition, cannot be directly validated. Anyone can propose extreme events. However, it is impossible to assign probabilities to these events, so we are unable to apply statistical tools. Another advantage of focusing on losses that occur once in 20 years is that we can validate such estimates with long-run studies of market returns.

How Should We Estimate Required Capital?

We should discontinue our focus on extreme downside losses to book equity. The best way to start is by focusing on losses with a less extreme confidence interval. We should also increase our focus on two key risk factors that currently receive too little attention in risk management:

1. **Earnings momentum.** Debt-rating agencies view earnings momentum as a primary driver of a firm's credit rating. As we evaluate earnings momentum, we should reduce our focus on position risk—for example, market risk and credit risk. In many cases, such losses are one-time events. Instead, we should increase our focus on operational risk and business risk because they represent the earnings franchise of the firm compared to its competitors. Furthermore, the market views operational and business risks as ongoing and thus able to reduce a firm's market value by a multiplier.

   Building on the ideas of Merton and KMV, a powerful quantitative measure of earnings momentum is the market value of the firm's equity (See Figure 1). The firm's market equity represents the market's valuation of the net present value (NPV) of the firm's cash flows in excess of the cash flows due on the debt. Interestingly, many firms use KMV as a tool to estimate expected default frequency. Few firms use these ideas to evaluate their own capital structure and business risk.

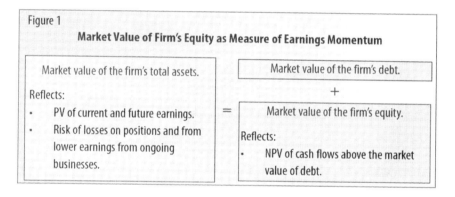

Figure 1

Market Value of Firm's Equity as Measure of Earnings Momentum

Market value of the firm's total assets.	Market value of the firm's debt.
Reflects: • PV of current and future earnings. • Risk of losses on positions and from lower earnings from ongoing businesses.	+ Market value of the firm's equity. Reflects: • NPV of cash flows above the market value of debt.

$=$

2. **Liquidity.** We need to focus on liquidity risk because it is the immediate cause of default for trading firms. Quantitative metrics and models of liquidity risk should be developed. We need to consider how a firm may be affected if normal collateral requirements are increased due to a lack of confidence by counterparties. Agreements to post more collateral if a firm is downgraded create similar risk because they are "wrong way" contracts in the firm's own liquidity.

Determining the Cost of Capital for the Firm

A simple way to define the cost of a firm's equity capital is:

Cost of equity capital = Amount of equity capital x Expected return on equity.

From a shareholder perspective, the cost of equity capital is more important than the amount of capital because:

▪ A firm maximizes shareholder value by maximizing the NPV of earnings less the cost of equity capital to produce those earnings. It does not maximize shareholder value by maximizing ROE.

■ The cost of equity capital allows managers to integrate the economics of risk into financial decisions along with other key financial variables such as revenue and expense.

On the positive side, most firms focus on the cost of equity capital rather than ROE. According to a recent RMA survey of 12 large banks and investment banks, only one firm focuses primarily on ROE. Most of the firms focus on earnings, less the cost of equity capital (often called EVA[1] or SVA). Unfortunately, the RMA study reveals that most firms (75%) use a fixed hurdle rate of return to determine the cost of equity capital.

Using a constant hurdle rate of return seems intuitive. Economic capital is defined as having the same default probability across various activities. Therefore, it must be equally risky. If the risk is the same, then the hurdle rate of return should be the same. Unfortunately, this simple view is flawed, leading to incorrect economic conclusions.

The flaw is that we define economic capital by focusing only on an extreme downside event (perhaps 99.9% or 99.97%). Shareholders evaluate the risk (and cost) of investments by focusing on all the investment returns—not a single, extreme downside event.

For example, if an economic capital framework leads to correct business decisions, then it should lead to correct decisions in simple situations. The simplest situation is the pricing of an equity option. In this case, we can validate the predictions of the economic capital framework.

Assume we have three investment strategies. We will invest in three different equity strategies (including cash positions and options) for a one-year horizon. We will hold the position open (unhedged), seeking a fair return on our risk. We consider three different strategies, all of which represent long equity positions with a positive expected return:

■ Long call on the S&P 500, with the strike at-the-money forward.
■ Long position in the S&P 500.
■ Short put on the S&P 500, with the strike at-the-money forward.

We make standard Black-Scholes assumptions, in particular that equity prices are log normally distributed. We define economic capital as the 99.97% downside. We assume a 4% risk-free rate and a 5% market risk premium. Table 3 presents a summary of the expected returns on the three investments over the one-year horizon.

We know that EVA is zero for any investment that can be duplicated by a passive market strategy, such as the ones above. Yet, these investments have ROEs that vary from 8% to 32%. How could they all have an EVA of zero?

Table 3	Expected Returns on Three Investments Over One Year				
Investment Strategy	Economic Capital	Expected Earnings from Risk Premium	Earnings on Capital at Risk-Free Rate	Combined Return: Risk-Free Rate Plus Risk Premium	Return on Economic Capital
Long call option	$10.35, due to lost option premium	$2.93	$0.41	$3.34	32.3%
Long cash position	$59.20, due to decline in price	$5.00	$2.37	$7.37	12.4%
Short put option	$48.85, due to decline in price less premium for option sold	$2.07	$1.95	$4.02	8.2%

The reason is that economic capital has been defined with respect to an extreme downside loss. For a call option, there is a lot of upside (causing a reasonably high beta) with a very low downside (just the loss of the option premium). In contrast, a put option has a very large downside, but the risk premium is actually somewhat lower than the call.

These examples can be extended to business activities. For example, a loan portfolio has the features of a sold put: a very large downside with a relatively low risk premium. This does not indicate that the lending business has a terrible ROE. It means that the business has extreme downsides (high capital), but a steady income stream in most situations (low beta).

The M&A business has the features of a long call. When times are good, it generates very high returns. In bad times, losses are limited because fixed expenses are limited. Such a business has a very high ROE, leading to the conclusion that it is adding shareholder value. A more appropriate conclusion is that such a business is expected to have a high ROE because it generates cyclical profits (high beta), combined with a low investment (low capital).

How do we measure the hurdle rate of return for each business? The best way is by reference to external firms in a similar business. For example, asset management activities should use the beta for asset managers (for example, Franklin Resources). Credit card operations should use the hurdle rate of return for a bank focused on credit cards. This is consistent with corporate finance principles for evaluating the hurdle rate of return for merger opportunities.

A second source of hurdle rates of return is expected market returns. The EVA is zero for investing in an asset that can be held by the market if the asset's return equals the market return.

This includes many corporate loans and equity investments. The market return for such assets is often visible in market spreads. If a market spread is used to estimate the target return, it is important to split the spread into the expected loss and the compensation for unexpected loss (the risk premium).

If there is no market proxy, a target return has to be developed from internal data. In general, this should be done based on the standard deviation, rather than the downside tail. The standard deviation captures the uncertainty of all the profits and losses. One approach to estimate the target return on equity is seen in Figure 2.

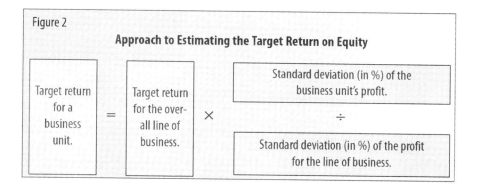

Figure 2

Approach to Estimating the Target Return on Equity

| Target return for a business unit. | = | Target return for the overall line of business. | × | Standard deviation (in %) of the business unit's profit. ÷ Standard deviation (in %) of the profit for the line of business. |

Conclusion

Current economic capital frameworks are seriously deficient. This problem is not going to be solved by more detailed risk models. We need to stop and take a fundamentally new approach. A key feature of this new approach is an increased focus on market values:

- Market value of equity.
- Volatility of the firm's market value.
- Market-determined rates of return for different asset classes.

Using this new approach, we will have a firmer foundation for reaching economically valid conclusions.

Note

1. EVA is a trademark of Stern Stewart & Company.

Convergence of Economic Credit Capital Models

BY MICHEL ARATEN

ignificant progress has been made in developing economic credit capital models. Economic capital determination is a function of both the input credit risk parameters and the way in which the models combine these parameters to estimate credit capital.

While new regulatory credit capital requirements under Basel II have been promulgated, these allow only firms following an advanced approach to submit their own estimates of key parameters as input into a single regulatory formula under Pillar I. The Basel Committee has expressed willingness to explore the use of bank internal models. Although regulators have not yet accepted their use, a review of the soundness of economic credit capital models is part of the supervisory process under Pillar II.

In furthering their objective of fostering research on credit risk capital modeling, the International Association of Credit Portfolio Managers (IACPM) and the International Swaps and Derivatives Association (ISDA) undertook a two-year project in 2004 to explore the convergence of economic credit capital models in use by their member firms.

The principal objectives of this study were twofold:

- To provide banks participating in this project with comparisons of the capital measures generated by different credit capital models—that is, expected loss for the portfolio and the amount of economic capital needed to support the credit risk of the portfolio at a specified confidence level. In addition to making portfolio-level comparisons and sensitivities to changes in key parameters, the study also sought to explore the assessment of credit capital allocated to individual exposures.
- To provide to external audiences, such as the Basel Committee and other interested parties, objective, verifiable, and reproducible comparisons of internal credit capital models for their review in assessing the appropriateness of using such models for regulatory purposes.

To this end, a representative portfolio of transactions was assembled with pre-specified data assumptions regarding their risk characteristics. The intent was to allow for modeling differences but not to allow for data assumptions to be the controlling variables, though some modeling differences may have resulted from data interpretation. Throughout this project an overriding consideration was to develop an understanding of the various model assumptions that would reconcile differences in capital estimates.

203

The overall conclusion from this study is that economic capital models employed by firms can, for the most part, be shown to converge in their estimates of portfolio-level capital requirements, given the same data assumptions. Where differences arise, a road map of the modeling assumptions can be used to reconcile these differences.

Sensitivity analysis of portfolio composition indicates that implementation of correlation assumptions may still contribute to some dispersion of results. As expected, while firm-level capital estimates have been shown to converge, how firms choose to allocate capital to individual transactions indicates significant dispersion, reflecting both the diverse purposes to which these estimates are used as well as the risk management practices specific to individual firms.

Project Participants and Governance

Members of IACPM and ISDA were invited to participate in this study. Twenty-eight large financial institutions elected to participate under the guidance of a Steering Committee.[1] An initial survey of the participants identified the types of credit capital models employed.

The three vended models were Moody's KMV *PortfolioManager (PM)*, RiskMetrics Group *CreditManager (CM)*, and Credit Suisse First Boston *CreditRisk+ (CR+)*. In addition to the vended models, project participants used either variations from vended models or internally developed models. The techniques used by the 28 participants in this study can be subdivided as follows:

- Twelve obtain their official economic capital measure directly from one of the vended models.
- Six obtain their official economic capital measure from an internal model that uses the output from one of the vended models.
- Eight obtain their official economic capital measure from an internally developed model that is similar to a vended model.
- Two obtain their official economic capital measure from an internally developed model that is significantly different from the vended models.

Test Portfolio

The $100 billion test portfolio[2] was comprised of two term loans to each of 3,000 obligors across a diverse set of industries (643 NAICS codes) and seven countries dispersed along eight whole-grade rating buckets with associated PDs and varying LGDs.

Exposure amounts varied from $1 million to $1.25 billion, and tenors ranged from six months to seven years. "R-squares" (the degree to which obligors exhibit systematic versus idiosyncratic risk) varied from 10% to 65%. Contractual spreads over a risk-free rate were chosen so that the mark-to-market value of the exposures at time zero relative to specified required market spreads associated with their credit quality and maturities would be par. The characteristics of the test portfolio are provided in Figure 1.

Figure 1	
Characteristics of the Test Portfolio	
Portfolio Size	
Exposures	6,000
Portfolio Size	$100 billion
Obligors	
Number of Obligors	3,000
Rating Scheme	8 ratings buckets
Credit Rating	Average = BBB
Industry Classifications	61 M-KMV industries 643 NAICS codes (6 digit)
Countries	7
Facilities (Term Loans)	
LGD	22% to 58% Average = 40.6%
Fixed vs. Floating	100% floating rate
Exposure Distribution by Facility	
Mean	$16.7 million
Standard Deviation	$101.7 million
Minimum	$1 million
Maximum	$1.25 billion
Tenor Distribution by Facility	
Mean	2.5 years
Standard Deviation	1.7 years
Minimum	6 months
Maximum	7 years
Correlation	
R-squared	Average = 20%

Project Phases

▨ *Phase 1* of the project was the analysis of key results from running the portfolio models in two modes—default mode and mark-to-market mode—using a set of standardized and pre-specified base settings. For comparative purposes, required capital under Basel II was also determined.

▨ *Phase 2* consisted of exploring changes to key data assumptions and related sensitivities of portfolio capital to explore how models reacted to data assumptions. Basel II capital was also recalculated based on the changed input data.

■ *Phase 3* consisted of comparing attributed capital to a small set of individual transactions. It was felt that while credit capital models might be shown to converge at the portfolio level, bank practices associated with allocating capital to individual exposures were likely to be highly varied.

Analysis Phase 1

The objective of Phase 1 was to compare the capital measures (at the portfolio level) generated by different credit capital models—that is, expected loss for the portfolio and the amount of economic capital needed to support the credit risk of the portfolio at various specified confidence levels.

All 28 of the project participants submitted Phase 1 responses. The responses were based on seven different types of credit capital models.

The initial inspection of the default-only[3] mode responses from project participants suggested that the results from *PM* and similar models, while consistent within models, were very different from the results from *CM* and *CR+* and similar models (Figure 2). The average expected loss and the average economic capital at the 99.90% confidence level generated by *PM* and similar models were significantly larger than those generated by *CM* and *CR+* and similar models.

However, it turned out that these results differ from the way the models treat the four quarterly interest payments in the event of a simulated default at the one-year horizon. In the case of *PM*, all of the coupons that were owed between time zero and the horizon are included in the loss in the case of default at the horizon.[4]

CM and *CR+* effectively presume that the obligor pays all of the coupons. In this instance, the loss is measured with respect to the principal and excludes the coupons between initial and horizon date. To demonstrate this, *PM* was rerun, with spreads and the risk-free rate set equal to zero. The results of this demonstration created as Working Group (WG) runs (Figure 3) illustrated that when spreads and the risk-free rate are set to zero, *PM* produces results that are very similar to those produced by *CM* and *CR+*.

Figure 2	Default-Only Base Runs			
Default Only ($MM)	**Expected Loss**		**Capital at 99.9%**	
	Mean	Standard Dev/Mean	Mean	Standard Dev/Mean
PM and Similar Models	789	3%	4,419	4%
CM and Similar Models	565	2%	3,816	10%
CR+ and Similar Models	563	0%	3,387	10%
Basel II (with caps/floors—minimum 1-year maturity and .03 bps PD)	606		3,345	

Figure 3	Default Only	
Default Only ($MM)	**Expected Loss**	**Capital at 99.9%**
WG Run of PM with Spreads and Risk-Free Rate Set to Zero	563	3,791
WG Run of CM	561	3,533
WG Run of CR+	563	3,662

The implication is that, if there are no coupons subject to loss in the default-only mode, the three models converge.

The difference in treatment of coupons in the definition of loss between the different types of models leads to such large differences in outcomes. This can be explained by the observation that expected loss and, to a lesser extent, economic capital are largely determined by the bad-quality credits in the portfolio. For these credits, the coupons were set quite high in order to let them price to par at the initial date.

Initial inspection of the mark-to-market runs provided results similar to those of the initial examination of the default-only mode responses (Figure 4). The average economic capital at the 99.9% confidence level generated by *PM* and similar models was significantly larger than that generated by *CM* and similar models. (*CR+* as a default-only model was not included.)

In addition to treatment of coupons, we expect a number of other variables to account for the differences. These would include the way in which correlations are applied, the translation of a term structure of PDs used for *PM* versus the transition matrix approach in *CM*, and the manner in which non-defaulted exposures are valued at the horizon.

To determine the degree to which LGD assumptions associated with coupons versus correlation assumptions accounted for the differences in economic capital, the portfolio was simplified by setting the maturities of all transactions to one year, thereby controlling for differences in market valuation methodologies between models. Alternative credit capital results were obtained by changing 1) the spreads and the risk-free rate and 2) the degree of diversification of the portfolio (Figure 5).

Figure 4	Mark-to-Market Base Runs			
Mark-to-Market ($MM)	**Expected Loss**		**Capital at 99.9%**	
	Mean	Standard Dev/Mean	Mean	Standard Dev/Mean
PM and Similar Models	789	3%	5,617	7%
CM and Similar Models	761	23%	4,823	10%
Basel II (with caps/floors—minimum 1-year maturity and .03 bps PD)	606		4,208	

Figure 5	Default-Only Runs							
Default Mode	Run 1		Run 2		Run 3		Run 4	
Spreads, Coupons, Risk-Free Rate	On		On		Off		Off	
Industry	All		"Unassigned"		All		"Unassigned"	
Country	All		U.S.		All		U.S.	
Model	CM	PM	CM	PM	CM	PM	CM	PM
Expected Loss	567	862	567	862	605	605	605	605
Capital (99.9%)	3,467	4,626	6,633	8,331	3,756	3,890	7,221	7,148

Again, we see in run 3 that when we eliminate all spreads, coupons, and the risk-free rate, we obtain capital convergence. We also see convergence in run 4, even where—in addition to eliminating spreads, coupons, and the risk-free rate—all exposures were assumed to be in a single unassigned industry within a single country. However, when the same contrasting portfolio composition assumptions were tested in runs 1 and 2 but spreads, coupons, and the risk-free rate were not eliminated, we see significant capital divergence. We can thus assume that the differences associated with LGD assumptions as found in default mode or when maturities are set to one year will carry forward in a mark-to-market mode with a full range of maturities.

In the same manner as in default-only mode, runs were made to isolate the effects of the LGD assumptions discussed above, correlations, and other modeling differences. In this analysis, as can be seen in Figure 6, it was determined that the LGD assumptions and correlation assumptions each contribute about 25% to the differences in model results, and modeling differences account for approximately 50% of the difference.

While initially mark-to-market capital differences in the base runs were as high as 25%, by controlling for LGD assumptions that impact coupons and by creating a simpler set of correlation assumptions, we reduced the capital differences to about 12%. Thus, while assumptions can be aligned as far as LGDs and correlations, we are still left with different modeling methodologies that may not be completely aligned. These would include PDs beyond the one-year-horizon and market-valuation methodologies.

Figure 6	Mark to Market							
Mark-to-Market Mode	Run 1		Run 2		Run 3		Run 4	
Spreads, Coupons, Risk-Free Rate	On		On		Off		Off	
Industry	All		"Unassigned"		All		"Unassigned"	
Country	All		U.S.		All		U.S.	
Model	CM	PM	CM	PM	CM	PM	CM	PM
Expected Loss	728	793	728	793	561	418	561	418
Capital (99.9%)	4,182	5,600	7,946	9,794	3,501	4,321	6,802	7,749

Analysis Phase 2

The objective of Phase 2 was to compare the sensitivities of the various credit capital models to changes in concentrations and parameters (Figure 7).

The sensitivities examined included the following:

- Separating investment-grade and non-investment-grade transactions into two separate portfolios, summing their separate capital and comparing this sum to the single combined portfolio's capital.

Figure 7	Sensitivities: Changes in Mark-to-Market Portfolio Capital from Base Levels			
Scenario		PM & Similar Models	CM & Similar Models	Pro Forma Basel II
Segment Portfolio into Investment Grade and Non-Investment-Grade Sub-Portfolios		7%	12%	No Change
Geographic Concentration	Change all countries to "U.S."	43%	19%	No Change
Industry Concentration	Change all industries to "Unassigned"	7%	32%	No Change
Geography and Industry	Change countries to "U.S." /Industries to "Unassigned"	80%	76%	No Change
Increase Individual Exposure	Increase 1 telecom exposure from 5MM to 5,005MM	3%	9%	2%
Probability of Default (PD)	Increase all PD by 20%	6%	6%	6%
Loss Given Default (LGD)	Increase all LGD by 20%	15%	15%	20%
R-Squared : Increase by 20%		15%	15%	No Change

- Concentration changes:
  - Change in geography and/or industry concentration.
  - Change in individual exposure concentration.
- Changes in parameters:
  - Change in probability of default.
  - Change in loss given default (LGD).
- Changes in R-squared (*PM*-type and *CM*-type models) or the volatility of the probability of default (*CR*+ type models).

The results of the sensitivity tests can be summarized as follows:

- *Segmenting the portfolio into investment-grade and non-investment-grade sub-port-folios:* In contrast to the Basel II approach, which is invariant to this segmentation, the economic capital obtained from the credit capital models used by participants increased.
- *Geographic and/or industry concentrations:* In contrast to the Basel II approach, all of the models used by participants are sensitive to changes in geography and/or industry concentrations.
  - Geographic concentration: *PM*-type models are more sensitive to this change than are the other model types.
  - Industry concentration: *PM*-type models are less sensitive to changing all industries to "unassigned."
  - Combining industry and geographic concentration: Changing all countries to "U.S." and all industries to "unassigned" has a dramatic impact on the concen-

tration of the portfolio. Economic capital numbers obtained from *PM*-type and *CM*-type models increase about the same amount, almost doubling.

- *Individual exposure concentration:* The models used by the participants are somewhat more sensitive to the changes we examined than is the Basel II approach.
- *Probability of default:* For a 20% increase in probabilities of default, the increases obtained from the models used by participants are approximately the same as with Basel II.
- *LGD:* The models used by the project participants produced changes that are similar but not quite as linear as those produced using the Basel II formula.
- *R-squared:* Basel II capital is invariant to this change; all the models used by project participants produced similar increases in economic capital.

The Phase 2 results led to the following conclusions:

1. The models that all participants use for their internal economic capital estimates are sensitive to changes in portfolio concentration. Such changes may arise from a change in the number of exposures in the portfolio, changes in geography and/or industry, or changes in the size of individual exposures. The results show that the effect of changes in concentration on economic capital can be very significant. This contrasts with the Basel II regulatory capital calculations, which are insensitive to changes in portfolio concentration.
2. The size of economic capital changes as a result of changes in portfolio concentration can differ significantly between models. The observed differences in concentration effects between models may point to differences in correlation estimates between the various models. Such differences in correlation can be structural in nature, such as whether industry or regional relationships are emphasized. Different participants may also use different data to calibrate correlations (for example, historical equity returns versus default rate data). Even if participants use the same type of data, calibrated correlations may differ if different historical time periods have been used in the calibration.
3. Most of the models used by the participants react quite similarly to changes in the input parameters—PD, LGD, and R-squared. The observed differences with the sensitivities of the Basel II regulatory capital calculations can, for some parameters, be attributed to the fact that they are not a direct input into the Basel II formula. The project has not explored further the reasons for the differing impact of the changes in PD and LGD, but these may be due to the role that portfolio concentration effects play in the internal models and/or the fact that internal models include uncertainty in the LGD while Basel II does not.

Analysis Phase 3

The objective of Phase 3 was to compare the risk contributions that different participants would assign to specific transactions and to defined cohorts of obligors.

Project participants were asked to provide capital allocation information concerning both individual transactions as well as industry cohorts.

In order to compare the risk contributions, project participants were asked to characterize their risk contributions:

- Mode: "default only" or "mark-to-market."
- Type of risk contribution: "standard-deviation based" risk contribution or "tail-risk based" contribution.
- Use of risk contribution: performance measurement or pricing.

The 23 Phase 3 submissions received suggest that there is very little consistency with respect to the risk contributions calculated by individual institutions. Within each of the groups of model types are many variants that could be used for either standard-deviation based or tail-risk-based contributions. How firms choose to allocate capital to individual transactions indicates significant dispersion, reflecting both the diverse purposes to which these estimates are used as well as the risk management practices specific to individual firms.

Conclusion

Credit risk modeling practices at major international financial institutions have been explored using a fixed set of data inputs. Across both vended and internal models, it can be shown that when loss assumptions are aligned, estimates of credit capital can be shown to converge at least in default-only models.

Differences in mark-to-market models also can be reduced, but not eliminated completely. Sensitivities to changes in parameters produce somewhat similar and expected changes in credit capital and stand in contrast to Basel II calculations, which are not sensitive to portfolio composition. Finally, as expected, there is a rather diverse set of internal practices when it comes to allocating overall portfolio capital to individual transactions in the portfolio.

Notes

1. Michel Araten from JPMorgan Chase chaired the Steering Committee with Gene Guill, of Deutsche Bank and chairman of IACPM, and David Mengle, head of Research, ISDA ex-officio. Charles Smithson of Rutter Associates provided consulting and assured confidentiality of data submissions.
2. A zipped file containing the data set and assumptions is available upon request to Som-Lok Leung (somlok@iacpm.org).
3. "Default only" was evaluated by capping the maturity of all exposures to one year without changing their contractual spreads. This produced a portfolio with higher spreads than what was required based on their shortened maturities.
4. Communication from M-KMV indicates that the treatment of these coupons has now been changed to allow user preferences.

Stressed LGDs in Capital Analysis

BY GARY WILHITE

he new Basel Capital Accord is built around concepts used in banks' economic capital systems. One feature of the accord that differs from many economic capital implementations is the required use of a stressed loss given default (LGD).

In both economic capital systems and the proposed Basel regulatory capital framework, risk capital is needed to cover the possibility of extreme losses. For credit risk, these losses include both those realized on defaulted loans and the loss of value for loans that have become riskier but have not yet defaulted. Risk capital methodologies typically estimate, for instance, a loss amount that would be exceeded in only one in 1,000 cases and require that at least that much capital be available to absorb losses.

Most, if not all, capital calculators consider the result of many loans defaulting and otherwise losing value at the same time. There is, however, much less uniformity in dealing with the risk that diminished recoveries (that is, higher LGDs) may magnify already high losses. Variations in LGD are especially important if they are influenced by the same factors that drive default rates.

In early capital models, LGD uncertainty contributed to the uncertainty of loan-level losses. This uncertainty was aggregated across the portfolio, considering the correlation of losses among loans. Although these approaches had several shortcomings, LGD uncertainty did influence the uncertainty of portfolio losses and thereby capital requirements.

More recent models typically consider the correlation not of losses but of the underlying value of borrowers—the value that enables borrowers to service their debt. Some of these models incorporate a measure of loan-level LGD uncertainty. Within this group, one approach relates LGD to asset values such that there is a systematic relationship between the default rate and the average LGD realized in each run of the simulation. Others have reportedly made the expected LGD in each run dependent on the realized default rate.

Another group of models assumes independence between the default rate and the realized LGDs. Since it is possible that some of the very largest defaults will experience above-average LGDs, idiosyncratic variation in LGDs can materially affect total losses and the need for capital.

There can be a significant difference in the amount of required capital, depending on whether the LGD distribution has a large variance (U-shaped, with most observations close to zero or 100%) or a relatively small variance (looking like a normal distribution centered on the expected LGD value), especially for "lumpy," low-default portfolios.

Finally, some models—including those used in the Basel Capital Accord—assume both uncorrelated LGDs and such granularity as to make LGD effectively a constant equal to the expected value. Uncertainty around LGDs does not affect required capital.

The suitability of each approach—along with any "adjustments" one may make to compensate for each approach's weaknesses—depends on the question one wants to answer.

Portfolio-level capital requirements. One question asks how much additional capital is required at the portfolio level to deal with LGD risk. Theoretically, the most appealing solutions directly use a relationship between default rates and LGDs. However, reliably estimating extreme losses with an expected LGD contingent on default levels requires understanding the relationship across the full range of economic conditions, not just the typical values where most of the data lies.

The two studies discussed below each offer *multiple* potential models for the relationship between default rates and LGD, with the differences between the models widening as one moves further into the tails of the distributions. Those who are not yet willing to rely on questionable relationships between extreme defaults and losses may compensate with alternative approaches. One common approach is to add conservatism to the expected value of LGD or to other parameters, such as the variance of individual LGDs or even the confidence level at which capital is determined.

Loan-to-loan variance. A related question asks how the risk of systematically elevated LGDs varies from loan to loan, so that the relative effect can be reflected in pricing. This area provides an opportunity for future research, especially in determining factors by which one can reduce the risk of elevated LGDs exacerbating losses in stressed periods.

One line worth pursuing might be the relationship between a loan's primary and secondary sources of repayment. Some anecdotal evidence suggests that situations where the two sources of repayment are closely related—for example, selling an office building as an alternative to collecting rents from it, selling specialized equipment or entire businesses rather than being repaid from the cash flow they generate, or collecting on a guarantee from someone whose entire net worth is tied up in the industry being financed—may be vulnerable to stronger correlations between default rates and LGDs.

On the other hand, secondary repayment sources that are relatively independent of the primary source appear less likely to suffer compounding effects. Examples would include selling assets with many alternate uses, selling financial collateral, or collecting from a guarantor whose wealth is independent of the asset financed.

Stressed LGDs in the Basel Capital Rules

The Basel rules attempt to address the effect of elevated losses given default on extreme losses by requiring the use of stressed LGD inputs into the capital function. Where the cyclical variability in loss severities is important, banks must use severities appropriate for periods of high credit losses.

In the U.S., the draft rules define this as the loss rate the bank would expect to incur "if default were to occur...during economic downturn conditions." In addition, the U.S. rule provides that expected loss (covered by reserves rather than capital) will be calculated using expected LGD rather than this stressed LGD, with the difference covered by capital.

Further, banks that do not convince their regulator that they have reliable estimates of stressed LGDs will use a formula for stressed LGD (8% + 92% x expected LGD). LGD has a linear effect on the regulatory capital function, so the formula would raise capital requirements by 45% and 15%, respectively (plus the LGD/ELGD/EL effect) if expected LGD were 15% or 35%.

The phrases used in these requirements may be difficult to put into operation. Some have remarked that the requirement for LGD to be matched to "downturn conditions" is reminiscent of the admonition to dress warm for a cold day. It's far from certain that two people will attach similar meaning to the phrase. Concern exists that no bank will be able to show that its LGD estimates are aligned with such vague requirements, leading regulators to always demand that the stressed formula be used, even for portfolios that exhibit little correlation between LGD and default rates. It is difficult to know how much higher "downturn condition" LGDs should be than ELGDs. Valid ELGD estimates must already be dominated by downturn conditions, since that is when the vast majority of defaults occur.

Illustrations

The following analysis is presented in order to make these concepts more concrete. It uses the formulas described in papers by Altman *et al.*[1] and Araten *et al.*[2], which study the relationship between default rates and LGDs. Both show correlation between LGDs and default rates, although the r^2 values indicate that 37% and 56% of the variance in the annual LGDs are *not* explained by the relationship to default rates.

Default rates are taken from beta distributions, which provide a reasonable approximation for the range of realized annual default rates. Beta distributions are often used to describe default probabilities, including in the Basel capital formula for securitizations under the Supervisory Formula Approach. Figure 1 shows that the distribution reasonably matches actual default rates for Altman's data.

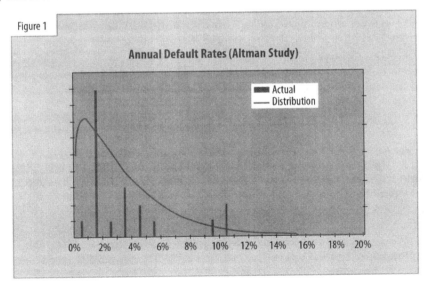

Figure 1

Annual Default Rates (Altman Study)

Table 1	LGD Relationship Studies		
Study for LGD Relationship	Altman	Araten	Hypothetical Study Lower LGD with Weak Correlation
Attributed default distribution Mean, standard deviation α, β	3.5%, 3.1% 1.2057, 33.24604	1.5%, 1.5% 0.97, 63.69667	1.0%, 1.1% 0.8082, 80.01
LGD relationship (from study)	LGD = 0.998 + 0.113 * ln(Def Rate)	LGD = 1.16 + 0.16 x ln(Def Rate)	LGD = 0.5 + 0.06 x ln(Def Rate)
LGD estimates Period-weighted LGD Default-weighted LGD (ELGD) Stressed LGD with formula Stressed LGD increase over ELGD	57.3% 65.9% 68.6% 4.1%	46.3% 59.4% 62.7% 5.5%	19.5% 25.3% 31.3% 23.6%
Equivalent default distribution percentile Default weighted LGD Stressed LGD with formula	75.7% 84.4%	85.5% 90.6%	79.9% 98.3%

Given a probability for each default rate and a link between the default rate and the expected LGD value, we can compute several expected values, as presented in Table 1. First, we can link a probability to each LGD value, thereby determining a period-weighted average LGD rate. In this computation, an equal weight is given to the average LGD realized in a good year, with lower LGDs but few defaults, as to the average LGD in a stressed year.

For forward-looking estimates, the default-weighted average is better. The default-weighted computation weights each LGD value by the probable number of defaults that will experience that LGD—the product of the probability of experiencing a default rate times the default rate. Since there are more defaults in stressed years, the default-weighted average is significantly higher than the period-weighted rate. Regulatory capital rules point toward the use of the default-weighted average as the expected LGD. One can then compute the stressed LGD rate by applying the stressed-LGD formula to the ELGD.

With these values one can determine the default rate (and where it lies on the default distribution) associated with the ELGD and stressed LGD values. Since the default-weighted average LGD primarily reflects periods with many defaults, it is not surprising that these values map to default rates well above the underlying unconditional probability of default—that is, to periods that exhibit stress.

For the Altman study column shown in Table 1, the ELGD value is equivalent to the LGD one would expect when default rates are at the 76th percentile of the default distribution; for the Araten study, at the 86th percentile; and in the hypothetical case, at the 80th percentile.

Applying the stressed-LGD formula to the ELGD value, we raise the LGD rate and the point at which one would expect the realized LGD rate to match the Basel parameter. For the Altman study, the stressed LGD is equivalent to the LGD expected in a year with defaults worse than 84% of all cases, and in the Araten study column the equivalence occurs at the 91st percentile of the default distribution. As bankers try to interpret the phrase "economic downturn conditions," one must ask if regulators really intended something like the worst year out of every 10 years in banks' histories, rather than the worst in four or five years.

It is important to note that the stressed-LGD formula has the biggest impact when LGD rates are least correlated to default rates. In the hypothetical study column in Table 1, stressing LGD produces a rate nearly 25% higher than ELGD and increases the point of equivalence from the 80th percentile to the 98th percentile. A very large move into the tail of the default distribution is needed to reach a point where the conditional LGD is so much higher than ELGD. This situation highlights the importance of being able to produce one's own estimates of stressed LGDs, especially when those LGDs are *not* substantially higher during economic downturn conditions. Likewise, it will be important for supervisors to grant permission to use an institution's own estimates in these cases and not insist on the formula "just to be safe."

In addition, the stressed-LGD formula produces a larger percentage increase in capital for loans with lower ELGDs than for loans with higher ELGDs. If the primary purpose of the formula is to require relatively more capital for loans with demonstrably more uncertainty, this may be justified. If the purpose is principally to increase capital requirements to protect against the unquantified risk of uncertain LGDs, then a simpler approach could be used with less confusion and expense and without distorting relative capital requirements from loan to loan.

The Problem of Insufficient History

With the default distribution and the expected LGD relationship, we can also construct a distribution of expected annual LGD rates, as shown in Figure 2 for the Altman model. (Actual annual LGD rates will be somewhat more dispersed due to the error term in the LGD models.)

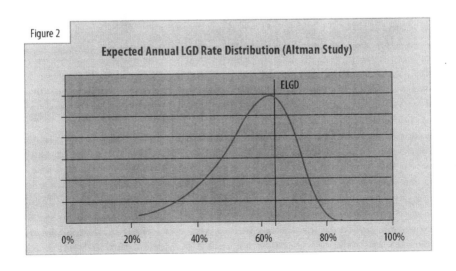

Figure 2

Expected Annual LGD Rate Distribution (Altman Study)

Note that significant portions of the LGD distribution are quite far from ELGD. One-quarter of the annual LGD observations are expected to be below 50%, although ELGD is over 65%. Although defaults and LGDs are random variables, they are not independent from year to year: Recessions occur periodically with stretches of good years in between.

Consequently, it is important to recall that ELGD must be estimated looking forward, keeping in mind the full range of default rates and LGDs. The stressed-LGD formula will not make up for a failure to realize that a few good years do not mean that low defaults and LGDs will continue forever. For this example, stressing a sample average LGD of 50% would produce a value of only 54%, still well under the 65% ELGD. Regulators should not use the stressed-LGD process to address a concern that some LGD rates have been estimated without adequately considering loan behavior over a full cycle.

Opportunity for Further Study

A benefit of implementing the Basel capital framework is that data will be captured to permit additional analyses of effects such as those discussed above. The industry will benefit from a deeper understanding of borrower and loan behavior.

Notes

1. See Edward I. Altman, Brooks Brady, Andrea Resti, and Andrea Sironi, "The Link Between Default and Recovery Rates," a paper extended from a report prepared for the International Swaps and Derivatives Association, April 2002 (revised September 2003).
2. See Michel Araten, Michael Jacobs Jr., and Peeyush Varshney, "Measuring LGD on Commercial Loans: An 18-Year Internal Study," *The RMA Journal*, May 2004.

Sources of Inconsistencies in Risk-Weighted Asset Determinations

By Michel Araten

It has been observed that measures of risk-weighted assets (RWA) and thus the ratios of RWA to capital vary considerably across banks subject to the advanced internal ratings-based (AIRB) treatment of the Basel rules. Industry participants have raised considerable concerns over the non-level playing field resulting from these differences.

Regulators have recently agreed to investigate the sources of these differences, to learn whether they are due to differences in credit profiles, estimation of input parameters, or varying supervisory review criteria across firms. To that end, they are considering providing benchmark portfolios as a way to control for credit profile differences. It should be noted that some industry associations have in the past conducted similar benchmarking surveys among their members.

This article explores some of the sources of the differences associated with the input parameters to the AIRB formula, confining itself to the traditional wholesale credit risk product portion of RWA determination. Supervisors will need to understand and account for these differences as they conduct benchmarking surveys and horizontal reviews of banks.

Banks with dissimilar client portfolios or different concentrations of risk types will have different empirical evidence driving their AIRB parameters and resultant RWAs. In addition, AIRB input parameters will be different among banks based on the way they perform forensic analyses of their historical defaults or the way they conduct their risk management practices. Banks with advanced data-capture systems are more likely to be able to better account for risk drivers that affect their default and recovery experience. Note that a key factor leading to differences in risk management practices is that the banks' dynamic relationship with their borrowers provides an opportunity to improve their position as borrowers slide into difficulty. Such opportunities are usually not available to investors in public bonds.

This article does not explore differences in AIRB risk parameters that may naturally arise when banks have different customer bases or credit underwriting standards and when they report parameters and RWAs based on their associated default and recovery experiences. Nor does it focus on differences that could arise from the manner in which supervisors across different regions or jurisdictions review these parameters at their assigned banks.

Two hypothetical firms best illustrate the potential differences in parameters and RWA. Bank Liberal (L) and Bank Conservative (C) have had identical portfolios and underwriting standards over a 10-year period that has been examined for historical default information. This data will be the basis for their estimates of the three key AIRB parameters: the probability of default (PD), the exposure at default (EAD), and the loss given default (LGD).

The objective of enumerating the various ways to measure these parameters is to make firms and supervisors aware that these different approaches may or may not have a material effect on AIRB parameters and RWA, yet it is important to at least study their possible impact. Where appropriate, this article identifies best practices to provide improved guidance and level the playing field.

Probability of Default

PD estimates contribute to RWA in a nonlinear manner. For example, with a 40% LGD, a five-year maturity, and a hypothetical set of PDs mapped to ratings, a one-notch improvement from an A-rated credit could reduce RWA by 7.5%, while a one-notch improvement in a B-rated credit could reduce RWA by 9.5%.

The manner in which historical data is extracted from a bank's internal default database can influence how PDs are determined and applied. This section explores how these calculations can differ among banks in response to differences in risk management practices and rating philosophies.

Nonaccrual Policy

Both Bank L and Bank C use an identical rating process with numerical grades ranging from 1 to 10, with pluses and minuses corresponding to rating agency grades (AAA, AA+, AA, AA-, etc., down to D for default). Bank L tended to wait until the borrower was 90 days past due, while Bank C would place borrowers on nonaccrual at the earliest sign of weakness.

For example, in the fourth quarter of 2007, Bank C placed on nonaccrual 10 out of the 1,000 borrowers whose grade at the beginning of the year was a 6. Meanwhile, Bank L waited until the first quarter of 2008 to place eight borrowers that actually moved into default status. It turned out that two of the borrowers identified by Bank C never actually incurred a payment default.

By the beginning of 2008, both Bank L and C originated 10 new borrowers. The early recognition of nonaccrual by Bank C continued in 2008. There were eight additional borrowers that actually defaulted in the third quarter of 2008, according to Bank L, while Bank C had again placed 10 borrowers on nonaccrual in the second quarter. Bank C's default rate calculation was 1% (10/1000) for 2007 and 2008, while Bank L's default calculation was 0% for 2007 and 1.6% for 2008. As will be shown, the placement on nonaccrual of two borrowers for whom no losses were incurred will also affect LGD calculations and the determination of downturn periods.

Definition of Default

In late 2009, several borrowers in the leveraged finance market experienced distress. And, while the banks had secured their exposures with significant over-collateralization, subordinated bond holders exchanged their debt for equity with substantial haircuts.

The rating agencies deemed the distressed exchange a default, which was reflected in their default statistics.

Bank L, however, did not classify the exchange as a default, because payments to the banks continued uninterrupted. In fact, it maintained its rating grade of 5 that was assigned in 2008 and agreed to by its supervisors. However, while Bank C had also assigned a grade 5, its supervisors mandated a downgrade to default status in 2009. The result of the difference in supervisory review is that Bank L would have a different default rate calculated for grade 5 in 2009 compared to that of Bank C.

Determination of Obligors for Calculating Default Rates

The customer base of the banks consisted of 1,000 clients. In addition, 100 of these companies had established nine legal entity subsidiaries for tax purposes. The parents, as well as all the subsidiaries, were borrowing entities. The remaining 900 companies had no subsidiaries. On a parent-only basis, there were 1,000 borrowers. Counting parents and subsidiaries, there were 1,900 borrowing entities.

In 2006, five of the obligors with multiple subsidiaries defaulted, along with each of their subsidiaries, as did 20 of the obligors that had no subsidiaries. Bank L calculated the default rate on the basis of parent observations as 2.5% (25/1000), while Bank C determined the default rate based on a parent and subsidiary count as 3.7% (70/1900). Here, one would argue that a default rate based on a parent basis is more appropriate.

Calculation of Default Rates Including or Excluding Withdrawn Obligors

Annual default rates for a particular rating are based on dividing the number of defaulters observed over a year's period by the number of obligors at the beginning of the year. A more complete migration analysis will reveal not only the number of defaulters but also those that migrated to a different rating at the end of the year.

However, there are usually a certain number of obligors whose rating status at the end of the year cannot be determined given that they are no longer customers of the bank. The rating agencies recognize this when they observe issuers whose ratings are withdrawn at the request of the borrower or those who may have merged with another firm or had their debt retired.

Typical withdrawn rates as reported by the rating agencies are on the order of 3% to 11%, depending on the grade. Banks have almost twice the withdrawn rates than bond issuers because banks can be more active risk managers with clients they no longer deem to be acceptable risks and they can encourage these clients to refinance elsewhere; in short, they do not renew their facilities. Once the borrowers are withdrawn, the banks have no information as to whether the borrowers defaulted with another creditor. However, they do know these borrowers did not default within the year on the credit that they extended.

As an example, assume that for rating class 5 there were 1,100 borrowers at the beginning of the year. Of this number, 11 defaulted and 100 were no longer customers at year-end for both Bank L and Bank C. Bank L could choose to calculate the default rate as 1% (11/1100) to include withdrawn obligors, while Bank C could choose to exclude them from the beginning population and calculate the default rate as 1.1% (11/1000), a 10% higher default rate.

It is appropriate to follow Bank L's analysis because it is clear that these withdrawn clients did not default on the debt extended by Bank L or by Bank C. Further, it should be clear that PDs should reflect actual default rates, consistent with loss rates and exposure amounts associated with defaulting borrowers. However, there are no loss rates or exposure amounts available since these borrowers did not default at these banks.

Different risk management practices could also affect PDs. Assume that Bank L has a highly vigilant risk management practice, and it was able to encourage 100 customers to refinance elsewhere. Meanwhile, Bank C retained these customers through the end of the year, though none of them defaulted but instead migrated to a lower rating. In this case, Bank L would include the withdrawn customers in the beginning of the year and calculate the default rate as 1% (11/1100); Bank C would observe no withdrawn customers and also arrive at a 1% default rate. However, if a number of these 100 customers actually did default, Bank L's default rate would still be 1%, while Bank C's default rate would be higher.

Borrowers without Risk Ratings

For a certain class of obligors, collateral—and not financial condition—is the prime basis for extending credit. Examples include private banking customers who are not willing to provide financial statements, but who will provide as collateral marketable securities whose value, even after haircuts, exceeds loan amounts by a factor of two or more. While an obligor rating is required to compute RWA, banks will assign a "fallback" rating.

For example, Bank L and Bank C may provide the same fallback rating of 5. In computing the internal default rates, Bank C has kept track of which obligors have a rating of 5 based on a credit analysis and which were assigned a fallback rating. Bank L, however, did not distinguish between these two groups. Assuming that none or very few of the obligors with fallback ratings of 5 will default, Bank L's determination of a PD for its obligors rated 5 will be appreciably less than Bank C's, given that Bank C eliminated those obligors with fallback ratings from its PD calculations. Fallback ratings should not be combined with valid ratings in determining PDs.

PD Implementation

Even if the experienced default rates of Bank L and Bank C are identical, application of the Basel rules could be different. For example, for one borrower whose rating is BB, a guarantee is provided by a third party whose rating is AA. Bank L may choose to use PD substitution based on the guarantor's AA rating, while Bank C may choose to use LGD substitution based on AA's LGD, with a different impact on RWA.

Point-in-Time versus Through-the-Cycle

While Bank L and Bank C have experienced the same internal default rates, Bank C chooses to use a point-in-time rating system that is informed by its estimates of PDs extracted from market credit spreads and vendor-supplied current default probabilities. Its ratings tend to bounce up and down in response to the credit cycle, as well as to idiosyncratic changes in the borrower's riskiness.

Bank L chooses to use a through-the-cycle rating system, which tends to examine the borrower's riskiness based on worst-case, "bottom of the cycle" scenarios. Accordingly, there is less volatility in this rating system. Assume that, over time, current market-based PDs equate to the average internally and externally experienced default rates.

To comply with long-run average requirements stated in the Basel rules, Bank C maps the average PDs to their ratings, though the mapping of point-in-time ratings and PDs to through-the-cycle estimates can vary by methodology. As a result, during downturns in the cycle, Bank C will most likely have downgraded ratings on its set of obligors to a greater extent than Bank L and will therefore have higher associated PDs. The opposite will occur during upturns in the cycle.

Exposure at Default

EAD impacts RWA in a linear manner, but there is relatively little research on what drives EAD. To some extent, the ability of borrowers to continue drawing on commitments as opposed to the banks' ability to reduce unused commitments is a function of the presence of covenants. However, while covenant information is available for publicly traded debt, banks generally do not track covenant behavior on a historical basis.

Measurement of EAD for unused contingent obligations is based on the commitment amount one year prior to default and the subsequent exposure at default. Some practitioners break the commitment into two components: the outstanding or "used" exposure and the "unused." They will measure the loan equivalent amount (LEQ) of the unused as the ratio of the additional used amount at default divided by the unused one year prior. The EAD is then the sum of the outstanding one year prior plus the LEQ.

Revolving Credit EADs

Bank L and Bank C evaluated the EAD associated with two revolving credit (RC) facilities, RC-1 and RC-2, to one of its defaulted obligors. RC-1 showed a drawdown prior to default, while RC-2 showed a decrease in outstanding at the time of default. Bank C calculated two LEQs, one for each of its facilities, flooring RC-2 to zero, since otherwise it would result in a negative LEQ.

Bank L, however, observed that the amount of the drawdown on RC-1 equated to the increase in outstanding on RC-2 and decided to pool the two facilities. Its resulting calculated LEQ was zero usage of the total unused commitment, a more appropriate measure.

Revolving Credits and Term Loans

Bank L and Bank C evaluated the EAD associated with one RC facility to one of its defaulted obligors where there was a 20% drawdown of the unused commitment prior to default. Bank C included this 20% in its reported LEQs. Bank L observed that the obligor also had a term loan and was in the process of workout. The obligor paid down the term loan by the same amount that resulted in the drawdown of the RC.

In reviewing these results, Bank L concluded that the LEQ for RC was zero. This situation could also have been observed if the RC was completely utilized one year prior and the RC commitment was increased just prior to default by the amount of the term loan's pay-down. The economic analysis of EAD as conducted by Bank L appears to be more appropriate.

Revolving Credits and Letters of Credit

Utilization by an obligor of a $10 million revolving credit was $7 million one year prior to default. Two months prior to default, a $3 million financial standby letter of credit (SBLC) was subsequently issued under the RC to a municipality to ensure that workers' compensation claims incurred by the obligor would be paid.

At the time of default, no additional cash was drawn down, but the utilization of the RC was deemed to be 100% owing to the issuance of the SBLC. During reorganization of the obligor, there was no drawing of the SBLC by the municipality as it simply wanted assurance that workers' compensation claims would be paid, if necessary. Bank L determined that, at the time of default, since no additional cash left the bank with respect to the $3 million unused commitment, the LEQ was zero. Meanwhile, Bank C calculated the LEQ as 100%.

Revolving Credit LEQs

A $10 million revolving credit was 98% utilized one year prior to default. At the time of default, the 2% unused commitment remained undrawn to an obligor who had been in workout over a two-year period. Bank C checked with its middle office and determined that even though 2% was available, covenant violations had prevented the borrower from drawing down the remaining amount; accordingly, it decided to exclude that observation from its data set.

Bank L, however, calculated the LEQ as zero since there was an unused commitment and there were no further drawdowns at the time of default.

Revolving Credits and Borrowing Bases

Commitments are often established for commercial or middle-market customers using accounts receivable or inventory as collateral. In addition, usage under the RC is limited to the lesser of the eligible collateral, known as the borrowing base (BB), and the commitment.

For example, with a $10 million RC and a BB of $8 million, there was $6 million outstanding one year prior to default, and an additional $1 million was drawn down at the time of default. The LEQ as calculated by Bank C was 25%. Bank L calculated an LEQ of 50% relative to the unused BB of $2 million.

In applying the calculated LEQs to their current portfolios, Bank L and Bank C applied their approaches with respect to a customer with an RC of $20 million with $5 million outstanding and a BB of $ 10 million. Bank C applied the 25% LEQ to the unused commitment of $15 million, resulting in a total EAD of $8.75 million. Bank L applied the BB LEQ of 50% to the unused BB of $5 million, resulting in a total EAD of $7.5 million. With the availability of BB information, Bank L's approach appears more appropriate.

Loss Given Default

LGD affects RWA calculations in a linear manner. And there are even more situations where differences in calculation approaches and risk management processes across firms can affect RWAs than those cited above for PD and EAD. A number of these arise from the same circumstances previously cited for PD. The following examples assume the recoveries are discounted at approximately 10%.

Nonaccrual Policy

As described in the PD section, if Bank C places 10 borrowers on discretionary nonaccrual prior to their actual default and only eight of these borrowers actually default, Bank C will record a higher PD than Bank L, which will wait until a payment default actually occurs.

However, assuming that the eight borrowers had an average LGD of 40% as determined by Bank L, the inclusion by Bank C of two borrowers with zero LGD will result in a 32% LGD.

Cohort Formation

It typically takes at least two years for workouts to completely resolve themselves, and those that resolve quickly tend to have lower LGDs, not only because it is likely that the collateral may be stronger, but also because the discount rate has less impact on the net present value calculation of the cash flows.

Assume that half the exposures resolve within a year and have an average LGD of 20%, that one-quarter resolve at the end of two years and have an LGD of 30%, and that the rest have an LGD of 50%. The banks have nine years of data. Bank L will include all nine years and report an average LGD of 27.6%, while Bank C will include only seven years, excluding the last two cohort years, and report an LGD of 30%. This practice is more consistent with conservative requirements in Basel.

Borrowers with Small Exposures at Default

Assume that both Bank L and Bank C are large global banks that also have middle-market and commercial business. While LGD analysis can often be segmented at the line of business (LOB) level to analyze losses based on types of loans, there are situations when large global banks, with exposures ranging between $5 million and $200 million, may also have many smaller exposures on the order of $50,000 or less.

In some cases, these smaller exposures are deemed "orphan" accounts and are no longer actively managed by the banks. In other instances, these are small, unsecured accommodation-types of exposures. Assume that the average LGD for these small exposures, based on 30 observations, is 66%, while for the more typical large exposures, the average LGD, based on 50 observations, is 40%.

Bank L may exclude these smaller observations on the basis that they are not representative and report a 40% LGD, while Bank C may include the smaller observations and report overall LGD as 50%. If these smaller exposures can be identified as a separate class, then separate LGDs should be calculated for them.

Collateral Applied Prior to Default

Bank L and Bank C have obtained collateral equal to 70% of the $10 million exposure for an obligor. Bank C has a more active risk management process. Realizing that the obligor is in technical default, it is able to apply the collateral to the loan three months prior to default; so by the time the obligor defaults, the bank's exposure is reduced to $3 million, of which there is a $1 million loss. Bank C will calculate an LGD of 33%. Meanwhile, Bank L, which did not apply the collateral prior to default, will report an LGD of 10%.

The Basel rule requires that the bank must demonstrate consistent historical experience during economic downturns in achieving pre-default reductions in exposure. If Bank C cannot demonstrate this, it will have to report the higher LGD.

Change in Collateral Status Prior to Default

Bank L and Bank C have unsecured loans to obligors that include maintenance covenants. Observing that an obligor has violated its covenants, Bank C is able to renegotiate and restructure the loan so that it has obtained collateral; yet, ultimately, the obligor defaults, resulting in a 30% LGD. The 30% LGD will be associated with a secured facility since that was its status at the time of default. Meanwhile, Bank L did not invoke the covenant violation and incurs a 40% LGD, but that LGD will be associated with an unsecured facility.

Even if both Bank L and Bank C experience the same LGD percentages of, say, 40%, these will be reported in two different categories. Specifically, Bank C will report a 40% secured LGD, while Bank L will report a 40% unsecured LGD.

Change in Exposure Prior to Default

Bank L and Bank C have unsecured loans of $100 million to obligors with deteriorating credit profiles. But Bank C has a proactive risk management process whereby, 18 months prior to default, it is able to convince its obligor to sell some assets and reduce its exposure down to $50 million.

Eventually, however, the obligor defaults, and the liquidation of the remaining assets results in a loss of $25 million, or an LGD of 50%. Bank L did not get any reduction in exposure, and its loss of $25 million measured against its EAD of $100 million results in an LGD of 25%.

Allocation of Cash Flows to Individual Exposures

Bank L and Bank C have two facilities to a borrower of $60 million and $40 million each, the former secured by accounts receivable and the latter by inventory. In the process of the workout, a total of $60 million was obtained from the borrower and $40 million was recorded as a loss.

Bank L decided to allocate the $40 million loss to the accounts receivable and inventory facilities in proportion to the EAD so that its LGD for both facilities was 40%. Bank C reasoned that two-thirds of the recovery should be allocated to the more liquid receivables facility, resulting in LGDs of 33% and 50% to the accounts receivable and inventory facilities, respectively.

Sale versus Workout Approach

Bank C has a policy of aggressively selling defaulted loans into the market as soon as possible following default, while Bank L prefers to work them out. Typically, Bank C obtains 60% recovery while Bank L, after two years, obtains an 85% recovery including workout costs. The LGD for Bank C, after taking into account a discount rate of 10%, is 40%, while Bank L's is 30%.

The sale versus workout approach could also have an impact on the degree to which there is a downturn LGD effect. Presumably, during periods of high default, a sale into a depressed market by Bank C is likely to result in a higher LGD during downturn periods, while during a period of low defaults Bank C may actually obtain a relatively high price if investors are looking to buy distressed loans. This will accentuate the downturn LGD effect for Bank C and require it to use LGDs that are experienced during downturn periods.

Bank L will receive cash flows over an extended period of time that may include economic recovery periods. As a result, it may be able to demonstrate that its LGDs have a lower correlation with downturn periods and be able to use its full complement of LGDs.

Resolution of Defaults

Workouts can extend over several years, and during that time banks reduce the book value through charge-offs as well as through receipt of cash flows. Banks will often declare a default "resolved" when the book value, as reported in their nonaccrual system, is zero, rather than wait for the legal balance to be zero. This can lead to a number of differences in measurement of LGDs:

- **Aggressive charge-offs.** For a $10 million loan, after two years Bank C has received $6 million of cash and has charge-offs of $4 million. Considering the default resolved, it will report an LGD of 50% (discount rate of 10%) and not pursue further repayments. Bank L will also receive the same $6 million of cash flows and, in the third year, receive an additional $2 million, then charge off the remaining $2 million. It will consider the default resolved after three years and report an LGD of 35%, using the same discount rate. Even if Bank C continues to pursue further repayments until the repayment is received, it will report the 50% LGD after two years as it considers the loan resolved. Meanwhile, Bank L will not yet report its LGD at the end of two years, as it will consider it unresolved. Eventually, Bank C may update its LGD estimate to incorporate the additional repayment received.
- **Capture of past-due interest.** Banks that rely exclusively on their nonaccrual reporting system to determine cash flows may not capture past-due interest that was ultimately received. Assume a $10 million loan that also has unpaid interest of $1 million for a total EAD of $11 million. The loan was repaid in full at the end of one year, and six months later the unpaid interest was also repaid. Bank C uses the differences in balances on its nonaccrual system to determine cash flows, recording resolution at the end of one year, at which point the loan will be removed from its system and the LGD determined to be 17%. The additional interest that was received will be recorded in its general ledger as "other income," not easily traceable to the specific loan. Bank L's system is more sophisticated and will track the recovered interest to the specific loan and recalculate the LGD following final resolution to be approximately 9%.
- **Capture of stock and warrants received.** The same result described above for the collection of past-due interest also arises when the bank receives securities, such as stock or warrants, for debt previously contracted as part of the workout, which

it sells at a later date. Bank C will have difficulty in attributing the cash received for these securities to the defaulted loan, recorded as "other income," and will ignore it in calculating the LGD. Bank L will be able to attribute the cash received to the loan and incorporate it into LGD estimates.

- **Valuation of stock, warrants, and real estate.** Even when banks have the ability to associate the receipt of stock, warrants, and foreclosed real estate as part of the workout, their valuations can be different. Generally, the balance of the loan on nonaccrual will be reduced by a combination of the payment received, the charge-off incurred, and the value of the stock, warrants, and real estate. At the point when the book value is reduced to zero, the value of the stock, warrants, and real estate will be transferred from nonaccrual to "nonperforming." Conservatism in these valuations can easily drive differences in the LGD. For stocks and warrants, there may be restrictions on when the stock can be sold or the warrants exercised. Even when there are no restrictions, the workout department may believe that the current values of the securities are depressed and choose to sell them at a later date. Assume the stock was valued at $100 at time of receipt, but the bank held it and then sold opportunistically two years later at $200. Bank L may choose to incorporate the $100 as a cash flow in its LGDs. When the stock is sold for $200, after properly applying the discount rate, the bank will revise the LGD. Meanwhile, Bank C would consider holding the stock to be a separate speculative investment decision and ignore the $200 value in determining its LGD.

- **Tail estimates of recoveries.** When workout periods are lengthy (for example, over three to four years), there is a desire to incorporate these defaults into the LGD estimation. However, the remaining book value may be relatively small, on the order of 15%. Assume Bank C decides at the end of year three to attribute no further recovery to the loan and calculates an LGD of 30% on the cash flows it has actually received. Bank L, however, has compiled extensive data on such loans and determines that two-thirds of the remaining book balance is obtained by the end of year four in 95% of cases. It will then add the 10% projected recovery at the end of year four and calculate its LGD at approximately 23%.

Conclusion

The differences in AIRB risk parameters have many sources. These sources include the various ways in which forensic measurements are constructed, as well as how banks approach risk management. The resulting differences in input parameters could well account for substantial divergence in RWA estimates among firms with identical credit profiles.

Sending out benchmark portfolios for horizontal reviews of RWA estimates must be accompanied by qualitative surveys that could facilitate a better understanding of why RWA estimates seem so dissimilar. Most of these differences in the cases cited above will not be resolved through prescriptive guidance, though there may be a number of instances where best practices can be identified.

Retail Credit Capital

E conomic and regulatory capital calculations have undergone radical changes over the last decade. The introduction of Basel II brought a new way of thinking about regulatory capital. The renewed focus on portfolio volatility simultaneously triggered new research into developing internal methods for estimating loss volatility, referred to as economic capital.

The adoption of Basel II for retail loan portfolios proved particularly troublesome. Retail loans have significant product-specific loss dynamics that do not conform easily to the strictures of the Basel II formulas. This led to a significant amount of research into how best to deploy Basel II and to the creation of better economic capital models. This section presents articles on both Basel II regulatory capital and economic capital calculation.

"Retail Economic Capital and Basel II," by Vandana Rao and Ashish Dev, provides an introduction to the concepts and terminology of economic capital along with the Basel II regulatory capital approach. Economic capital generally is about measuring the width of the loss distribution between the expected loss (EL) and the desired solvency level, 99.xx%. This difference is also called the unexpected loss (UL).

The Basel II formula is a structural model, meaning that a loss distribution is determined a priori and then calibrated to the available data. Portfolio input values of probability of default (PD), exposure at default (EAD), and loss given default (LGD) are combined with regulatory parameters to obtain regulatory capital estimates.

The article provides an overview of the derivation of the Basel II distribution and how it is employed. Asset-value correlation (AVC) is a key component of the Basel II formula, so it is discussed in detail in the context of retail loans and how it scales with credit quality.

"Economic Capital for Consumer Loans," by Gary Wilhite, makes the case for creating economic capital models based on effective expected-loss models. The article provides pros and cons for several classes of economic capital models: mean-variance models, asset-value correlation models, and econometric models.

For mean-variance models, the portfolio is segmented into a large number of homogeneous risk pools. Within each segment, capital is estimated as a multiple of the loss variance. Asset-value correlation models are structural models with an assumed distribution shape. The Basel II formula is the best known of these. Econometric models start with a portfolio loss forecasting model. Given a sufficiently extreme macroeconomic scenario, economic capital is the corresponding loss amount minus the loss amount obtained from an average scenario.

The article concludes that no single approach has been found superior. Although the article was written in 2006, that situation has not changed. Regulators have embraced multiple approaches, with AVCs used for regulatory capital and econometric models used for confirmation via stress testing.

Whereas the first article focused on structural models and the second on expected-loss models, "Economic Capital Estimation for Consumer Portfolios," by Fang Du, provides a detailed discussion of estimating economic capital using Monte Carlo simulation. The simulation is wrapped around an expected-loss framework including a loss-rate estimation, standard deviation for the rates, and a covariance matrix for the product segments. The technique is demonstrated for an unsecured consumer portfolio, with detailed discussion around incorporating the covariance structure of the portfolio.

"Universal Laws of Retail Economic Capital," by Joseph Breeden, employs a Monte Carlo-based approach similar to that described in the previous article, but develops the expected-loss model from the vintage forecasting techniques described in the section on retail credit modeling. The article presents results of a multi-institution, multi-product study looking for rules of thumb in economic capital that could serve as guides to practitioners developing their own models.

Three primary results were reported: 1) Volatility decreases as the loss rate increases, 2) volatility increases with time at a rate greater than a random walk, and 3) volatility decreases as the age of the loan increases.

Notably, a presentation in Edinburgh a couple of years later by Elizabeth Mays, head of consumer risk modeling and analytics at JPMorgan Chase, repeated this study in-house, but split the results by auto, card, and mortgage. Her results showed that the variation seen in Figure 1 of Breeden's article could be captured by segmenting according to product category. Within each product segment, the same "law" was observed as reported in the article.

"Best Practices in Mortgage Default Risk Measurement and Economic Capital," by David Kaskowitz, Alexander Kipkalov, Kyle Lundstedt, and John Mingo, is the executive summary of a much larger study sponsored by Washington Mutual. The study included panel data models, first-generation default mode (FGDM) models, Merton-type models, and roll-rate models. The panel models are equivalent to the mean-variance models described earlier, where the segments are intended to represent homogenous risk pools. The FGDM model combines an expected default model with a correlation model. The Merton-type model was an asset-value correlation model. The roll-rate approach leveraged a common loss forecasting technique to simulate the future loss distribution.

This article concludes that, in the end, the roll-rate approach was preferred because it incorporated more known portfolio dynamics and was in the middle of the range of the answers produced: Economic capital was estimated at 1% of outstanding balances.

The article was written in 2002 in response to the emerging Basel II guidelines and argued that the Basel II numbers were much too pessimistic about the risks in mortgage lending. Although the U.S. mortgage crisis weighed in with the opposite conclusion, the study itself provides useful details on how these models are created.

This section concludes with an article by Daniel Rösch and Harald Scheule, "Modeling Systematic Consumer Credit Risk: Basel II and Reality." Like the previous article, this one presents a study of annual delinquency rates for 400 U.S. banks from 1984 to 2002 and macroeconomic data to review the key parameters in the Basel II formula. Macroeconomic models of industry loss rates were created, from which correlations and default probabilities were estimated. The results showed that the Basel II values were conservative, but might be justifiable relative to the study's results, since the study did not include maturity adjustments or model risk. Since publication of this article, model risk has become a topic unto itself.

Economic capital and stress-testing articles have been segregated into two separate sections. However, the Monte Carlo simulation articles here were actually stress-test models given a broad range of scenarios. In an ideal world, a correctly chosen scenario run through a stress-test model is an economic capital estimate. Since a good stress-test model should be derived from a robust forecast model, and forecast models can now be taken to the loan level, we are beginning to see a path where scoring, forecasting, stress testing, and economic capital can be merged into a single modeling framework.

Retail Economic Capital and Basel II

By Vandana Rao and Ashish Dev

Although retail *and* corporate portfolios of most U.S. financial institutions today are about the same size, the management of these portfolios has been uneven.

Best-practice banks have long been managing the risk in their retail portfolios by product category, customer score, and other segmentation, which has led to common standards and terminology. However, far fewer institutions use this information to compute retail portfolio *economic capital* (EC), and the methodologies in use to determine EC also vary much more among retail product categories than among commercial product categories. Thus, there are no common standards and terminology as yet.

The retail credit business generally is divided into several broad product categories: mortgages (purchased money), home equity loans and HELOC, auto loans and leases, student loans, boat and recreational vehicle loans, unsecured bank loans, and revolving credit cards. In the language of economic capital, each product category may be characterized as having a narrow band of loss given default (LGD) and a correlation.

Basel II deals with minimum regulatory capital rules that are based on risk sensitivity and internal models. There is considerable convergence between banks' internal economic capital methodology and Basel II. The consultative paper issued in 1999 at the very beginning of the process did not have an explicit methodology for capital adequacy for retail portfolios. CP2, the consultative paper issued in January 2001, set forth capital adequacy formulation for retail portfolios, but many details were missing.

A working paper issued in October 2001 provided details of the standardized and internal ratings-based (IRB) approaches. The risk weight curve was the same for all retail products. Another working paper, issued in October 2002, introduced different risk weight curves (essentially different portfolio correlations) for three different product categories within retail. It also introduced correlation as a decreasing function of credit quality. CP3, issued in April 2003, incorporates these changes.

The Basics of Economic Capital

Economic capital is a common currency for measuring diverse financial risk. In the case of credit risk in retail lending, it captures the unexpected losses from a credit portfolio. The risk arises from the unexpected nature of the portfolio loss as distinct from the portfolio's *expected loss* (EL), which is considered part of doing business and covered by reserves and income.

EC covers all unexpected events except the catastrophic ones, for which it is too expensive to hold capital. The most important conceptual difference between EL and EC is that the EL of a portfolio is simply the sum of the ELs for each of the constituent loans in the portfolio. In that sense, EL is similar to such variables as revenue and expense.

But the same does not hold true for EC. EC in a portfolio has to take an important additional variable into account: *correlation*. Correlations can exist between default behavior of one loan and another (intra-portfolio correlation) or between one portfolio and another (inter-portfolio correlation). Typically, intra-portfolio correlations are much lower for retail portfolios than for wholesale portfolios. Lower correlation means lower EC and, consequently, lower EC (for the same EL).

Another way of saying this is that a retail portfolio is more diversified than a wholesale portfolio. This is at the root of the sometimes counterintuitive result that a portfolio may have a higher EL but a lower EC. For example, a highly granular portfolio of diversified customers' credit card loans may have an EL of 4.5%, while a commercial real estate portfolio consisting of a limited number of large projects concentrated in certain geographies may have an EL of 1.2%. Yet the EC required to support the credit card portfolio may be less than the EC required to support the CRE portfolio.

Economic capital is the potential unexpected loss of economic value for a portfolio over one year, calculated at a specified confidence level. The level of confidence is anchored by the desired bond rating of the bank. Most banks have a rating of BBB to AA, which translates to one-year default probabilities of 0.5% to 0.03%. The confidence level is therefore very high, ranging from 99.50% to 99.97%. No one can be sure of the actual loss that can occur in a portfolio of retail loans over the next year. But it is possible to derive a loss distribution. Figure 1 shows a typical loss distribution for a diversified retail portfolio. EC is the difference between the 99.xx percentile loss and the EL.

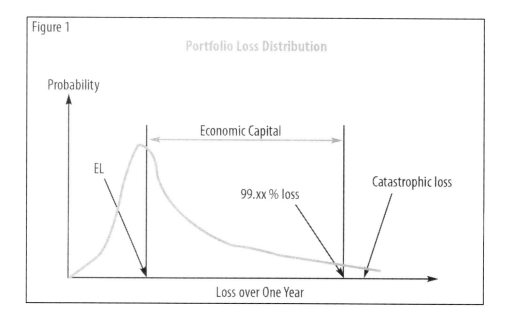

Since the introduction of EC in best-practice banks about a decade ago, it has become an important tool for the following:

- Measuring and managing risk.
- Risk-adjusted pricing, so that the bank is adequately compensated for all risks taken.
- Customer/relationship profitability.
- Strategic planning and optimum allocation of relatively expensive capital.
- Performance measurement for shareholder value creation.
- Determining compensation strategies.

In other words, EC (whether for retail businesses specifically or for all areas in general) now plays a significant role in major functions performed in a sophisticated bank. Enterprise risk management (ERM) is steadily becoming a very important part of the way banks are managed. A well-established EC framework is a prerequisite and the cornerstone of ERM in a financial institution.

Structural Models of EC and the Basel II IRB Approach

There are three fundamental ways to model EC for credit risk: structural models, empirical models, and intensity-based models. For retail portfolios, the first two are more common. Of late, structural models have gained prominence. The Basel II advanced internal ratings-based approach (AIRB) falls into this broad category. A description of the formulation of Basel II standardized and AIRB approaches to capital adequacy rules for retail credits is too detailed to include here, and this article also avoids mathematical equations. The interested reader is referred to Dev (2004) or to the actual Basel Accord document, both listed in the References.

Structural models have their origin, one way or the other, in a framework developed by Robert Merton. Merton assumed a firm with a stock and a single zero coupon debt. Default occurs when the value of the assets falls below the face value of the debt.

Many enhancements of the Merton model have been developed since 1974. From the perspective of EC, the most important adaptations of Merton's model have been done by Oldrick Vasicek, who applied the Merton framework to a portfolio of borrowers. These models can be classified as the Merton-Vasicek framework. They form the foundations of well-known products such as KMV's PortfolioManager ™ and JPMorgan Chase's CreditMetrics™.

A special but very important case of the Merton-Vasicek framework is when the portfolio losses are driven by a single risk factor and the portfolio is infinitely fine-grained. This is known as the *asymptotic single risk factor* (ASRF) framework. Michael Gordy showed that this is the only case in which the portfolio EC is not dependent on the portfolio composition. Basel II capital adequacy formulas are based on the ASRF framework. It is pertinent to note that retail portfolios are much closer to satisfying the condition of finely grained portfolios than are commercial portfolios, since the size of the largest loan in a retail portfolio represents a minuscule fraction of the total portfolio size.

The basic parameters of a Merton-Vasicek-Gordy type structural model for EC are:

- Exposure at default (EAD).
- Probability of default (PD).
- Expected loss given default (LGD or ELGD).
- LGD distribution (volatility of LGD).
- Default correlation or, equivalently, asset value correlation (AVC).
- Correlation between PD (default event) and LGD.

PD is the likelihood that a given borrower will default within one year. PD is also the fraction of borrowers defaulting in a very large portfolio of similar borrowers. It is common in risk management of retail portfolios to segment the portfolio by such score bands as FICO or bureau scores. Everything else being the same, each score band has an associated good:bad odds ratio.[1]

There is a mathematical relationship between PD and the good:bad odds ratio: Odds ratio = (1 − PD) / PD. LGD is a measure of the severity of loss once a loan has defaulted. It is simply 1_recovery rate. Recovery rate is the fraction of outstanding principal recovered, in present-value terms, by the bank from a defaulted loan.

Conceptually, LGD is similar to net-to-gross charge-off.[2] Often, retail practitioners focus on loss rate, which in technical terms is expected loss (EL in %) in the future, based on past loss data. This combines PD and LGD into one dimension (EL% = PD x ELGD). Furthermore, loss rate is not the same as EC. That loss rates for retail portfolios are fairly stable over time is also not a valid assumption.[3]

The structural model has an intrinsic advantage over any data-based empirical model. Regulatory capital as well as EC need to be calculated at a very high confidence level with a one-year horizon. This means that the model should be able to estimate an annual portfolio loss, which happens, on average, once in 1,000 years.

Very few banks have enough data to build an empirical model capable of describing such rare events. However, a conceptual model based on sound fundamental principles needs only a moderate amount of data to calibrate its parameters. After calibration, it is capable of estimating losses at any confidence level.

The Basel II model generally satisfies this criterion. It is one thing to estimate PD of a consumer based on several (say, five to seven) years of default data, and it is a very different thing to estimate a high percentile from observing annual losses over the same period. The former is statistically robust; the latter is not. Furthermore, it is a rare bank that has a long history on consistent and stable segments of retail portfolios.

The development of empirical models of EC for retail credits is natural, given the long history of empirical methods used in consumer scoring models. The three types of empirical methods are 1) the EL-sigma approach, 2) the nonparametric approach, and 3) an approach fitting a prespecified closed-form distribution to observed loss data.

The EL-sigma approach consists of computing the standard deviation (sigma) of the loss observations and calculating EC as a multiple of the standard deviation. It can be shown that the multiple depends nonlinearly on PD, the level of asset correlation, and the level of confidence. Therefore, the multiple has to be determined carefully, which is rarely done in an empirical implementation. Certainly, using a fixed multiple for different segments is not correct. The nonparametric approach does not estimate the parameters of a loss distribution. Instead, it directly assesses loss through simulation.

One problem with the nonparametric approach is its overdependence on data for variables that are subject to accounting rules and jugglery and do not reflect economic values. And fitting a prespecified distribution leaves a lot to be desired conceptually, since there is no a priori economic reason for portfolio losses to follow such a distribution.

Correlation as an Important Factor in Retail EC

Default events are correlated—the well-being of all obligors is affected by the same macroeconomic factors as well as by individual circumstances. Correlation is a measure of the extent to which default of one obligor goes hand in hand with the default of another obligor. Correlations between default events are responsible for heavy tails of portfolio loss distributions. EC, as a tail percentile of the loss distribution, is very sensitive to the level of correlations.

In the Merton-type structural models of EC, an obligor defaults whenever its asset value falls below a certain threshold. Asset correlation is the correlation between returns on the assets of two obligors. Asset returns have two components: systematic (related to the state of the economy, the same for all obligors) and idiosyncratic (reflecting individual circumstances of each obligor). Asset value correlation (AVC) is a measure of relative weight of the systematic component in asset returns. A typical retail portfolio consists of small loans to a large number of consumers who are employed in diverse professions, in diverse industries, and often living in different geographies. As a result, the financial status of these consumers is not strongly correlated. This lower correlation not only leads to lower EC, but also makes EC more sensitive to the values of correlation. For example, given a retail credit card portfolio with a PD of 1.0% and ELGD of 90% (this corresponds to an odds ratio of 99:1 and a loss rate of 0.9%), the portfolio EC is as low as 2.7% when the AVC is 4% and as high as 7.2% when the AVC is 12%.

If two consumers belong to a homogenous group sharing the same default correlation, its value can be determined from a time series of defaulted and nondefaulted loans of this group without any assumptions except that of stationarity. However, in the case of corporates, estimates may suffer from small sample bias because the available time series of default rates is rather short, and defaults are few in many periods. This problem does not exist for retail portfolios. There are a sufficient number of defaults (as well as credit transition states, such as 30-day and 60-day delinquencies) observed in almost every period for consumers of different segments, each with homogeneous credit quality.

On the flip side, unlike publicly traded corporates, retail consumers have neither observable stock price or option-implied volatility nor bond or credit default swap trading in the market. Therefore, the methodology typically used to estimate default and asset correlations is less useful than an econometric estimation. A *maximum likelihood estimation* (MLE) technique applied directly to time-series data on defaulted and nondefaulted consumers can yield an efficient default correlation estimate. In the case of retail credit data, corrections for a small sample are generally not necessary. The econometric estimation method yields default correlation first, from which AVC can be derived. The mathematical relationship is beyond the scope of this article.

Asset Correlation as a Function of Credit Quality

There is considerable industry data available on publicly rated bond defaults. Estimates of default correlations and asset correlations from Moody's historical default rates show that asset correlation decreases significantly as credit quality deteriorates. The results may also include the manifestation of size effect, since better-quality commercial firms are larger, on average, than poorer-quality ones. It is not a big leap of faith to then assume that a similar pattern (decreasing asset correlation as the credit rating worsens) holds for a portfolio of wholesale or retail loans. The Basel II IRB formulation did exactly that for corporate credits and for retail credits other than mortgages and revolving credit cards.

There also can be conceptual arguments for asset correlation to decrease as PD increases.[4] Consider a poorly rated (very high PD) consumer earning hourly wages in an unskilled job and a highly rated (very low PD) consumer with a professional white-collar job. The former may get drunk and not show up for work for more than a day. He or she may get fired, fail to find another job easily, and end up defaulting on a loan. This is idiosyncratic behavior, and another poorly rated consumer is not likely to do the same thing at the same time. A similar idiosyncratic behavior on the part of a highly rated customer is not likely to result in a loss of livelihood and default. He or she is more likely to default because a sector of the economy is doing badly. In other words, the proportion of idiosyncratic components in total credit risk is lower for highly rated consumers than for poorly rated consumers—this is the equivalent of saying that asset correlation is lower for poorly rated consumers.

This argument does not imply that either the total credit risk or the systematic component is lower for poorly rated consumers. Both will be higher for poorly rated consumers than for highly rated consumers, which is a PD effect. The observation that many more poorly rated consumers default (seemingly together) when the economy sours than do highly rated consumers is a result of this effect. The asset correlation effect is different. It is the relative proportion of the systematic part to the idiosyncratic part that is lower for poorly rated consumers and higher for highly rated consumers.

Basel II (CP 3) has posited an AVC function (decreases as PD increases) for corporate, small and medium-sized enterprises, and retail exposures other than mortgages. This function was slightly simplified for application in the United States. Later, the AVC function for credit cards was simplified to a constant AVC of 4%. Mortgages also have a constant AVC of 15%. All other retail products have an AVC function that exponentially goes down from 16% to 3% as PD increases. The AVC values used by Basel II AIRB are not robustly estimated parameters from historical data.[5] That is why the parameters of the AVC function (also referred to as risk weight curve) have changed more than once during the Basel II process, as new but not conclusive evidence has come up.

The correlation between PD and LGD in secured retail lending can be motivated by the following examples:

1. Default can be triggered by a drastic drop in home values in certain neighborhoods, which implies a poorer recovery after foreclosure.
2. When a consumer gets into monetary difficulties and ultimately defaults, he or she is less apt to take care of a car or even a home.

This correlation increases EC. Internal EC models of some banks have PD-LGD correlation explicitly in the models. But the Basel II AIRB does not. Instead, the effect is sought to be incorporated partly by using stressed LGD (which is higher than expected LGD) in the Basel II formulations.

EC for Securitization of Retail Credit

Much more so than for wholesale loans, banks securitize many of their retail loan portfolios. Securitization is the process of pooling a number of loans and then packaging the receivables into securities with levels of priority and selling the securities to investors. The priority of payments is known as the waterfall. The securities are known as tranches.

In a three-tranche securitization, the senior tranche has priority over the mezzanine tranche, which, in turn, has priority over the lowest tranche (also known as first loss piece). In retail securitizations, usually the issuer bank holds the first loss piece and also provides servicing to the underlying borrowers.

Securitizations are so prevalent among retail lenders (especially monoline credit card issuers) that EC for securitization is intimately tied to EC for retail portfolios. Moreover, banks hold (typically highly rated) securitization tranches in their investment portfolios.

Securitization tranches are rated by the rating agencies just as bonds are. Except for being part of a waterfall, a tranche note's cash flows are similar to bond cash flows. Not long ago, it was almost universally believed that a rated (say, AAA or BB) tranche has the same credit risk characteristics as a bond or loan of the same rating. However, more rigorous models for credit risk in securitizations now show that this is not true. In the case of a highly granular portfolio of retail loans, a AAA-rated (senior) tranche requires much less EC to support it than does a AAA-rated bond or loan. In contrast, a BB-rated (mezzanine) tranche attracts many times more EC than does a BB-rated bond or loan. The thinner the tranche in the waterfall, the higher the EC. The Basel II regulatory capital for securitizations incorporates the results of these models.[6]

These recent models seem to show the following:

- Models of EC developed for credit risk in a portfolio of loans and bonds are not directly applicable to securitization tranches.
- EC for a tranche depends on 1) the granularity of the underlying pool of loans, 2) thickness of the tranche, and 3) rating. For securitization of retail portfolios, granularity is usually high, as each loan is small in comparison with the pool; even then, however, the extent of granularity does matter.
- Investors in non-investment-grade (typically mezzanine) tranches are generally getting relatively low coupons compared with investors in highly rated tranches, once the coupons have been adjusted for the true relative ECs required to support them.
- Banks buying non-investment-grade (typically mezzanine) tranches, with apparent high coupons, are actually getting much lower risk-adjusted returns than commonly thought. This is especially so for commercial loan securitization (for example, CMBS) mezzanine tranches with a limited number of loans in the underlying pool.

- Highly rated tranches (for example, a senior CMO tranche) in a bank's investment portfolio actually earn much higher risk-adjusted returns than usually given credit for.
- Public ratings reflect much more than a tail measure (for example, EC) of credit risk. Therefore, one cannot expect a one-to-one relationship between rating and EC across all kinds of structured products.

In Brief: EC for Residual Value Risk in Retail Leases

Leasing has progressively become a fairly large business for many retail banks and automobile "captive" financing companies. In addition to the credit risk of lessee default, there is considerable risk in the residual value of the asset being less than the stated value. There is also the uncertainty of whether or not the lessee decides to return the asset at the end of the lease or buy it at the stated residual value.

A model developed by Michael Pykhtin and Ashish Dev addresses the risk in auto lease residuals and the EC required to support the auto lease portfolio's residual risk. In simple terms, the model can be described as follows. The incidence of a car being returned is modeled in a manner similar to the incidence of default (PD). The shortfall of actual asset value from the stated residual value is akin to LGD. However, LGD can be positive or negative in this case. Since a rational customer is more likely to return the car if its value is less than the stated residual value, there is a very strong correlation between PD and LGD.

Also, the customer has more information about the car (whether it is a lemon or not) than the lessor. This asymmetry of information causes an idiosyncratic term that is correlated to the incidence of return. The latter makes solving the model mathematically complex. Many of the characteristics of this model can be applied to residual risk in other types of leases.

Conclusion

Consumer lending is a big part of the business for many banks in the United States. Risk management, pricing, and performance of these retail portfolios are very important determinants of many banks' overall financial performance. Economic capital (EC) is a common measure of all risks in a portfolio. It has become an extremely useful tool, not only in measuring and managing risk but also in risk-adjusted pricing, so that the bank is adequately compensated for 1) all risks taken, 2) customer profitability, 3) strategic planning and optimum allocation of relatively expensive capital, and 4) performance measurement for shareholder value creation.

An important area of EC for retail portfolios that has not been addressed here is validation of input parameters and assumptions in the EC model. While principles and methods for validating consumer scoring models have been well established, they are only being developed for EC models of consumer credit portfolios. In fact, these will have to be developed in short order and satisfied by banks in order to qualify for AIRB under Basel II.

One element of validation (if not actually forming part of the calculation of EC) is stress testing, which has been emphasized in the Basel II Accord. Stress testing adds important value to risk management well beyond regulatory requirements. While stress testing is common in market risk, there are not yet industry standards for stress testing (retail) credit EC models.

Notes

1. Owing to the sheer number of individual consumers (and defaulted consumers) in the database (of, say, Fair Issac), the econometric estimation of the odds ratio for retail consumers is more robust than the econometric estimation of PD for non-publicly-rated commercial firms.

2. Both the terms "odds ratio" and "net-to-gross charge-off" are far more familiar to retail practitioners than the terms "PD" and "LGD," respectively. However, the actually reported charge-off numbers are subject to differing rules for write-down and ignore timing of recovery.

3. An excellent discussion of input to an EC model can be found in Araten (2004); see References. Generic formulas for EL and EC can be expressed as EL = EAD x PD x ELGD and EC = EAD x F(PD, ELGD, volatility of LGD, correlations; level of confidence).

4. The IRB retail formulation in the Basel II January 2001 consultative paper (CP2) implied a constant AVC asset correlation. While in discussions relating to inordinately high capital for low-quality retail portfolios with high LGD (such as credit cards and subprime auto loans) in CP2, KeyCorp suggested a decreasing asset correlation function (as PD increases) to U.S. regulators active in the Basel II Pillar 1 formulation as early as June 2001, based on conceptual reasoning and data.

5. Most banks also do not have robust estimates of AVC (or default correlation) for their retail portfolios. One reason for this is changes (not infrequent) in the way segmentation is done.

6. For example, the capital requirements under the predominant ratings-based approach of Basel II are calibrated to Pykhtin and Dev (2002, 2003a); see References. See also Peretyatkin and Perraudin (2003) for details. The Supervisory Formula Approach is based on Gordy and Jones (2003).

References

Araten, Michel, 2004, "Conceptual Framework for Economic Capital Models and Required Inputs," in *Economic Capital: A Practitioner Guide*, Risk Books.

Basel Committee on Banking Supervision, 2001, "The New Basel Capital Accord," Consultative Document (CP2), January.

Basel Committee on Banking Supervision, 2003, "The New Basel Capital Accord," Consultative Document (CP3), April.

Breeden, J., 2004, "Stress Testing 2004-05 Retail Organizations," *The RMA Journal*, September.

Dev, Ashish, 2004, "Basel II Capital Adequacy Rules for Retail," in *Basel Handbook*, Risk Books.

Gordy, Michael, 2003, "A Risk-Factor Model Foundation for Ratings-based Bank Capital Rules," *Journal of Financial Intermediation* 12(3).

Gordy, Michael and David Jones, 2003, "Random Tranches," *Risk,* March.

Merton, Robert, 1974, "On the Pricing of Corporate Debts: The Risk Structure of Interest Rates," *Journal of Finance* 29.

Peretyatkin, Victor and William Perraudin, 2003, "Capital for Asset-backed Securities," working paper, February.

Perli, Roberto and William Nayda, 2004, "Economic and Regulatory Capital Allocation for Revolving Retail Exposures," *Journal of Banking and Finance* 28 (4).

Pykhtin, Michael and Ashish Dev, 2002, "Credit Risk in Asset Securitisations: Analytical Model," *Risk,* May.

Pykhtin, Michael and Ashish Dev, 2003(a), "Course-Grained CDOs," *Risk,* January.

Pykhtin, Michael and Ashish Dev, 2003(b), "Residual Risk in Auto Leases," *Risk,* October.

Vasicek, Oldrich, 1987, "Probability of Loss on Loan Portfolio," KMV Corporation.

Economic Capital for Consumer Loans

By Gary Wilhite

o single economic capital approach has yet emerged as best practice for consumer lending, the late bloomer in the family of credit risk capital models.

It's not surprising that commercial loans were first to receive attention from capital modeling pioneers. After all, loans to corporations are larger and represent bigger individual risks compared to consumer loans. Moreover, commercial loan losses had historically been more volatile than consumer loan losses.

The size of commercial loans justified the collection and analysis of more borrower-specific information, and the market provided observable information about the estimated ability of public companies to generate cash flow to repay debt as they built value for shareholders.

Modeling for consumer lending, on the other hand, developed in a different direction. Although lenders were reluctant to rely on commercial loan default models, consumer lending presented an ideal environment for the application of scorecards and other default-prediction techniques.

Most banks had far more consumer loans than commercial accounts and numerous defaults. Many wanted to avoid the expense of individually analyzing the information they collected on their consumer borrowers, and this data was easily amassed in databases where analysts could identify patterns and link behavior to characteristics of the borrower or loan. Such expected loss models were especially important to support securitization activities, which developed both to fund these loans and to avoid the regulatory capital required for low-risk consumer assets.

Indeed, understanding expected behavior remains by far the most important element in managing the risk of consumer lending. Consumer loan losses are not nearly so vulnerable to swings in the economy as commercial loans, but large, unexpected losses have unfortunately cost quite a few banks' shareholders plenty. In most cases, these losses occurred not because the economy hurt otherwise healthy borrowers, but because the borrowers were not as healthy as originally believed (or hoped).

Adequate modeling identifies the characteristics that differentiate performance and segments accordingly so that the lender knows when performance is likely to change. Good risk management is aware of the competitive environment, sensitive to changes in acceptance rates, and on guard against adverse selection. Changes in product offerings are tested in a disciplined fashion so that high losses are limited to test cells. It's also necessary to understand the timing of losses to avoid being misled by the fact that most consumer loans have lower loss rates in their first months on the books than in their second and third years.

The expected behavior of consumer loans must also consider the role of prepayments—a factor that is not as important in commercial lending. Estimating lifetime loss rates requires a projection of future losses and future balances.

Further, as many lenders discovered in 2003, higher-than-expected prepayments do not come evenly from all parts of the portfolio. Good customers are often more likely to refinance, leaving a shrinking pool of paying customers to offset charge-offs. In such cases, a bank must extract additional revenues from the remaining portfolio—through additional usage fees, or increased interest rates—or risk having losses overtake their margin income. Even if prepayments have only a modest effect on loss rates, the value of high-quality consumer loan portfolios may be driven more by prepayment rates than by credit losses.

It is difficult to overstate the importance of modeling expected behavior for consumer lending. The best capital models will produce meaningless results if the inputs are wrong. But good analytics provide a solid basis on which capital models can be built. Few, however, have integrated sophisticated expected-loss modeling with the analysis of unexpected losses needed to determine economic capital requirements.

Economic Capital Models for Consumer Loans

Several model types are currently used for consumer loans. There are three main categories, and additional approaches combine elements from multiple categories. Each of the three main categories has strengths and weaknesses.

Mean variance models. Here the portfolio is segmented into pools with similar loss characteristics. The mean default rate for each pool is determined, and capital is a multiple of the standard deviation of the loss rate.

The capital multiplier may be determined in several ways. The earliest approaches used rules of thumb, based loosely on results from more sophisticated commercial loan models. Losses also can be described with some probability distribution (a beta distribution is sometimes used), with the capital multiplier calculated to get to the 99.x percentile of the distribution.

Advantages of this technique include its simplicity and the ease with which results can be tied to actual performance. A variation of this method uses a modeled value for the expected loss rate, with the variance computed around the predicted value.

A weakness for some implementations is an assumption that each pool has a constant expected loss rate so that all variation is "unexpected loss." The risk in the most rudimentary approaches is that the lender may overlook changes in the portfolio's characteristics that should lead to increased expected losses.

Another potential problem is that pools must be large enough to generate meaningful statistics. A process to allocate capital must therefore be developed if expected default (or loss) rates are assigned to more granular segments than those that were used to determine variances.

Asset value correlation (AVC) models. This is the form used in the Basel Capital Accord. It is based on the most common framework used for commercial loans. The concept is that each consumer has an ability to pay debts from income and wealth, just as a corporation has a value based on its ability to generate cash flow in the future and its current cash position.

Changes in asset value—or the consumer's ability to pay debts—are caused by economic factors and individual circumstances. The volatility of losses depends on the degree to which the change in ability to pay is determined by systematic factors. Higher correlation with systematic risks means more defaults and higher losses when the economy performs poorly. The strength of the AVC model is that it is relatively simple and works at an individual loan level. Expected inputs and the correlation are all that's needed.

The problem is that asset value correlations are quite hard to estimate. They can't be observed directly as public companies can. They can only be inferred by observing variations in default rates.

Correlation values for consumers are typically lower than for commercial borrowers. Large RMA member banks were surveyed in an effort to support the association's Basel efforts.[1]

Consumer asset value correlations were typically highest for real-estate-secured loans, probably because a dependence on house prices adds systematic risk to these credits. Median correlations were in the range of 7.5% to 10%. The lowest correlations were used for credit card lending, with median values of 2.0% to 3.5% reported. Other secured and unsecured consumer loans lie in between, with median AVCs of 4% to 6%.

Capital is quite sensitive to correlation. Figure 1 shows the effect of changing the correlation input to the Basel capital model. Although this model is by no means the indus-

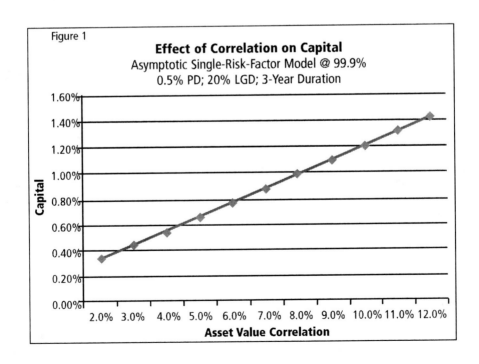

Figure 1

Effect of Correlation on Capital
Asymptotic Single-Risk-Factor Model @ 99.9%
0.5% PD; 20% LGD; 3-Year Duration

try standard for economic capital, it demonstrates the relationship between correlation and capital.

An increase in correlation from 8% to 10%, for example, would increase the attributed capital rate for the illustrated loan from about 1.0% to 1.2%.

Econometric models. These models predict defaults or losses as a function of external economic variables, such as home prices or the unemployment rate. Such a model can directly estimate defaults or losses, or can determine the vectors in a dynamic migration matrix, which sets the transitions between delinquency states. In either case, using these techniques for capital modeling requires estimation of the probability distribution for each of the economic inputs, the correlation among them, and the likelihood that the results will differ from the predicted value.

Depending on the modeling approach used, these techniques can estimate losses for pools or for individual loans over the full range of simulated economic scenarios, producing useful what-if results along with extreme values for capital purposes. Certain forms of these models—those with detailed models of home-price values, for example—can support analyses of geographic concentrations within the portfolio.

Complexity and the resulting validation challenges are the main difficulties with these approaches. Models also require sufficient data on the credit quality of the individual borrowers to detect changes that will affect the portfolio over and above the influence of external factors.

Which Approach Will Become Best Practice?

No single approach has yet emerged as best practice. Many of the methods used today are useful, but each has considerable room for improvement. The lack of consensus on a preferred approach can be good if it stimulates innovation and additional development along several fronts.

Strengthening the estimates of the capital multiplier used in mean-variance models clearly will require a better understanding of the relationship between extreme events and year-to-year volatility. Additional research also would be useful in generating better estimates for the asset value correlations used in AVC models. And there's no end to the work that could be done with econometric models to investigate the drivers of consumer loan losses and the interrelatedness of geographic and other consumer segments.

Since all the techniques described above have strengths, a combination of techniques holds the promise of a model with more benefits than any single current approach. One idea that deserves attention borrows from the most common commercial credit risk capital models. These models are expressed in terms of capital and unexpected loss, but they work in terms of portfolio value.

The expected value of the portfolio is calibrated to expected loss, and lesser values are measured as unexpected losses. The difference between the expected value and the value at the 99.x% level is required capital. Such an analysis of consumer loans could consider value losses from both higher-than-expected credit losses and higher-than-expected prepayments.

Decisions about the portfolio could simultaneously consider that different parts of the portfolio have different sensitivities to these risks. Some hedging can be done across risks within the portfolio, which is generally a cheaper alternative to external hedging. Such models could also be used to test the portfolio against specific stress scenarios.

The designation "best practice" remains free for the taking. Diligent research and innovative thinking can still bring significant improvements to this area, and those who advance the state of the art are likely to earn rewards for their shareholders. As model builders seek improved understanding of unexpected losses, they can't overlook the importance of understanding expected behavior, since even the best model will mislead its users if its inputs are incorrect.

Note

1. For more information, visit www.rmahq.org, click on "Regulatory Relations," then click on "RMA's Basel Response."

Economic Capital Estimation for Consumer Portfolios

BY FANG DU

Both regulatory capital and economic capital focus on a bank's risk of insolvency in the face of adverse events. A bank, for example, maintains regulatory capital or economic capital as a financial source to protect itself against insolvency.

Theoretically, regulatory capital and economic capital should converge because both cover the asset loss due to credit risk, market risk, operational risk, interest risk, reputational risk, and so forth. In reality, these two measures show not only a difference but also a dramatic divergence.

Most banks currently use a top-down approach to assign economic capital to their consumer portfolios, which include residential mortgages, home equity loans and lines (also known as closed-end and open-end home equity loans), automobile installment loans, student loans, credit cards, and others. Under this approach, the credit risk for each consumer loan within the same consumer portfolio is assumed to be homogeneous, regardless of its credit score, loan-to-value (LTV) ratio, debt-to-income ratio, tenure, and sensitivity to macroeconomic conditions.

In other words, all of the valuable information reflecting each customer's creditworthiness is ignored under this approach.

In consumer credit, most banks and financial services firms commonly use a FICO credit score (a generic credit score to predict a customer's default probability) to assess each borrower's creditworthiness. Generally speaking, a customer with a FICO score of 800 has a much lower probability of defaulting within the coming 12 months than a customer with a FICO score of 500 for the same time horizon. Unfortunately, the top-down approach does not distinguish differences in creditworthiness between these two customers.

In the same fashion, another noticeable risk factor—the LTV for secured consumer portfolios—plays no role in the economic capital allocation process. The top-down approach treats a customer with an LTV of less than 50% the same as one with an LTV of 100%. Therefore, the effectiveness of all risk factors, such as remaining time to maturity, the position according to credit cycle, and payment performance, is not taken into account when using a top-down approach.

The process of setting economic capital for consumer portfolios is progressing at differing rates among banks. Some banks, for example, treat home equity loans differently from home equity lines because of different lending policies and repayment schedules between outstanding balance and exposures.

Several national banks are evolving faster in this area by not only assigning the economic capital at the sub-portfolio[1] level but also differentiating capital by decomposing

247

the risk characteristics. Therefore, even within the same equity sub-portfolio, different capital rates are assigned according to risk levels. The majority of banks set a uniform capital number or ratio for each of their consumer sub-portfolios defined by product type.

The categorization for sub-portfolios is much broader. Some banks treat the home equity loans the same as the home equity lines, and the automobile installment loans the same as other secured installment loans. The worst case is that a number of banks assign only one capital ratio to their entire consumer portfolio regardless of whether they are secured or unsecured sub-portfolios. This approach implies that the credit card sub-portfolio possesses the same credit risk as the secured mortgage sub-portfolio.

Yet another problem caused by the top-down approach is that it ignores the variance and covariance between individual consumer loans. The variance-covariance matrix depicts the quantitative measure of how two loans behave over time: whether they move in the same or opposite directions or have no association pattern at all. This relationship also can be measured by the product of correlation coefficient and the standard deviations of individual loans. The concept of correlation coefficients plays a significant role in portfolio management.

In the U.S. equity market, the typical correlation coefficient falls into the 0.6-0.7 range for two stocks. This correlation coefficient is relatively high but not perfectly linearly related, so a portfolio manager chooses a position by carefully picking diversified securities to compose a portfolio. This type of security selection results in a portfolio with an associated risk level that will be less than any single asset included in the portfolio relative to the return of the portfolio and individual securities.

That is exactly what Markowitz's portfolio theory advocates. The analogous relationship should be expected for consumer loan portfolios as well. Since each consumer portfolio includes at least several thousand individual loans, the risk at the portfolio level is expected to be much smaller than the weighted sum of individual asset risks. For a consumer portfolio, only the systematic risk caused by macroeconomic factors is expected to exist, because the unsystematic risks or unique risks cancel each other out.

In the real consumer credit world, unfortunately, the information depicting the relationships among consumer loans is neglected, due either to the limited knowledge in this area or to avoidance of heavy and lengthy calculations. The economic capital requirement is increased dramatically because of the incorrect assumption of a perfect linear relationship between individual loans. In other words, portfolio theory plays no role in this circumstance.

Any banks using a top-down approach to quantify economic capital should recognize these drawbacks.

Regulatory versus Economic Capital

Some banks set capital by following the regulatory requirements and may not focus on whether this requirement accurately reflects the underlying portfolio risk. The distinction, however, between economic capital and regulatory capital is quite clear.

Regulatory capital is a fixed minimum capital requirement (from the 1988 Basel Accord) that banks have to hold. Fixed minimum capital requirements are defined as the ratio of capital to total risk-weighted assets. Until Basel II goes into effect, banks are required to maintain a minimum capital of 8% of weighted exposure.

Economic capital is the capital needed to offset the bank's combined credit risk, market risk, and operational risk, based on estimates of unexpected loss. A bank volunteers to hold the economic capital to cover losses in the unlikely, but fully possible, case of an unexpected adverse event and still meet the insolvency target. These are voluntary versus involuntary issues.

As mentioned earlier, the risk management techniques, practices, and skills are quite divergent among banks. This divergence becomes more significant in the consumer credit risk world. While some banks may make only limited use of credit scores, others already fully utilize the automated score decision, credit-limit assignments, and account payment monitoring system. While some banks use only a generic or standard score system, other banks extend the risk management scope by implementing new computer programs, such as a neural network or artificial intelligence, to explore a new marketing regime or mimic the fraud patterns in their fraud protection programs.

The 1988 Basel Accord cannot provide any incentive for those banks with sophisticated risk management tools and knowledge because its very nature is one-size-fits-all. Basel II comes closer to recommending a risk-based approach. The credit risk embedded in assets is measured by three approaches: 1) the standardized approach, 2) the foundation internal ratings-based approach, and 3) the advanced internal ratings-based approach.

Both regulatory capital and economic capital deal with the solvency issue. A target insolvency rate usually is chosen to be consistent with a bank's desired credit ratings for its liabilities. For instance, the solvency rates are 7 basis points, 3 basis points, and 1 basis point, respectively, for banks with single-A, double-A, and triple-A risk-rating liabilities. A number of banks choose a 0.05% solvency rate for their consumer portfolios. Robert Giltner recommended three standard deviations of loan-loss estimate to set sufficient economic capital.

Huge discrepancies exist between regulatory capital levels and experts' opinions about economic capital. Why? What are the major factors causing this gap? Many national banks inherently have a significant amount of portfolio diversification. This is especially true in consumer loan portfolios. All the portfolios within a bank are not perfectly correlated given the nature of the lines of business.

One reason that regulatory capital is higher than economic capital is the exclusion of the diversification effect. According to Markowitz's portfolio theory, the risk for any portfolio is smaller than the sum of risks of the individual assets included in the portfolio with an imperfect linear relationship.

Using the risk of one individual mortgage loan to infer the risk of a mortgage portfolio or using the risk in a consumer sub-portfolio to infer the risk of a whole consumer portfolio overstates the capital requirement, because risky assets in the portfolio are not perfectly related linearly. Generally speaking, there are several thousand loans—if not tens or hundreds of thousands—in a consumer sub-portfolio, and there is little chance of all loans defaulting at the same time. The risk existing in the portfolio is smaller than the weighted sum of individual risks.

Uneven sophistication of risk management systems is another factor causing regulatory capital to differ from economic capital. Banks with a sophisticated risk management system and a strong risk management team are able to monitor the credit quality frequently—daily, weekly, or at least monthly—and to make strategy adjustments as necessary. In contrast, some banks are still hanging on to outdated risk management systems because of the tremendous costs to replace them. Their risk monitoring systems cannot elicit warning signals in a timely fashion. A new risk management tool or instruments cannot upload into the systems because of capacity and programming constraints.

As a consequence, the aggregate risk could be much higher, even though the individual risk levels are similar. Basel II will partially correct this issue by allowing some banks to evaluate their credit risk using internal bank information if they have the ability to estimate their credit risk fairly and in an unbiased manner. Therefore, if a bank has sophisticated internal credit rating models that reflect the true credit risks, the regulatory agency would be more likely to support a bank's internal credit capital assessment. If a bank lacks risk management systems and models, the regulatory agency will recommend the standard regulatory capital as the optimal solution.

Credit Risk in the Consumer Portfolio

Some years ago, most national banks started to pay close attention to collecting and storing consumer-credit-related information, such as credit scores at loan origination, updated credit scores, payment history time series, and other consumer credit application information. At the beginning of the data collection process, the scope for using the data was narrower, focusing only on asset quality reporting or monitoring.

Although some banks enlarged the collection of detailed information in customers' payment performances, it was done mostly on an ad hoc basis and not updated regularly or stored properly. For example, tapes containing updated credit scores from the credit bureau stayed in a risk manager's drawer for months and were discarded afterwards. Therefore, the data quality may be questionable in the first one or two years of collection.

The norm of reliable data history on consumer portfolios is seven to eight years, although some banks may have longer histories. In addition, data quality is not always uniform for different consumer sub-portfolios. There may be more historical information on residential mortgages than on credit cards. Another issue is that the data quality is directly related to hierarchy levels. It's common to find a longer history at an aggregate level but less information when drilling down to a more detailed level for a consumer-specific portfolio.

Moody's, Standard and Poor's, and Fitch Investors Service possess much longer historical credit information on investment-grade bonds, high-yield bonds, and nonrated bonds. Fleet uses Moody's eight bond ratings—spanning 30 years, from 1970 to 1999—to test the three standard deviations of unexpected loan-loss estimates. Results show that the three-standard- deviation criterion is only good enough to cover the worst-year loss for bonds rated B or Ba.

For bonds rated Baa or better, three standard deviations are not sufficient to cover the worst credit stress.

Due to the non-normal nature of default risk, five standard deviations should be used for rating Baa bonds and six standard deviations for rating bonds of A or above. Of course, these results are derived based on historical data sets and are time sensitive, but at least they provide a guideline or direction for setting economic capital. Therefore, combining the knowledge and information about commercial credit risks will correct for the defect of a short history of consumer credit data.

Before using this publicly available information, practitioners have to ask themselves the following questions:

- Should commercial loans and consumer loans be treated in the same way or differently?
- What are the similarities and differences between commercial and consumer loans?
- What are the risk characteristics for commercial and consumer loans?
- How do macroeconomic factors impact commercial and consumer loans?
- How will commercial loan information be used to make a fair reference to consumer loans?

To date, these issues have not been discussed in the literature.

Another remedy for lack of data at a particular bank is to use the aggregated and pooled consumer information from other sources. Although aggregated data cannot fully represent the characteristics of consumer portfolios in a particular bank, at least they provide a directional benchmark by covering a longer consumer credit history.

Fleet collaborated with the FDIC's credit card research group to explore consumer credit data from 1984 to 1999. The average net charge-off rate was 180 basis points, and the volatility measured in standard deviation equaled 57 basis points for consumer products in aggregate. In this period, the minimum and maximum net charge-off rates were 61 and 286 basis points, respectively.

Three standard deviations as a proxy of the economic capital requirement are good enough to sustain the worst-year loss based on this 15-year period. Notably, using three standard deviations as a criterion to set the economic capital is suitable only for a consumer portfolio as a whole and is not good for a specific consumer sub-portfolio, such as mortgages, home equity loans, automobile installment loans, and credit cards. It's important to remember that this three-standard-deviation criterion as an economic capital proxy is data dependent or data sensitive. Using a different historical data set may yield a different conclusion.

Fleet conducted another study using Fitch's securitized credit card data. There were 119 monthly annualized charge-off observations from January 1991 to November 2000 in this data set. Three, six, and eight standard deviations were equal to 284, 596, and 758 basis points, respectively. The worst loss within this period was 693 basis points. Obviously, eight standard deviations would be required to properly assign the economic capital in this case.

The most notable phenomenon is that the FDIC data does not support the assumption that the expected default is smaller during economic expansion than during recession. The default rate for an aggregated consumer portfolio for the most recent eight years of economic boom (1992-2000) actually is higher than the past 16 years' default rate, which covers at least two economic recessions—a minor recession in 1987 and a severe recession in 1991. Therefore, when dealing with consumer portfolios, practitioners must understand their characteristics and differences from the commercial portfolio and the impact on the macroeconomy.

Most banks currently use logistic regression with dichotomy of a dependent variable—say, default or no default—to estimate the default probability for their consumer portfolios. Factors change corresponding to consumer sub-portfolios. The LTV ratio plays a significant role in a secured consumer sub-portfolio, but is ineffective in an unsecured consumer sub-portfolio. In addition, the sensitivities for the same factor differ among consumer sub-portfolios.

For example, the impact of credit scoring on a mortgage is definitely not the same as for a credit card. If the resource and computational systems are sufficient, it's preferable to conduct detailed studies, sub-portfolio by sub-portfolio. When several sub-portfolios are lumped together, valuable information is lost and this can cause inaccurate credit risk estimation.

Even within the same sub-portfolio, different loans carry different credit characteristics. Generally, every consumer sub-portfolio includes thousands of loans. It may not be worth it to use detailed analysis of each loan, because gains diminish due to intensive computation and time consumption. Clustering loans with similar credit risk characteristics into several segments to be treated as synthetic securities is feasible and offers a large benefit while losing little information.

The intersegment risk scale does not increase in a linear fashion. In other words, you cannot say that the risk will increase by 10% when the credit score worsens by 10%. A consumer with a credit score above 750 behaves quite differently from another with a score of 550. For evenly distributed credit score bands, the credit risk increases exponentially. Therefore, the credit risk characteristics should be explored not only for different sub-consumer portfolios but also within the same sub-portfolio. Fleet used 1992-2000 data to study several secured and unsecured consumer sub-portfolios. The research results support this argument.

Table 1 shows the estimate of annualized default probabilities on an unsecured consumer sub-portfolio measured in basis points.

Table 1 **Default Probability—Unsecured Consumer Sub-portfolio A**			
	Expected Default Rate		
	Factor 2		
Factor 1	Segment 1	Segment 2	Segment 3
Segment 1	28	62	95
Segment 2	76	173	253
Segment 3	156	363	494
Segment 4	373	640	859
Segment 5	573	1,148	1,318

Variance-Covariance Matrixes

The first step in determining economic capital for a commercial portfolio is to explore how these commercial loans react to adverse occurrences. Analogously, the reaction— as measured by correlation coefficients—toward external effects for loans in a consumer portfolio should be estimated at the very beginning. Theoretically, it is possible to estimate correlation coefficients for every pair of loans within the same consumer portfolio.

Let's assume a hypothetical consumer portfolio of 10,000 loans. To fully explore the association within any pair of loans, we need to estimate 49,995,000 correlation coefficients.[2] These coefficients can be estimated, but the calculation task could be arduous and costly.

The most feasible and efficient approach is to synthesize the loans based on their credit characteristics by using a bottom-up approach. Loans that fall into each segment are assumed homogeneous, measured by several credit-related factors such as credit score, LTV ratio, loan tenor, and delinquency status. Let's define aggregated loans in the same segment as a synthetic security, then estimate the correlation coefficients for each pair of synthetic securities using historical and projected information.

If banks have over 30 years of historical default data at the consumer sub-portfolio level, the estimation of the correlation coefficients between consumer sub-portfolios and between individual loans within the same sub-portfolio would be feasible. However, it's doubtful that any bank stores this much data on any of its consumer portfolios. For the estimation purpose, the minimum of three years, at least, of trailing 12-month default history can be used to estimate the variance-covariance matrix.

The first problem is that this estimated variance-covariance matrix depicts the historical relationship. As most financial practitioners know, the future financial relationship among these consumer loans may not be a repetition of their history.

The second problem is that the relationship derived from the historical data may be time dependent and unstable. In other words, the magnitude of variance-covariance may change when using a different time period. For instance, a variance-covariance matrix based on a recessionary period may yield a very different picture from one based on a strong economic period. Which relationship should the bank adopt? Risk managers should be aware of these issues when attempting to calculate correlation coefficients. Fleet adds the scenario analyses, particularly the macroeconomic changes, into variance-covariance matrix estimation.

Monte Carlo Simulation

Techniques for estimating credit risk, market risk, and operational risk have evolved rapidly, although some techniques appear to be state-of-the-art and some appear theoretically sound but inapplicable in practice. If the credit, market, operational, and interest risks can be measured accurately, the task of setting an economically sustainable provision for economic capital becomes much easier.

A handful of studies have been related to credit risk and economic capital for big commercial banks, but nearly all studies focus on commercial loan portfolios. The economic capital model for the consumer portfolio is rarely seen. In the consumer credit world, models are concentrated on default, bankruptcy, fraud, and line assignment. Default models are commonplace, but mark-to-market methods are almost nonexistent.

Although the research on estimating and forecasting the expected default rate and loss amounts started more than 30 years ago in the consumer credit world, there is almost no research geared to the estimation of unexpected losses. While most risk managers in charge of consumer portfolios understand the concept of expected credit loss very well, they have little quantitative knowledge about loss volatility. The majority of commercial banks have chosen a constant parameter to assign the economic capital rates to their consumer portfolios, but cannot rationalize the link between this parameter and the underlying loss distribution.

A Monte Carlo simulation methodology can be used to simulate the potential loss distribution for each consumer sub-portfolio. Before starting this process, there must first be an estimation of the expected loss rate and the standard deviation of the loss rates for each segment, as well as the covariance between all pairs of segments using historical information and scenario analysis results.

We assume a normally distributed loss rate in every segment, although the descriptive statistics such as *mean* and *variance* vary dramatically from one segment to another. In general, the sample size is large enough for most segments. But the small sample size and non-consumer credit history could be an issue in estimating the variance-covariance matrix, and risk managers and modelers should adjust estimates. Weights assigned to each segment are determined by their outstanding exposures. The portfolio is randomly simulated using 100,000 trials for each consumer sub-portfolio. Every trial must meet the condition of distribution at each segment as well as the correlation coefficient between these segments.

The last step in the simulation process is to test the loss distribution based on these 100,000 generated observations. Two sequential null hypotheses are proposed. The first assumption is that the simulated distribution is normally distributed. If this hypothesis is rejected, the simulated results do not support the normally distributed loss distribution.

The second hypothesis then comes into the picture by assuming that the simulated distribution is a gamma distribution. All six simulated loss distributions except one fail to reject the gamma distribution hypothesis. Two parameters, *alpha* and *beta*, are estimated. The maximum losses are provided and correspond to the bank's risk tolerance. Most banks chose the likelihood of solvency at a 99.95%, 99.97%, or 99.99% confidence interval. The economic capital (value at risk, or VaR), is measured by the difference between this maximum loss and expected loss. Figure 1 shows a simulated distribution for a secured consumer sub-portfolio. The vertical axis represents frequencies and the horizontal axis represents the loss rate measured in basis points.

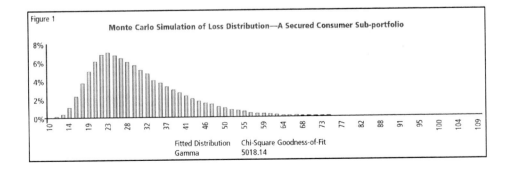

Conclusion

The methodology introduced in this article estimates and allocates economic capital for consumer portfolios better than the constant capitalization rate now used by most banks.

First, the default probability, default probability volatility, and the covariance relationship between loans can be estimated to reflect a bank's consumer portfolio credit profile.

Second, using a longer history than is available in a bank's own consumer portfolio offers greater reliability. As a result, the economic capital calculations not only cover the portfolios under economic boom conditions but also include considerations of economic recession in both minor and severe scenarios. Economic capital rates derived in this manner better represent the credit risk embedded in consumer portfolios.

Third, modern portfolio theory helps consumer portfolio diversification analyses as it did with commercial loan, equity, bond, derivatives, or combinations of portfolios. Currently, most banks assume that all loans in the consumer portfolio default at the same time. The diversification effect is totally ignored.

Finally, using the Monte Carlo simulation after synthesizing the homogeneous loans makes it feasible to estimate economic capital. VaR is easily calculated by using simulated loss distribution.

Notes

1. A particular consumer product—for example, a residential mortgage—is defined as one consumer sub-portfolio.
2. The number of permutations of n things k at a time $[n/k] = n/(n-k)!k!$

References

Basel Committee on Bank Supervision. 2000. "Credit Ratings and Complementary Sources of Credit Quality Information," Basel Committee on Banking Supervision Working Papers, no. 3, August.

Carey, Mark. 2000. "Dimensions of Credit Risk and Their Relationship to Economic Capital Requirements," NBER Working Paper no. 7269.

Giltner, R. C. 1998. "Using Profitability Data to Price for Risk," *Commercial Lending Review* 13, no. 2, Spring.

O'Connor, Ronan, James F. Golden, and Robert Reck. 1999. "A Value-at-Risk Calculation of Required Reserves for Credit Risk in Corporate Lending Portfolios," *North American Actuarial Journal* 3, no. 2: 72-83.

Universal Laws of Retail Economic Capital

By Joseph L. Breeden

This article employs results from a modeling approach that leverages the unique dynamics of retail portfolios to establish three laws of retail economic capital.

Many companies around the world are currently using this technology or other nonlinear decomposition approaches for scenario-based forecasting of revenue and losses and for stress testing. By combining a scenario-based forecasting engine with a Monte Carlo scenario generator, each portfolio can be analyzed independently to measure the distribution of future losses and make some discoveries about the nature of retail lending volatility.

Basel II was created to answer a very specific question: "How much capital do I need next year to cover the loans currently on my books?" While this is certainly the primary capital question for the finance function, other groups within a lending institution require more information in order to harness capital-based decisions for originations and risk.

For example, to properly price new loans, it is important to consider lifetime capital requirements. Similarly, planning for next year's originations requires computing incremental capital requirements.

Both of these issues are beyond the scope of the Basel II formulas, yet even the basic question of how much capital is required for retail portfolios has been problematic. Early iterations of the Basel II formulas struggled with calibrations for card portfolios, while capital for all subprime products is under scrutiny under the new guidelines.

Using a simulation-based approach to computing capital requirements, Strategic Analytics has developed some universal laws of retail economic capital. Simulation-based approaches, commonly used for economic capital in market-traded instruments, are rarely used in retail lending.

Unlike the Basel II formulas, simulation-based approaches have the advantage of being able to incorporate the known dynamics of the problem, such as life cycles and seasonality. A simulation-based approach also can create loss distributions for measuring the credit risk component of economic capital without making any a priori assumptions about the shape of the loss distribution.

The results shown in this article use the ratio of unexpected loss (UL), as measured directly from the loss distribution at the 99.9% solvency level, to expected loss (EL), which is the median of loss distribution. The UL/EL ratio measures the uncertainty of future losses relative to the predictable loss level.

Result #1: Volatility decreases as loss rate increases.

In plain words, subprime portfolios have high loss rates, as measured by

$$\frac{UL}{EL} = \frac{\lambda}{\sqrt{\text{Loss Rate}}}$$

EL / Total Receivables, but relatively low volatility as measured by UL/EL. Prime first mortgage portfolios have very low loss rates, but their volatility is much higher than what would be observed in the subprime portfolios.

The plot shows volatility versus loss rate using one point for each portfolio analyzed with a best-fit line overlaid. Every major type of retail loan is represented in the data shown in Figure 1: cards, auto, mortgage, home equity, personal loans, retail purchase financing, and small business loans. Also, these results cover multiple countries and the full spectrum from prime to subprime.

Much of the variation in the fit is due to other factors unique to each portfolio, but the best-fit line shows that commonalities are strong across retail products. The lambda factor in the formula is the product calibration. The square root in the denominator was measured experimentally and has a 12% uncertainty band.

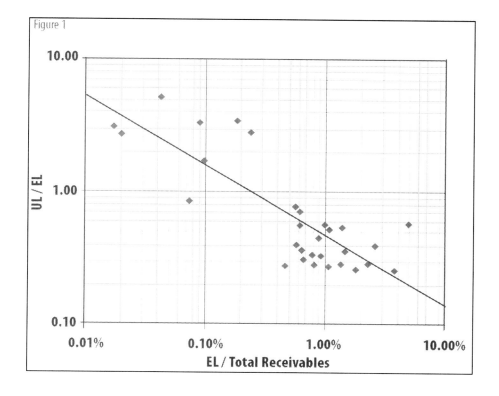

The obvious impact of this result is that high losses do not imply high volatility. A true economic capital calculation must be able to distinguish between predictable and unpredictable losses and only assign capital to the latter.

Result #2: Volatility increases as the 2/3 power of time.

There is a well-known rule of equities trading that volatility grows as the square root of time.

$$\left[\frac{UL}{EL}\right]^T = \left[\frac{UL}{EL}\right]^1 T^{2/3}$$

This is easily proven theoretically if one assumes that successive returns are uncorrelated. Thus, the annual volatility of a stock is $\sqrt{250}$ times the daily volatility, because there are 250 trading days each year.

With retail lending, however, losses month-to-month are correlated. Consumer behavior is driven in part by the macroeconomic environment, and the economy does not swing randomly from recession to expansion each month. Economic cycles have transition times, and those lead to monthly correlations in consumer behavior. By incorporating this autocorrelation into the Monte Carlo scenario generator, one can run forecasts many years into the future in order to measure lifetime capital requirements, as shown in Figure 2.

The experimental result is that the proper exponent for retail lending is 2/3 instead of the often used 1/2. As with the first law, this result holds again for all product types, all risk categories, and in all countries tested thus far. The 2/3 exponent has an uncertainty of 4%.

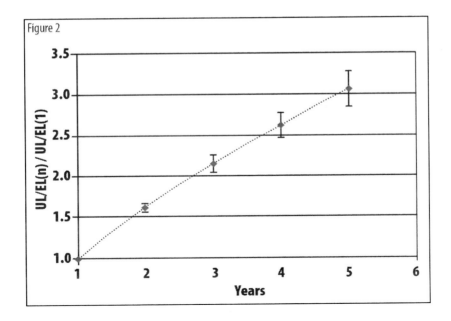

Figure 2

With this result, a manager can take a one-year capital estimate and multiply by the number of years to the 2/3 power to estimate how much capital is required over a five-year horizon.

Result #3: Volatility decreases as the age of the vintage increases.

Younger accounts are more volatile than older accounts. As with the first result above, this is a fairly obvious outcome, but it is beyond what would be found in the current Basel II guidance.

$$\frac{UL}{EL} = \frac{\lambda}{(\text{Months-on-Books})^{1/5}}$$

Many groups implementing the straight Basel II formula include segmentation by months-on-books—for example, first year, second year, and years three and beyond. This vintage segmentation will capture the fact that accounts of different ages have different loss rates, but it does not capture the way in which volatility changes with account age.

For most retail products, the first year has relatively low loss rates because of the maturation or seasoning process. However, from a volatility perspective, that first year carries a great deal of uncertainty because of the volatility in attrition and balance growth. The simulation approach employed in Figure 3 includes attrition and balance dynamics in addition to the usual Basel II variables PD, LGD, and EAD, so such effects are captured.

Figure 3 shows the one-year-forward estimate of UL/EL comparing young vintages to older vintages. Every product segment will have a different lambda factor, but for

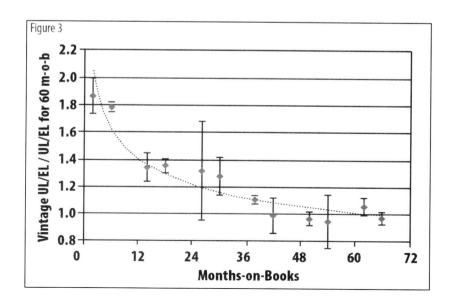

plotting purposes, the values were all normalized to the UL/EL value for vintages at 60 months-on-books. As with the previous two results, the 1/5 factor was measured experimentally from the best-fit line shown in the plot. The uncertainty in that factor is 11%. Once again, this result includes a range of products, demographics, and geographies.

Therefore, new accounts are not an equal replacement for old accounts from a capital perspective, even if the expected loss rates were the same. Purchasing older accounts is different from originating new accounts when estimating economic capital requirements.

Conclusion

As lenders around the globe implement new economic capital solutions for retail loans, rules of thumb are in high demand. Compare these results against your own to see if they make sense. For many groups, Results #2 and #3 go beyond what a straight Basel II implementation can compute, so these rules might serve as a way of expanding the value of economic capital calculations to other purposes within the bank.

The primary intent of Basel II is to make capital calculations useful for business decisions. The studies done here are intended to be expansions of that mandate so that the marketing and credit functions can join with finance in obtaining results suitable for planning and risk-based pricing.

References

Breeden, J. 2002. "Becoming a Better Vintner," *The RMA Journal*, September.

Breeden, J. 2003. "Portfolio Forecasting Tools: What You Need to Know," *The RMA Journal*, October.

Best Practices in Mortgage Default Risk Measurement and Economic Capital

By David Kaskowitz, Alexander Kipkalov, Kyle Lundstedt, and John Mingo

A number of models are currently in use to estimate unexpected losses for mortgages. A study sponsored by Washington Mutual compared four basic classes of models and benchmarked their results against those of best-practice institutions. The classes include the following:

1. The "panel data" models.
2. The first-generation "default mode" (FGDM) models.
3. The Merton models.
4. The "roll rate" (RR), or "state-transition" models.

The purpose of the study was to help both practitioners and regulators evaluate the results of these models through two separate empirical experiments. The first experiment involved establishing estimates of the loss distributions for important cohorts of the market portfolio, using two large databases of prime and subprime loans. Shortcomings were observed in the panel data and FGDM models, and the most complete was found to be the state-transition models.

The second experiment used a more detailed analysis on a randomly drawn sample to establish parameters for the model adopted by regulatory agencies, using the economic capital results from a best-practice model.

Principles of Credit Risk Measurement and Economic Capital

Risk practitioners use a number of common terms. An understanding of these terms helps set the stage for any discussion of the various credit risk models used for first-mortgage products.

Economic capital (EC). EC, a statistic that summarizes the institution's measurement of portfolio risk, serves many purposes, including helping to establish a general level of capital adequacy within the bank. EC also is used in the denominator of risk-adjusted return on capital (RAROC) calculations. The institution attempts to invest in activities for which the calculated return to allocated economic capital exceeds some targeted rate, generally taken to be the weighted-average cost of capital. Only by investing in such high RAROC activities can the bank maximize shareholder value-added (SVA), defined as the excess of returns over the market rate of return required for the level of capital needed to maintain the bank's targeted soundness level.[1]

Soundness. No bank can manage to a zero probability of insolvency, so a bank needs to decide the level of insolvency probability it wishes to manage. Some banks manage to a high soundness standard (high bond rating, low insolvency probability), while others manage to a lower soundness standard with a correspondingly higher insolvency probability. Soundness is generally defined as a particular probability of insolvency, over a particular horizon, to which the bank aspires. Often, this targeted insolvency probability is expressed in terms of a targeted bond rating for the institution's debt. In this theoretical framework, EC is the level of capital that, given the bank's portfolio, is sufficient to reduce to an acceptable level the probability that losses will exceed that level of capital.

Loss probability density function. When measuring EC to maintain the targeted soundness, the bank must estimate the probability that any particular bad loss on the portfolio will actually occur. The risk practitioner thinks of this as *estimating a loss probability density function*, more commonly referred to as a "loss distribution," for the bank's current portfolio. Such loss distributions, estimated for credit risk, are notoriously fat-tailed—the thicker the tail of the distribution, the riskier the portfolio.

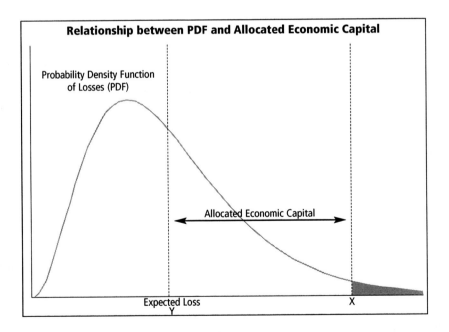

Unexpected loss. Mean or expected credit losses do not, in this framework, represent a true risk—such expected losses (EL) can be priced so that yields on performing assets can "cover" the losses on those assets in the portfolio that actually default. Rather, risk involves the chance that portfolio losses will exceed this expected amount. Economic capital, in turn, is defined as the portfolio loss that would occur with the targeted small probability—for example, 1-2% over a five-year horizon—less the expected loss level covered by the yields on good assets. This difference—loss at the chosen "confidence interval" on the loss distribution *minus* EL—is equivalently called unexpected loss (UL) by many practitioners.

For purposes of this study, the same confidence interval to measure EC—a confidence interval of 98.18% over a five-year horizon—is used for every model. Longer time horizons (for example, five years) are more appropriate than the typical one-year horizon used for measuring credit risk in corporate loan portfolios.

Further, this study uses the Basel assumption that all banks should, in effect, adhere to a minimum soundness standard of at least the equivalent of a BBB (investment grade) rating. Thus, the confidence interval shown above is used because 1 minus the confidence interval (1.82%) is the long-run historical average percent of BBB-rated corporate bonds that would default over any given five-year period. This assumes that the targeted insolvency probability and the chosen time horizon of the hypothetical bank using our EC estimates are 1.82% and five years, respectively.

Models for Estimating Unexpected Losses for Mortgages

Basically, four classes of models have been examined: the panel data models, the first-generation default mode (FGDM) models, the Merton models, and the roll rate (RR) or, equivalently, state-transition models.

1. **Panel data models** use an extensive "cohorting" process to break up the portfolio into many "buckets" or cohorts—each bucket being assumed to represent a group of fairly homogenous loans. For each bucket, the analyst measures the historical losses, say, over each quarter, for as many quarters as are available in the database. The mean and standard deviation of these historical loss observations is then assumed to be the mean and standard deviation of the "true" underlying loss distribution. Moreover, this true underlying distribution is assumed to be of a particular, tractable "shape" (for example, the Beta distribution). After estimating such a distribution, the analyst measures the loss at the 98.18% confidence interval and then subtracts mean losses (EL) to arrive at the EC estimate.

2. **The FGDM** model may also use cohorting to segment the portfolio. In this model, however, the analyst is required to measure the default probability (PD), or equivalently the expected default frequency (EDF), for the "typical" asset in the cohort. Additionally, a loss given default (LGD) must be estimated for the asset. Finally, an estimate must be made for the degree to which defaults across loans are *correlated*. For any given PD and LGD characteristics, the higher the default correlation, the thicker the tail of the loss distribution (the riskier the portfolio or the cohort).

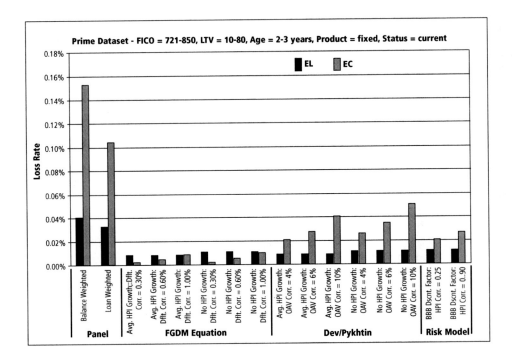

3. **A Merton-type model,** like the FGDM model, does not necessarily need any cohorting to be done; it relies on an estimated PD and LGD for each loan in a portfolio. However, rather than use a loan's *default* correlation with other loans to help estimate the loss distribution, the Merton model relies on a stylistic view of the default process for each obligor. In this process, the obligor (homeowner) is assumed to default only when, and always when, the value of the obligor's assets (the house price) falls below the value of the obligor's liabilities (the outstanding balance on the mortgage loan). Under this assumption, the analyst needs to estimate the distribution of house prices and, especially, the degree to which house prices are correlated across obligors. To distinguish between the FGDM model and the Merton model, think of the former as a *loan default* correlation model and the latter as an *obligor asset value* (OAV) correlation model.

4. **A roll rate, or state-transition, model** is the final class considered. In such models, there is no particular need to estimate "defaults." Rather, the analyst uses a much more complex process in an attempt to estimate the probabilities that any particular loan will "transition" from its current state—for example, "current" or "30 days past due"—to any other state (such as foreclosure). These various probabilities of transitioning to any particular state are expressed in a transition matrix or, equivalently, a roll rate matrix. Since, theoretically, each loan faces such a probability matrix at the start of any given month, it is possible to use computer-intensive techniques to *simulate* the future path of each loan or a portfolio of loans. When any loan enters, through simulation, a state that could involve a loss (such as foreclosure), the

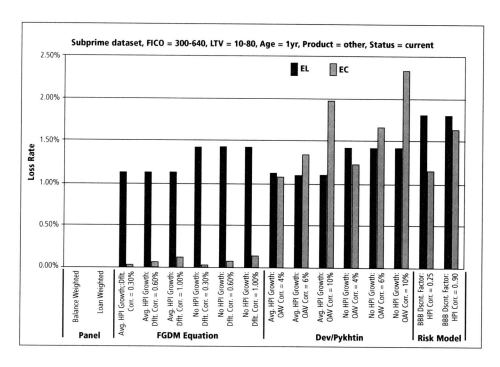

analyst may apply a separately estimated loss model to estimate the present value of the losses attributable to the loan entering into the state of default. The study uses a particular form of state-transition model—the LoanPerformance RiskModel™—in all cases that compare the performance of such models vis-à-vis the performance of other models.

Empirical Experiments: Using Credit Risk Models to Estimate Economic Capital

Two separate empirical experiments were used in this study. The first experiment involved establishing estimates of the loss distributions for important cohorts of the market portfolio by using the LoanPerformance databases for prime and subprime loans—consisting of 16.6 million and 510,000 individual mortgage loans, respectively. These two large databases were "cohorted" into buckets based on several characteristics of the loan: FICO, original LTV, age of the loan, product type (fixed rate versus "other"), and loan status (current versus noncurrent).

There were 180 different cohorts, resulting from using five FICO ranges, three LTV ranges, three age ranges, two product types, and two loan status categories (5 x 3 x 3 x 2 x 2 = 180). Twenty-one of these cohorts were chosen, and their characteristics varied systematically over the selected characteristics. Credit loss distributions were estimated for each of these cohorts and for each of the four model types. In general, the Merton model and the state-transition model produced similar results, while the panel data approach produced very high EC estimates relative to the other models, and the FGDM approach produced very low estimates of EC.

In general, the analysis from this study concludes that shortcomings in the panel data and FGDM models render them less than "best practice," calling their EC results into question.

In particular, the panel data approach necessarily assumes that the "true" underlying loss distribution for the portfolio remains constant (stable) throughout the entire history of the database—an assumption that does not comport either with common sense or with other empirical studies in other lending businesses, such as commercial lending. The FGDM model, on the other hand, tends to use estimates of default correlation that are either educated "guesses" or estimated by particular applications of the panel data approach—thus subjecting the FGDM model to the same criticism associated with the panel data approach.

The remaining two models are much more satisfying analytically, and they are becoming much more widely used by practitioners, having established themselves as current "best practice" processes. The relative downside of the Merton model, however, is that the analyst still must independently estimate the obligor-asset-value correlations, and these are notoriously difficult to estimate.

The state-transition model, however, can employ an estimated transition-probability matrix without needing to estimate explicit correlations (the actual correlations are embedded within the transition matrix). These matrices, moreover, can be based on all of the historical information—obligor characteristics such as FICO, loan characteristics such as loan type and age, and so forth—associated with each loan. Furthermore, the model can employ assumptions regarding future probabilistic paths of key macro variables such as interest rates and housing prices on a state-by-state or MSA-by-MSA basis. For this reason, the state-transition models, as a class, are the most "complete" of the models examined.

Focusing on these two classes of models—the Merton models and the state-transition models—the results, as applied to the LoanPerformance databases, suggest that EC for credit risk is in the range of *less than 1%*, expressed as a percentage of the underlying loan balances, for the portfolio as a whole. Different percentage capital allocations would apply to different cohorts, depending on FICO score, LTV, and so forth. Thus, these best-practice estimates of capital for credit risk are considerably below the current regulatory requirement and, indeed, are below the planned Basel requirements for capital for mortgage credit risk (that is, capital exclusive of capital for interest rate risk or capital for operating risk).

A second empirical experiment involved a more detailed analysis on a randomly drawn sample of approximately 108,000 loans from the LoanPerformance universe, which represented the market of active loans. The aim of the second analysis was to help parameterize the Merton model, using the EC results from the LoanPerformance model (which we consider to be the best-practice model among those analyzed). Regulatory agencies have decided to use a Merton model in calibrating future Basel capital requirements for mortgage credit risk, and the modeling staff of Basel is seeking help in choosing the "best" obligor-asset-value correlations to be used in the regulatory version of the Merton model.

The study suggests a range of correlations that are below 4%—assuming a five-year horizon in a Merton model, in which the bank inputs an estimated five-year PD for each cohort of the portfolio. Additional findings are that these asset-value correlations *decline* as the PD of a cohort rises, and the simulated LGDs rise as PD increases. While such information is of little use to the practitioner using a state-transition model, it should assist the users of Merton models (for example, Basel) and also provide some basis for comparing the results of state-transition models with the results of Merton models.

Note

1. SVA is analytically related to RAROC. SVA = revenues - expenses - expected losses - m*EC, where m is the weighted average cost of capital (at the desired soundness level). RAROC - [revenues - expenses - expected losses] / [economic capital]. In other words, the bank maximizes SVA when it invests in all business lines that yield RAROCs greater than the targeted rate of return.

Modeling Systematic Consumer Credit Risk: Basel II and Reality

By Daniel Rösch and Harald Scheule

he Basel Committee on Banking Supervision in April 2003 issued its third proposal for a revision of the standards for banks' capital requirements.[1] A significant part is devoted to the evaluation of credit risk in retail loan portfolios. Two important input parameters are default probabilities and correlations.

For the internal ratings-based approach, the capital requirement is calculated as the product of exposure at default (EAD), loss given default (LGD), and conditional default probability (CDP). The CDP can be interpreted as a "very bad case" default probability. It depends on the unconditional probability of default (PD) and the asset correlation (k).

$$\text{Capital Requirement} =$$

$$\text{EAD} \times \text{LGD} \times \Phi \left[\frac{1}{\sqrt{1-k}} \left(\overbrace{\Phi^{-1}(PD)}^{\text{unsystematic component}} + \overbrace{\sqrt{k}\Phi(0,999)}^{\text{systematic component}} \right) \right]$$
$$\underbrace{\qquad\qquad\qquad\qquad\qquad\qquad\qquad}_{\text{CPD}}$$

where $\phi(.)$ denotes the cumulative standard normal distribution function and $\phi^{-1}(.)$ its inverse.

The model assumes that a default event happens if the value of a borrower's assets falls short of the value of debt.[2] The asset returns are driven by a systematic and an unsystematic risk component. The weight of the systematic risk driver is given by √k. It describes the impact of common risk sources on asset returns. Thus, the correlation of the asset values of two borrowers is an indicator for the degree of co-movements. Default correlations can be analytically derived from the asset correlations.

This capital requirement formula is based on a value-at-risk (VaR) approach. It is assumed that the value of the common risk factor is more or equally adverse than 99.9% of all possible outcomes. Thus, asset returns are jointly driven downward and default probabilities upward, leading to capital charges that seek to cover losses caused by this adverse environment.

While banks are permitted to provide their own estimates for default probabilities, the correlations are prescribed by the Basel Committee due to limited empirical evidence on their magnitude. Figure 1 shows that asset correlations specified by the Basel Committee depend on the default probability and exposure class:

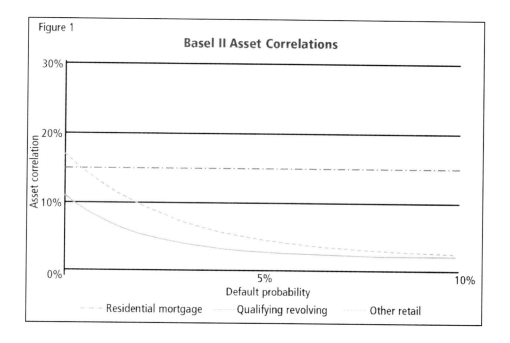

Figure 1

Basel II Asset Correlations

- - - Residential mortgage   ——— Qualifying revolving   ······ Other retail

- 15% for residential mortgage exposures.
- Depending on the PD, 2% to 11% for qualifying revolving exposures (such as credit card loans).
- Depending on the PD, 2% to 17% for other retail exposures.

If time series of default observations are available, asset correlations can also be empirically estimated.[3] Therefore, this article uses the annual delinquency rates filed by 400 representative U.S. banks in the period from 1984 to 2002. We assume that the delinquency rate is a good approximation of the default rate for a given year. The delinquency rates are filed by the American Bankers Association[4] and are published separately for the categories shown in Figure 2.

In addition, we extend the data by U.S. macroeconomic risk factors obtained from the Organization for Economic Cooperation and Development.[5] They serve as proxies for the business cycle and cover the following areas:

- Demand and output.
- Wages, costs, unemployment, and inflation.
- Supply-side data.
- Savings.
- Fiscal balances and public indebtedness.
- Interest and exchange rates.
- External trade and payments.
- Miscellaneous.

Figure 2		
Loan Categories by Basel II:		
Retail Exposure Classes		
Residential Mortgage	**Qualifying Revolving**	**Other Retail**
Home equity and second mortgage	Bank card	Automobile, direct
	Home equity lines of credit	Automobile, indirect
	Revolving credit (noncard)	Education
		Marine financing
		Mobile home
		Property improvement
		Personal, unsecured
		Recreational vehicle

As is common in econometrics, changes of macroeconomic variables are taken as risk factors, where appropriate, and all risk factors are lagged by one year. The risk factors used in the analysis are as follows:

- Current account balance in terms of GDP.
- Average real wage index.
- Change in consumer prices.
- Change in government consumption.
- Change in import prices.
- Change in unit labor costs.
- Lending interest rate.
- Change in exports of goods and services.
- Deposit interest rate.
- Gross national savings in terms of investments.
- Unemployment rate.
- Real effective exchange rate.

As a first step, we assume that the default probabilities are constant over time (through-the-cycle rating). In a second step, we assume that the default probabilities change during a business cycle and thus can be explained by observable macroeconomic risk drivers (point-in-time rating). As a matter of fact, the presented risk factors represent the respective point in time of the business cycle and are not necessarily responsible for the default probabilities themselves. Figure 3 shows the realized and estimated de-

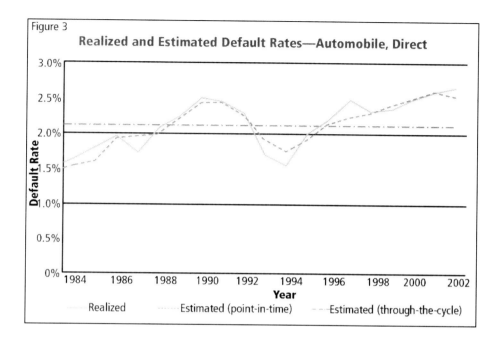

Figure 3

Realized and Estimated Default Rates—Automobile, Direct

Realized · · · · Estimated (point-in-time) – – Estimated (through-the-cycle)

fault rates of the exposure category "automobile, direct" for the two rating approaches.

We tested the economic plausibility of all macroeconomic variables—for example, that an increase of GDP leads to a lower default rate in the next year. Figure 4 shows the estimated average default rates and asset correlations for the two ratings systems.

In a through-the-cycle rating, any cyclical pattern is attributed to the asset correlations, while a considerable part of the correlations in a point-in-time rating can be explained by macroeconomic risk factors. For example, the estimated asset correlation of "automobile, direct" loans decreases from 0.42% to 0.09% when macroeconomic variables are included in the model. As a matter of fact, asset correlations depend on the point-in-time calibration of default probabilities. Thus, correlations and default probabilities should always be estimated simultaneously. Note that the length of the observation period is critical to the validity of the estimates, so banks missing a sufficient data history could use the estimates presented in Figure 4 as temporary input for their internal portfolio models.

In addition, the empirically estimated asset correlations are a lot smaller than the ones proposed by the Basel Committee. They also differ within the residential mortgage, qualifying revolving, and other retail exposure classes. A dependency between the default rates and the asset correlations cannot be observed. However, the conservative assumptions of asset correlations by the Basel Committee might still be justifiable since we did not take maturity adjustments or estimation and model risks into account. Nevertheless, a future adjustment of the regulatory asset correlations could be based on empirical values.

Figure 4
**Estimated Average Default Rates and Asset Correlations
in %, 1984-2002**

Loan Category	Average Default Rate	Asset Correlation Through the Cycle	Asset Correlation Point in Time
Home equity and second mortgage	1.67	0.42	0.29
Bank card	3.08	0.66	0.36
Home equity lines of credit	0.79	0.27	0.21
Revolving credit (noncard)	2.60	1.42	0.64
Automobile, direct	**2.11**	**0.42**	**0.09**
Automobile, indirect	2.50	0.49	0.21
Education	8.93	1.55	0.98
Marine financing	0.59	0.59	0.08
Mobile home	4.21	1.67	0.35
Personal, unsecured	3.40	0.27	0.08
Property improvement	2.15	0.26	0.11
Recreational vehicle	2.18	0.47	0.25

Notes

1. See Basel Committee on Banking Supervision, New Basel Capital Accord, Third Consultative Document, April 2003.
2. For details on the model, see M.B. Gordy, "A Risk-Factor Model Foundation for Ratings-Based Bank Capital Rules," *Journal of Financial Intermediation* 12, 2003; and C.C. Finger, "The One-Factor CreditMetrics Model in the New Basel Capital Accord," *RiskMetrics Journal* 2, no. 1, 2001.
3. For details on the estimation of asset correlations, see D. Rösch and H. Scheule, "Forecasting Retail Portfolio Credit Risk," *Journal of Risk Finance* 5, no. 2, 2004.
4. See http://www.aba.com.
5. See http://www.oecd.org.

Portfolio Management and RAROC

he new tools for estimating economic capital provide a basis for adjusting returns to incorporate risk in the form of capital, thus providing a key metric to manage credit portfolios. Banks no longer have to settle for balance sheets populated by credits that reflected their marketing, industry, or geographic specializations.

For the last 15 years, many banks have developed a philosophy of origination for the purposes of distribution, recognizing that often the loan product, with its limited upside potential, could be viewed as a loss leader with respect to more profitable fees for service products. Economic capital considerations can be viewed as a driving force in shaping loan portfolios through sales in the secondary market, syndication, and hedging through credit default swaps.

The article "Managing Credit Portfolios by Maximizing Risk-Adjusted Returns," by Charles Smithson and Gregory Hayt, describes the new paradigm for managing bank credits. Behaving like an asset manager, the bank must maximize the risk-adjusted return to the loan portfolio by actively buying and selling credit exposures, where possible, and otherwise managing new business and renewals of existing facilities.

This leads immediately to the realization that the principles of Modern Portfolio Theory (MPT)—which have proved so successful in the management of equity portfolios—must be applied to credit portfolios. To evaluate risk and returns, one cannot rely on probability distributions as being normally distributed or symmetric. For a loan portfolio, the emphasis is on extreme outcomes—the "tail" event—to determine economic capital, and portfolio models need to be developed.

"Retail Portfolio Optimization," by Joseph Breeden, presents a brief review of how to measure risk-adjusted returns in the context of MPT. Most retail products have high degrees of correlation, making it difficult to construct well-diversified retail portfolios. For retail portfolios, it is important to note that management decisions regarding marketing or product characteristics can distort the historical measures of profit volatility and correlations among retail products. Therefore, emphasis should be on future losses based on macroeconomic scenarios. Trade-offs of profitability versus profit volatility can be explored using simpler approaches compared to more complicated optimization models.

"Managing Corporate Credit Risk: Catalytic Effects of Basel II," by John McQuown, argues that, with Basel II's emphasis on capital, banks need to manage their capital more efficiently by using new credit risk technology. The analysis of diversification in loan portfolios is of paramount importance, as are accurate measures of default likelihood and loss severity.

At the same time, banks must make substantial investments in improving data collection and risk measurement systems. With regulators' increased emphasis on validation and compliance, banks have recently devoted significant resources to improving their underlying data systems. The author's prediction of the importance of secondary markets for loans has been realized with the attendant emphasis on mark-to-market measures.

"RAROC: A Tool for Factoring Risk into Investment, Pricing, and Compensation," by Rocky Ieraci, provides cautionary advice for using the results of RAROC models. Different inputs to RAROC models can be selected, depending on the application of the models. Rating philosophies and horizons can vary, depending on the line of business. The evaluation of relationship profitability for middle-market customers will incorporate different criteria and also longer time periods than what may be used for large corporate customers, who may occasionally offer bond underwriting and short-term trading opportunities. It is always important not to use quantitative tools blindly.

"Designing and Validating Your RAROC Framework," by Robert Duran, Yan An, and Robert Mark, continues in the same vein as the prior article with respect to not only validating the inputs to RAROC models but also implementing the model. By evaluating the sensitivity of inputs to RAROC results, one can better focus on improving data quality and model assumptions. In some instances, more careful examination of losses in the tail of the distribution is appropriate, while other risks such as market, operational, and reputational are often overlooked. Most importantly, qualitative assessments of PDs and LGDs should be employed in addition to their historical measures, and constant attention should be given to whether the quantitative assessments make sense.

Given the degree of conservatism regulators now employ in validating the risk parameters used in regulatory capital, as well as the increases in the amounts of regulatory capital now required, the question arises as to the role of economic capital, loan portfolio management, and RAROC today. Basel III's regulatory capital also incorporates liquidity requirements, leverage (which is a non-risk-based measure), and stress testing.

While some banks are continuing to use their economic capital models to drive portfolio and transaction decisions, others are substantially more focused on the impact on regulatory capital. A movement is now beginning to view portfolio management as a constrained optimization problem. In other words, banks are asking how they can maximize the economic risk-adjusted return on their portfolios in the face of numerous and sometimes conflicting regulatory constraints.

Managing Credit Portfolios by Maximizing Risk-Adjusted Return

BY CHARLES W. SMITHSON AND GREGORY HAYT

he lending function is undergoing critical review at all financial institutions, and many institutions are in the process of changing the way in which the credit portfolio is managed. Visible evidence of the change is found in the rapid growth in secondary loan trading, credit derivatives, and loan securitization.

Less obvious—but far more important—is the fact that banks are abandoning the traditional transaction-by-transaction "originate and hold" approach, in favor of the "efficient portfolio" approach of an investor.

Forces Leading to the Changes

Market realities are the primary reason for the changes. Banks have experienced declining margins on loans, due to disintermediation caused both by nonbank competitors and by changes in the structure of the markets. Figure 1 tracks the spreads to Libor for A-rated and BBB-rated U.S. borrowers. Despite the uptick in spreads during 1998 and 1999, the trend in spreads has been steadily downward. Consequently, banks have found it increasingly difficult to earn an economic return on, for example, high-grade corporate loans.

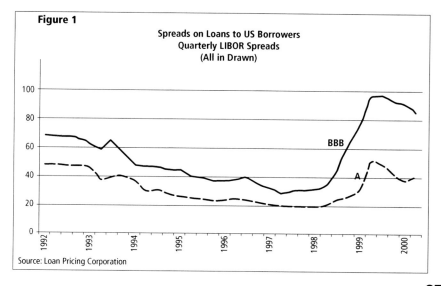

Figure 1

Spreads on Loans to US Borrowers
Quarterly LIBOR Spreads
(All in Drawn)

Source: Loan Pricing Corporation

Bank supervisors have also been pressuring banks for changes in their loan portfolio management practices. The 1988 Capital Accord represented the first step toward risk-based capital adequacy requirements; however, the "blunt instrument" nature of the 1988 Accord gave banks an incentive to engage in "regulatory arbitrage," that is, using credit derivatives and loan securitization to decrease the percentage of the credit extended to high-credit-quality obligors (which attract too much regulatory capital).

In response, the Basel Committee on Banking Supervision (comprised of national supervisors from the U.S. and 11 other countries) opened a discussion about revising the Accord. Regardless of whether the Basel Committee proposes a new set of rules wherein regulatory capital is determined by the credit rating of the obligors or permits regulatory capital to be determined by the bank's "credit portfolio model," the result will be more focus on credit portfolio management by the banks.

Banks as 'Investors' in Loans

As Figure 2 illustrates, investors are increasingly displacing banks as the final holders of loans. These new investors—insurance companies, hedge funds, and mutual funds—look at bank loans as an asset class. Consequently, banks must manage their lending activity as objective investors and adopt a risk-adjusted return approach to the loan portfolio (and the loan "business").

Moreover, the bank must be able to perform a rigorous analysis of the economics of originating, trading, and investing in loans. As investors in loans, banks must earn a sufficiently high economic return on the capital that supports the loan portfolio; if not, the bank should shift the capital to some other business. In addition to managing quantitative aspects, banks also face major organizational challenges in moving to this more ac-

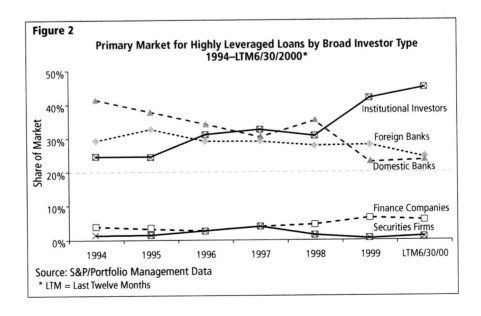

Figure 2

Primary Market for Highly Leveraged Loans by Broad Investor Type 1994–LTM6/30/2000*

Source: S&P/Portfolio Management Data
* LTM = Last Twelve Months

tive approach. For example, the active approach will affect the traditional relationship between banks and their corporate borrowers.

Applying Successful Equity Portfolio Techniques to Loan Portfolios

The new market realities mean that the "credit function" must transform into a "loan portfolio management function." Behaving like an asset manager, the bank must maximize the risk-adjusted return to the loan portfolio by actively buying and selling credit exposures where possible, and otherwise managing new business and renewals of existing facilities. This leads immediately to the realization that the principles of Modern Portfolio Theory (MPT)—which have proved so successful in the management of equity portfolios—must be applied to credit portfolios.

The central message of MPT is that, by recognizing the effects of correlation, the investor can increase the expected return for the portfolio, without increasing the riskiness of the portfolio.

To see this, suppose that two assets are available to the investor. As illustrated in Figure 3, Asset A has a lower expected return than Asset B; but Asset A also is less risky than Asset B. (Risk is measured by the standard deviation of the returns. An asset whose return distribution is wider—that is, more likelihood of very high or very low returns—is more risky.)

Now suppose that the investor combines the two assets into a portfolio. The expected return for the portfolio is simple: It is the weighted average of the expected returns of Asset A and Asset B. The riskiness of the portfolio is, however, more complex. It depends on the riskiness of Asset A and the riskiness of Asset B, but it also depends on the correlation of the returns for Assets A and B—that is, the degree to which Assets A and B move in unison or oppositely.

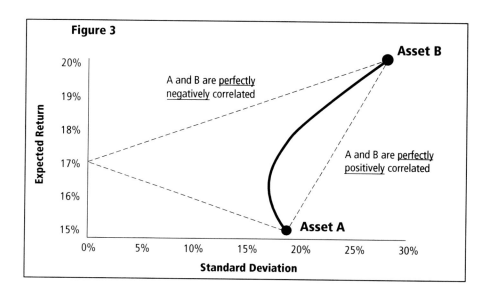

Figure 3

The dotted line in Figure 3 illustrates one extreme: If Assets A and B were perfectly positively correlated—in other words, if they moved in lockstep—there is no advantage to combining the assets into a portfolio, because the risk of the portfolio is simply the weighted risk of the two assets. The dashed line in Figure 3 illustrates the other extreme: If Assets A and B were perfectly negatively correlated—that is, if the movement of one counteracted the movement of the other—there is a portfolio (a combination of Assets A and B) that would have no risk but would have an expected return that is higher than the risk-free return.

Either of these extremes is unlikely. The normal relation between assets is that they are less than perfectly positively correlated. Such a situation is illustrated by the solid line in Figure 3. By combining the assets in the portfolio, the investor ends up with a risk that is lower than the weighted average of the risks of the two assets.

The implication of this is dramatic. By applying the tenants of MPT, an investor can increase expected return, without increasing risk. Not surprisingly, MPT-based investing has come to dominate equity investment over the past 40 years.

The Challenges in Applying MPT to Loan Portfolios

Applying MPT to portfolios of credit assets is not as simple as it might first seem. Despite its intuitive appeal, MPT is built on the critical assumption that the security returns are jointly normally distributed.

As it turns out, when they are examined empirically, equity returns do not precisely fit normal distributions. This is illustrated for IBM in Figure 4. However, equity returns are at least symmetric, so the techniques of MPT are generally employed without modifications. However, bank loan returns—particularly viewed on a hold-to-maturity basis—are neither normally distributed nor symmetric. Loans have strong option-like characteristics. As illustrated in Figure 4, the limited upside and potential 100% loss due to defaults results in a highly skewed loss distribution. Consequently, we cannot directly apply the mean/variance-based techniques of MPT to portfolios of loans.

Implementation of a MPT-based approach to loan portfolio management is further complicated by data limitations. To put loan data into a portfolio system, it would be necessary to have data on default and credit migration probabilities and the percentage loss in the event of default—not to mention data on the volatilities and correlations between defaults or downgrades for individual obligors.

Moreover, loan portfolio management requires more than a mean/variance view of the world. For a loan portfolio, the emphasis is on extreme outcomes—the "tail" event—to determine economic capital and credit rating. And the loan portfolio manager must deal with complex business relationships with borrowers.

Finally, it appears that diversification "works differently" for loans. The available empirical evidence suggests some good news and some bad news. The bad news is that, in comparison to portfolios of equities, portfolios of credit assets would have to be larger to achieve the full effect of diversification. The good news is that the potential diversification effect is larger for credit portfolios than for equity portfolios.

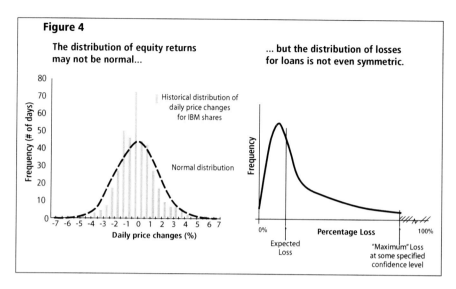

Figure 4

The distribution of equity returns may not be normal...

... but the distribution of losses for loans is not even symmetric.

The Question Is Capital

In contrast to equity portfolio managers who focus on risk-adjusted return measures (for example, the Sharpe ratio), banks tend to focus on measures of risk-adjusted return to capital (RAROC measures). The problem is in determining the amount of capital necessary to support a loan portfolio.

Since banks hold capital to provide a cushion against unexpected losses, the amount of capital a bank needs is a function of the riskiness of the bank's portfolio. In the context of the distribution of credit losses illustrated in Figure 4, the bank's reserves are determined by the expected loss for the portfolio. Unexpected loss is a measure of the volatility of actual losses around their expected value. For capital purposes, banks typically specify a multiple of unexpected loss such that the probability of losses exceeding capital is extremely remote—for example, 5 to 15 basis points. This point is identified as the "maximum" loss in Figure 4, where maximum is in quotes to emphasize that there is a small probability of exceeding this amount.

References

Basel Committee on Banking Supervision, 1988, "International Convergence of Capital Measurement and Capital Standards," July.

Basel Committee on Banking Supervision, 1999, "A New Capital Adequacy Framework," Consultative Paper, June.

Federal Reserve System Task Force on Internal Credit Risk Models, 1998, "Credit Risk Models at Major U.S/ Banking Institutions: Current State of the Art and Implications for Assessment of Capital Adequacy," May.

Merton, Robert C., 1974, "On the Pricing of Corporate Debt: The Risk Structure of Interest Rates," *Journal of Finance* 29(2).

Office of the Comptroller of the Currency, 1998, "Loan Portfolio Management," *Comptroller's Handbook*, April.

Retail Portfolio Optimization

By Joseph L. Breeden

Despite a 54-year history, modern portfolio theory and the benefits of diversification still have a ways to go to be effective in many banking institutions. Besides data issues, failure to change old perceptions of loss and risk continues to hamper institutions.

Optimization carries many different connotations throughout a banking institution, but portfolio optimization focuses on strategic questions around how to obtain the best possible performance for the organization. Although the results from portfolio optimization impact many aspects of the organization, we can summarize the goal in one question:

> What is the ideal blend of products to maximize profit while minimizing capital requirements and profit volatility?

When considering the matrix of possible products offered to each consumer segment, the goal is to make the proper trade-off between risk and reward. The most common mistake in retail lending is to equate loss rate with risk. Loss rates are not a measure of risk. They are one component of reward. Risk refers to the uncertainty in being able to obtain the expected reward.

So why do we care about volatility? Why not just maximize return? The answer is that companies are valued both on their historical rate of return and the certainty of those returns. Many studies indicate that the market places a higher value on companies that demonstrate reliable returns over time (low volatility) than those with volatile returns. One study of bank stock performance showed that a one-standard-deviation increase in volatility of corporate profits corresponded to a 32% lower stock price.[1]

Because the ultimate goal of any publicly traded company should be to maximize its market value, decreasing the volatility of profits is the often-overlooked aspect of growing value.

Modern Portfolio Theory

Harry Markowitz initiated modern portfolio theory with his landmark paper in 1952. The question was essentially the same as stated above. How does one choose the optimal investment blend across a set of different opportunities?

His insight was that the optimal portfolio is one that maximizes return while simultaneously minimizing the volatility of returns. The ratio of return over volatility is referred to as the *Sharpe ratio*. For a set of investment opportunities,

$$S_i = \frac{r_i - r_f}{\sigma_i}$$

where S_i is the ith Sharpe ratio for the ith investment opportunity, r_i is the expected return, σi is the expected volatility, and r_f is the risk-free rate of return, such as from a U.S. government bond. In retail lending: 1) return would be the expected margin for the loan or pool of loans, 2) the portfolio's hurdle rate should be substituted for the risk-free rate, and 3) the volatility is the uncertainty in obtaining the anticipated margin.

The answer so far would be quite simple, but Markowitz also recognized the importance of the correlation between investment opportunities and included this in his solution. In retail lending, it would not be sufficient to determine that five mid-tier credit card segments all had the highest profit-volatility ratio, because they are likely to move in unison relative to the economy. Placing all the portfolio's growth in those five segments would not be optimal because it does not confer any *diversification benefit.*

The idea behind a diversification benefit is that the less correlation there is between investments, the lower the overall volatility of the portfolio. If two products provided equal returns but were highly anti-correlated,[2] the best answer would be to invest in both equally. The average return would be unchanged, but the net volatility would be much lower.

Unfortunately, anti-correlated products rarely exist in retail lending. The retail book in total might be anti-correlated to other bank products and services, but for now let's focus our discussion on creating the optimal blend within the retail book. Within retail, the best we can usually hope for is to identify uncorrelated products so that we can avoid amplifying the volatility by being concentrated in correlated products.

Figure 1 shows three retail loan portfolios through a typical economic cycle. In general, all products will be affected by the economy, but with differing lags and severity. When comparing across products, the result is that some products (mortgage) may look less correlated to the rest (auto and card).

Markowitz provided a simple solution to this optimization problem. Subsequent work incorporated the notion of business constraints so that more realistic solutions can be derived. Many commercial packages are available to compute the ideal portfolio blend using Markowitz's theory, as long as the user provides the expected profit and volatility for each instrument and covariance between instruments. More on this issue later.

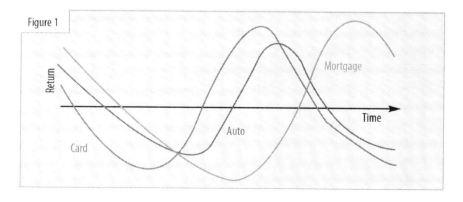

Figure 1

The efficient frontier. One of the most interesting results of Markowitz's work was the concept of the efficient frontier (Figure 2). A large body of literature exists on this topic, but the simple answer is that there is no single solution to the problem Markowitz posed. Rather, a plot of the possible solutions in profit versus volatility shows a line capturing the optimal blend of the available instruments. The portfolio manager can set any point along the upper half of this line as a goal.

The reality is that the efficient frontier is never reached. Business constraints and estimation problems make this a theoretical ideal that one should constantly strive to achieve.

Predicting returns, volatility, and covariance. Almost all the literature around modern portfolio theory[3] focuses on its application to market-traded instruments, such as stocks and bonds. However, the reader might be surprised to learn that many research papers exist to explain why portfolio optimization is a bad idea.[4] If fact, this author's own experience with forecasting tradable instruments is that uniform weighting usually performed better in real life than the "optimal" solution from portfolio theory.

The difficulty comes from trying to estimate *expected* return, volatility, and covariance.[5] Predictive models of stock price movements are notoriously unstable: As soon as a given structure is widely known, it is traded away. Predicting returns is synonymous with being able to forecast the financial markets. Predicting volatility or covariance is no less challenging because those quantities are also tradable through options contracts and are therefore inherently unstable.

So why spend so much time on something that is unusable? The answer is that, as usual, retail is different. Retail loan consumers, for the most part, do not care what you might predict about their behavior. Consumers know that credit scores exist to predict their behavior, but they do not take financially unreasonable actions to defeat those scores. Consumer balance sheets are not tradable instruments, so retail loans do not have the same forecasting instabilities as stock portfolios. When a recession comes, retail loans will default with much higher forecast accuracy than anything obtainable in the stock market. The same holds true for volatility and covariance, as long as sufficient data exists to create the estimate.

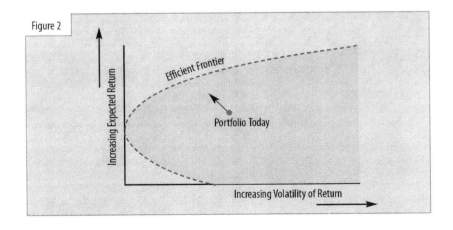

Figure 2

Increasing Expected Return

Efficient Frontier

Portfolio Today

Increasing Volatility of Return

Unique Retail Dynamics

Retail portfolios are predictable only if the unique dynamics of those portfolios are taken into consideration. Previous articles in *The RMA Journal* have explained how models of retail portfolios must consider loan maturation, credit risk, and environmental impacts.[6,7]

As long as those elements of the retail portfolio dynamics are incorporated in the model, the profit forecasts should be sufficiently accurate.

Unfortunately, many portfolio-optimization implementations use historical averages for the rate of return. Taking such a backward-looking view of the portfolio has led to some of the major portfolio failures of the last decade. If no reliable forecasts are available, portfolio optimization should not be attempted.

The largest uncertainty in a retail portfolio model will always be the future macroeconomic environment. Macroeconomic scenarios tend to provide a reasonable scenario for the first 12 months. Beyond that, a relaxation to historical averages is most appropriate (Figure 3).

For purposes of portfolio optimization, the most important feature of any macroeconomic scenario is that the *same* scenario must be used for all product and segment forecasts.

Correctly estimating volatility and covariance. The profit volatility of product segments and the covariance between them are challenging to measure but only because practitioners do not usually think of it correctly. Remember that we are trying to estimate the *expected future* volatility. Taking the historical profitability time-series and computing the volatility does not correctly reflect future volatility because of the impact of marketing.

Consider an auto loan portfolio that management decides to grow dramatically. In one year, the portfolio grows 30%. Because of the maturation process surrounding loan delinquency, we expect the loss rate to fall and the profitability to rise for the portfolio during this year and into the next. However, within 18 months and continuing another one to two years, loss rates will rise dramatically, simply because those loans are reaching peak delinquency. About three years after booking, we expect the impact of that program to be disappearing and loss rates to be stabilizing.

All of this volatility is artificial and has nothing to do with our expected future volatility for the current portfolio. Volatility derived from macroeconomic cycles (reces-

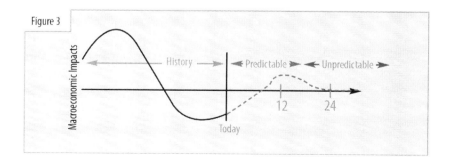

Figure 3

sions) is the kind of uncertainty we expect to see persist irrespective of marketing campaigns or management actions.

Now imagine that the manager of the mortgage portfolio, not to be outdone by auto, implemented a similar growth strategy, increasing the mortgage portfolio's receivables by 20% over the same period. This portfolio would go through a similar boom-bust cycle, again driven purely by the marketing plan. Computing the correlation between the profitability time series for those two products would show them to be highly correlated, when again this is just a management artifact that cannot be expected to recur.

Therefore, to compute the proper metrics for portfolio optimization, the historical profitability series must be normalized for the volume of bookings and the maturation process ("seasoning") of those originations. In the end, we are looking for the volatility and covariance derived primarily from the macroeconomic environment. However, there will always be unexplained noise in the historical data coming from day-to-day management actions on the portfolio. These are typically left in the volatility calculations because it is assumed that minor management impacts, both good and bad, will continue to occur in the future.

Economic capital. Although this article focuses on computing economic capital, it must be pointed out that everything discussed so far would still apply if the term losses were substituted for profit. The preceding discussion of how past marketing actions can distort expected profit volatility is equally true when computing expected future loss volatility. The best economic capital systems will normalize for artificially introduced volatility derived from past marketing plans.

Various definitions are possible for these metrics, but in general they can be viewed as follows:

$$RAROC = \frac{Return}{Economic\ Capital} = \frac{Revenue - Losses - Expenses}{Economic\ Capital}$$

$$RORAC = \frac{Revenue - Expenses}{Risk\text{-}Adjusted\ Capital}$$

$$Risk\text{-}adjusted\ Capital = \frac{1\ standard\ deviation\ of\ Earnings}{r_f}$$

$$Earnings = Revenue - Losses - Expenses$$

Alternative metrics. If the Sharpe ratio is so useful, why do most retail loan portfolios use something else? Actually, almost all retail portfolios today use intuition rather than optimization to guide portfolio management. Historically, this made sense because the available models and data were insufficient to support true optimization. Performance metrics have been computed by finance departments for decades, but these are almost universally retrospective measures of how things have performed in the past—not how they will perform in the future. As mentioned above, performing optimization based on historical average performance metrics is dangerous at best.

RAROC/RORAC. Some may consider it strange to describe RAROC (risk-adjusted return on capital) and RORAC (return on risk-adjusted capital) as alternate metrics, since collectively they are probably the most popular metrics in use. Because economic capital is so often used as the "volatility" of the portfolio, both of these metrics could be viewed as approximations of the Sharpe ratio.

Both metrics can be used for portfolio optimization analogous to what has been described so far. The appropriate covariances would also need to be computed, but products exist for performing the optimization given the appropriate inputs.

Maximizing Profit

Optimizing the portfolio to maximize profit is an obvious approach and common at an intuitive level. EVA (economic value added) and SVA (shareholder value added) both fall into this category. They adjust for hurdle rates or the cost of capital, but they do not explicitly consider the profit/volatility trade-off.

$$EVA = Net\ Return\ after\ Taxes - Economic\ Capital\ ^*\ r_f$$
$$SVA = (Return\text{-}on\text{-}equity - r_f)^*\ Average\ Equity$$

Volume or loss rate. The most common approach performed on a daily basis is perhaps the worst. Too often, management objectives are stated in terms of maximizing portfolio growth or minimizing loss rate. Most of the famous portfolio failures of the last decade have occurred for exactly this reason. Growth without regard to losses or profitability can lead to disaster. Minimizing loss rate alone causes portfolio under-performance by failure to assume reasonable risks. In the best cases, different groups are given competing objectives and forced to negotiate toward the kind of risk-reward trade-off represented explicitly in the preceding discussion.

Optimizing without an optimizer. One can easily become immersed in technology when discussing portfolio optimization and forget that enormous gains can be achieved just by implementing part of the solution. A good first step is to compute true expected profitability and profit volatility for each product segment and make a plot. Figure 4 shows a hypothetical example, with one point for each product segment indi-

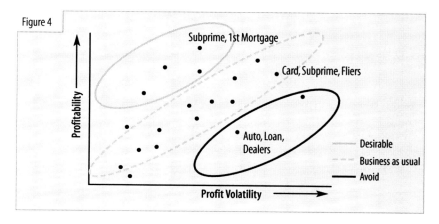

cating the expected profitability and profit volatility for each. A few points are labeled for discussion. Three main categories emerge when examining the plot.

1. In the upper left are product segments that produce abnormally high returns relative to the amount of volatility. Called the "desirable" category, such segments will be the most difficult to find.
2. Through the middle, in a roughly diagonal band, is the "business as usual" region. Most products are expected to be priced such that riskier products provide higher returns.
3. The lower right represents the "avoid" category. Product segments in this region are not producing a high enough expected return relative to the volatility they bring to the portfolio.

While examining this plot, remember that loss rate is not volatility. Subprime segments typically have higher loss rates, but often are less volatile than prime products relative to the macroeconomic cycle.

Optimizing the portfolio intuitively given the information in Figure 4 is relatively straightforward.

- Add more from the "desirable" category.
- Curtail originations in the "avoid" category.
- Maintain a blend across the "business as usual" category.
- Be wary of concentrations in a certain product or segment (shifting purely into cards or subprime).

With any optimization exercise, be aware that product segments will move in this diagram. Competitive pressures will cause changes in the profitability of product segments that can significantly alter the perspective. Whether managing intuitively or with an optimizer, reevaluate the answers quarterly or annually to make sure the portfolio is still steering along the correct path.

Get Started

Most organizations need to improve their techniques around portfolio optimization. The theory is well known. The issues are all around execution. Regardless of where your organization is today, consider the following points to make the next step:

- Collect time-series data at least at the product/segment/vintage level suitable for computing profitability over time for each campaign.
- Implement models incorporating known retail portfolio dynamics to predict profit and profit volatility across products and segments using consistent macroeconomic scenarios.
- Either perform judgmental optimization through comparative plots or employ optimization software incorporating the product segment covariances.
- Align management objectives with sound portfolio performance metrics.

Notes

1. G. Allayannis, B. Rountree, and J. Weston, "Earnings Volatility, Cash Flow Volatility, and Firm Value," a paper presented at the American Accounting Association's 2006 annual meeting, August 6-9, 2006, Washington, D.C.

2. When two products are correlated, it means that their ups and downs occur at the same time. If they are anti-correlated, it means that their returns usually move opposite to each other. Uncorrelated products have an apparently random and unpredictable relationship.

3. B. Scherer and D. Martin, *Introduction to Modern Portfolio Optimization*, Springer Press, 2005.

4. See, for example, R. Michaud, "The Markowitz Optimization Enigma: Is 'Optimized' Optimal?" *Financial Analysts Journal*, January 1989; and J. Jobson and B. Korkie, "Putting Markowitz Theory to Work," *Journal of Portfolio Management*, Summer 1981.

5. Covariance is similar in concept to correlation. It measures the cross-volatility between two instruments. If the correlation is positive, the covariance will be positive. A negative correlation coincides with a negative covariance. Correlation is essentially a normalized measure of covariance.

6. J. Breeden, "Retail Loan Portfolio Dynamics: Becoming a Better Vintner," *The RMA Journal*, September 2002.

7. J. Breeden, J., "Portfolio Forecasting Tools: What You Need to Know," *The RMA Journal*, October 2003.

Managing Corporate Credit Risk: Catalytic Effects of Basel II

By J. A. McQuown

Diversification control is a requirement of any economically sound bank. This article describes the management of corporate risk—not according to today's "best" practices but rather tomorrow's "next" practices.

The measurements that inform diversification decision-making beyond Basel II's required reporting ratios include 1) the coming of secondary markets in corporate credit; 2) the more general benefits of marking to market, whether or not it is disclosed; and 3) the key changes required of bank management to meet these challenges.

Basel II as a Springboard to 'Next' Practices

Although this may change, Basel II has thus far remained silent on perhaps the most important risk management issue facing banks today: diversification. Banks that focus on unsettled compliance requirements miss the immediate economic opportunity to better diversify their corporate credit portfolios.

Decision support technology makes it feasible to substantially improve the risk-return trade-off in corporate credit portfolios—that is, to substantially improve diversification. Capturing this opportunity also will prepare a bank to comply with the emergent Capital Accord, whatever that turns to be, because the fundamental debate surrounding the Accord is about how to put corporate banking on an economically sound footing, not simply how to prevent bank failures. Obviously, economically sound banks do not fail—Accord or no Accord!

Basel II compliance will prove costly, just given the data management requirements alone. However, decision support technology represents just a small incremental outlay beyond the minimums to reach compliance and allows banks also to reduce unexpected losses, improve profitability, increase risk-carrying capacity, and undertake more originations.

A Dearth of Diversification: The Core Problem with Corporate Credit Portfolios

Historically, banks have originated corporate credit exposures and then "passively" held them until the obligors either paid or defaulted. More recently, syndication and distribution businesses have emerged in corporate credit, creating the potential for banks to spread their originated risks. However, large concentrated retained portfolios are still more rule than the exception.

Relationship management remains the dominant strategy employed by virtually all banks. Incentive compensation is often proportional to the volume of credit originated, regardless of whether it is retained or distributed and whether obligors pay off or default. Rather than toppling the relationship management paradigm, however, diversification management is complementary to it.

Credit distress in banks can be traced predominantly to under-diversification in corporation credit portfolios. Diversification has the power to reduce risk without diminishing expected returns, thus affecting risk-adjusted profitability. Retained corporate exposures require "active" management through portfolio diversification.

Adoption of diversification management has been slow, even though it does not conflict with managing interpersonal and institutional relationships between lender and borrower. Lack of appropriate data and perspective, limitations of some existing tools, a prevalent buy-and-hold culture, and insufficient appreciation of the benefits of diversification have all hampered its use.

Moody's KMV has examined the corporate portfolios of 80-plus major banks and reached a clear and unambiguous conclusion: *The "expected return per unit of risk" (that is, the Sharpe ratio) of corporate credit portfolios retained by banks is seriously inferior to that delivered by other managers of corporate credit portfolios.* Corporate credit portfolios retained by banks exhibit Sharpe ratios of between 0.1 and 0.3. Non-originating asset managers of corporate credit often achieve Sharpe ratios of well over 0.5. Some serious-minded managers assemble corporate credit portfolios, from secondary markets, with Sharpe ratios of over 1.0.

The Cost of Not Diversifying

Many bankers argue that extending credit to major corporations is a "loss leader" and that the "relationship" only becomes acceptably profitable when noncredit services are included. However, it's unlikely that noncredit services can overcome the Sharpe ratio deficiency of portfolio concentrations. The economics of corporate credit, and therefore the relationship, are largely dictated by the consequences of "unexpected losses" that diversification could materially diminish. Beyond a doubt, improved diversification would materially reduce opportunity cost and correspondingly increase the profitability of all corporate credit relationships.

Interestingly, most banks will find themselves in compliance with the mandates of Basel II *while still suffering the opportunity cost of substantial under-diversification.* It is likely that Basel II will remain silent on diversification. It does not follow that these bankers should be content with the under-diversification opportunity cost they are asking their shareholders to carry.

Distributing concentrations improves diversification and more generally opens additional origination capacity. In one instance, a U.K. bank was able to triple its originations to large corporations without altering its capital base as a direct consequence of improved diversification. Diversification diminishes the economic pressure on capital; concurrently, diversification of assets improves the quality of bank-issued debt. Buying the originations of others expressly for diversification also increases banks' sensitivity to where the market is pricing risk.

Capturing the Benefits

Under-diversified portfolios (concentrations in too few names) lead to credit losses that are too large in relation to the scale of the portfolio. Concentrations increase the chances that a substantial fraction of a bank's capital can be consumed by unexpected losses. On the other hand, when a portfolio's Sharpe ratio is increased by a factor of three, which is often possible, its losses per portfolio-dollar could be diminished by a factor of three. The U.K. bank referred to earlier recently estimated that its benefits—in terms of net losses avoided—from active diversification management have exceeded its costs (that is, the expense of systems, personnel, hedging, and transacting) by a factor of six.

Two complementary sets of actions are required to capture the benefits of diversification. First, concentrations require thinning: The largest exposures need to be sold down or hedged (by buying "protection" through credit default swaps). Second, the proceeds from selling and hedging need to be reinvested in appropriate corporate credit acquired from secondary markets. Appropriate diversifying exposures are those with default probabilities that are comparatively uncorrelated with the thinned portfolio. The net result of these trades will leave the overall portfolio with approximately the same contribution to reported earnings per share and a higher Sharpe ratio after transactions costs are accounted.

However, the new Accord has not, so far at least, addressed the use of technology required by active portfolio management, or diversification management, per se. The banks themselves need to realize that the road to compliance is not necessarily the road to active portfolio management.

Critical Measurements: The State of the Art

The ability to accurately measure and frequently monitor the default risk in corporate obligors has taken a quantum jump since the early 1990s. As a result, the bulk of the conversation around Basel II has focused on which internal-ratings-based (IRB) default measurement models to implement. In short, what is feasible today in default measurement was unthinkable a decade ago.

Diversification requires the following critical risk-related measurements, all but one of which will likely be required by Basel II compliance:

- *Default probabilities.* Expected default frequencies (EDF) are available for corporates, both quoted and privately held.
- *Loss given default (LGD).* While bankers have not kept sufficiently detailed records of nonperforming exposures, workable ways to estimate LGD are emerging. The secondary-market price history of bonds traded shortly after default or bankruptcy announcements is very helpful, as is collateral quality.
- *Exposure at default (ED).* Here again, the historical record would be helpful. The available data suggests that bankers can do much better at detecting and limiting borrower access to lines of credit as default becomes increasingly imminent.
- *Unexpected loss (UL).* This is a new concept for many bankers. If an exposure has an expected loss, then that loss, given the reality of uncertainty, also has an unexpected component. UL can be well estimated, too.

■ *Default correlations.* Contrary to some early opinions, default correlations exist and can be measured well. However, it requires advanced technology that leverages the information contained in equity prices.

The only above risk-related measurement required by active diversification management that is not required by compliance is the final one: default correlations. These default correlations must be purchased, given that it is not economic for a single bank to estimate them.

The analytics required for regulatory capital attribution from Basel II also can be used to actively manage diversification. There is, however, one missing ingredient: Banks need to measure the spreads and fees that exposures earn, expressed not at their origination value but as ongoing market values. This means that originated spreads and fees need updating to the values the current market would command. The technology to achieve this is termed MTM—mark-to-market (or, more accurately, marked-to-model).

With today's state-of-the-art credit technology, these critical measurements can be made with sufficient precision such that the benefits of active portfolio management can be realized. Those bankers contemplating the imposition of Basel II's capital requirement will come to realize that the technology used in active portfolio management will play a critical role in literally managing the bank's capital. The choice of what to buy or sell in order to adjust capital depends on measuring the risk-return trade-offs of all trades contemplated. Therefore, the pressure that Basel II will inherently impose is to actually manage capital more efficiently, which means toward a higher Sharpe ratio. While the sufficiency of capital is certainly important, the efficient managing of capital provided by shareholders is paramount.

Beyond Compliance: Leveraging the Value of Data Gathering

While financial institutions have, for decades, spent princely sums on computing and data management systems, the expenditure has typically been in two areas:

1. Consumer banking, as reflected by consumer touch-point technologies such as call centers, websites, and ATM networks.
2. Product accounting and general-ledger systems to comply with regulation.

Notably, neither achievement provides the basis for risk analysis required to support economic decision-making. Credit decision-making largely remains an art form, divorced from analytics, because clean, historical time-series data does not yet exist. Demand for data to support decision making is emerging more from the requirements of active portfolio management than from Basel II reporting requirements.

Demand to record and maintain obligor risk ratings arose only in the past decade at most banks. Even today, few banks have systems in place to measure recovery rates from the collection of nonperforming obligors. Credit analysts have only recently had systems for recording their own assumptions and analyses that permit quantitative and qualitative reflection.

It follows that too few banks understand the real economics of the business of extending and investing in corporate credit. Critically, no single bank's individual experience can provide a statistically significant credit experiment on which to vet either default frequencies or recovery rates. Banks need to commingle their experiences (i.e., data) to reach sufficient sample densities.

Thus, banks are on the brink of substantial spending to upgrade their data management systems to comply with the risk management requirements of Basel II. But compliance data falls short of the requirements of diversification management and offers no return on investment. Diversification management will produce a material incremental return. In addition to more data, diversification management requires analytics and an appropriate organizational division of responsibility. But once the credit decision-making responsibilities are properly organized and analytically supported, the incremental cost to calculate capital ratios, as required by compliance, will be virtually negligible.

The Road Extends to Market-Based Valuations

It would be unfair to assess bankers' mastery of active portfolio management unfavorably in contrast with that of other asset managers. After all, credit has generally been the relatively ignored step-cousin of equity. The lack of accurate measures of default probabilities and recoveries and related correlations has surely contributed to credit's lesser status.

Over the past 25 years, energy expended on equity performance measurement has transformed the way equity portfolios are managed. Equity performance measurement was possible because historical price data from every equity market on the planet is abundant and inexpensive. In contrast, transactions prices of corporate credit exposures of all types are nearly nonexistent. One reason is that secondary-market transactions in corporate debt are so sparse, in part a circular consequence of the unavailability of prices on transactions that have occurred. Portfolios of corporate loans carried by banks only recently have begun to trade at all, but they remain about as price-opaque as bonds.

Bank corporate loan portfolios have not succumbed to the scrutiny wrought by the dictates of performance measurement. Part of the reason is the lack of transactions prices, and another part is the comparatively greater complexity of loans. Further, the culture of banking has not been market-value oriented. There are perhaps three most-cited reasons for this:

1. The MTM would reveal "unrealized" losses.
2. Markets do not exist for loans anyway.
3. The necessary data and technology are not available to "synthesize" MTM with sufficient accuracy.

While the first of these statements is probably true, the second and third are losing currency by the day. Today, bankers are awakening to the necessity of marking-to-market their retained portfolio of corporate exposures for the purpose of managing risk. Active portfolio management requires exposures be marked-to-market, regardless of whether or not the results are publicly disclosed.

MTM is a critical prerequisite of the decision-making process designed to improve diversification and therefore Sharpe ratios. Actually, MTM is a model that quantifies the dollar-value impact on a loan grown riskier without a compensatory increase in spread, and vice versa. Banks do recognize, of course, the extreme case: When credit quality deterioration leads to default, the loan is "revalued" to an estimate of its recovery value, and write-downs are taken.

The enormous middle ground between origination at or near par and default presents the opportunity to bring critical information to the decision processes. Monitoring, reserving, restructuring, hedging, or selling must all be based on estimates of market value, independent of what is publicly disclosed. At renewal, pricing and collateral requirements can be aligned with the current riskiness. MTM provides the basis for diversification management.

The most voluminous secondary market for corporate credit media is probably the corporate bond market, however thinly traded it remains. The secondary bank loan market has less trading volume. It appears, however, that the credit default swap (CDS) market is overtaking traded volumes in both bond and loan secondary markets. There is sufficient trading in these markets taken together to permit the evolution of a technology capable of quite accurate "modeled marks," answering the question: At what price (spread) would these exposures trade if they did trade? MTM can thereby provide the foundation on which diversification decision-making needs to rest.

MTM technology is conceptually simple. Whatever trading occurs in markets serves to put a value on a "unit" of default risk. The challenge is to estimate the number of "units" of default risk that exist in a given obligation. This can be accomplished by assessing bond market price data, CDS spread data, and syndicated loan spreads. The result is a mark on default risk of virtually all obligors' obligations that has been separated from both call (and other) options and interest rate risk.

Active portfolio managers, when they transact, do so at market values, not book values, and the analysis leading to these decisions requires market values. Accordingly, the most progressive bankers like these modeled marks and use them in three ways:

1. When a trade of a particular position is being considered, MTM provides a context for the negotiation.
2. The sum of MTMs across an entire portfolio produces a highly accurate picture of the total portfolio's market value.
3. When setting spreads on originated credit exposures that do not enter syndication, MTM technology can ensure that loans are appropriately priced.

To date, few if any banks are disclosing these marks to their shareholders, but that evolutionary shift is not far off.

Needless to say, widespread active diversification management of banks' corporate credit portfolios will require a marketplace where default risk, in many forms, can be bought and sold. A variety of historical impediments to the development of these secondary markets are falling by the wayside. Surely, one such impediment has been the invisibility of transaction prices. The Securities and Exchange Commission only recently required dealers to begin disclosing corporate bond transaction prices.

MTM technology has reached ample precision. As the practice of risk management matures, progressively more decision makers are becoming comfortable with the value that diversification management can add. The cultural distinction that separated default asset management at banks from other forms of asset management is melting away.

Arguably, the most important recent propellant has been the emergence of the CDS market, which is enjoying substantial growth as more obligors are traded and as a progressively wider array of institutions invest. For example, one major bank claims that it has used mostly derivative transactions to successfully hedge some 40% of its retained portfolios' default risk. Another large bank is routinely discussing in the public forum its growing success from active portfolio management.

Even middle-market loan portfolios are receiving more diversification attention. When it is not feasible to buy and sell these obligations one obligor at a time, portfolios, or fractions of portfolios, are beginning to be sold or swapped in bundles or baskets. In a recent example, a single swap transaction was engineered between two geographically dispersed banks' middle-market loan portfolios. The result? Both banks' portfolios became better diversified.

In fact, there are few remaining impediments to limit the extent of diversification that can be achieved. Before secondary markets, credit derivatives, and basket swaps emerged, the opportunities to improve diversification were limited. Yet, ironically, many banks have ignored the opportunity to diversify.

The Means to the End: The Role of Credit Risk Technology

Over the past 10-plus years, the advances from financial analysis, computers, data systems, and telecommunications have converged on the doorstep of corporate banking. Notably, tools—built around the critical measurements outlined above—are now available and can help banks fulfill the Basel II requirement of coherent "business use, compliance, and disclosure." Banks adopting a best-practices approach to IRB will reap rewards.

But the "next" practice will almost surely be active diversification management, and it will reap significantly greater rewards. In fact, extracting real value from IRB models will necessitate active diversification management, because that is where the critical buy-hold-sell decisions are made.

As the equity investment community inevitably takes note of these changes, banks employing next-generation practices will be rewarded with higher and less volatile share prices. Leading-edge institutions are today deploying the state-of-the-art risk management tools residing at the heart of this revolution. Midsized and even smaller banks will increasingly recognize that they, too, can capture the same economic benefits from improved measurement and active management of corporate default risk. More generally still, all financial institutions that manage portfolios of corporate credit risk stand to benefit economically from the recent advances in credit risk measurement and management technology. Credit risk technology is destined to transform the practice of managing portfolios of corporate credit risk.

When coupled with the emergence of more transparent and deeper secondary markets, particularly credit default swaps, the opportunity cost of under-diversification will be wrung out of the system. That is, the cumulative effect of progressively more portfolio managers maximizing their Sharpe ratios will be to eliminate price/quantity mismatches. In the process, interest rate risk and credit default risk will become fully decoupled, such that investors are able to invest independently in the two fundamental fixed-income risk sources.

Overall, the dynamic movement toward elimination of previously unrealized opportunity cost should materially reduce the composite cost of leverage for corporations, but by no means uniformly. Some corporations will pay more while others pay less. Surely, the Sharpe ratios of credit portfolios will rise well above what today's investors earn.

RAROC: A Tool for Factoring Risk into Investment, Pricing, and Compensation

By Rocky Ieraci

Banks need to find better ways to factor risk into their decision making, and they are turning to risk-adjusted return on capital (RAROC) models as part of the answer.

For over a decade, these models have been used by large banks to explore the balance of risk and reward, especially when lending to large corporations. Now they are fast becoming popular in smaller banks specializing in middle-market and small and medium-sized enterprise (SME) lending (Table 1).

By measuring the amount and cost of the risk capital associated with a bank transaction and comparing this to the bank's returns, RAROC helps banks make better decisions when approving, structuring, and pricing deals. It also helps them in assessing business-unit performance and risk-adjusting compensation.

The RAROC equation is simple in concept (see left side of Figure 1), but there are plenty of devils in the details. In particular, it is easy for inconsistencies to arise between what

Table 1	
Key Differences between Large Corporate and Middle Market/SME Lending	
Large Corporate	**Middle Market/SME**
Nonhomogeneous pools of obligors common	Homogeneous pools of obligors the norm
Large exposures	Smaller exposures
Portfolios weighted to low PD obligors	Sub-investment-grade obligors the norm
Specialized and often complex deals	Standard products and terms
Lengthy decision process attributable to size and nature of deals	Volume-oriented and highly automated decision tools
Fair amount of discretion allowed in pricing individual deals	Pricing matrix common base on product type and obligor rating
Credit risk dominant risk type	Operational risk significant

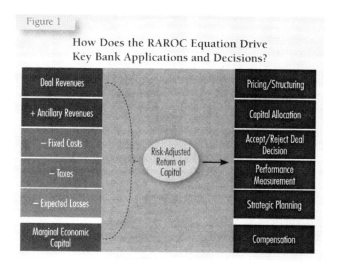

Figure 1

How Does the RAROC Equation Drive
Key Bank Applications and Decisions?

RAROC-based results are taken to mean by decision makers and what they actually mean, which is driven by the many inputs and assumptions that underlie the RAROC model.

Confusions creep in because RAROC is the culmination of the bank's various attempts to measure and analyze risks, costs, and revenues. As such, inputs must be drawn from all over the bank and are themselves often dependent on an underlying risk model; for example, economic capital usually depends on the bank's internal risk-rating system. For RAROC to be meaningful, all the inputs must be consistent with one another and with a clearly set goal for RAROC—for example, "a one-year forward assessment of risk-based profitability" or "risk-based profitability over the life of the deal."

For reasons we'll discover, RAROC results can be especially fragile when the bank uses them to compare the profitability of different lines of business and when there are turning points in the economic cycle. So banks should be particularly vigilant in the current period.

Banks must learn to ask, "Are our RAROC results measuring what we think they measure?" While the perfect RAROC model may prove elusive, banks should make sure that flaws are taken into account when making important decisions.

Let's look at some specific pitfalls when building RAROC models in areas ranging from capital allocation processes to monitoring how RAROC results are used.

How Do Capital Allocation and a Changing Risk Appetite Drive RAROC?

Economic capital models calculate the amount of risk capital the bank requires after taking into account various concentration costs and diversification benefits at the enterprise level. To support RAROC applications, the bank then has to allocate a portion of this firm-wide capital amount to each of its businesses, activities, and individual exposures.

This allocation process is fraught with difficulties. Unfortunately, a single "correct" allocation model does not exist and institutions must understand the implications of their modeling choices. For example, if a bank with a largely North American loan portfolio set up an international lending group to make loans in Brazil, the new business group might well attract massive capital benefits from risk diversification. These in turn will drive the new group's deal RAROCs up to startlingly high numbers. It is not uncommon to see RAROCs over 100% owing to diversification benefits attributed by capital models.

These hypothetical returns are really due to modeling inaccuracies and lack legitimacy from a more fundamental credit perspective. The new group should be working hard to differentiate between the risk-adjusted profitability of Brazilian borrowers, rather than getting a free ride from diversification benefits arising from the whole bank's portfolio composition.

Our point here is that banks should not *inadvertently* allow diversification benefits and other quirks of capital allocation to distort their assessment of business-unit performance. Their use of the numbers to make decisions should be conditioned by a deep understanding of RAROC drivers and by sound business intuition. Similarly, model developers make important choices, largely hidden to the users of RAROC results, about how the bank's risk appetite should drive capital allocations.

The classic example of this problem concerns how a portfolio of loans with a low probability of default but large exposure amounts (for example, lending to large corporations or financial institutions) compares with another portfolio that exhibits higher probabilities of default but smaller exposures (for example, SME loans).

As Figure 2 illustrates, the SME portfolio will look relatively risky if capital is allocated based on how much each exposure contributes to the loss distribution around the mean (that is, one standard deviation, or "unexpected loss"). By this measure, the SME portfolio's RAROC will look relatively low compared with the large corporate portfolio since the latter does not contribute significantly to the loss distribution in this region. (In reasonably normal

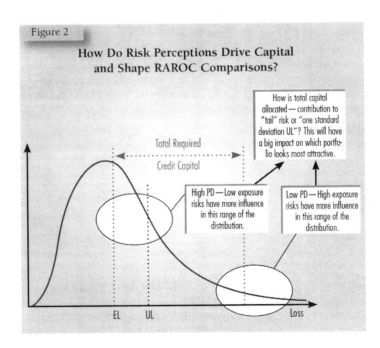

Figure 2

How Do Risk Perceptions Drive Capital and Shape RAROC Comparisons?

How is total capital allocated — contribution to "tail" risk or "one standard deviation UL"? This will have a big impact on which portfolio looks most attractive.

Total Required Credit Capital

High PD — Low exposure risks have more influence in this range of the distribution.

Low PD — High exposure risks have more influence in this range of the distribution.

EL   UL   Loss

times, large corporations are not expected to default.)

On the other hand, if the model allocates capital based on how much a portfolio contributes to severe downturn risk (tail risk), then the capital allocated to the large corporate portfolio will be much higher (and thus less capital will be allocated to the SME portfolio). This will, in turn, make the large corporate portfolio look relatively less attractive in RAROC terms compared to the SME portfolio.

How Should the Nature of the Bank's Business Drive Its RAROC Modeling?

It's easy for banks to fall into the trap of using a generic RAROC approach that does not reflect the risk profile of their various lending businesses. Take, for instance, the two problems of loan maturity and risk-type coverage.

Loan maturity is an issue because RAROC models with a one-year time horizon—often chosen because the bank's economic capital has been calculated using a one-year horizon—can be biased against longer-terms deals; for example, they underestimate the true profitability of a five-year loan compared with a one-year loan.

The problem arises because credit capital models, which account for the major portion of economic capital for lending exposures, often assign a term premium for longer-dated exposures in the first year of the deal. While longer-term deals are indeed "riskier" than shorter-term deals, the magnitude of this premium and the fairness of comparing the front-loaded first-year capital of a five-year deal to the capital of a one-year deal are problematic.

Furthermore, the longer-dated deal will attract less and less one-year capital as it matures (Figure 3). By the last year of the term, the one-year RAROC of a matured deal may look much greater than the RAROC of the one-year deal it was originally compared to!

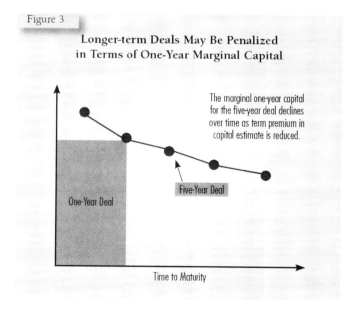

Figure 3

Longer-term Deals May Be Penalized in Terms of One-Year Marginal Capital

The marginal one-year capital for the five-year deal declines over time as term premium in capital estimate is reduced.

One-Year Deal

Five-Year Deal

Time to Maturity

The problem can be countered by calculating the whole-of-life risk of the loan, in addition to pure one-year measures (which are still important for certain deal-comparison purposes), or by using average one-year capital usage over the life of a deal. Alternatively, the bank can take account of the bias in a judgmental way when making decisions based on RAROC.

Risk-type coverage is another significant issue. In the ideal world, a RAROC model would take account of all the risk costs associated with a given deal, commonly defined as market, credit, operational, and business risk. In reality, bank RAROC models rarely cover all types of bank risk due to methodology or operational constraints, and some are driven entirely by credit risk.

How much this matters depends on how the bank is using RAROC. The focus on credit risk may be legitimate if the results are used mainly to compare the risk-adjusted profitability of lending transactions within a portfolio of large corporate loans.

Problems arise, however, when we consider other kinds of portfolios or make comparisons across business lines. For example, middle-market and SME lending may be largely model-based and automated with only limited underwriter oversight. Here, there is a considerable risk that something systematic will go wrong in the bank's decision making that is not accounted for in its credit risk calculations. This kind of risk usually is classed as an operational risk, and it will account for a larger percentage of total economic capital in an SME portfolio than in a portfolio of large corporate exposures.

Therefore, the bank needs to make some estimate of the operational risk associated with its approach; otherwise, it may overestimate business line profitability and under-price transactions for SME-like portfolios.

This example points to a more general lesson: Banks need to understand what drives their RAROC model in light of the model's application to a diverse set of portfolios. Incorporating the full picture of risk (credit, operational, and market) becomes important when assessing risk-adjusted returns at the consolidated bank level to ensure optimal allocation of the capital a bank needs to carry on its balance sheet.

Does Our Credit-Rating Approach Distort RAROC Results over the Economic Cycle?

The credit-rating philosophy that underpins a bank's estimates of credit risk capital can also drive RAROC in unexpected ways.

For example, some banks adopt a "through the cycle" approach to determining internal risk ratings and the probabilities of default associated with them. These banks' internal ratings reflect a long-term, cycle-neutral measure of borrower default risk. But this may not align with the bank's RAROC approach if the RAROC model adopts a one-year forward horizon.

Other inputs into the RAROC model will be in alignment, such as estimates of spread revenues plugged into the model. As the economy goes into a downturn, spread revenues will rise to reflect the general tightening in bank lending; at the same time, the bank's through-the-cycle risk estimates (and therefore marginal capital estimates) will not rise in line with present realities, owing to the bank's choice of rating philosophy (Figure 4).

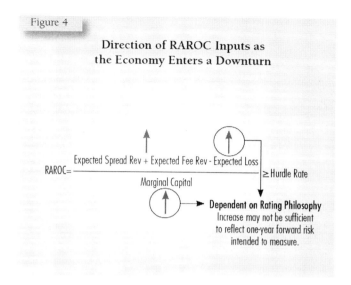

Figure 4

**Direction of RAROC Inputs as
the Economy Enters a Downturn**

$$RAROC = \frac{Expected\ Spread\ Rev + Expected\ Fee\ Rev - Expected\ Loss}{Marginal\ Capital} \geq Hurdle\ Rate$$

Dependent on Rating Philosophy
Increase may not be sufficient
to reflect one-year forward risk
intended to measure.

The result might be a model that underestimates RAROC during the early part of an expansionary period, but then overestimates RAROC as the economy goes into a downturn.

From a RAROC perspective, the loss-given-default estimates used in models of bank credit risk could also be problematic, because they usually reflect average losses for particular types of products, structures, and collateral over many years, rather than being a current estimate in line with a typical RAROC model's one-year forward time horizon.

Banks may not be keen to change their rating philosophies to make them consistent with RAROC calculations, but they can gauge the extent of the potential problem so that decision makers can take this into account. There is no one-size-fits-all solution to the challenges faced in aligning rating philosophies with the various uses of performance-measurement tools such as RAROC. Many banks are realizing that they may need more than one variation of the standard RAROC measure to properly assess their complex range of products and businesses.

Regulatory Capital and Risk-Adjusted Decision Making

Using regulatory capital as a substitute for economic capital in RAROC calculations is now widely recognized as poor practice because regulatory capital, particularly Basel I, is not a very accurate or sensitive risk measure. But banks can't simply ignore regulatory capital in their risk-adjusted decision making. Regulatory capital has an economic cost attached to it so long as the bank's regulatory capital requirements are higher than its economic capital requirements.

There are various ways to take the cost of regulatory capital into account. For example, to the extent that its regulatory capital requirement is greater than its economic capital requirement, a bank might allocate a portion of the gap back to each business line and product. Or the bank can insist that deals exceed a given hurdle in terms of *both* RAROC and return on regulatory capital.

The important thing is that the cost of supporting regulatory capital is recognized in some fashion when calculating or interpreting RAROC numbers.

Relationships Have a Value

At its best, banking is about building long-term relationships with customers across different product areas. However, the simplest approach to RAROC is to measure the RAROC of each transaction independently of its links to other bank business.

This is frustrating for bankers who can see that a specific deal is the gateway to a much larger transaction or a wider relationship, or who think that offering low-margin deals in one product area is a way to bring in profitable business. An example would be a company that wants a low-margin revolving loan today, but says it will need a large, higher-margin construction loan in a few months.

There are various ways to incorporate the value of relationships into RAROC analysis. One approach is to look at RAROC on a whole-relationship basis over a given period. Another is to factor some portion of the benefits of future business into the reported RAROC for the initial deal. For example, the bank might allow the RAROC for one deal to include a percentage of the profit from a future linked deal, after taking into account the lender's estimate of the probability that the deal will actually happen.

Of course, lenders may be tempted to overestimate the chance of future business to help push the RAROC of the initial deal over the bank's deal-acceptance hurdle rate. This issue can be resolved by tracking outcomes in terms of realized deals and profitable relationships and comparing them to the original estimates. The result might be tougher haircuts for particular lenders or for certain kinds of relationship business.

Monitoring Model Operations and Performing Outcomes Analysis

It is important for banks to monitor how RAROC results are produced and used at a day-to-day operational level. The bank can track how RAROC numbers are used in decision making (for example, the number of times a below-hurdle RAROC deal is approved). It also can look at the average RAROC by segment for new deals and watch for unexplained trends. If RAROC is used to decide whether to accept or reject a deal, the bank can compare initial RAROC estimates with current estimates using actual balances and updated risk information.

Banks also should periodically conduct data-integrity tests. For example, are the specified model inputs actually being used when calculating RAROC? And have the underlying systems been validated—for example, the bank's internal ratings system?

Back-testing deal-level RAROC isn't always practical, but we can ask whether the predicted profitability of segments and portfolios turns out to be broadly accurate (see, for example, Figure 5). This kind of analysis should not prompt the bank to make a simple reject-or-accept decision about the RAROC model. Instead, the results are diagnostic and should prompt investigation into what's driving any misalignments; the variables that are tested indirectly include expected income, expected loss, utilization, and planned capital usage.

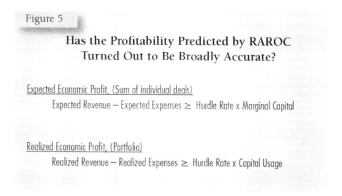

Figure 5

Has the Profitability Predicted by RAROC Turned Out to Be Broadly Accurate?

Expected Economic Profit, (Sum of individual deals)

Expected Revenue − Expected Expenses ≥ Hurdle Rate x Marginal Capital

Realized Economic Profit, (Portfolio)

Realized Revenue − Realized Expenses ≥ Hurdle Rate x Capital Usage

RAROC estimates also can be rerun using benchmark models to see if an independent model or methodology produces results similar to those generated by the bank's RAROC model, given the same inputs. Similarly, banks can benchmark their model via a consortium, whereby different banks run a sample of representative deals through their RAROC pricing model and share the anonymous results. The intent of these comparisons is not to accept or reject a bank's RAROC model, but rather to understand key differences and work continuously to refine the overall approach to risk methodologies.

Conclusion

Models of risk-adjusted return on capital can provide a great advantage to banks, but they are easy to get wrong. Too often these models are created by quantitative experts working at some distance from business lines and from the senior executives who will use the results.

RAROC needs to be approached carefully to ensure alignment between expectations about what its results mean and the model's inputs and assumptions—particularly with regard to how capital is calculated and allocated, the bank's rating philosophy, its risk appetite, and the nature of the bank's portfolios. For example, if banks simply apply generic RAROC models built for large corporate portfolios to calculate the RAROC of SME portfolios, they are particularly likely to make poor decisions.

There is no magic answer to some of the practical challenges encountered when implementing RAROC, so users of its results must be made aware of the potential biases and their impact. Users must be able to ask the right questions and allow for the correct margin of error in their interpretation of the model's results.

Despite these challenges, banks must not put off investing in RAROC. Used wisely, the right RAROC tool will help a bank factor risk into its investment, pricing, and compensation decisions throughout the economic cycle. As well as creating long-term competitive advantage for individual institutions, RAROC may be the best way for the banking industry to avoid the boom-and-bust conditions we see in many banking markets today.

Designing and Validating
Your RAROC Framework

BY ROBERT DURANTE, YAN AN, AND ROBERT MARK

he task of identifying where banks make money after risk costs are taken into account has become urgent, given unprecedented credit losses and an upcoming increase in the amount and quality of bank risk capital. The Basel III phase-in period (2013-19) is about to begin.

However, existing approaches to risk-adjusted return on capital (RAROC) and related shareholder value-added metrics are under critical review in light of the banking crisis (Figure 1). RAROC needs to take better account of tail risk and stress testing, embrace a more comprehensive set of risks, and more accurately measure credit costs during downturns.

Meanwhile, regulators concerned about model risk say that banks must show they have adopted best practices in developing, implementing, and using any model that underpins key management decisions—RAROC models included.[1]

Banks can best meet these challenges by adopting a three-step approach:

1. Look again at their RAROC framework to make sure key conceptual judgments are in line with best practice and the bank's goals.

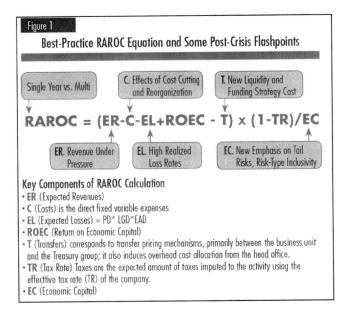

Figure 1

Best-Practice RAROC Equation and Some Post-Crisis Flashpoints

Single Year vs. Multi

C. Effects of Cost Cutting and Reorganization

T. New Liquidity and Funding Strategy Cost

$$RAROC = (ER-C-EL+ROEC - T) \times (1-TR)/EC$$

ER. Revenue Under Pressure

EL. High Realized Loss Rates

EC. New Emphasis on Tail Risks, Risk-Type Inclusivity

Key Components of RAROC Calculation
• ER (Expected Revenues)
• C (Costs) is the direct fixed variable expenses
• EL (Expected Losses) = PD* LGD*EAD
• ROEC (Return on Economic Capital)
• T (Transfers) corresponds to transfer pricing mechanisms, primarily between the business unit and the Treasury group; it also induces overhead cost allocation from the head office.
• TR (Tax Rate) Taxes are the expected amount of taxes imputed to the activity using the effecttive tax rate (TR) of the company.
• EC (Economic Capital)

2. Pay special attention to the input variables in the RAROC equation that are most critical. For commercial lenders, these are often estimates of probability of default and loss given default.
3. Create an independent, ongoing process for validating the RAROC model in accordance with regulatory guidelines, making sure gaps have not sprung up between the bank's RAROC concept and day-to-day RAROC calculations.

Looking Again at RAROC Frameworks: Conceptual Judgments

When building a RAROC framework, it is important to recognize the central role judgment plays in making important conceptual decisions. Table 1 identifies 10 key conceptual judgments that should be considered when validating a RAROC framework.

There are no universally correct standards. Instead, choices must be made within the context of the bank's risk profile and ambitions, how the bank plans to use its RAROC output, and the extent of the bank's knowledge about best industry practices.

We can explore this in light of two issues that have become particularly worrisome for banks since the 2007-08 crisis:

- Solvency standards and tail risk capital.
- Risk types included in RAROC.

Table 1
Ten Key Conceptual Judgments
1. Setting the solvency standard and the treatment of downturn/tail risk.
2. Defining the risk types included in the risk capital cost calculations.
3. Defining risk capital for RAROC — economic versus regulatory versus available; stand-alone versus diversified versus marginal.
4. Identifying risk-type correlations.
5. Determining the treatment and allocation of diversification benefits.
6. Establishing RAROC granularity: RAROC at the enterprise, business unit, relationship, and deal level.
7. Deciding when to use RAROC versus SVA (share value added).
8. Setting the hurdle rate, discount rate, and overhead allocation.
9. Determining the appropriateness of the funds transfer pricing (FTP) system.
10. Determining the appropriateness of the PD and LGD model.

Solvency Standards and Tail Risk Capital

Banks need to build a better understanding of how judgments about risk appetite and tail risk affect their approach to RAROC.

Given the new regulatory focus on risk-appetite setting, there should be congruence between the bank's risk appetite, its target rating, and the solvency standard applied in its economic capital model (for example, 95% versus 99%).

For instance, if a bank hopes to obtain a AA rating for its debt offerings, then this implies a probability of default of 2 to 3 basis points, corresponding to a confidence level in the range of 99.97% to 99.98%. Table 2 shows the one-year default rates associated with various Standard & Poor's rating grades.

However, there is an important trade-off here between bank soundness and risk-adjusted profitability. The choice of solvency standard determines the amount of the tail of the loss distribution included in the calculation of capital costs. Setting a lower confidence level can reduce the risk capital allocated to an activity and boost its apparent profitability, especially when the institution's risk profile is dominated by tail-risk-heavy operational, credit, and settlement risks.

Even economic capital analyses with 99% confidence intervals could fail to capture the risk that lies in the very tail (say, 1%) of the probability distribution. Increasingly, banks may elect to capture this tail risk by applying specialist value-at-risk (VAR) methodologies such as *conditional* value at risk (CVAR), which incorporates a measure of the expected loss of the tail of the distribution. Figure 2 highlights the economic cap-

Table 2	
S&P Default Rate by Rating	
S&P Rating	One-Year Default Rate
AAA	0.00%
AA	0.02%
A	0.08%
BBB	0.24%
BB	0.90%
B	4.49%
CCC	24.16%
CC	55.68%
C	66.67%

Source: S&P Capital IQ's CreditPro database

Note: One-year default rate from 1981 to 2011; each risk grade includes all rating buckets (for example, B categories include B-, B, and B+).

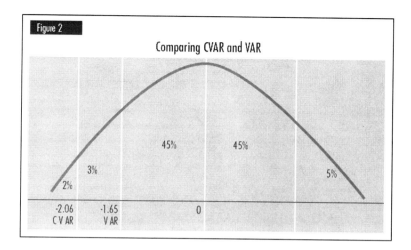

ital implications of applying a CVAR analysis versus a VAR analysis. Observe that CVAR for a normal probability density function based on a 95% confidence interval is 2.06 standard deviations from the mean.

In addition to applying CVAR, banks should consider attributing capital in light of stress and scenario testing, including macroeconomic scenario testing. Best-practice stress scenarios combine periods of projected normal market conditions with periods of market crises characterized by large price changes, high volatility, and a breakdown in the correlations among risk factors.

Setting conservative solvency targets and adding stress capital may pull down the RAROC associated with an activity. The answer to this is analytical flexibility: The bank needs to be able to see its RAROC numbers with (and without) different kinds of conservatism to reach a balanced judgment. For example, some banks may find that a CVAR-based economic capital analysis based on a confidence interval of 95% for a normal distribution yields a lower economic capital number—and higher RAROCs—than a VAR-based analysis using the 99% confidence interval.

Risk Types Included in RAROC

At the moment, banks vary in the risk types they include in the economic capital component of their RAROC analysis. Many include market, credit, and operational risks, while others try to include a wider spectrum of risk types, as shown in Table 3.

The principle that RAROC modelers ought to consider a wide spectrum of risks is sound. However, the way in which these risks enter the RAROC equation should vary in line with particular bank practices, and it may not be sensible to attribute a capital cost to every risk given the difficulty in measuring the risk or its relative importance. Again, a degree of judgment is required.

For example, lending activities will expose the bank to market risk in the form of interest rate risk and funding liquidity risk. The usual assumption is that interest rate risk

---

Table 3

Best-Practice Spectrum of Risks Considered for the EC Component of RAROC

EC = MRC + CRC + ORC + BRC+ RRC+ SRC-PEC

Key:

- **EC** Economic Capital (EC)
- **MRC** Market Risk Capital* (MRC)
- **CRC** Credit Risk Capital* (CRC)
- **ORC** Operational Risk Capital* (ORC)

- **BRC** Business Risk Capital (BRC)
- **RRC** Reputational Risk Capital (RRC)
- **SRC** Strategic Risk Capital (SRC)
- **PEC** Portfolio Effect Capital (PEC)

*Risk types included in Basel II capital adequacy calculations

---

and its costs are managed by the treasury function. The business is then charged a price for funds through the funds transfer pricing system in line with the costs incurred by the treasury for raising funds for the business and conducting any interest rate hedging.

Some banks "encourage" strategic businesses by offering them cheap funds in a way that can distort their RAROC analyses. From a RAROC point of view, it is better to charge the business the true cost of funds and then make a call on the strategic value of the business once the true RAROC is known.

The transfer price must also include a charge for the loan's impact on the liquidity of the bank. Charging for liquidity is not an exact science, but the bank should, at a minimum, make sure that charges are directionally correct (for example, that a five-year loan incurs a greater liquidity charge than a three-year loan).

In the future, banks that develop an active credit portfolio management capability may also want to transfer credit risk into a credit portfolio management group and include it in the bank's transfer pricing system.[2]

Paying Attention to Critical Variables in the RAROC Equation

The headline components of the classic RAROC equation (EC in Figure 1, for example) are driven by a number of critical subcomponents. For commercial lenders, RAROC tends to be particularly sensitive to the probability of default (PD) and loss given default (LGD) subcomponents.

Therefore, one of the most effective ways for lenders to improve RAROC calculations is to analyze the sensitivity of RAROC output to changes in estimated PD and LGD and then make targeted improvements to their risk estimation systems (such as the internal rating systems).

PD and RAROC

PD is an important factor for estimating expected losses (EL = PD*LGD*EAD) and for calculating the amount of economic capital associated with an activity.

The sensitivity of the bank's RAROC to PD estimates depends on the nature of the bank's obligors (Figure 3). For example, a change in one rating grade for a high-quality obligor (that is, one with a rating above A) tends to have only a minor impact on PD and therefore on expected losses.

However, a change in the rating of a less creditworthy obligor makes a much bigger difference. As an example of the potential impact, a change from B to B- leads to an increase in one-year PD from 5.49% to 8.65%; if we assume an exposure at default of $5 million, and an LGD of 30%, then the expected loss associated with this loan in the RAROC equation would increase by 58%, to $129,750 from $82,350.

PD is also used to estimate economic capital in the denominator of the RAROC formula. Figure 4 offers an analysis for an illustrative but reasonably typical loan, showing how a change in PD from low to high increases the economic capital and expected loss associated with the loan (while reducing RAROC).

This kind of analysis clarifies the relationship between obligor ratings and loan profitability, but also underlines the importance of improving and validating internal rating systems and the PD estimates used for calculating RAROC. Table 4 identifies key factors in designing a PD rating system.

The challenges faced by our clients when designing internal PD rating systems include the following:

- **Separate PD and LGD rating systems.** Some clients do not possess separate PD and LGD rating systems. Instead, they combine both risk assessments into a single "transaction rating." This means that the bank cannot later distinguish PD risk from LGD risk.

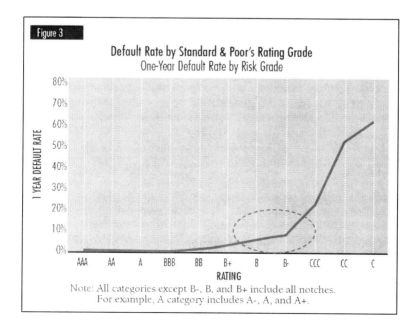

Figure 3

Default Rate by Standard & Poor's Rating Grade
One-Year Default Rate by Risk Grade

Note: All categories except B-, B, and B+ include all notches. For example, A category includes A-, A, and A+.

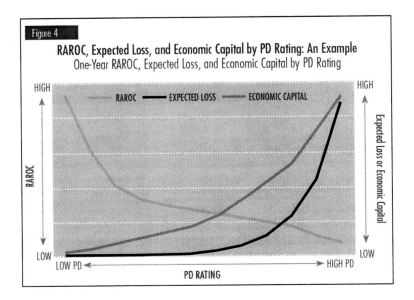

Figure 4

RAROC, Expected Loss, and Economic Capital by PD Rating: An Example
One-Year RAROC, Expected Loss, and Economic Capital by PD Rating

- **Qualitative versus quantitative risk factors.** Ideally, PD scorecards should incorporate both quantitative risk factors (such as financial ratios) and qualitative risk factors (such as assessments of market position or management quality). However, some clients rely solely on quantitative risk factors in their PD scorecard. Furthermore, the quantitative risk factors should usually cover risk dimensions such as profitability, capitalization, liquidity, and cash flow. However, we find that some clients employ only a few profitability ratios and do not put enough emphasis on liquidity and leverage.
- **Scoring guidelines.** Some clients incorporate qualitative risk factors but do not offer their analysts detailed guidance on how to score these risk factors. For example, in the interest of operating efficiency, the scoring guidelines might divide the scores into "strong," "average," and "weak," but fail to offer descriptions that help the analyst decide which category is most appropriate for the obligor. As a result, analysts in different regional teams might attribute "strong" and other scores inconsistently.
- **Override.** Some of our clients' analysts employ many overrides when applying their banks' scorecards. When this happens, it is usually best to conduct research and convert the override element into a risk factor.
- **Parent/government support.** Some scorecards do not take into consideration the support of a parent company or government, even though this can be highly significant.
- **Point-in-time (PIT) versus through-the-cycle (TTC):** Realized transition and default probabilities vary over the years, depending on whether the economy is in recession or expanding (Figure 5). It therefore makes a large difference to RAROC calculations whether the bank attempts to estimate the default rate (PD) at a particular point in time or over a longer period such as the economic cycle. A complication here is that the rating agencies typically rate obligors from more of a

---

Table 4

Eight Factors That Can Distort RAROC

PD Rating System Design Factor

1. Make sure the bank applies the right number of sector-specific models,[3] which should be driven by the similarity (or otherwise) of obligor risk profiles.

2. Find the right balance between financial ratio analysis and the analysis of nonfinancial risk factors such as economic risk (stability and structure of a country's financial system, level of credit risk in the system, etc.), industry risk (intensity of competition, relative profitability of the industry, concentration of the market, etc.), competitiveness, and management quality.

3. Score risk factors, especially nonfinancial risk factors, in an objective way, using scoring guidelines with detailed attributes to promote consistency.

4. For low-default sectors such as large corporates, consider applying a scorecard approach that can combine statistical analysis with expert judgment.

5. Draw out the impact of structural features such as parental support with carefully designed overlay scorecards.

6. Map ratings carefully to external agency ratings, such as Standard & Poor's, which can be associated with a long and rich history of default data, taking into account any methodological differences between the bank's rating approach and the source of external ratings.

7. Consider how the ratings-derived PD number relates to the RAROC number the bank is trying to calculate—say, in terms of whether the PD is based on a point-in-time or a through-the-cycle analysis (then analyze the sensitivity of the bank's RAROC numbers to this choice).

8. Generate an accurate rating transition matrix to help estimate, for example, the economic capital for deals with maturities of longer than one year.

TTC perspective, while many bank analytic modelers typically rate the obligor from a PIT perspective (capturing the PD in the short term). The different approaches introduce an inconsistency that must be tackled (such as when banks apply average historical transition probabilities derived from rating agencies' historical data). The approach adopted also needs to be thought through in relation to the particular application of the RAROC numbers (such as current pricing versus longer-term strategic decisions).[3]

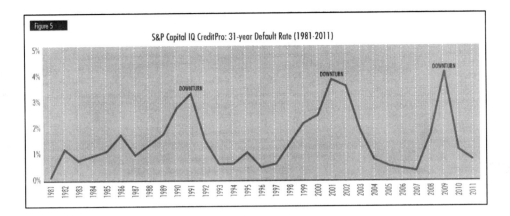

LGD and RAROC

Some components of the RAROC calculation tend to be estimated in a broad-brush way that prevents banks from differentiating between the profitability of given activities.

This is particularly true of LGD, largely because banks feel they lack the large amounts of detailed internal recovery data that would allow them to estimate statistically the LGDs associated with different kinds of deals.

The reasons for unavailable internal data vary considerably. For example, some clients have LGD data that covers a full economic cycle, but this data is not associated with detailed information about the facility and collateral. In the case of real estate facilities, the bank may not have recorded the location of the real estate or the type of appraisal for the real estate. Other banks record the value of the collateral at the time of issuing the loan, but do not record the value of the collateral at default. Finally, banks might not track the recovery cash flow after default, or they may track the cash flow but fail to differentiate between different types of cash flow, such as recovery cash flow versus recovery cost.

Recently, banks have begun to build new hybrid approaches to LGD estimation that combine statistical analysis—based on available internal data and carefully selected external data[4]—with expert judgment in a rigorous manner.[5] The hybrid approaches have become the latest modeling trend for commercial portfolios because they:

- Recognize that the available data does not always identify all known and plausible risk drivers.
- Combine the available empirical data with expert judgment.
- Allow for different LGD treatments for different segments—for example, using statistical models as an input into the hybrid model with the addition of a qualitative overlay.

Figure 6 sets out a decision-tree hybrid approach to LGD estimation that combines both quantitative and qualitative techniques. Here, the decision tree sets out a series of

---

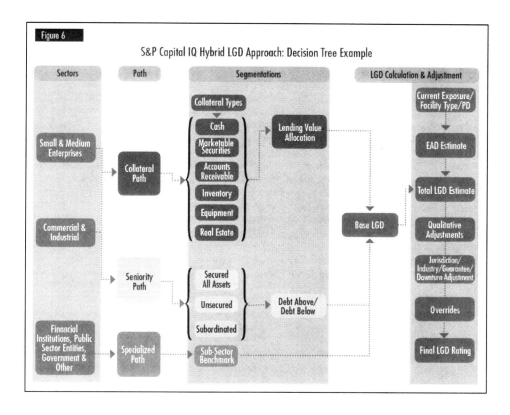

Figure 6

S&P Capital IQ Hybrid LGD Approach: Decision Tree Example

analytical paths (collateral path, seniority path, specialized path) that help the bank adopt the most appropriate way to estimate LGD in different kinds of portfolios. The results of each appropriate statistical analysis can then be benchmarked against industry-wide data and adjusted using panels of experts from the relevant divisions of the bank (an example would be adjustments for construction real estate LGD versus permanent real estate lending).

There are many challenges to overcome when developing an LGD model. For example, best-practice approaches should consider the impact of economic downturns on LGD.

If the bank has a long history of LGD data, it should use this internal data to estimate downturn LGD. Some of our clients, however, have only three or four years of data available.

There are various ways to approach this problem. For example, banks can use an industry database of loss statistics to define a downturn in terms of the raised rate of default. They can then use a database of industry LGD data to compare the time-weighted average LGD associated with defaults in this downturn period against the cycle-average loss rates (Figure 7). It is important to adopt a best-practice approach because LGD estimates make a big difference to the bank's RAROC analysis. In Figure 8, as LGD increases

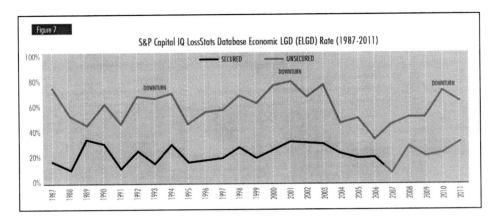

Figure 7

S&P Capital IQ LossStats Database Economic LGD (ELGD) Rate (1987-2011)

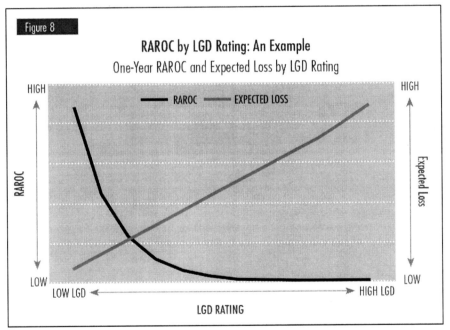

Figure 8

RAROC by LGD Rating: An Example
One-Year RAROC and Expected Loss by LGD Rating

from a low to a high risk grade, the expected loss value associated with the deal rises and RAROC declines significantly.

Figure 9 shows how the combination of PD and LGD rating has a particularly significant impact on RAROC value. However, we can also think of this chart as a demonstration of what might happen when one factor (PD or LGD) is held constant and the other factor is incorrectly estimated. This issue highlights the importance of validating all key aspects of the RAROC model.

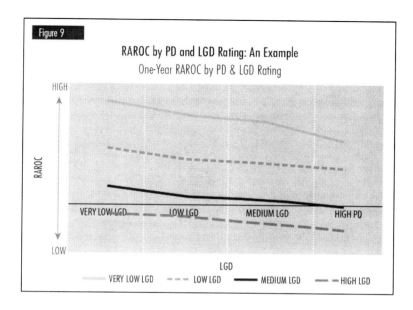

Designing an Operationally Sound, Validated Approach

As RAROC becomes more and more entwined in business decisions—deal approval as well as bank strategy—it has become critical for banks to regularly validate their RAROC systems.

Figure 10 sets out a framework for RAROC validation in line with the latest regulatory guidance on model risk management, which embraces issues ranging from conceptual soundness to model governance.

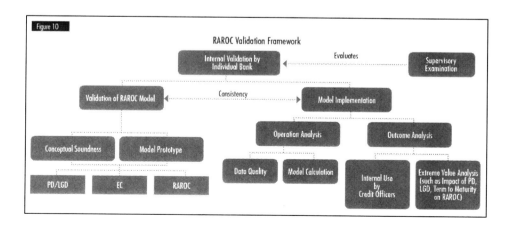

Among the many aspects of RAROC model validation, perhaps the operational challenges are the most overlooked. Banks must ensure that the validated conceptual RAROC approach has been implemented appropriately in the rolled-out RAROC system.

One way to do this is to build the conceptual model in a spreadsheet—closely mapping the variables in the spreadsheet to the bank's RAROC methodology documentation—and see whether the numbers the spreadsheet model produces are the same as the numbers generated by the bank's day-to-day production model across a range of deals. Some of our clients have found that this can reveal significant discrepancies.

Banks also need to make sure that subsystems such as the internal rating system (PD, LGD, etc.) and FTP system—which feed data into the RAROC model—have been validated and that all the data entering the RAROC model is authenticated by tracing it back to its original source. Some of S&P Capital IQ's clients have found that data in a source system can assume a different value when transferred into the RAROC system database. This may happen when variables (such as calendar dates, for example) are handled in a slightly different manner.

The bank will also need to test the RAROC system output. To a limited degree, outcomes analysis may take the form of comparing *a priori* RAROC numbers (say, at the point of deal approval) with *ex post* RAROC numbers (such as RAROC calculated for the same deal two years down the road).

However, the challenges inherent in RAROC back-testing mean that outcomes analysis depends heavily on a rigorous series of judgmental cross-checks to make sure the bank's RAROC numbers make sense. For example:

- Does the RAROC output change in a directionally correct manner as variables are altered? For instance, as PD rises, does a deal become less profitable?
- What is the effect of extreme input values on the output? In other words, when does the RAROC output become unreliable?
- Does the RAROC output at deal level roll up to the entity and relationship level in a consistent way, taking portfolio effects into account?
- Are outcomes reasonably consistent with management expectations about the profitability of customers and products?

The bank will also want to check how the RAROC output is being used. For example, do users understand the various conceptual judgments that shape RAROC output? And can the bank present evidence that RAROC is applied to deal selection (such as an analysis of the RAROCs of accepted versus rejected deals)?

Conclusion

In a world of scarce and expensive capital, banks must learn to identify the businesses, deals, and relationships that bring long-term profitability. First, though, the bank has to build a best-practice RAROC model that incorporates:

- Sound judgments about key concepts.
- Improved accuracy in terms of key variables such as PD and LGD.
- Robust operational and validation procedures.

Meeting this challenge is not simple, however, and improvements to RAROC will at times prove contentious. But banks that succeed will be able to risk-adjust their strategic and tactical decisions with confidence and in ways that preserve profitability in the new tougher, capital-intensive banking environment.

Notes

1. See, for example, Office of the Comptroller of the Currency, "Supervisory Guidance on Model Risk Management, OCC-2011-12, April 4, 2011.
2. See Michel Crouhy, Dan Galai, and Robert Mark, *The Essentials of Risk Management*, McGraw Hill, 2006.
3. The CreditPro database contains 31 years of global default data, which can be segmented by geographic region, country, industry, and year. The default data can be used to benchmark the internal probability of default and transition matrix and also to validate the bank's choice of point-in-time versus through-the-cycle PD rates within its RAROC framework.
4. The LossStats database is the largest of its kind in the industry. It currently includes over 4,000 defaulted bank debt and high-yield bonds with $800 billion defaulted principals for more than 800 public and private U.S. companies that have defaulted since 1987. The database can be used to develop LGD estimates by industry and collateral types.
5. S&P Capital IQ has developed several hybrid LGD/EAD scorecards in the past few years, based on a combination of the analytical process of Standard & Poor's, the most recent regulatory guidance, and the best industry practices and data.

Stress-Testing Methodologies

rior to 2009, *The RMA Journal* featured only one article per year on stress testing, reflecting a corresponding lack of interest from most lenders. Stress tests during that period usually ran along the lines of "What would happen if our roll to bucket 1 went up 10%?" or "What if our PD rates return to the levels of the last recession?" The *Journal* articles during that time were lamenting this weakness and urging lenders to build true stress-test models. But very little changed.

In the four years that followed, the *Journal* published 16 articles on stress testing, reflecting a sea change in the regulatory and lending landscape resulting from the U.S. mortgage crisis.

The core technologies behind stress-test models have not changed over the time span of these articles, but regulatory standards and levels of practice within the top lenders have improved dramatically. In August 2013, the Federal Reserve published "Capital Planning at Large Bank Holding Companies: Supervisory Expectations and Range of Current Practice," which made clear that the old ways are no longer acceptable. Modern stress-test models must be forecast models that capture all the key portfolio drivers and add economic drivers for stress testing.

This section begins with the article "Stress Testing Is a Critical Tool in Risk Management," by Jim Clarke, which serves as an introduction to the topic of stress testing. Four key principles are described for effective stress testing. Specifically, the stress test should 1) be tailored to the specifics of the lender, 2) incorporate multiple approaches, 3) be forward-looking and flexible, and 4) be clear and actionable.

The article introduces interest rate risk, liquidity risk, and credit risk as key areas to be studied. Notably, the article's introductory comments address community banks, which are not currently required to create credit risk stress-test models. However, lenders of all sizes are realizing that they will need to have stress-test models someday soon.

In "Stress-Testing Methodologies and Tools," William Nayda introduces some of the types of credit risk stress tests commonly used, including benchmarking, historical shock analysis, factor analysis, and grade migration. Benefits and limitations are provided for each and examples given for various retail loan portfolios. These stress-testing tools are compared for their coverage of bank-level risks, portfolio-level risks, and loan-level risks.

Compared to the Fed's 2013 publication on stress-testing practices, the list of categories given in this article is not exhaustive. Rather, it includes the types of models a lender might build in the first or second year of stress testing. This is the first step on a stairway leading to models that will incorporate an understanding of the full range of portfolio drivers, resulting in more accuracy.

We have seen evidence that a weak stress-test model can be worse than no model because of the false sense of security it imparts. "Stress the Stress Testing," by Yakov Lantsman and David Shu, highlights two key weaknesses of stress-test models in use during the 2007-09 crisis: 1) Risks and markets are highly correlated, and 2) stress testing was not stressful enough. The crisis showed that we need to hold these models to a higher standard than was done previously.

The authors propose more comprehensive behavioral understanding of the market players in order to better understand correlations. To address the second weakness, the models need to account for the time horizon of the market participants, consider horde behavior, all for dynamic changes in correlation structures, better analyze tail risk, and develop more defensible scenarios. To illustrate these concepts, the article describes, for each major risk category (liquidity, market, credit, operational, and macroeconomic), specific events from the U.S. mortgage crisis.

To move beyond generalities, we must discuss specific asset classes. The best model for a credit card portfolio will not be the same for commercial and industrial lending. Different loan behaviors, different amounts of data, and different management guidelines require different techniques. *The RMA Journal* has not covered all asset classes, but "Stress Testing the Credit Risk of Commercial Real Estate Mezzanine Lending," by George Pappadopoulos, provides an example of creating stress-test models in one area.

The article builds a model with the debt service coverage and loan-to-value ratios as the primary inputs. This model is then used to estimate portfolio net returns under different economic scenarios in order to determine if the lender is properly pricing for risk. In short, it focuses on making operational use of a stress-test model.

For retail lending, we have the oldest article in the section, "Stress Testing 2004-05 Retail Originations," by Joseph Breeden. Although the article discusses a specific point in the credit and economic cycle, it does so in the context of how to leverage robust retail-lending forecast models for portfolio stress testing. Nothing has changed in that regard.

The article employs an age-period-cohort-style model of portfolio performance, which measures life cycle as a function of the age of the loan, credit quality by vintage (including any adverse selection), and macroeconomic impacts. Unemployment, interest rates, and real GDP were the key macroeconomic drivers. With this model, industry scenarios were tested in order to assess potential losses. Further, the article describes how stress-testing models can be employed to assess the fragility of loan pricing under various economic conditions.

The final article of this section, "Reverse Stress Testing: A Structured Approach," by Maurice Kilavuka, develops a methodology through which a lender can start with a feared disaster scenario and trace backward through the failure mode, possible causes, and necessary preconditions.

The article borrows from engineering to take a failure mode approach. The key failure modes identified for loan portfolios are 1) sudden events leading to rapid failure, 2) sudden events leading to sudden failure, 3) sustained stress leading to sudden failure, and 4) sustained stress leading to gradual failure.

Reverse stress testing is referred to as a "many to one" problem. Many causes and preconditions can create the same failure. The article presents a management process for identifying some of these primary failure paths.

The stress-testing articles presented here serve as a starting point, particularly for those who have never been required to create stress-test models. However, the regulatory environment is clearly such that all lenders will eventually need such models, and stress-test models at even the most sophisticated lenders must continually improve. Unlike with scoring, where the models are mature after decades of development, we have not yet seen a model blessed as "good enough." Continual improvement is our path for the foreseeable future.

Stress Testing Is a Critical Tool in Risk Management

By Jim Clarke

Stress testing has been in vogue since the financial crisis of 2008, but the concept is not new to bank financial managers. Community banks have been stress testing their balance sheets for interest rate risk since at least 1996, and thrift institutions were testing as far back as the 1980s.

Only in the past four years has stress testing been extended and formalized to encompass liquidity and credit risk management. The crises faced by Bear Stearns and Lehman Brothers in 2008 were the impetus for liquidity stress tests introduced in 2009. Meanwhile, concern over systemic risk posed by the largest banks led to the introduction of credit stress testing.

In 2009, the Basel Committee on Banking Supervision proposed guidelines in a document that laid out general principles for stress testing.[1] Regulators have provided specific guidelines for interest rate stress tests, but they have been hesitant to articulate specific requirements for liquidity and credit risk stress testing.

The following general principles should apply to all stress tests:

Principle 1: A banking organization's stress-testing framework should include activities and exercises that are tailored to and sufficiently capture the banking organization's exposures, activities, and risks.

Principle 2: An effective stress-testing framework employs multiple and conceptually sound stress-testing activities and approaches.

Principle 3: An effective stress-testing framework is forward-looking and flexible.

Principle 4: Stress-testing results should be clear, actionable, and well supported and should inform decision making.

These principles were initially intended for institutions with consolidated assets of more than $10 billion, but they should apply to all banking organizations in all of the various stress tests they currently conduct or will be expected to conduct. These principles represent the regulators' views of best practices and form the expectations of examiners.

This article will apply these principles to interest rate and liquidity stress tests, which are currently required of community banks. It will also address credit risk stress testing, which also will be required for all banks, probably within the next two years.

Stress Testing of Interest Rate Risk

Stress testing for interest rate risk was formally introduced to all community banks in 1996[2] with the release of the "Interagency Statement on Interest Rate Risk," which was

322

updated in 2010.[3] Interest rate risk can be defined as the impact of a change in market interest rates on a bank's financial statements. Stress testing for interest rate risk is very specific in its requirements and outcomes.

In all testing, it is necessary to create events that would put stress on the bank's financial statements. The outcome is focused on the event's impact on a bank's capital or income. In this type of stress testing, the event is straightforward. Specifically, banks are required to simulate an increase and decrease in market rates of +/- 100 to 400 basis points.

In the opinion of this author, interest rate stress testing within community banking effectively addresses the principles developed by the Basel Committee. The first principle addresses the need for the stress-testing framework to include activities and exercises that are tailored to and sufficiently capture the banking organization's exposures, activities, and risks. In other words, the testing should reflect the complexity of the bank's balance sheet.

Interest rate stress testing is accomplished through sophisticated simulation models, and the guidelines provided by the Federal Financial Institutions Examination Council (FFIEC) focus on the robustness of these models. There are differences in the models' capability to handle complexity, however. Note that complexity is normally correlated to embedded options in the balance sheet, or negative convexity. The least complex balance sheets in community banking are those of small commercial banks, whereas the greatest complexity would be found in large savings and loan associations.

The second principle advises that effective stress testing should employ multiple and conceptually sound stress-testing activities—effectively achieved with the current modeling approaches used in community banks. The FFIEC guidelines require 1) income statement simulation for years one and two focused on net interest income (NII) sensitivity, and 2) balance sheet sensitivity focused on the economic value of equity (EVE).

The guidelines also emphasize scenario analysis, which addresses yield curve risk. Most models currently used in the industry are adaptable to various scenarios or yield curve shifts. The most common approaches used by community banks are parallel instantaneous changes in the yield curve (referred to as shocks) and ramping up of the curve over time.

The third principle emphasizes that an effective stress-testing framework is forward-looking and flexible. Interest rate stress testing is clearly forward-looking as it is a simulation of future interest rates showing the result on financial statements over at least the next two years.

The fourth principle states that the stress-testing results should be clear, actionable, and well supported and that they should inform decision making. Interest rate stress-testing results are clear and therefore should be actionable; in fact, the bank's board is required to establish limits on the degree of volatility acceptable for both net interest income and EVE.

The value of stress testing for changes in market rates, as with all modeling, depends on the quality of the input and the modeling assumptions. The quality of the input usually comes down to the complexity of the balance sheet. The greater the balance sheet complexity, the greater the need to refine data, especially detailed investment and loan portfolio data. The FFIEC guidelines are very specific with respect to assumptions requiring back-testing and validation.

Interest rate risk modeling and stress testing have come through almost two decades of refinement, and overall they represent a good example of the best practices the Basel directive is trying to achieve. This is not the case for liquidity and credit stress-testing approaches, however, as both are in formative stages.

Liquidity Stress Testing

For community banks, liquidity stress testing is an outgrowth of the 2008 financial crisis. Bear Stearns and Lehman Brothers were systemic concerns, but the failure of Indy Mac Bank and the problems faced by the Federal Home Loan Banks (FHLB) brought the crisis to the level of community banking. The run on deposits at Indy Mac in July 2008 was a reminder to all banks and regulators that liquidity matters. The FHLB system is a major source of liquidity management in the community banking industry, and its health was a concern.

In 2009, regulators introduced the concept of liquidity contingency planning, which involved conducting a stress test. For this type of stress test, it's necessary to create scenarios or events that place pressure on a bank's liquidity position. At the community banking level, a negative impact on liquidity is most likely to come from credit problems associated with the loan portfolio that result in higher levels of nonaccruals and charge-offs. If serious enough, these problems could lead to a bank becoming less than well capitalized, with negative impacts on deposit insurance premiums, credit rating (for example, Bauer Financial ratings), and repo and other debt covenants. These negative signals could potentially lead to an outflow of deposits or other drains on liquidity.

Table 1 presents a quarterly cash flow pro forma. In this example, the bank's cash position is increasing quarterly as cash inflows exceed cash outflows. The sample bank has been common sized to $1 billion; therefore if we focus on the ending balance, the liquidity ratio as a percentage of assets increases from 10.3% to 14.3%. The sample bank is experiencing increasing liquidity quarter after quarter based on the pro forma.

Table 1				
Quarterly Cash Flow Pro Forma				
	March	June	September	December
Securities — Maturity & Call	2,000	5,000	7,000	11,000
Cash Flow from MBS	5,400	5,400	5,500	5,700
Loan Payments (Amort + Prep)	58,700	59,800	61,900	62,400
Deposits	18,800	19,400	19,600	21,400
Borrowings	------	------	(6,000)	(4,000)
Total Cash Inflow	84,900	89,600	88,000	96,500
Investment Purchases	(15,000)	(22,000)	(18,000)	(21,000)
Loan Funding	(56,000)	(62,000)	(60,000)	(60,000)
Total Cash Outflow	(71,000)	(84,000)	(78,000)	(81,000)
Net Income [including Adj.]	2,840	2,710	2,830	2,960
Net Change in Cash	16,740	8,310	12,830	18,460
Beginning Balance	86,800	103,540	111,850	122,680
Ending Balance	103,540	111,850	122,680	143,140

To conduct a stress test, we will use the pro forma analysis shown above, but impose a negative event that resulted from a serious increase in credit problems. Based on this negative event, the following assumptions are imposed on the cash flow pro forma:

- Deposit inflow slows by 40% versus budget.
- Net income declines 60% versus budget.
- Loan repayment slows by 40% versus budget.

Table 2 represents the new cash flow pro forma. The change in liquidity (ending balance) is primarily the result of the decline in deposits and the loan repayments. The liquidity ratio has declined to less than 1% by the fourth quarter.

Liquidity contingency policy requires bank management to report the results of the stress test to the board (preferably quarterly) and to recommend potential resolutions of the problem either through asset adjustments (for example, reducing investment purchases) or liability solutions (such as borrowing or deposit strategies). Note that the pro forma needs to be rolling forward to show at least four quarters or 12 months. Also, management should show more than one event, basically by increasing the impact of the assumptions.

The principles developed by the Basel Committee need to apply to liquidity stress testing. The first principle addresses the need for the stress-testing framework to include activities and exercises that are tailored to, and sufficiently capture, the banking organization's exposures, activities, and risks. The cash flow pro forma shown in Table 1 is fairly typical for a community bank, although each bank should modify the analysis to more closely fit its balance sheet.

The second principle addresses effective stress testing, and it indicates that organizations should employ multiple and conceptually sound stress-testing activities and approaches. This was relatively straightforward in the example for interest rate risk, but more difficult to capture in a liquidity stress test. A cash flow analysis is likely the best approach

Table 2

Impact on Quarterly Cash Flow Post Assumptions

	March	June	September	December
Securities — Maturity & Call	2,000	5,000	7,000	11,000
Cash Flow from MBS	5,400	5,400	5,500	5,700
Loan Payments (Amort + Prep)	35,220	35,880	37,140	37,440
Deposits	11,280	11,640	11,760	12,840
Borrowings	------	------	[6,000]	[4,000]
Total Cash Inflow	53,900	57,920	55,400	62,980
Investment Purchases	[15,000]	[22,000]	[18,000]	[21,000]
Loan Funding	[56,000]	[62,000]	[60,000]	[60,000]
Total Cash Outflow	[71,000]	[84,000]	[78,000]	[81,000]
Net Income (including Adj.)	1,140	1,080	1,130	1,180
Net Change in Cash	[15,960]	[25,000]	[21,470]	[16,840]
Beginning Balance	86,800	70,840	45,840	24,370
Ending Balance	70,840	45,840	24,370	7,530

for analyzing liquidity and potential changes in liquidity. There is no standardized approach. Three assumptions are recommended here that would impact cash flow and liquidity, but there are other possible assump-tions. The only real commonality among banks would be deposit outflows. Therefore, without definitive regulatory guidelines, as was the case with interest rate risk, each bank must establish its own assumptions.

The third principle emphasizes that an effective stress-testing framework is forward-looking and flexible. Liquidity stress testing, as presented in this article, is clearly forward-looking as it is a simulation of cash flow pro forma.

The fourth principle states that the stress-testing results should be clear, actionable, and well supported and that they should inform decision making. Liquidity stress testing should be actionable. A bank's board should establish limits on the degree of volatility acceptable for liquidity ratios and noncore funding dependency.

Credit Risk Stress Testing

The stress testing of bank capital for credit risk is relatively new to community banking and, for banks with assets of less than $10 billion, there are no specific requirements or guidelines. The Dodd-Frank Act requires stress testing for banks with assets above $10 billion, but it's the opinion of this author that stress testing will be required of all banks within the next three years. Based on what is required of large banks, this article will build a framework for stress testing a typical community bank. The example represents a $1 billion bank with the following characteristics:

- Assets = $1 billion.
- Capital = $90 million [9%].
- Nonperforming = $34.9 million.
- ALLL = $8.54 million [coverage ratio – 24.5% of nonperforming].
- Noncurrent [30-90 days] = $36.8 million.

Event 1: A Mild Recession
To conduct the stress test, we need to simulate an event that would likely have a negative impact on credit quality. The first level of event is a mild recession (such as the one in 2001). The current coverage ratio for nonaccrual loans is 24.5%; however, in a mild recession, optimal coverage will need to be 40% of nonaccruals (this assumption and all others are subjective).

- 0.4% x $34.9 = $13.96 million.
- Shortfall—$13.96 million minus $8.54 million = $5.42 million.

Instantaneous impact on capital—$90 million minus $5.42 million = $84.58 million, or an 8.46% capital ratio.

Event 2: A Serious Recession
In a more serious recession (such as in 1981-82 or 2007- 09), a 60% coverage ratio will be required as the loan portfolio deteriorates—plus 20% additional coverage for noncurrent loans that may become nonaccrual.

- 0.6% x $34.9 = $20.9 million.
- Nonaccrual shortfall—$20.9 million minus $8.54 million = $12.4 million.
- Noncurrent = $7.36 million.
- Instantaneous impact on capital—$90 million minus [$12.2 million + $7.36m] = $70.4 million or a 7.04% capital ratio.

The example above provides a basic framework for a stress test of credit risk. As the model is refined and tailored to capture the banking organization's exposures, activities, and risks, it will eventually satisfy the principles established by the Basel Committee. Nevertheless, credit stress testing at the community bank level is a work in progress.

Conclusion

Stressing testing has become an important tool in financial risk management at all levels of banking. But it is important for bankers and regulators to understand that it is only one tool of risk management and perhaps not the most important. Credit risk remains the industry's major risk, making effective loan portfolio diversification and underwriting essential tools. The level of bank capital is another key to determine the bank's safety and soundness.

Notes

1. Basel Committee on Banking Supervision, "Principles for Sound Stress Testing Practices and Supervision," May 2009.
2. Federal Deposit Insurance Corporation, Board of Governors of the Federal Reserve System, and Office of the Comptroller of the Currency, "Interagency Statement on Interest Rate Risk," June 1996.
3. Federal Financial Institutions Examination Council, "Advisory on Interest Rate Risk Management," January 2010.

Stress-Testing Methodologies and Tools

By WILLIAM NAYDA

I n consulting with banks, I often get asked the following questions: Which stress-testing method should I be using? Which vendor model should I buy? Which method or system do the regulators want me to use? What level should I stress: loan or portfolio?

The answer to all of these questions depends on the type of risk you are trying to measure and prevent. So the selection of a tool or system first starts with asking *this* question: What risk am I trying to examine and control? Keep that in mind as you read this article. Then you can determine which tools are best for your bank. Table 1 is a good place to start.

Table 1 Determining the Best Tools for Your Bank	
What risk do I want to better understand?	Tools
Bank-level risks	• Qualitative analysis • Disaster recovery drills • Aggregate lower-level stress tests for a prescribed event • Use of benchmarks (such as operational risk)
Portfolio-level risks	• Historical severe loss rates • Asymptotic single-risk-factor models • Multifactor models • Value at risk • Benchmarks (such as using SCAP or CCAR loss rates)
Loan-level risks	• Grade migration • Multifactor models • Asymptotic single-risk-factor models

Stress-Testing Methodologies and Tools

There are many different types of stress-testing methodologies and tools. Figure 1 aggregates them into four broad categories based on their underlying methodology: benchmarking, historical analysis or simulation, factor analysis, and grade migration. I recommend that banks use multiple methodologies in their stress-testing efforts because stress testing is not an exact science. In fact, in large simulation efforts, banks may be required to use a combination of all the methodologies described here when developing their level of stress.[1]

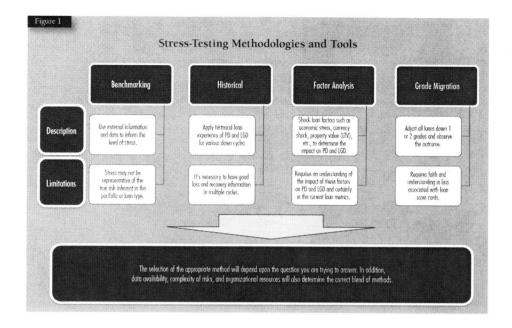

Figure 1

Stress-Testing Methodologies and Tools

	Benchmarking	Historical	Factor Analysis	Grade Migration
Description	Use external information and data to inform the level of stress.	Apply historical loan experience of PD and LGD for various down cycles	Shock loan factors such as economic stress, currency shock, property value (LTV), etc., to determine the impact on PD and LGD.	Adjust all loans down 1 or 2 grades and observe the outcome.
Limitations	Stress may not be representative of the true risk inherent in the portfolio or loan type.	It's necessary to have good loss and recovery information in multiple cycles.	Requires an understanding of the impact of these factors on PD and LGD and certainly in the current loan metrics.	Requires faith and understanding in loss associated with loan score cards.

The selection of the appropriate method will depend upon the question you are trying to answer. In addition, data availability, complexity of risks, and organizational resources will also determine the correct blend of methods.

Benchmarking

The stress-testing technique of benchmarking uses available public information, rules of thumb, and consultant-provided or consultant-developed shocks and ratios to determine the level of stress. Because the estimate of shock is provided by an external source, benchmarking can be one of the easiest methods for a bank to use. However, banks must not be naïve in using benchmarks and should try, when possible, to tailor the results to the institution so as not to be overly conservative or aggressive in the level of stress.

An important external benchmark was provided by the regulatory agencies and Treasury Department in their release of the base and adverse scenarios by loan type in the Supervisory Capital Assessment Program (SCAP).[2] This stress test is of critical importance to U.S. banks because it provides a window into regulators' thinking and expectations around stress testing. Further, it provides regulator-vetted stress-testing assumptions that banks can use to determine their level of stress.

The SCAP process started with regulators providing the 19 largest banks with a range of loss experience by loan type, as shown in Table 2. These were the outcomes projected to occur over the forecast period of 2009-10. More importantly, the SCAP specified the level of stress in an adverse economic situation that was equivalent to—or, in some cases, worse than—that experienced during the Great Depression.

As shown in the table, the ranges can be quite large, so banks should be judicious in their application. As an example, the SCAP rates for multifamily commercial real estate (CRE) range from 10% to 11%. However, the same rates for the individual banks range from 2% to 45%. A bank would have to examine these ranges carefully and custom-tailor them to its own underwriting and macroeconomic experience.

Table 2 Indicative Loss Rates Provided to BHCs for SCAP (cumulative two year, in percent)	Baseline	More Adverse
First Lien Mortgages	5 – 6	7 – 8.5
Prime	1.5 – 2.5	3 – 4
Alt- A	7.5 – 9.5	9.5 – 13
Subprime	15 – 20	21 – 28
Second/Junior Lien Mortgages	9 – 12	12 – 16
Closed-end Junior Liens	18 – 20	22 – 25
HELOCs	6 – 8	8 – 11
C&I Loans	3 – 4	5 – 8
CRE	5 – 7.5	9 – 12
Construction	8 – 12	15 – 18
Multifamily	3.5 – 6.5	10 – 11
Nonfarm, Nonresidential	4 – 5	7 – 9
Credit Cards	12 – 17	18 – 20
Other Consumer	4 – 6	8 – 12
Other Loans	2 – 4	4 – 10

Source: The Supervisory Capital Assessment Program: Overview of Results, Federal Reserve Board, May 2009.

For example, a bank portfolio containing agricultural land in the Midwest, which is currently enjoying a booming economy thanks to high commodity prices, might have lower levels of stress than a bank with a portfolio containing significant construction loans in a hard-hit area. So, in using these rates, banks should consider their own loss experience in relation to the loss levels experienced by the 19 largest banks and adjust the shock accordingly. Further, a bank should examine its historical charge-off experience in relation to the SCAP levels of stress to determine if the level of stress is aggressive or conservative.

Analysts responsible for conducting stress tests in their bank should refer to the SCAP instructions and results. This is especially true if the bank wants to conduct a full SCAP-type analysis, which requires an estimate of pre-provision net income over the next two years and ending reserves after the two-year stress period. The analysis also requires an understanding of the current capital position and the post-stress position. The details on how to conduct the test are provided in the SCAP documents.

Historical Shock Analysis

The next most widely used methodology for a single-factor stress test is to use historical data, which can come from the bank and also from public sources.

Bankers often ask: How much stress is appropriate? In my practice, I often see banks using simple rules such as 5%, 10%, or 25% levels of loss. Then they begin to question the basis for their shocks and start wondering about the appropriate levels for moderate, medium, or severe stress.

Banks can use their internal experience with stressed losses to determine the appropriate amount of stress to apply to a portfolio. I recommend that, when running a stress test, an analyst should perform simple statistical techniques in Excel® on the historical data to inform the appropriate level of stress.

There are limitations in using internal data, however, and they have to do with the amount of history available to the bank and the quality of the data. Does the data capture a partial instead of a full credit cycle? Is the data no longer representative of the portfolio? If these limitations are present, banks sometimes can use a combination of internal and public data to infer the loss. For instance, a de novo bank or a bank with limited loss experience in a particular portfolio may wish to combine institutional experience with industry shocks.

The example in Figure 2 uses historical CRE loss rates on all banks to derive the level of stress. The historical data is available from the Federal Reserve's data download program, which includes loss rates for various types of commercial and consumer loans. The data is presented merely for expository purposes, as the banks' own data or peer data can be used to determine the level of stress.

A simple nonstatistical method for determining the appropriate level of stress is to use the maximum loss experienced over the history of the data as the severe level of loss—which in this case is a 2.87% loss rate, or a two-year loss rate of 5.74%. Note that this observed loss rate is lower than that recommended in the SCAP, indicating the severity of the SCAP assumptions.

Another simple method is to examine the changes between peak and trough and determine the multiple. During the trough period, the average level of loss is 0.17%; how-

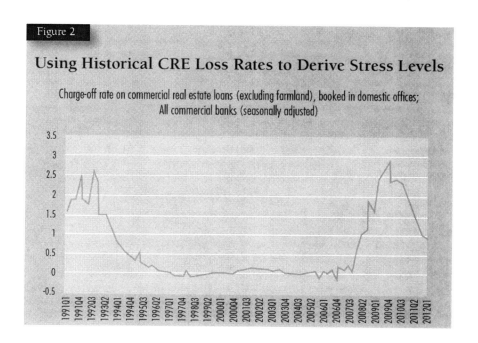

Figure 2

Using Historical CRE Loss Rates to Derive Stress Levels

Charge-off rate on commercial real estate loans (excluding farmland), booked in domestic offices; All commercial banks (seasonally adjusted)

ever, in the peak period, the loss experience is 1.9%. That's roughly a tenfold increase in losses experienced be-tween the peak and trough. Therefore, a bank may wish to stress its portfolio with a 10x loss rate during benign credit environments in order to determine how it would perform under a stressed environment.

Statistical analysis indicates the mean loss rate for the series to be 0.7% and the standard deviation to be 0.86%. Analysts can easily calculate the mean of the data series in Excel by using the =AVERAGE() function or the standard deviation by using the =STDEV() function. Therefore, if an analyst wanted to determine a moderate level of stress, he or she could add the one standard deviation to the average level of stress. In this instance, a moderate level of stress would be the mean plus one standard deviation, or 1.56% (0.7%+0.86%). Using the industry CRE data during average times, a moderate level of stress is equivalent to a doubling of the bank's average CRE loss rate. A severe stress may be akin to a three-standard-deviation move. In this instance, the severe stress would be 3.28% (0.7%+3*0.86%). Therefore, a severe stress would be equivalent to a 5x increase in the average level of loss.[3]

These rates are based on national data, though, and regional data may be quite different. Community banks whose portfolios are exposed to a single industry, employer, or region may wish to examine peer-level data from a hard-hit region. For example, if a community bank is located next to a military base, the closure of that installation would have a significant impact on the bank. So this bank, in order to determine the appropriate level of stress—and therefore the appropriate mitigation techniques—may wish to examine peer data from banks that were exposed to similar situations.

The drawback in using historical data is that past performance is not always indicative of future events. For example, in the peak loss event of the early 1990s, losses topped out at 2.57%. During the 2007-09 financial crisis, however, they peaked at 2.87%. The height of the peak is only one consideration, however: The duration of the elevated stress event should be considered as well. Ultimately, banks should have all of their scenarios approved by management and the board to ensure that the analysts are applying the appropriate level and duration of stress and that management fully understands the limitations of the analysis.

Factor Analysis

The stress-testing technique of factor analysis shocks individual drivers to determine what the overall impact on loss rates might be. For example, in analyzing the impact of drivers of credit loss in commercial real estate, the analyst may shock factors such as property value, debt service coverage, vacancy rates, net income, and cap rates. In analyzing consumer credit losses, factors to shock could be income, unemployment, debt-to-income ratio, and change in loan-to-value.

It might also be useful to shock interest rates or foreign exchange rates, then follow up with an investigation into the impact those events might have. This method can be one of the most difficult to conduct because of the level of data and analytics required to develop robust scenarios. Multifactor analysis is the methodology currently used in the large banks when conducting the Comprehensive Capital Analysis and Review, or CCAR.[4]

One drawback of factor analysis is the often limited ability of the practitioner to fully understand the relationship between the factor and subsequent loss. Trying to develop the relationship can quickly morph into the need for something more sophisticated—usually regression analysis, which is required to understand the main drivers and their relationships. These models can be difficult to develop and often require long histories of rich data before the analyst can fully understand the relationships.

However, in the case of plain-vanilla portfolios, simple relationships can be drawn and assumptions made. For instance, a bank may wish to examine the impact of a rise in interest rates and related credit risk on variable-rate loans. The analyst could examine the change in the debt service coverage ratio from a rate shock, and then make an inference about the number of loans that may go into delinquency and others that may go into default. Simple analyses like these can reveal the degree to which the portfolio is sensitive to factor shocks. Again, the conversations that will take place in trying to determine the relationship are just as important as the stress. Analysts, product managers, and management should discuss what is appropriate and which factors have the greatest impact on performance and risk.

A great resource for banks wishing to conduct a multifactor analysis is the information provided in the CCAR (assuming the regulators continue to release their expectations publicly). The CCAR released in November 2011 contained the regulators' projections for a multitude of economic in-dicators under baseline and severe stress scenarios. The following indicators provided in the CCAR are relatively comprehensive and can be used by community banks to infer potential loss:[5]

- Real GDP growth.
- Nominal GDP growth.
- Real disposable income growth.
- Nominal disposable income growth.
- Unemployment rate.
- CPI inflation rate.
- Three-month Treasury yield.
- Ten-year Treasury yield.
- BBB corporate yield.
- Mortgage rate.
- Dow Jones Stock Market Index.
- Market Volatility Index (VIX).
- House Price Index.
- Commercial Real Estate Price Index.
- Plus additional euro, Asian, U.K., and dollar indices.

As an example, the unemployment rate from the CCAR is regressed against a sample bank's credit card charge-offs.[6] Then, using the regression coefficients and the CCAR forecast of future unemployment rates, the analyst can produce a baseline and stressed forecast of credit card charge-offs. It's important to include an upside forecast as well. An easy way to generate that forecast is to use the results produced using the lower 95% confidence interval from the regression, as well as the baseline unemployment data. Table 3 presents the regression analysis and the forecast of charge-off.

Table 3	Regression Results				
Regression Statistics					
Multiple R	0.818469201				
R Square	0.669891834				
Adjusted R Square	0.661840415				
Standard Error	132.1735868				
Observations	43				
ANOVA					
	df	SS	MS	F	Significance F
Regression	1	1453522.047	1453522.05	83.2017138	2.03003E-11
Residual	41	716264.1395	17469.8571		
Total	42	2169786.186			
	Coefficients	Standard Error	t Stat	P-value	Lower 95%
Intercept	-65.50119962	70.50237783	-0.92906369	0.35829392	-207.8836402
Unemployment	97.69411438	10.7103155	9.12149734	2.03E-11	76.06419342

As a refresher, in a linear regression, the result or estimate is to take the intercept plus the slope coefficient times the independent variable. In this instance, the intercept is -65.5, the slope is 97.7, and the independent variable is the projected unemployment rate. As shown in Table 4, the baseline unemployment rate for the fourth quarter of 2011 is 9.1%. Therefore, the forecast rate for the fourth quarter of 2011 would be 824, or -65.5+97.7*9.1. Similarly, the upside charge-offs would be -65.5+76.1*9.1. Table 4 provides the calculations, and Figure 3 shows the differences in trajectories and assumptions.

Grade Migration

Grade migration examines the impact on loss as loans migrate to lower buckets. It is a relatively straightforward exercise for the bank to complete. Grade migration may shock a portfolio of loans down one or two risk grades and determine the worst-case impact on reserves and capital. A more realistic case is to pick something in between; for example, 33% of the loans remain in the current bucket, 33% migrate down one grade, 33% migrate two grades, and 1% migrate up one grade. Depending on its conservatism, management can pick and choose a scenario that is relevant to the bank's risk appetite.

Banks looking to conduct this exercise in Excel should start with a snapshot of the loan book from their data provider. Load the snapshot into Excel and make varying assumptions about the potential migration and subsequent loss rates. Be sure to keep track of the loans' status and rating, and aggregate the amount of loans within each bucket. Then consider the impact the loss rates might have on reserves and capital. An

Table 4 Unemployment and Charge-offs in Various Circumstances					
	Baseline Unemployment	Baseline Charge-offs	Stressed Unemployment	Stressed Charge-offs	Upside Charge-offs
Q42011	9.1	824	9.68	880	627
Q12012	9.1	824	10.58	968	627
Q22012	9	814	11.4	1,048	619
Q32012	8.9	804	12.16	1,122	611
Q42012	8.9	804	12.76	1,181	611
Q12013	8.69	783	13	1,205	595
Q22013	8.48	763	13.05	1,209	580
Q32013	8.27	742	12.96	1,201	564
Q42013	8.06	722	12.76	1,181	548
Q12014	7.93	709	12.61	1,166	538
Q22014	7.78	695	12.36	1,142	526
Q32014	7.63	680	12.04	1,111	515
Q42014	7.48	665	11.66	1,074	503

example of a migration table is shown in Table 5. (All data used in the following tables is fictitious.) As the table indicates, the first step is to determine the loan balances in each bucket and the expected loss associated with each grade. The sum product yields the aggregate expected loss.

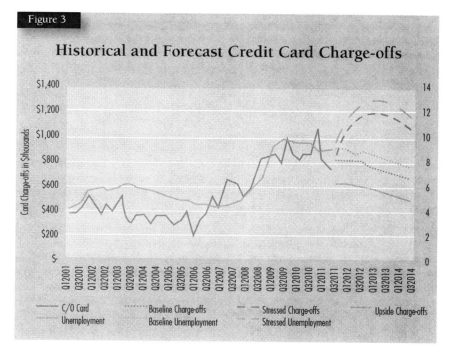

Figure 3

Historical and Forecast Credit Card Charge-offs

Table 5

			Starting Balances									
					Future							
			Pass						Special Mention	Sub-standard	Doubtful	Loss
		1	2	3	4	5	6	7	8	9	10
Current		1	$300,000									
		2		$400,000								
	Pass	3			$500,000							
		4				$1,000,000						
		5					$700,000					
		6						$600,000				
	Special Mention	7							$250,000			
	Substandard	8								$350,000		
	Doubtful	9									$300,000	
	Loss	10										$100,000
	Totals		$300,000	$400,000	$500,000	$1,000,000	$700,000	$600,000	$250,000	$350,000	$300,000	$100,000
	Loss Factor		.10%	.15%	.25%	.50%	.75%	1.0%	1.5%	2.5%	5.0%	10.0%
												Sum
	Expected Loss		$300	$600	$1,250	$5,000	$5,250	$6,000	$3,750	$8,750	$15,000	$10,000	$55,900

The next step is to apply the stress. This example assumes a loss migration of 1% up one grade, 33% down one grade, and 33% down two grades. This is reflected in the balance migration in Table 6. In this example, the starting expected loss was $55.9 million, and, after the stress, the expected loss increased to $91.7 million, an increase of almost $36 million.

Note that these changes only consider loss in the current balance. Typically, as a loan approaches default, the borrower starts to draw down on the open lines. These open lines can be considered using a credit conversion factor that translates the open line into principal balance in order to determine the overall exposure. This adds an additional step, because the bank must calculate the balance in undrawn lines and then apply a factor (say, 75%) to determine the amount that would translate into additional exposure.

Data Considerations

Data availability is a critical consideration in tool selection. Any model is only as good as the inputs contained in that model. The old adage still holds: Garbage in, garbage out! Indeed, data integrity is critical to any stress test. Banks should consider the quantity and quality of data they have prior to embarking on a formal stress-testing exercise. If the bank has a limited loss history, or if the history is from a benign period, then the internal data should be combined with data from the industry for a more robust stress on defaults.

Data is also very important because it defines the severity of the stress. If the data is not representative of potential future losses, the results could indicate a level of stress well within the expected bands, and the bank will gain a false sense of security. Therefore, part of any stress-testing program should be a process to back-test the results.

Management should always challenge the results of the stress test, especially during periods of benign loss. Similarly, they should challenge it during periods of high loan

Table 6											
Ending Balances after Migration											
				Future					Special Mention	Sub-standard	Doubtful	Loss
			Pass									
			1	2	3	4	5	6	7	8	9	10
		1	$102,000	$99,000	$99,000							
		2	$4,000	$132,000	$132,000	$132,000						
	Pass	3		$5,000	$165,000	$165,000	$165,000					
		4			$10,000	$330,000	$330,000	$330,000				
		5				$7,000	$231,000	$231,000	$231,000			
Current		6					$6,000	$198,000	$198,000	$198,000		
	Special Mention	7						$2,500	$82,500	$82,500	$82,500	$115,500
	Substandard	8							$3,500	$115,500	$115,500	$198,000
	Doubtful	9								$3,000	$99,000	$100,000
	Loss	10										
	Totals		$106,000	$236,000	$406,000	$634,000	$732,000	$761,500	$515,000	$399,000	$297,000	$413,500
	Loss Factor		0.10%	0.15%	0.25%	0.50%	0.75%	1.00%	1.50%	2.50%	5.00%	10.00%
	Expected Loss		$106	$354	$1,015	$3,170	$5,490	$7,615	$7,725	$9,975	$14,850	$41,350
	Change		$(194)	$(246)	$(235)	$(1,830)	$240	$1,615	$3,975	$1,225	$(150)	$31,350

Expected Loss Sum: $91,650
Change Sum: $35,750

losses because those periods could also produce results detrimental to the organization. I see many zealous bankers, some at the encouragement of their examiners, who are using today's stressed losses and then adding a severe level of stress to already elevated losses. The results are magnitudes above what could happen in reality. The danger here is that management will not believe in the results of the test and therefore will not actively mitigate the risks.

The second peril is in using these elevated unexpected losses as inputs into pricing models. The high levels of capital associated with the super-stressed losses may cause new loans to appear to be under the hurdle, and therefore the bank will make few (if any) new loans and will continue to shrink.

This causes an equally dangerous situation in that earnings risk becomes a greater concern than credit risk. Clearly, it is a fine balance that must be maintained between being too conservative and too aggressive in the assumptions.

And finally, the bank needs to have enough data to determine the relationship between economic factors and loan performance. Small institutions with limited loss history, as well as de novo banks, may not have a rich enough historical database to build a credible relationship. In this instance, the bank may wish to consider using benchmarks or rules of thumb for their stress testing. Regardless, the quality of data will determine the quality of the results, and the stress and management's actions should reflect the bank's risk appetite.

Conclusion

This article provided an overview of the methodologies and tools available to community banks wishing to conduct a stress test. It's been shown here that banks can perform simple stress tests in Excel without having to purchase sophisticated vendor models.

Recall the most important question to ask prior to selecting a tool: What risk or risks am I trying to control or mitigate?

The answer to this question will dictate the appropriate tool. Banks should determine if they are interested in the overall bank-level risk, portfolio-level risk, or loan-level risk. And they should ultimately consider performing multiple sets of stress tests because the science is not exact. Using multiple types of techniques provides multiple levels of information to compare and contrast, further enriching the discussions around stress testing as staff, management, and the board debate the outcomes. Most importantly, examining these multiple dimensions can reveal weaknesses in the bank's strategy.

In summary, stress testing is a cornerstone of a well-functioning ERM program. Banks of all sizes should be considering the benefits of a stress-testing program and either starting the function internally or enhancing current efforts.

Notes

1. This article provides an overview of the various methodologies and tools. For a more in-depth explanation, including detailed examples and a practical how-to guide, see *RMA's Scenario Analysis and Stress Testing for Community Banks: A Basic Guide.*

2. Board of Governors of the Federal Reserve System, "The Supervisory Capital Assessment Program: Overview of Results," Washington, D.C., May 2009.

3. RMA and bankstresstesting.com have additional information and tools to help analysts use the statistics and infer the appropriate level of stress.

4. Board of Governors of the Federal Reserve System, "Federal Reserve System Comprehensive Capital Plan Review," Washington, D.C., November 2011.

5. Banks may wish to supplement this national data with state or other local information consistent with their operating geography.

6. The data is derived from an amalgamation of several community banks with credit card portfolios, based on call report data. The data is masked to protect the identity of the banks.

Stressing the Stress Testing

By Yakov Lantsman and David Shu

arket volatility and extreme distress have occurred since the beginning of capitalism. The Tulip Mania in 1637 and the South Sea Bubble in 1720, dubbed the "Enron of England," were among the most infamous in the early days.[1,2]

Centuries later, we continue to witness financial distress that destroys considerable amounts of wealth while leaving ill-prepared market participants in shock. Major financial incidents have become much more frequent in recent times, with 2008 marked by a large number of failures in the financial industry.

While the recent crisis has similarities to its major predecessors, there is a notable exception. Computer-generated risk models are more influential than ever before in decision making. Lenders, rating agencies, and investment banks relied heavily on these risk models. Financial companies across the globe use similar models deemed as reliable and sufficient to measure risk. Confidence in these models grew after long periods of relatively benign economic and financial conditions while memories of the last major market distress faded.

During the economic expansion of 2002-07, the derivatives market ballooned to an unprecedented level of $600 trillion, the equivalent of almost $100,000 per person on earth.[3] Certain highly complex financial instruments, such as collateralized credit default swaps (CDS), were unregulated and poorly understood, resulting in banks' and investors' widespread miscalculations of the actual risk inherent in those instruments. While the risk models were useful under "normal" market conditions, ultimately they proved inadequate under extreme market distress.

Many attribute model failures to insufficient stress testing. Although banks performed frequent stress tests in the past, the financial crisis led many banks and regulators to question whether these stress-testing practices were adequate to cope with a rapidly changing environment. In particular, not only was the crisis far more severe than reflected in the banks' stress-testing parameters, but possibly it was compounded by weaknesses in stress-testing practices in reaction to the unfolding events.[4]

The U.S. government's stress-test undertaking, or Supervisory Capital Assessment Program (SCAP), was designed to assess if major U.S. banks have sufficient capital to buffer against losses that could occur under conditions more stressful than expected. Banks were asked to estimate their potential losses on loans, securities, and trading positions, as well as pre-provision net revenue and the resources available from the allowance for loan and lease losses under two alternative macroeconomic scenarios.[5]

While the usefulness of SCAP is beyond the scope of this article, it is important to note that it is but *one measure* of potential stresses—an estimate fraught with assump-

339

tions and risks. These risks include underestimating the potential severity and duration of stress events and insufficiently identifying and aggregating risks on a firm-wide basis.

Nout Wellink, chairman of the Basel Committee on Banking Supervision and president of the Netherlands Bank, noted that "stress testing is an important risk management tool. It plays a critical role in strengthening not only bank corporate governance but also the resilience of individual banks and the financial system." He added that "the financial crisis has demonstrated the importance of stress testing as an integral part of any bank's risk management, liquidity, and capital planning process."[6]

Lesson 1: Risks and Markets Are Highly Correlated

Many financial institutions did not perform stress tests that took a holistic view across risks, geographies, and different portfolios. Stress tests insufficiently aggregated risks and failed to recognize the interdependencies among the many types of institutions in modern-day financial markets. Consequently, banks did not have a comprehensive view across the credit, market, liquidity, and operational risks of their various businesses.

Additionally, stress events often were based on historical events, such as the 1987 stock market crash or the Asian crisis in the 1990s. Organizations struggled to create stress tests based on hypothetical scenarios and events. Imagine management's reaction to a chief risk officer who in 2005-06 suggested modeling a 25% decline in the housing price index or the failure of a number of the largest Wall Street investment banks.

Furthermore, existing correlation modeling methodologies were based on a static view of the interdependencies among markets, products, and institutions. Comprehensive statistical analysis of corresponding correlation structures reveals a significant element of periodicity in correlation behavior. Another way of describing this is "regime change," in which abrupt changes in otherwise stable correlation structures can be observed. Suddenly and unexpectedly, portfolios started moving in one "wrong" direction with accelerated speed.

When correlation assumptions based on a history of stability or "normality" break down, the correlations tend to swing to the extremes. In 1998, Long-Term Capital Management (LTCM) collapsed following Russia's default on its debt. LTCM's complex models used a Gaussian copula, or connecting curves of normal distribution, that assumed no contagion across markets.

In the recent crisis, the behavior of collateralized debt obligations (CDO) clearly is not inde-pendent as they are all affected by the same general market conditions. In fact, they turned out to be highly correlated. The risk was systematized by using Gaussian copula model functions to rapidly price these instruments based on the price of related CDS. This approach assumed that the price of CDS was correlated with and could predict the correct price of mortgage-backed securities.

Because the models were highly tractable, they rapidly came to be used by a huge percentage of CDO and CDS investors, issuers, and rating agencies. The entire pricing model was based on a misconception of the real estate market and did not reflect the level of systematic risks. This pricing approach was an accident waiting to happen. According to FT.com, it has been estimated that "from late 2005 to the middle of 2007, around $450bn of CDOs of ABS [asset-backed securities] were issued. ... Of that pile, around $305bn of the CDOs are now in a formal state of default. ...."[7] In the first quarter of 2008 alone, rating agencies announced more than 4,000 downgrades of CDOs.[8]

Existing modeling methodologies based on well-documented concepts of efficient markets, where all participants act rationally to maximize their utility functions across different products and time horizons, cannot be adapted easily to reflect the phenomenon of regime change that results from bubble bursts. Reconsidering these methodologies may enable model builders to make another quantum leap in understanding and explaining the collective behavior of market participants.

In our view, two major components are necessary to build a more realistic modeling framework. One component is a more comprehensive behavioral understanding of the market players and their goals, risk appetite, horizons, regulatory environment, and anticipated changes. A more technical component is developing a more robust and reality-oriented modeling framework that consistently reflects several critical factors, including the following:

- Account for market players' horizons. What could be a devastating loss event for a day trader or hedge fund manager could be a buying opportunity for a pension fund or insurance company.
- Develop mechanisms to trigger horde behavior, where investors defy the laws of rational behavior and stampede to exit the market.
- Develop a statistical modeling framework that incorporates dynamic changes in correlation structures.
- Provide more systematic insights into modeling tail-risk behavior.
- Develop a consistent and realistic mechanism for stress testing based on educated, challenged, and defensible scenarios (to reduce the ad hoc nature of many scenarios).

To see the regime change in the correlation structure, recall how rapidly high-quality paper consisting of senior tranches of CDOs and RMBSs imploded. The major result of downgrading these instruments was a snowballing of foreclosure and delinquency rates, a direct reflection of the surge in correlation between individual exposures.

Today's market participants are trying to digest the controversial reality of highly correlated value-at-risk (VaR) losses. According to the modeling methodologies that underlay the "efficient market" concept, the market could be correlated (even significantly) in the middle part of the loss distribution, but not at the extreme tails. The location of this efficient-market correlation is where information symmetry breaks down and where participants should consider independent behaviors. The often-used modeling structure is a Gaussian copula with corresponding characteristics of highly concentrated correlations in the middle part of the loss distribution and a lack of correlation at the extreme tails. In the realm of the Gaussian copula, it is virtually impossible to impose meaningful correlations at VaR levels of 99.95% and higher. But today's market proved to be operating at this level of losses.

In other words, if we are trying to assess the aggregate impact of three risks (for example, products, portfolios, and markets) at an extreme level of events at 99.95% (one in 2,000 years) and significant correlation, we will end up with the joint probability of 99.99999% (one in 10,000,000 years) for all three events to happen. A completely independent case results in a VaR level of one in 80,000,000 years.

Table 1	
What Happened in Each Risk Area	
| Liquidity risk |	All markets experienced dramatic drops in liquidity—and, through new linkages, multiple markets became illiquid at the same time. Access to funding was restricted significantly owing to contraction in the interbank lending markets as well as to retail depositor concerns that led to runs on some banks. Market liquidity dried up, and banks could no longer hedge their portfolios.
| Market risk |	Negative yield curve and market downturn. The negative yield curve shift severely impacted interest rate risk and portfolio risk. We observed large standard deviation moves in the market—moves of 5, 6, 7 standard deviation or greater. Additionally, basis risk became severe as relationships between various benchmark rates moved well away from historical relationships.
| Credit risk |	Dramatic increases in mortgage and credit card defaults (and loss given default). The lack of confidence quickly turned into a credit crunch in which some banks could not fund existing loans and most banks were unwilling to extend new credit. The credit market was nearly frozen in September 2008.
| Operational risk |	Extreme operational losses occurred or were alleged to have occurred due to rogue trading or alleged fraud. Losses were greatly amplified by the negative market conditions. Most notable examples included Madoff Securities ($50 billion), Allen Stanford ($8 billion), and Société Générale ($7 billion).
| Macroeconomics |	By September 2008, average U.S. housing prices had declined more than 20% from their mid-2006 peak.[9] Energy prices skyrocketed during the summer of 2008. Many portfolios were simply bets on favorable macroeconomic conditions in the U.S. and the world. Hence, the structural changes and shocks in macroeconomic and sociopolitical factors led to a crisis of confidence; to pressures on currency values, interest rates, and capital flows; and to the sudden worsening of economic conditions that caused spectacular losses.

However, today's events demonstrate that the reality assesses the likelihood of joint events at a level of at least 99.97% to 99.99% (3,000 to 10,000 years), literally putting all correlation at the extreme tail. This discussion demonstrates that currently employed modeling techniques cannot be used to measure aggregate loss in a world where correlation assumptions are changing dynamically—thus the importance of rethinking stress-testing analyses.

It seems evident that the existing stress testing was not structured for systematically testing dependencies across risk areas and between portfolios. With regard to funding liquidity, stress tests did not anticipate the structural changes in financial markets that evolved over time and led to the systemic nature of the crisis, nor did they foresee the magnitude and duration of the disruption to interbank markets.

We advocate a comprehensive modeling framework that addresses the shortcomings stated above by introducing modeling concepts based on the ideas of multifractal theory, pioneered by Benoit B. Mandelbrot. Multifractal capital market theory (MCMT) considers capital markets not as homogeneous trading and risk-managing activities with similar goals, time horizons, and risk appetites, but as scalable constructs with properties taken from observing large natural and social systems. With MCMT, it is conceptually and technically natural to incorporate market triggers to assess probability of large price swings or changes in correlations. The stress testing of individual risk components is a logical extension of fat-tail distributions employed by fractal scaling.

Lesson 2: Stress Testing Was Not Stressful Enough

Financial models attempt to predict market reactions to a range of anticipated inputs. Unfortunately, the market is simply the aggregation of human actions and reactions, and the entire range of inputs cannot be anticipated adequately. The fundamental reason for systemic failure was the overreliance on models with what turned out to be deeply flawed assumptions.

Modeling experts and their business leaders used their models to justify risk-based returns, tweaking risk tolerances and, at times, throwing common sense out the window. As the U.K. Financial Services Authority stated, "… many firms have previously been over-optimistic in evaluating the severity and impacts of adverse scenarios."[10] This level of optimism eventually led to underpricing risk.

The requirements for timely, comprehensive, and complete data along with realistic market scenarios pose enormous technical challenges. Modelers often resort to using historical data and set prices and make decisions based on expected market moves. Additionally, the last deep recession occurred in the late 1980s to early 1990s, whereas most historical data goes back only five to seven years.

Furthermore, in the 20 years since, many banks have consolidated away from multi-bank holding companies to more centralized one-bank holding companies, consequently wiping out considerable amounts of data. Meanwhile, new and highly complex investment products and services have been introduced with no historical precedents. The fundamental question for modelers and risk managers is this: *Would you predict the future using only the rearview mirror?*

A critical component of a risk manager's job is to help business leadership look beyond the "good old times" and devise strategies for what will inevitably come—bad times and a down cycle. Because risk models are only as good as their inputs and assumptions, challenging deal valuations, credit estimates, and VaR results is paramount. We recognize that many risk managers likely expressed these views. It is more important than ever that risk professionals be supported and heard within an organization and that downside scenarios be vetted thoroughly when making business decisions.

Figure 1 demonstrates the stress-test scenarios used by regulators during SCAP. Many believe these scenarios are realistic in the current environment, yet anyone who suggested them two years ago would have been ridiculed or ignored. Acceptance of these radical scenarios requires leadership and involvement by senior management. Executive involvement is the foundation of successful risk management—stress testing in particular.

Senior management should seek to foster a culture where consideration of risk is second nature and personnel are expected to identify key risks. Managers must use their business knowledge to identify scenarios that are stressful enough to identify extreme moves and construct scenarios in which such extreme losses would occur.

For example, what might cause a 5-, 6-, 7-, 8-, 9-, or 10-standard-deviation loss event? As long as the events are possible, no matter how unlikely, they should at least be consid-

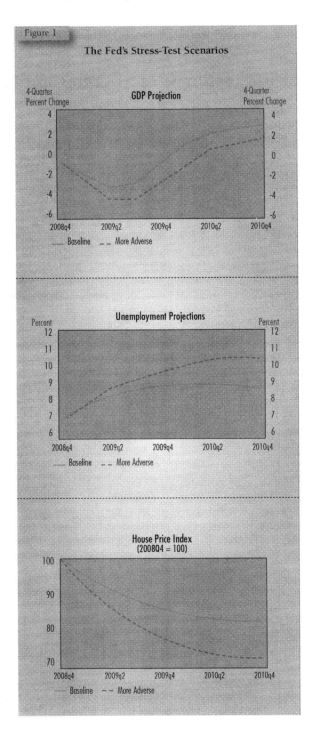

Figure 1

The Fed's Stress-Test Scenarios

ered. Smaller moves are not relevant for stress testing and are addressed in risk and capital measures. Some of the macroeconomic scenarios might include the following:

- Hyperinflation.
- A sharp devaluation of the dollar.
- Sudden collapse of a major economy, such as China, Russia, or Japan.
- Global pandemic illness.
- Category-4 hurricanes up the U.S. East Coast.
- An 8.0 Richter-measured earthquake on the U.S. West Coast.
- An energy bubble bursting.
- Downgrade of U.S. sovereign debt.

Management should always challenge assumptions and overly optimistic model outcomes. Historical data should not be relied on entirely for investment decisions—it can too easily be manipulated to see what you want to see. Management should apply common sense to stress testing and never be intimidated by mathematicians. Challenging them only makes them better.

What's Next?

Most bank stress tests were not designed to capture the extreme market events we have experienced. Scenarios tended to assume mild shocks with shorter durations and underestimated the correlations between different risk types and markets. Stress testing failed in large part because of overly optimistic assumptions.

Overreliance on computer-generated models is most certainly a major problem. While we devise models that attempt to better understand market phenomena, these models will always be limited. *They must be used and tested with discretion and sensitivity to their limits.*

Stress testing should be embedded in regular management dialogue and decision making. No risk management program can prevent all losses, but the firms with the best practices can minimize surprises and position themselves to succeed in crisis situations. Stress testing, when used properly, is a powerful means of anticipating and preparing for shocks and the resulting potential losses.

According to the Basel Committee on Banking Supervision, stress testing will help risk management achieve the following objectives[11]:

- Provide forward-looking assessments of risk.
- Overcome limitations of models and historical data.
- Support internal and external communication.
- Feed into capital and liquidity planning procedures.
- Inform the setting of a bank's risk tolerance.
- Facilitate the development of risk mitigation or contingency plans across a range of stressed conditions.

Risk managers should continue to evaluate and revise stress-testing practices to improve the quality of their risk models. New regulatory standards will be more demanding, and their implementation will create significant challenges for financial services firms. The question is not only how risk management generates better scenarios and more reliable model results, but also how these results are best communicated, validated, and transformed into strategic decisions.

Notes

1. See "South Sea Bubble," available at http://www.stock-market-crash.net/south sea.htm.
2. "History of Greatest Market Crashes," *The Korea Times*, April 22, 2009.
3. "Bring Back Link between Gold and Dollar," *Financial Times*, November 23, 2008.
4. Basel Committee on Banking Supervision, "Principles for Sound Stress Testing Practices and Supervision," January 2009.
5. Board of Governors of the Federal Reserve System, "The Supervisory Capital Assessment Program: Design and Implementation," April 24, 2009.
6. Bank for International Settlements, "Principles for Sound Stress Testing: Basil Committee Issues Consultative Paper," press release, January 6, 2009, available at http://www.bis.org/press/p090106.htm.
7. "Insight: Time to Expose the True Value of CDOs," FT.com, February 26, 2009.
8. "CDO Deals Resurface but Down 90 Pct in Q1-Report," Reuters, April 9, 2008.
9. "A Helping Hand to Homeowners," Economist.com, October 23, 2008.
10. Financial Services Authority, "Stress and Scenario Testing," December 2008.
11. Basel Committee on Banking Supervision, January 2009.

Stress Testing the Credit Risk of Commercial Real Estate Mezzanine Lending

By George Pappadopoulos

t's the old question that continues to haunt us: What's the proper balance between risk and pricing?

It's particularly hard to answer that question in a dynamic and highly competitive environment coinciding with the peak of the credit cycle. This article suggests a way to determine the proper pricing for commercial real estate mezzanine lending.

In their search for higher-yielding investments in the tough competitive environment of 2006, commercial real estate (CRE) lenders moved outward on the risk spectrum. According to the Mortgage Bankers Association, CRE mezzanine loans, second mortgages, and preferred equity increased almost 300% in 2005, substantially narrowing the previously high yields of these instruments. Things didn't get any better in 2006. The good news, to date, is that delinquencies continue to be very, very low, but that picture could change in 2007.

As the intermediate financing piece in the capital structure, mezzanine investments are expected to provide returns that exceed those of the senior debt. As with many financial instruments, the increased return comes at the expense of increased risk. The key question is this: What level of excess return is appropriate compensation for the excess risk (increased downside exposure)?

Mezzanine loans provide financing that bridges the gap between a senior mortgage and borrower equity. As such, the security of the mezzanine lender is subordinate to the senior mortgage; that is, the mezzanine investor will bear losses ahead of the senior lender, and the downside protection of the mezzanine loan is smaller.

Increased competition in this sector has pushed lenders farther out on the capital stack. The overall leverage available to borrowers from mezzanine financing has gone from 75-85% to a riskier 80-90% and can range as high as 95% of the capital structure in some cases.

Borrowers are willing to pay up for the increased leverage available from mezzanine financing. In fact, there appears to be a very sizable market. As a result, mezzanine investment spreads can range from a few hundred basis points to 700 or more, depending on how much of the capital structure is covered.

Totals Returns versus Net Returns

Returns of up to 700 basis points or more are certainly attractive, especially in today's environment. The question remains, however, as to the level of *net* returns after default losses. Being higher in the capital structure means mezzanine investments have less cushion from loss (higher loan-to-value); that is, the borrower's equity slice is smaller, so these investments can encounter losses earlier and to a larger degree than senior mortgages.

Another important factor regarding the risk of mezzanine investments is that they are inherently leveraged. Because it is a smaller slice of the capital structure (typically 5-20%) and is subordinate to other financing, *full* mezzanine principal is hit by loss before the first dollar loss occurs to the senior position. So mezzanine could experience a 100% loss, but it's highly unlikely that the senior mortgage would.

  ▪ Example: Assume a $100 property has a $75 senior lien and an additional $10 mezzanine loan. A $50 default recovery due to a decline in the property value means a complete principal loss for the mezzanine loan but only a 33% principal loss for the senior loan (($75-50)/$75). The smaller the piece of the capital structure represented by the mezzanine tranche, the more severe this issue becomes.

Obviously, quantification of expected loss is a critical component in understanding the risk of mezzanine loans. Since individual metropolitan-level and property-type cycles are a major driver of default, let's focus on assessing credit risk through the integration of three key systematic risk factors:

  ▪ Metropolitan-level and property-type volatility.
  ▪ Expected metro and property-type growth for NOI and value.
  ▪ Loan structure protection.

Creating a Model

We should be able to assess meaningful expected losses by *calibrating* a model based on systematic factors that influence the performance of the underlying real estate collateral. A number of critical considerations go into the analysis of a commercial mortgage portfolio—for example, various levels of debt service coverage ratios (DSCR) and loan-to-value (LTV), assorted changes in the ratios through time, and a diverse range in the uncertainty of such changes.

The model allows us to develop an informed *proactive* opinion about the relative riskiness of different loan structures in different markets and property types.[1] Since our approach outlines a time series of periodic loss expectations, we can appropriately assess the expected *yield degradation*.

  ▪ We can calculate the risk-adjusted cash flow stream by applying loss expectations for each period.
  ▪ The internal rate of return for the risky cash flows is the risk-adjusted yield, and the difference between the risk-adjusted yield and the non-risk-adjusted yield is the *yield degradation*.

Using this consistent, forward-looking framework, we can quantify the credit cost differences across market and submarket, property type, and loan structure. By modeling several alternate loan structures across four property types in 54 of the largest metropolitan areas, we can gain a broad-based understanding of the credit costs associated with mezzanine lending.

Figure 1 outlines the summary statistics for the yield degradation incurred for each loan structure across all 216 metro and property-type combinations. We can determine the increased risk associated with the general upward move in the capital stack by having the structures compare a more conservative 85% LTV with several higher-risk 90% LTV tranches.

- On average, we can expect a 69-basis-point impact from credit loss for an older-style (Structure A) 20% mezzanine tranche of a four-year, 85% LTV, and 1.2 DSCR loan. Meanwhile, 90% of the markets can expect to see an impact of less than 126 basis points. So a large pool of well-diversified real estate loans of this structure is expected to perform very well on a credit-risk-adjusted basis. That is, the excess yield generally available for this type of structure should be more than enough to compensate for average loss expectations at the portfolio level.

- As we would expect, the increased leverage (and reduced DSCR) of newer 90% LTV mortgages (Structure B-1) stresses loss expectations. Yield degradation for a 20% mezzanine loan behind a 70% senior loan is nearly 50% more than the lower-leverage alternative of Structure A (98 versus 69 basis points). Furthermore, narrowing the mezzanine tranche to 15% and then to 10% successively increases the average expected yield impact to 130 and 197 basis points. In addition, some markets experience some very harsh loss numbers. On average, a loss impact of more than 350 basis points is worrisome, except when compared with the high pricing levels that can be achieved in the marketplace for such originations. Double-digit returns mean that mezzanine investors are, on average, receiving substantial excess returns for this level of credit risk. Especially if some of the riskier markets can be avoided, there appear to be solid risk-adjusted opportunities even with a small tranche at this high level in the leverage hierarchy.

- On the other hand, what if we see more drastic deterioration in the underlying economic conditions? The results shown in Figure 1 are based on the most likely trend for the economy, but what if we are mistaken in those assumptions? If a severe downturn ensues, these higher-leverage instruments will see highly exacerbated losses. This is because an economic downturn will certainly place a lot of pressure on property markets and thereby erode the protective cushion—slim as it is in this case—available to the lender.

Figure 1	Yield Degradation—Base Case			
Base Case	**Structure A**	**Structure B-1**	**Structure B-2**	**Structure B-3**
Senior Tranche	65%	70%	75%	80%
Mezzanine Tranche	20%	20%	15%	10%
Total Loan LTV	85%	90%	90%	90%
DSCR	1.2	1.1	1.1	1.1
Yield Degradation (bps)				
Average	69	98	130	197
Maximum	245	328	440	670
90th Percentile	126	162	217	327

Figure 2	Yield Degradation—Recession Scenario			
Recession Stress Case	**Structure A**	**Structure B-1**	**Structure B-2**	**Structure B-3**
Senior Tranche	65%	70%	75%	80%
Mezzanine Tranche	20%	20%	15%	10%
Total LTV	85%	90%	90%	90%
DSCR	1.2	1.1	1.1	1.1
Yield Degradation (bps)				
Average	119	200	268	408
Maximum	412	704	961	1,513
90th Percentile	179	307	414	631

Figure 2 illustrates the impact on these investments under a stress scenario of severe recession. It is clear that the newer-style mezzanine originations do indeed see a substantial increase in overall loss expectations, and the thinner tranches of Structures B-2 and B-3 bear the huge brunt of such a downturn. Although this economic scenario is unlikely to occur, the numbers are still worrisome and important to consider. Nonetheless, if appropriate underwriting can avoid high leverage exposure to a number of high-risk markets, then downside exposure for diversified mezzanine loan portfolios may be covered by high yields, and highly negative returns can then be avoided.

Proceed, but with Caution

In general, the underlying credit risk of mezzanine investing increases significantly over its whole-loan alternatives, and the risk certainly increases with decreasing size of the first-loss tranche. That said, investors appear to be well compensated for originating a well-diversified, appropriately underwritten pool of mezzanine loans, even under some of the increased-leverage assumptions. The risk-adjusted yield for mezzanine commercial real estate mortgages as a whole compares very favorably with other, more traditional fixed-income investments, and an appropriate allocation to this sector appears justified. So after appropriate stress testing and careful deliberation, commercial real estate lenders should continue to participate in and be rewarded for mezzanine investing.

Note

1. See George Pappadopoulos and Jun Chen, "Commercial Real Estate Loan Default Frequency," *Journal of Portfolio Management,* fall 2002.

Stress Testing 2004-2005 Retail Originations

By Joseph L. Breeden

A few years back, lots of people used the words "stress testing," but not many knew how to stress test portfolios. Then came Basel II and a ready response to "Why stress test?" But more recently, we've come to see the business value in stress testing, and this article offers both the rationale and the basics. Although stress testing is often discussed in relation to model stability or operational risks, the emphasis here is on macroeconomic stresses.

Retail lenders frequently hear the question "What good is stress testing?" The current favorite answer is "to satisfy Basel II requirements." But there are more bottom-line factors to consider than just regulatory compliance. While it's true that Basel II requires stress testing as a check on capital adequacy, the *business value* of stress testing can be significant. Stress testing existing portfolios and pricing new loans against a range of possible future environments is a critical piece of strategic management information. It answers the question "Is my portfolio robust to any change?"

The response might still be "Who cares? I can't do anything about the environment!" Here, the rejoinder is that it's necessary to take *fragility* into account.

Forecasting is used today to set product pricing, features, and policies. The baseline forecast is created using a baseline economic scenario representing the midpoint of possible futures—the 50/50 scenario.

We assume that the product is properly priced relative to the baseline scenario. But what if the future does not unfold as planned? We assume that better future environments are to our advantage, at least relative to losses, but what about the other 50%? How fragile is our product to macroeconomic futures that do not match our expectations? In some situations, even a small downturn in the economy can create troublesome situations for management.

Can we price our products to be profitable under all possible future environments and still be competitive in the market? This is the core question in product design and Basel II.

Retail Stress-Testing Basics

Stress testing for retail lending, although conceptually similar to commercial lending, is unique in its details. Stress testing is usually viewed as one of the following:

1. Stressing the structure (parameters) of forecast models.
2. Testing the impact of operational events.
3. Testing the impact of extreme macroeconomic environments.

Although the first two are important, the third type of stress testing—considering macroeconomic changes—gives us an opportunity to change product terms, pricing, and segment mix to make profitability more robust to the environment.

Stress testing starts with scenario-based forecasting. The point of introducing stresses is to see how future performance will be impacted. Thus, a forecasting model is required. To introduce the stresses, the forecasting model needs to be able to take these as inputs. Therefore, explicit scenario-based forecasting is required.

Creating a scenario-based forecasting model is where retail lending diverges from commercial lending. Previous articles in *The RMA Journal* have focused on the details of creating such models. To summarize, all models either intuitively or explicitly incorporate three primary factors:

1. Quality of the loans booked.
2. Maturation process for the risk-return characteristics.
3. External (macroeconomic) impacts on loan performance.

These factors can be incorporated into models of default risk, revenue generation, and expenses. Apparently, such models can be created with equal fidelity at either the account or vintage/segment level. The trade-off is greater processing speed for vintage models but greater dynamic drill-down capability for account-level models. For stress testing involving multiple scenarios, processing speed probably is more valuable.

Controlling Product Fragility

Stress testing tends to be viewed as a regulatory checklist item because it is not connected to anything operational. However, if we know that a 5% deterioration in the macroeconomic environment can cause our loans to become unprofitable, immediate action should be taken. Portfolios fail during recessions because they were too fragile to macroeconomic changes.

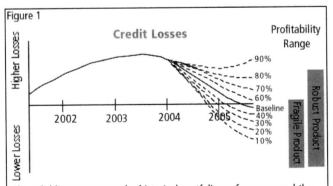

Figure 1

The solid line represents the historical portfolio performance and the baseline scenario for future performance under a range of macroeconomic environments. The dashed lines are alternate scenarios for future performance. The product bars at right show what range of environments can be withstood and maintain profitability.

So if we run our stress test and find, as in Figure 1, that our portfolio is fragile, how do we take corrective actions? Line-of-credit products tend to be more flexible than installment products. Credit lines can be adjusted, balance-transfer programs altered, and interest rates changed. For both loans and lines, we often can change penalty fees and grace periods. In all cases, we must focus on the product terms and pricing at origination—where we have the most flexibility to make changes.

Although the above paragraph offered the usual list of control knobs for account originations and management, we also want to include the changing cost of funds, recovery rates, attrition, and prepayment. The point is that we need to look *beyond* setting product control knobs just to meet margin goals under a baseline scenario. As we consider making changes, we need to rerun the stress test and ask how fragile a proposed pricing model will be to possible changes in the macroeconomic environment.

Looking Backward

Peering back into the past—say, January 2000—the baseline economic scenario was not set for recession. Some scenarios assumed flat growth and others were wildly optimistic about the death of the business cycle. A few lonely voices warned of a possible recession, but not many people noticed until the stock market declined.

Even after the recession set in, most retail loan portfolios continued to book loans aggressively. Credit scores continued to look reasonable during this period, but the 2000 vintage proved to be one of the highest-risk vintages in many years. One reason cited is adverse selection by consumers: The best consumers were startled by the stock market difficulties and started protecting their balance sheets. Those willing to take on new debt may have known they were in trouble before it appeared in their credit scores.

The problem is that retail loans take time to mature. This is the second of three factors in retail loan modeling mentioned earlier. For most loan products, peak default risk occurs about two years after origination—in this case, around 2002. That put the worst vintage in years maturing during the worst environment in years.

An unexpectedly bad vintage maturing in an unexpectedly bad environment caused trouble for many portfolios. Although many reported record profits because of the low cost of funds, others were not so fortunate. Again, the question is one of product fragility. Some portfolio managers got lucky. Others planned ahead or reacted quickly.

Looking Forward

The relevant question now is this: What about 2004? The environment looks good. Everyone's baseline scenario is for continued steady improvement in the economy and therefore in default rates. But the loans booked today will be maturing in 2006 and 2007. Are we certain that the environment two to three years from now will improve as much as we think? Pricing calibrated to an improving economy is equivalent to placing a bet on the economy.

Rather than placing a bet on the advice of your favorite economist, why not try a range of possibilities. See how robust those new bookings and the portfolio overall will

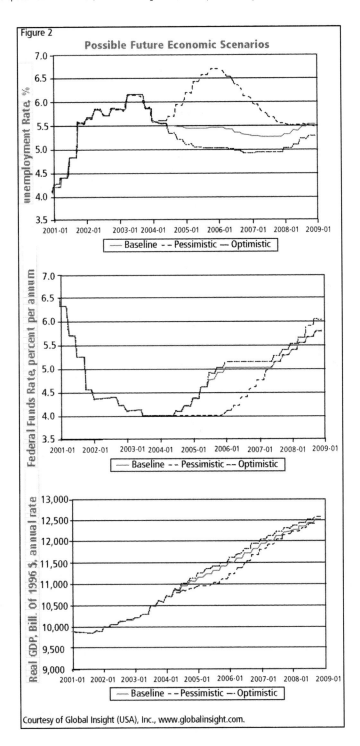

Figure 2

Possible Future Economic Scenarios

Courtesy of Global Insight (USA), Inc., www.globalinsight.com.

be to possible deterioration in the economy. Most economic data vendors offer a range of scenarios for the future macroeconomic environment. Three primary U.S. macroeconomic scenarios are provided in Figure 2 for purposes of our discussion here.

The *baseline* scenario is the slow but steady growth that everyone is discussing. Interest rates start to rise by the end of this year and, by 2007, industry delinquency levels reverse course.

The *optimistic* scenario differs in that inflation stays low so the Federal Reserve keeps interest rates low through 2005. This results in more economic growth before the brakes are applied.

The third scenario, labeled *pessimistic*, calls for a "growth recession" in 2005. This is not a true recession in the sense of negative GDP growth, but a burst of unemployment would have a negative impact on consumers.

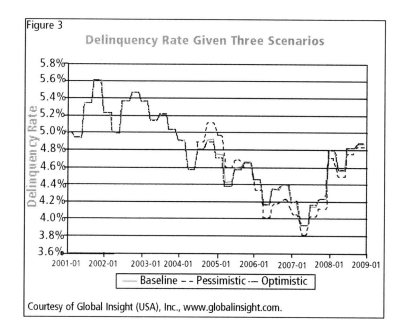

So how will your portfolio perform under the pessimistic scenario? How much are you willing to pay in adjustments to your product pricing to buy insurance against such a downturn? If you have a scenario-based forecasting system in place, then you have the tools necessary to answer this question. If your portfolio struggles given just this moderately pessimistic scenario, changes may be in order.

Viewing stress testing as just a regulatory requirement misses important business value. Stress testing is at the heart of managing a portfolio through the uncontrolled ups and downs of the future economic environment.

Reverse Stress Testing: A Structured Approach

By Maurice Kilavuka

I n recent years, regulators have introduced new requirements for reverse stress testing. Conceptually, reverse stress testing is meant to analyze situations in which a firm's business model would be rendered unviable owing to occurrences of predefined events. In such a state, the firm either fails completely or incurs major supervisory intervention.

The objective is not to assess the amount of capital required to avert the failed state indicated by the scenarios. Rather, the goal is to provide senior management with insight into how, or even if, it can strengthen its risk management and business operations to contain some of the potential risks.

If done properly, reverse stress testing can close existing gaps between the firm's risk and business strategies. When firms understand the potential pitfalls, they should be able to adjust their risk strategies accordingly. The result of these adjustments naturally leads to an increase in the certainty of delivering on the chosen business strategy.

Meeting the Challenge

The challenge for firms is to develop credible and comprehensive scenarios that can play a role in informing a firm's risk management practices. Regulators point out that the key benefit derived from reverse stress testing lies in the thought process involved in developing the scenarios. Quantitative measures demonstrate the potential impacts, but are not the ultimate goal in themselves.

This article offers some insight into the approach that firms might take in reverse stress testing. The primary focus is on defining the scenarios rather than the numerical analysis that often accompanies scenario analysis. Readers might find it useful to review the literature on stress testing to gain an understanding of approaches to quantitative analysis.

For reverse stress testing, we are principally concerned about failure scenarios—that is, scenarios that would lead to the failure of a business model (although the firm might be able to survive in a different form). For such scenarios to materialize, preconditions must be satisfied. Some of the preconditions will be unknown or unobservable. Others will be uncontrollable or nonspecific to the firm (what we call environmental conditions).

Regardless of the conditions, a trigger event or combination of events sets off the materialization of the scenarios. Subsequent actions and reactions, coupled with existing control mechanisms, then determine the ultimate effects of the scenarios. Clearly, the path from cause to a failed state is nonlinear; several influence points need to be considered in the scenarios' evolution process.

Thinking of Failure Modes

It is helpful to approach the development of failure scenarios from an engineering angle. Borrowing from mechanical and material engineering, let us consider the mode of failure of a component. The way the failure happens may be equated to the failure of a system, process, procedures, or operations in a firm. We are interested in the causes and the likely end states of a failure scenario.

The failure mode tells us how a failure occurred. From the failure mode, we can then determine which events precipitated the failure, why those events happened, and what the results might be. Hence, our approach is to start by imagining all possible failure modes and then go on to develop the possible scenarios.

For each failure mode, we need to describe the failure conditions and hypothesize on the proximate and ultimate causes of the failure. Then we analyze the process leading to the failure and its development patterns. Separately, we need to estimate likelihood and frequency of occurrence. Lastly, we need to work out the likely effects and therefore the severity of the failure.

The following discussion illustrates the types of scenarios that should be considered based on the failure modes.

1. Sudden Events Leading to Rapid Failure (Brittle Failure)

This failure mode is generally characterized by minimal indication of stress to the system. The failure is also sudden. We can imagine some scenarios that fit this description. Here are two examples:

- Sudden loss of reputation due to a serious breach by the firm that leads to almost all its counterparties withdrawing business from the firm. This event needs to happen within a few days to fit the pattern and must lead to the complete cessation of the firm's business activities.
- A major operational failure at the firm that renders continuing and future business impossible. We assume there can be no recovery of operations within a period that enables the firm to regain the trust of its clients and partners.

2. Sudden Events Leading to Gradual Failure (Ductile Failure)

In contrast to brittle failure described above, this mode allows for some residual operations after the events. For instance, if a withdrawal of significant clients and business partners were to occur, we assume that the firm retains a few of them but that the business model is unsustainable with the reduced numbers. Therefore, the firm fails within a few months of the event's occurrence. Similar to the brittle failure, however, the stress induced on the system would have been unobservable prior to its occurrence, hence its sudden nature. Two examples might be the following:

- Failure of some operational systems that greatly erodes the marketplace's trust in the firm, leading to its quick withdrawal from certain products. The ramp product lines are insufficient to sustain the firm.
- Sudden collapse of some significant part of the firm's market that terminally limits its options for future business streams.

3. Sustained Stress Leading to Sudden Failure (Buckling)

These scenarios imagine developing events that put enormous stress on the firm's viability. The stress gradually increases. Eventually, at some trigger moment, the stress suddenly overwhelms the firm's resistance and it fails. The key point here is that the stresses are observable. Indeed, the firm may be actively trying to mitigate the stress, but it eventually succumbs at some breaking point. The failure that follows needs to be sudden—for example, taking just a few days to materialize. Up to this point, it might appear that the firm could survive the stresses. Had the final "straw" not occurred, in all likelihood the firm would have survived.

For example, assume that the firm is experiencing trading or credit losses over a number of reporting periods. All along, the firm is able to manage through the losses and retain market confidence. Finally, at the occurrence of a market event (possibly nonspecific to the firm), confidence collapses suddenly, leaving the firm unable to continue trading. The business model unravels and the firm's remaining business is no longer viable.

4. Repeated or Sustained Stress Leading to Gradual Failure (Creep and Fatigue)

This failure supposes that the firm experiences high levels of stress over a long period of time. The result is that the business operations are altered slowly to accommodate the stresses. The failure is not immediate, but the changes to the business are permanent. Additionally, cracks begin to appear in the systems or operations of the firm. Eventually, as a result of the accumulated strain, the business fails. This gradual failure (possibly observable) distinguishes creep or fatigue failure from brittle and buckling failures.

For example, consider a firm facing stiff competition in its marketplace. The firm tries to adapt its strategy in a bid to improve its financial position. The new, more aggressive strategy does not fit its risk management capabilities. Consequently, it begins to experience large credit and operational losses. The firm's reaction to the changing situation helps fix some problems, but new ones continue to emerge. After several attempts to change its operations, the firm continues to lose business, and stakeholders' confidence in the firm declines. Finally, investors begin to withdraw and the firm slowly winds down.

Retracing the Paths to Failure

Given the failure mode, we can then explore two paths: The first leads to the proximate causes of the failure; the other traces the ultimate development and effect of the failure.

Stage 1

The causal relationships must be clearly established between the event and the failure mode. First, we address the simple question of the occurrence of the event and the mechanism of failure. For instance, a hidden fault in a system design under certain specific but rare conditions leads to a complete system failure, the consequences of which are eventual business failure.

Having established the cause (the design fault), we can then explore the preconditions for the existence of the fault and for the failure to occur. The preconditions might take different forms: technical, organizational, cultural, environmental, or human error. Thus, we construct a picture of the prevailing conditions that lead to the failure via a specific mode. There may be several variants of events that generate the same failure mode, and each will have its own unique preconditions.

The second question addresses how the failure develops. Once the trigger event occurs, it sets off a collection of attendant events, some of which are sequential and others concurrent. For each event, we need to explore how the event might present itself and the patterns it might follow, including any subsequent events it might trigger. By considering the factors that could exacerbate or mitigate the potential effects, we can draw up a prognosis of the end state.

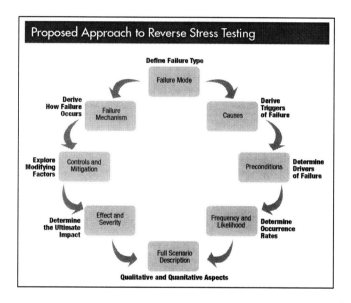

Stage 2

In the second stage, we need to pursue the two paths plotted in Stage 1 in order to determine the final components of the failure scenarios—that is, occurrence rates and severity. These two components enable us to derive some quantitative measures of the scenarios.

The occurrence rate is a function of two measures:

- The likelihood of the existence of the necessary preconditions.
- The frequency at which the triggering event occurs given the preconditions.

These two parameters need not be related directly. For example, it is possible to conceive of a situation in which the conditions may exist often, but the triggering event occurs only rarely and sporadically.

The severity is a quantification of the ultimate impact of the scenario once it has fully developed. The degree of severity will differ by failure type and environmental factors (from partial to complete failure). We need to take into account several aspects of the failure effect:

- The ultimate financial impact on the firm and its stakeholders.
- The ultimate financial impact on the industry, partner firms, and the wider economy.
- The nonfinancial impact on the firm, industry, and society.

Clearly, the failure of a systemically important institution will have a greater effect across the board; in the case of smaller firms, probably only their immediate stakeholders will be affected.

Once the causes and preconditions have been identified, it should be a straightforward exercise to derive the parameters for the quantification of the severity. In effect, we would have reached the starting point of the traditional stress-testing approach. For instance, we might have determined that one of the preconditions was a large movement in interest rates. It then follows that we require interest rate shocks of various degrees to produce the expected results. By applying simulations across multiple factors, we can discover what the probable degrees must be.

Finally, we can combine all of the findings to define the failure scenarios. The description will include the following:

- The assumptions and preconditions.
- The triggering events that cause the failure.
- The nature of the failure (failure mode).
- How the events developed and resulted in ultimate failure.
- Any controls and mitigating actions, as well as reactions, to the developing events.
- The scenario's frequency of occurrence.
- The severity of the scenario, including both qualitative and quantitative aspects.

The figure summarizes the proposed approach, starting from the failure mode and extending to the full scenario description.

An Example

The approach can be illustrated by this scenario involving a bank. It is a national bank with wholesale and retail divisions, although its capital market operations are relatively small. It has a significant share of the mortgage lending market in the country. Thus, its mortgage book represents the largest source of risk. For this scenario, we will assume that the macroeconomic environment is challenging for the financial sector in general.

The bank is experiencing stress from a credit, liquidity, operational, business, and reputational risk perspective. Earnings have been under considerable pressure over a five-quarter period due to loan losses. Nonetheless, the bank remains profitable (albeit profits are greatly reduced) because the other business lines continue to perform well.

1. Failure Mode
Buckling: The firm faces funding pressure due to the stressed performance of its loan book. As a result, market and public trust in the firm declines gradually, then reaches a

critical point when key funding on the wholesale market suddenly ceases. Depositor withdrawals accelerate and the firm collapses quickly.

2. Causes

The management is unaware of the true risk of its lending strategy. Furthermore, the risk is amplified by the unexpected failure of its risk policies, governance, and controls. The contributing factors include:

- Overconcentration exists in certain product types whose susceptibility to an economic downturn was previously untested.
- Underwriting standards and policies are weaker than anticipated. The controls and governance structures fail to prevent the introduction of riskier loans into the bank's book. As a result, a significant portion of the loans causes the bank to exceed its stated risk appetite.
- Third-party intermediaries break underwriting guidelines, resulting in the acquisition of riskier-than expected loans.
- The risk controls, systems, and governance are not fully integrated, thus reducing the bank's ability to monitor the total risk or understand how the risks interrelate. This is further exacerbated by high turnover in the risk management team and a break in continuity of risk measurement or monitoring.

Due to unfavorable public perception of the firm's financial position and the challenging marketplace, the firm is unable to raise new capital or sustain its liquidity to fund its continuing operations.

3. Preconditions

- The housing and mortgage markets collapse, leading to loan losses that had not been forecast.
- The firm's borrowing capacity is severely limited over a period of three months, and its stock price is depressed significantly compared to the same period in the prior year.
- Over a period of six months, press reports continue to spread rumors of the bank's poor financial position. Clarifying statements fail to convince investors and the general public, possibly owing to the general malaise in the industry and the febrile atmosphere.
- In the prior year, the strategy in place seemed to support aggressive growth. The market appears stable and thus does not indicate any major underlying risks.
- Over time, the bank has been transforming its product mix to incorporate new loan products that increase earnings in concordance with the industry shift.
- The bank is unable to provide adequate oversight of third-party intermediaries and cannot detect the underwriting breaches at source.
- Strong competition gradually steers the bank's portfolio to overconcentration in certain regions, which are subsequently impacted by a macroeconomic crisis.

4. Failure Mechanism

The firm begins to experience loan losses from its risky products. Loan charge-offs and reserves are recorded for four consecutive quarters, depressing earnings by 75%. At the same time, the share price declines to 25% of its peak value.

The liquidity position begins to exhibit stress. The firm responds by raising capital at considerable cost. However, the bank's liquidity position is further weakened by significant deposit withdrawals as customers react to unfavorable press reports.

The market experiences a serious crisis that leads to failures of some firms, which adds to the bank's stress. The market begins to restrict the bank's borrowing capacity. Within a one-week period, the bank suffers 20% of net deposit outflows, thus compounding the liquidity crisis.

Unable to raise funds to improve its liquidity position in the face of depositor withdrawals and poor market perceptions, the bank effectively collapses.

5. Controls and Mitigation

Management actions to strengthen internal controls come too late to affect the portfolio composition. Riskier product lines are closed and new, enhanced processes are introduced.

The liquidity position is improved through inward investment, which provides temporary relief. Further losses and the decline in the share price continue to stress the bank's position. In order to attract deposits, the bank has to offer deposit rates that are higher than those of competitors.

The bank holds frequent investor briefing sessions in an attempt to calm the market. Failures of similar institutions create inordinate public suspicion and overreaction.

The fragile position leads to a collapse in employee morale, thus reducing the efficacy of management plans and responses.

6. Frequency and Likelihood / Effect and Severity

This is a subjective exercise unique to the firm. Some points to bear in mind include the following:

- Use historical events as a guide, but apply judgment on the necessary modifications.
- Consider the preconditions and sequence of events to help develop a hypothesis on the occurrence rates and outcome.
- Evaluate the likely efficacy of the controls and of management or supervisory actions that might arrest the failures or reduce their impact.

Conclusion

Stress testing and reverse stress testing have different starting points: The first assumes particular inputs, and the second presupposes an outcome. Nonetheless, they retain significant commonality. The structured approach to reverse stress testing proposed here has the natural effect of identifying potential parameters for traditional stress testing. Indeed, we can conceive of a self-perpetuating process: reverse stress testing leading to new stress tests, and vice versa. Therefore, the two exercises complement each other as risk management tools.

Historically, firms have viewed stress testing as an exercise for determining the levels of required capital. It is anticipated that reverse stress testing will highlight the fact that the level of residual capital is not the sole determinant of a firm's survivability. By identifying the wider set of risk factors, firms should be able to readjust their risk strategies and develop corrective actions based on their risk appetite.

The approach described here seeks to help firms identify their true universe of risk. The key benefit is a structure that can ease the process for composing a sufficiently representative set of scenarios. The use of the results is critical to realizing the full benefits. A firm may seek to mitigate some of these risks, but not necessarily all of them. Those that remain must therefore be reconciled with the firm's risk appetite. With the right approach, firms can transform both types of stress-testing exercises from a regulatory requirement into an effective business tool.

About the Editors

MICHEL ARATEN is head of Credit Risk Capital Advisory. After 40 years, he recently retired from JPMorgan Chase as managing director with a focus on regulatory issues. He has developed credit risk capital models for global retail, wholesale, and capital markets. In addition, he has published widely in journals, authored chapters in books, and is a frequent speaker at conferences and seminars. He has been an adjunct lecturer at Columbia University, Fordham University, and New York University Polytechnic School of Engineering and holds a doctorate in operations research from Columbia University.

JOSEPH L. BREEDEN, PH.D., is chief executive officer of Prescient Models LLC. Breeden has designed and deployed risk management systems for loan and deposit portfolios since 1996. He co-founded Strategic Analytics in 1999 and Prescient Models in 2011. In those 18 years, he created models for every major international financial crisis. He has published over 40 academic articles, and the second edition of his book, "Reinventing Retail Lending Analytics: Forecasting, Stress Testing, Capital, and Scoring for a World of Crises," was published by RiskBooks in 2014.